Modern Methods for AI-Integrated Language Curriculum

Nayef Jomaa
University of Technology and Applied Sciences, Salalah, Oman

IGI Global
Scientific Publishing
Publishing Tomorrow's Research Today

Vice President of Editorial Melissa Wagner
Director of Acquisitions Mikaela Felty
Director of Book Development Jocelynn Hessler
Production Manager Mike Brehm
Cover Design Phillip Shickler

Published in the United States of America by
IGI Global Scientific Publishing
701 East Chocolate Avenue
Hershey, PA, 17033, USA
Tel: 717-533-8845
Fax: 717-533-7115
Website: https://www.igi-global.com E-mail: cust@igi-global.com

Library of Congress Cataloging-in-Publication Data

Library of Congress Cataloging-in-Publication Data

Names: Jomaa, Nayef, 1979- editor.
Title: Modern methods for AI-integrated language curriculum / edited by Nayef Jomaa.
Description: Hershey, PA : IGI Global Scientific Publishing, [2025] | Includes bibliographical references and index. | Summary: "This book is an attempt to identify to what extent Artificial Intelligence can be integrated with the modern methods of teaching and learning languages"-- Provided by publisher.
Identifiers: LCCN 2024057403 (print) | LCCN 2024057404 (ebook) | ISBN 9798369396063 (hardcover) | ISBN 9798369396070 (paperback) | ISBN 9798369396087 (ebook)
Subjects: LCSH: Language and languages--Study and teaching--Technological innovations. | Artificial intelligence--Educational applications. | LCGFT: Essays.
Classification: LCC P53.855 .M326 2025 (print) | LCC P53.855 (ebook) | DDC 418.0078/563--dc23/eng/20241230
LC record available at https://lccn.loc.gov/2024057403
LC ebook record available at https://lccn.loc.gov/2024057404

British Cataloguing in Publication Data
A Cataloguing in Publication record for this book is available from the British Library.

Table of Contents

Detailed Table of Contents

This study investigates the impact of AI-integrated vocabulary learning on EFL Omani students, focusing on their academic performance and English proficiency. A quantitative approach was employed, employing data collection through a survey distributed to 500 students, with 236 valid responses analysed. SPSS version 26 was used in the analysis. The findings revealed that EFL Omani students generally perceive AI tools as beneficial for vocabulary acquisition and learning, with higher proficiency and academically stronger students demonstrating greater trust, ease of use, and motivation to engage with AI-driven learning. However, lower-proficiency students and those with weaker academic performance reported more challenges in using AI tools and exhibited lower trust in AI-generated vocabulary recommendations. Though general trends indicate a positive correlation between proficiency level and AI learning effectiveness, statistical analyses showed no significant impact of academic performance on AI-assisted vocabulary acquisition.

This chapter discusses the role of artificial intelligence in transforming curriculum development and content creation for language education. In fact, with institutions of learning under increased pressure to ensure that learners have more personalized, inclusive, and culturally sensitive learning experiences, AI emerges as a powerful tool in addressing such demands. The chapter examines how AI technologies enable adaptive learning pathways, in-class real-time feedback systems, and support for diverse learning styles using multimodal content delivery. It is intended to further examine such implementation of the use of AI-driven solutions for developing culturally responsive materials while maintaining the highest pedagogical standards. Discussions will involve key areas: personalization strategies, frameworks for the inclusivity of cultures, accommodation in terms of learning styles, and analytics for continuous improvement in real time.

This chapter explores the evolving role of teachers in an AI-driven language learning environment. With the rapid advancement of AI, traditional methods of language education are undergoing significant transformation. AI tools offer personalized learning experiences, real-time feedback, and adaptive assessments, enhancing the efficiency and accessibility of language instruction. However, the role of the teacher remains essential in guiding, supporting, and interpreting AI-generated data to ensure a holistic and human-centered learning experience. This chapter discusses the shifting roles of teachers as facilitators, mentors, and ethical leaders in an AI-enhanced classroom. It emphasizes the need for teachers to develop AI literacy, adapt pedagogical strategies, and foster emotional connections with students. The integration of AI in education also raises ethical considerations related to equity, privacy, and bias. Ultimately, the future of language education lies in the synergy between AI tools and human expertise, ensuring effective and inclusive language learning.

The advent and integration of artificial intelligence (AI) in higher education have become invaluable. The pursuit of learning foreign languages has been a continuous and significant human effort, motivated by the desire to enhance cross-cultural interaction, enhance job prospects, and promote cognitive growth; there has been a growing focus on integrating artificial intelligence technologies into different educational domains, including language learning recently. Nevertheless, the utilisation of these technologies also presents obstacles and possible drawbacks. Grounded in the theory of constructivism, this study aims to identify and analyse

Preface

INTRODUCTION

The primary goal of this volume is to investigate how Artificial Intelligence can enhance modern methods of teaching and learning languages. By opening submissions to include insights across all languages and AI tools, we have curated a diverse and forward-thinking collection of contributions. These chapters examine theoretical foundations, pedagogical strategies, classroom applications, and emerging technologies that are shaping the future of language education.

This book is intended as a valuable resource for researchers, curriculum designers, educators, and learners who are navigating the rapidly changing landscape of both AI and language instruction. Whether you are developing AI-driven educational tools, implementing AI-enhanced teaching strategies, or simply exploring new possibilities in language learning, this volume offers insights and inspiration for your journey.

I extend my heartfelt thanks to all the contributors whose work and vision have made this collection possible. Together, we hope to inspire innovation and foster collaboration between the fields of Artificial Intelligence and language education for years to come.

ORGANIZATION OF THE BOOK

Chapter 1: Utilizing AI in Learning English Vocabulary Among EFL Omani Students: The Relationship of Academic Performance and English Proficiency

In this chapter, the authors investigate the influence of AI-integrated vocabulary learning on English as a Foreign Language (EFL) students in Oman. Drawing on a survey of 236 students, the study highlights how AI tools are perceived by students with varying levels of academic performance and English proficiency. The findings suggest that AI tools are viewed as beneficial for vocabulary learning and acquisition, particularly by higher-proficiency and academically stronger students. However, lower-proficiency students encounter challenges in using these tools and demonstrate lower trust in AI-generated recommendations. This study provides a nuanced view of how AI can impact language learning based on students' performance, with key insights for educators aiming to optimize AI-based vocabulary learning tools.

Chapter 2: Using AI for Curriculum Development and Content Generation: Enhancing Diversity, Inclusion, and Adaptability in Language Education

This chapter explores the transformative potential of AI in curriculum development and content creation within language education. The authors highlight how AI can support personalized, inclusive, and culturally responsive learning experiences, accommodating diverse learning styles and ensuring that content is adaptable to various educational contexts. By leveraging AI technologies such as adaptive learning pathways and real-time feedback systems, this chapter emphasizes how AI can enhance the inclusivity and cultural sensitivity of language curricula. It also provides a framework for educators to implement AI-driven solutions that address the varied needs of students while upholding high pedagogical standards.

Chapter 3: The Role of Teachers in an AI-Driven Language Learning Environment

As AI technologies revolutionize language education, this chapter examines the evolving role of teachers in an AI-enhanced classroom. While AI tools offer personalized learning experiences and real-time feedback, teachers remain integral to guiding students through the learning process. This chapter underscores the importance of AI literacy for teachers, exploring how they can use AI tools effectively while maintaining emotional connections with students and addressing ethical concerns, such as privacy and bias. It argues that the future of language education lies in the synergy between AI tools and human expertise, ensuring that both technological and human elements work together to create effective learning environments.

Chapter 4: The Key Obstacles to Using Emerging Artificial Intelligence Tools in Foreign Language Learning: A Systematic Review

In this chapter, the authors conduct a systematic review to identify the key obstacles hindering the integration of AI tools in foreign language learning. Grounded in the constructivist theory, the study reveals challenges, such as lack of access to technology, insufficient understanding of AI's pedagogical applications, and barriers related to affordability. By analyzing existing literature, this chapter provides a comprehensive overview of the challenges facing AI adoption in language education and offers suggestions for overcoming these barriers to enhance the effectiveness of AI tools in the classroom.

Chapter 5: Evolution and Future Trends in Artificial Intelligence in Education (AIEd)

This chapter takes a broad view of Artificial Intelligence in Education (AIEd), tracing its evolution from early instructional software to advanced systems like intelligent tutoring and adaptive learning technologies. The authors explore how AIEd is increasingly aligned with cognitive science theories and immersive learning technologies such as AR/VR. Looking forward, this chapter discusses the future applications of AIEd, including lifelong learning solutions and the integration of AI with other educational disciplines. It serves as a forward-thinking reflection on the trends shaping the future of AI in education, particularly in language learning.

Chapter 6: Enhancing Educational Future by Integrating Artificial Intelligence in Language Curriculum

This chapter discusses the profound impact of AI on language curricula, transforming traditional teaching methodologies and offering new ways to support diverse learning needs. The authors highlight key AI-driven tools, such as natural language processing, intelligent tutoring systems, and speech recognition, which can enhance student learning and personalize the educational experience. They also address the ethical considerations and training challenges faced by educators in adopting these technologies. This chapter serves as a comprehensive guide for educators and policymakers looking to incorporate AI in language curricula to improve students' outcomes.

Chapter 7: Developing AI-Enhanced Task-Based Language Learning (TBLL) Activities

In this chapter, the authors explore how AI can be integrated with Task-Based Language Learning (TBLL) to create innovative, personalized, and learner-centered language education experiences. The chapter emphasizes the role of AI technologies, such as adaptive learning platforms and immersive virtual environments in facilitating dynamic tasks that encourage meaningful communication and real-time feedback. While offering a wealth of opportunities for improving language learning, the authors also discuss the challenges posed by ethical concerns, algorithmic biases, and the digital divide, suggesting ways to balance these issues while maintaining the communicative focus of TBLL.

Chapter 8: Challenges of Integrating Artificial Intelligence with Language Curriculum: Addressing Pedagogical, Technological, and Ethical Barriers

This chapter offers a critical examination of the challenges involved in integrating AI into language curricula, focusing on pedagogical, technological, and ethical barriers. The authors not only discuss how AI can personalize and enhance language learning, but also highlight the obstacles educators face, including alignment with curriculum goals, teacher readiness, and assessment challenges. The chapter further explores technological issues, such as access disparities and the adaptability of AI tools, as well as ethical considerations such as data privacy and algorithmic bias. The authors provide practical insights on how to navigate these challenges to create a balanced, effective, and inclusive AI-enhanced language curriculum.

Chapter 9: A Comprehensive Survey on Text Mining from Theory to Practice

This chapter delves into the field of text mining, exploring both its theoretical foundations and practical applications in Natural Language Processing (NLP). The authors provide a step-by-step guide to the text mining process, covering key algorithms and methodologies used in extracting meaningful information from unstructured text data. The chapter serves as a valuable resource for researchers and practitioners looking to apply text-mining techniques in various domains, offering detailed insights and code examples to facilitate implementation.

CONCLUSION

In conclusion, the chapters presented in this reference book collectively highlight the transformative potential of artificial intelligence in language education. As we navigate the evolving educational landscape, AI is emerging as a powerful tool to enhance learning experiences, from vocabulary acquisition to curriculum development. The contributions within this volume not only shed light on AI's capacity to personalize learning and foster inclusion but also critically examine the obstacles and ethical considerations that accompany its integration. The intersection of technology and pedagogy offers both immense opportunities and challenges, underscoring the need for a balanced and thoughtful approach to adopting AI-driven solutions.

From the exploration of AI-enhanced task-based language learning to addressing the barriers of AI integration, each chapter contributes valuable insights that help educators, researchers, and policymakers better understand the dynamic role AI will play in shaping the future of language education. As we continue to embrace and innovate with AI, this book serves as a guiding resource, encouraging ongoing reflection on how these technologies can be leveraged responsibly and effectively. It is our hope that this volume inspires future research, fosters collaboration, and ultimately leads to more inclusive, adaptable, and engaging learning environments for all students.

Chapter 1
Utilizing AI in Learning English Vocabulary among EFL Omani Students:
The Relationship of Academic Performance and English Proficiency

Nayef J. Jomaa
https://orcid.org/0000-0001-8952-5812
University of Technology and Applied Sciences, Salalah, Oman

Salim Al Maashani
https://orcid.org/0009-0004-9970-6798
Infrastructure University Kuala Lumpur, Slangor, Malaysia

Ahmed Almaashani
University of Bristol, Bristol, UK

ABSTRACT

This study investigates the impact of AI-integrated vocabulary learning on EFL Omani students, focusing on their academic performance and English proficiency. A quantitative approach was employed, employing data collection through a survey distributed to 500 students, with 236 valid responses analysed. SPSS version 26 was used in the analysis. The findings revealed that EFL Omani students generally perceive AI tools as beneficial for vocabulary acquisition and learning, with higher proficiency and academically stronger students demonstrating greater trust, ease of

DOI: 10.4018/979-8-3693-9606-3.ch001

use, and motivation to engage with AI-driven learning. However, lower-proficiency students and those with weaker academic performance reported more challenges in using AI tools and exhibited lower trust in AI-generated vocabulary recommendations. Though general trends indicate a positive correlation between proficiency level and AI learning effectiveness, statistical analyses showed no significant impact of academic performance on AI-assisted vocabulary acquisition.

INTRODUCTION

Advancements in mobile technology and artificial intelligence have opened limitless possibilities for overcoming communication barriers (Moxon, 2024; Rusmiyanto, Huriati, Fitriani, Tyas, Rofi'i, & Sari, 2023). In other words, technological progress has significantly impacted various fields, particularly English Language Teaching (ELT), because of the essential role technology plays in education (Keerthiwansha, 2018; Rao, 2019). Research findings indicate that technology-based language acquisition and learning surpass traditional methods, demonstrating a substantial and meaningful impact on language learning processes (Attamimi, 2025; Eragamreddy, 2025; Fajaruddin, Retnawati, Setiawan, Apino, Arlinwibowo, & Rachman, 2024; Jomaa, Attamimi, & Al Mahri, 2024, 2025; Jomaa, 2025; Kheder, 2025). However, learning a foreign language remains challenging for learners, primarily due to their limited vocabulary (Jomaa, Attamimi, & Alghafri, 2025; Oktadela, Elida, & Ismail, 2023). As a result, mobile technologies, particularly communication and language applications, have drawn the interest of researchers (Hasan, Fakih, Seraj, & Hasmirati, 2022). For instance, WhatsApp can be effectively utilized in educational settings by English language teachers, who are encouraged to incorporate it into their teaching practices. This integration may inspire students to use WhatsApp as a valuable tool for interacting with peers and engaging with other English learners beyond their immediate social circles. Additionally, Lafleur (2024) found that gamified applications offering daily rewards yield more favorable learning outcomes compared to traditional teaching methods. Currently, the integration of artificial intelligence (AI) into online learning represents a significant opportunity for advancing professional English education (Wang, Liu, & Zhou, 2024). Studies exploring the use of AI tools in English learning highlight both promising learning prospects (Aldawsari, 2024) and potential challenges (Rouabhia, 2025). Similarly, Amin (2023) emphasizes that incorporating AI in EFL education elicits both excitement and notable limitations. Despite these developments, limited research has examined students' attitudes toward AI tools for learning English, particularly vocabulary, within the Omani context. Recognizing this gap, Syahrin and Akmal (2024) argue that understanding the viewpoints of key stakeholders—including students, instructors, and university administrators—is essential for guiding AI integration in Oman's academic landscape (p. 86). With increasing attention on evaluating the effectiveness of emerging educational technologies, such as Memrise, in vocabulary learning and acquisition, Aprizal and Wachyudi (2024) emphasize the need for further research to explore diverse learning environments and address technical challenges (Jomaa, Attamimi, & Al Mahri, 2025). Consequently, this study investigates the perspectives of EFL Omani students regarding AI tools in vocabulary learning, identifying independent factors, such as English proficiency and academic performance to determine their potential influence on AI-based vocabulary learning.

LITERATURE REVIEW

Advanced technologies have greatly enhanced the language teaching and learning process, making it more appealing, engaging, and diverse. Several studies on technology in education suggest that incorporating ICT (Information and Communication Technologies) can boost students' motivation and interaction in the classroom (Alwahoub, Azmi, & Jomaa, 2020; Lim & Chai, 2004; Mooij, 2007; Özyildirim & Jomaa, 2023). For instance, mobile learning has been shown to improve foreign language learning when compared to traditional methods (Jomaa & Kamal, 2023; Lu, 2008). Additionally, Wang, Teng, and Chen (2015) found that using apps on iPads significantly increases students' engagement in learning English. It was also noted that students felt more confident when learning vocabulary through these applications. However, factors such as students' age, emotional state, and language proficiency should be considered when integrating technology into language instruction (Yu & Tainin, 2022).

Vocabulary acquisition and learning play a crucial role in mastering any language, especially for university students. The depth of their academic vocabulary knowledge often correlates with academic success, as it helps them better understand specialized texts and lectures (Alsahafi, 2023). Further, Elder and Von Randow (2008) emphasized that the size of students' vocabulary is a strong predictor of academic success. Other studies have also linked vocabulary size to overall academic performance (Cloate, 2016; Daller & Phelan, 2013; Harrington & Roche, 2014).

As a result of advanced technology, particularly AI tools, learning foreign languages has become much easier. A study on the use of AI in language learning found that ChatGPT positively influences writing skills, encourages students in online learning environments, and promotes interactive language learning. However, its impact on speaking, grammar, and word skills is limited. Moreover, ChatGPT helps expand students' cultural awareness and enhances their creativity and thinking skills (Eragamreddy, 2025; Karataş, Abedi, Gunyel, Karadeniz, & Kuzgun, 2024).

In another study, Rusmiyanto et al. (2023) demonstrated that AI tools significantly enhance English communication skills. These findings suggest important pedagogical implications, such as personalized learning and greater learner autonomy. In Saudi Arabia, the use of chatbots has been shown to improve English for Specific Purposes (ESP) vocabulary, with experimental group students outperforming control group students in learning ESP terms (Qasem, Ghaleb, Mahdi, Al Khateeb, & Al Fadda, 2023).

AI tools can serve multiple purposes, and Alsadoon (2021) found that translation tools and dictionaries were highly rated for vocabulary learning. In comparison, Hendrawaty, Yuliati, and Haryanti (2024) found that YouTube was the most common tool among foreign learners to study vocabulary, followed by Quizzis, Duolingo, and Kahoot. This suggests that students prefer learning vocabulary when it is fun, engaging, and self-selected rather than forced upon them. Aprizal and Wachyudi (2024) further showed that Memrise positively influences vocabulary learning, highlighting the importance of factors, such as mobile app preferences, technical considerations, autonomy, motivation, and gamification. In their studies, Alharbi and Khalil (2023) and Jomaa et al. (2024) found that students had a positive attitude toward using AI tools in English vocabulary learning. Similarly, Sumakul et al. (2022) reported that students were generally receptive to AI tools in the classroom. For effective English language teaching and learning, regular training courses should be provided to participants (Oktadela, Elida, & Ismail, 2023). Based on encouraging results, Wang, Teng, and Chen (2015) recommended using various ICT tools to teach English, especially vocabulary, in the classroom to meet the needs of foreign language learners. Yu and Trainin (2022) suggested exploring the impact of technology-assisted incidental L2 vocabulary learning through qualitative research. Lu (2008) advocated incorporating mobile phone usage with interactive features, a feasible option with current technological advancements, including language mobile applications and AI tools that can be installed on smartphones for foreign language learning. In his research on ChatGPT in English teaching, Al-Khresheh (2024) noted that ChatGPT can provide students with real-time, adaptive feedback, enabling immediate adjustments and clarifications. Oktadela, Elida, and Ismail (2023) observed that the Chatbot application led to increased happiness and enthusiasm among students, boosting their English vocabulary through conversations with the chatbot. However, in the Omani context, few studies have examined the perspectives of EFL students toward using AI tools to learn English vocabulary. Therefore, the aim of this study is to address two research questions that consider two independent variables, namely English proficiency and academic performance.

1- To what extent does English proficiency affect the use of AI tools to learn English vocabulary among EFL Omani students?

2- To what extent is academic performance associated with the use of AI tools to learn English vocabulary among EFL Omani students?

RESEARCH METHODOLOGY

A quantitative approach was employed in this study to investigate the perspectives of EFL Omani students regarding the use of AI tools in vocabulary learning. The questionnaire was distributed online via Google Forms to 500 EFL Omani students at the Preparatory Studies Center, with 236 valid responses received. The questionnaire was divided into two sections: the first section gathered demographic information, including gender, age, English proficiency level, and academic performance. Regarding the English proficiency level, students must complete four preliminary English levels at the Preparatory Studies Centre before advancing to specialized courses. However, some students may directly enter levels 2, 3 or 4 based on their English placement test results or by passing recalibrative exams during the semester. As for the academic performance, the students were divided into three groups (group 1: students who got less than 10 marks, group 2: students who got between 11 and 20 marks, and group 3: students who got 20+ marks). The second part of the questionnaire included 20 closed-ended questions, using a five-point Likert scale ranging from 1 (Strongly Disagree) to 5 (Strongly Agree). Eight of these items were adapted from a previous study by Alharbi and Khalil (2023), whereas 12 items were developed by the researchers in this study to enhance the questionnaire's comprehensiveness. A pilot study with 50 students was conducted to test the reliability of the survey, with Cronbach's Alpha yielding a strong correlation of .936.

Table 1. Reliability statistics of the pilot study

Reliability Statistics (50 EFL Omani students)		
Cronbach's Alpha	**Cronbach's Alpha Based on Standardized Items**	**No. of Items**
.936	.937	20

Using SPSS version 26, the reliability statistics for the main sample of 236 EFL Omani students showed a Cronbach's Alpha correlation of .942, indicating a high level of reliability.

Table 2. Reliability statistics of the main study

Reliability Statistics (236 respondents)		
Cronbach's Alpha	**Cronbach's Alpha Based on Standardized Items**	**No. of Items**
.942	.943	20

Descriptive statistics, including means, standard deviations, and frequencies, as well as the highest and lowest means, were reported using SPSS version 26. The survey was randomly distributed online via Google Forms to 500 EFL Omani students enrolled in the General Foundation Program at the Preparatory Studies Center at a public university in Oman. 236 students responded, and their questionnaires were deemed valid for analysis. The respondents varied in terms of age, gender, levels of study, English proficiency level, and academic performance. To ensure ethical standards, the respondents were given clear instructions about the study's objectives before completing the questionnaire. All data collected were securely stored without any personal identifiers, with the respondents assured that their responses would solely be used for research purposes.

FINDINGS

This section addresses the findings related to the possible effect of two variables, namely English proficiency and academic performance on AI-integrated vocabulary learning.

Part One

The effect of English proficiency on AI-integrated vocabulary learning is represented by dividing the students into four groups; group one included students who did not pass the replacement test and had to study all levels starting with level one. Group two included students who could achieve a high score and skipped level one, whereas students who achieved a higher score were placed in level three because they could skip levels one and two. Other students whose marks were higher than group two could skip levels one, two, and three; therefore, they were placed in level four.

Table 3. Effect of English proficiency on AI-integrated vocabulary learning among EFL Omani students

Question items		Mean	Std. Deviation	95% Confidence Interval for Mean Lower Bound	95% Confidence Interval for Mean Upper Bound
Q1- Using AI for vocabulary learning is effective and beneficial for me.	I studied all levels	4.0521	.74509	3.9011	4.2031
	I skipped level 1	3.8690	1.06171	3.6386	4.0995
	I skipped levels 1 and 2	3.7708	1.03635	3.4699	4.0718
	I skipped levels 1, 2, and 3	3.8750	1.35620	2.7412	5.0088
	Total	3.9237	.95121	3.8017	4.0457
Q2- I am completely comfortable with using AI-based tools or apps for vocabulary learning.	I studied all levels	3.7917	.96154	3.5968	3.9865
	I skipped level 1	3.7024	.95413	3.4953	3.9094
	I skipped levels 1 and 2	3.8333	1.05857	3.5260	4.1407
	I skipped levels 1, 2, and 3	3.8750	.99103	3.0465	4.7035
	Total	3.7712	.97554	3.6461	3.8963
Q3- I believe the advantages of using AI for vocabulary learning over the traditional method are: faster learning, more personalized learning, better retention, fun and engaging methods, etc.	I studied all levels	3.7500	.88258	3.5712	3.9288
	I skipped level 1	3.6190	.93015	3.4172	3.8209
	I skipped levels 1 and 2	3.6250	.98121	3.3401	3.9099
	I skipped levels 1, 2, and 3	4.0000	.75593	3.3680	4.6320
	Total	3.6864	.91511	3.5691	3.8038
Q4- I have not encountered any challenges or difficulties when using AI for vocabulary learning.	I studied all levels	3.5417	1.05548	3.3278	3.7555
	I skipped level 1	3.4524	1.02269	3.2304	3.6743
	I skipped levels 1 and 2	3.6875	.92613	3.4186	3.9564
	I skipped levels 1, 2, and 3	3.3750	1.40789	2.1980	4.5520
	Total	3.5339	1.02880	3.4020	3.6658
Q5- Especially compared to traditional vocabulary learning methods, I consider AI-based vocabulary learning more effective.	I studied all levels	3.6146	1.06987	3.3978	3.8314
	I skipped level 1	3.3929	1.02989	3.1694	3.6164
	I skipped levels 1 and 2	3.6042	1.04657	3.3003	3.9081
	I skipped levels 1, 2, and 3	3.6250	1.30247	2.5361	4.7139
	Total	3.5339	1.05735	3.3983	3.6695
Q6- I completely trust the vocabulary words or phrases recommended by AI tools.	I studied all levels	3.5625	.91551	3.3770	3.7480
	I skipped level 1	3.3095	1.05255	3.0811	3.5379
	I skipped levels 1 and 2	3.4583	.94437	3.1841	3.7326
	I skipped levels 1, 2, and 3	3.7500	1.38873	2.5890	4.9110
	Total	3.4576	.99054	3.3306	3.5847

continued on following page

Table 3. Continued

Question items		Mean	Std. Deviation	95% Confidence Interval for Mean	
				Lower Bound	Upper Bound
Q7- I often use AI tools or applications for vocabulary learning.	I studied all levels	3.7396	.95416	3.5463	3.9329
	I skipped level 1	3.5714	.98526	3.3576	3.7852
	I skipped levels 1 and 2	3.7083	.92157	3.4407	3.9759
	I skipped levels 1, 2, and 3	3.2500	1.38873	2.0890	4.4110
	Total	3.6568	.97457	3.5318	3.7818
Q8- I would recommend AI-based vocabulary learning tools to my peers.	I studied all levels	3.7083	1.00438	3.5048	3.9118
	I skipped level 1	3.4881	.99993	3.2711	3.7051
	I skipped levels 1 and 2	3.7083	1.05100	3.4032	4.0135
	I skipped levels 1, 2, and 3	3.5000	1.30931	2.4054	4.5946
	Total	3.6229	1.02196	3.4918	3.7539
Q9- I would recommend AI-based vocabulary learning tools to my peers because of their ease of use.	I studied all levels	3.8333	1.03280	3.6241	4.0426
	I skipped level 1	3.6071	.94446	3.4022	3.8121
	I skipped levels 1 and 2	3.7500	.93399	3.4788	4.0212
	I skipped levels 1, 2, and 3	3.3750	1.40789	2.1980	4.5520
	Total	3.7203	.99689	3.5925	3.8482
Q10- Using AI tools for vocabulary learning is interesting.	I studied all levels	3.8958	.83954	3.7257	4.0659
	I skipped level 1	3.6905	.91804	3.4912	3.8897
	I skipped levels 1 and 2	3.8958	.88100	3.6400	4.1516
	I skipped levels 1, 2, and 3	3.6250	1.40789	2.4480	4.8020
	Total	3.8136	.89869	3.6983	3.9288
Q11- I easily understand the exercises of new vocabulary presented by AI tools.	I studied all levels	3.5625	.94938	3.3701	3.7549
	I skipped level 1	3.5357	.91106	3.3380	3.7334
	I skipped levels 1 and 2	3.6458	.81187	3.4101	3.8816
	I skipped levels 1, 2, and 3	4.1250	.99103	3.2965	4.9535
	Total	3.5890	.91123	3.4721	3.7058
Q12- I want to spend much time and effort using AI tools to learn new vocabulary in English.	I studied all levels	3.6146	.99863	3.4122	3.8169
	I skipped level 1	3.3214	.98373	3.1079	3.5349
	I skipped levels 1 and 2	3.5417	1.07106	3.2307	3.8527
	I skipped levels 1, 2, and 3	4.0000	.75593	3.3680	4.6320
	Total	3.5085	1.00844	3.3791	3.6378
Q13- I will use AI tools frequently in the future to learn new vocabulary in English.	I studied all levels	3.7708	.90005	3.5885	3.9532
	I skipped level 1	3.6548	.95051	3.4485	3.8610
	I skipped levels 1 and 2	3.7083	.98841	3.4213	3.9953
	I skipped levels 1, 2, and 3	3.8750	.83452	3.1773	4.5727
	Total	3.7203	.93067	3.6010	3.8397

continued on following page

Table 3. Continued

Question items		Mean	Std. Deviation	95% Confidence Interval for Mean	
				Lower Bound	Upper Bound
Q14- I use AI tools because I am interested and motivated to learn new vocabulary in English.	I studied all levels	3.6146	.95554	3.4210	3.8082
	I skipped level 1	3.5000	.98788	3.2856	3.7144
	I skipped levels 1 and 2	3.6458	.97827	3.3618	3.9299
	I skipped levels 1, 2, and 3	3.6250	1.40789	2.4480	4.8020
	Total	3.5805	.98385	3.4543	3.7067
Q15- I use AI tools to increase my vocabulary in English.	I studied all levels	3.9896	.85218	3.8169	4.1623
	I skipped level 1	3.6310	.97905	3.4185	3.8434
	I skipped levels 1 and 2	3.9583	.87418	3.7045	4.2122
	I skipped levels 1, 2, and 3	4.2500	.46291	3.8630	4.6370
	Total	3.8644	.90779	3.7480	3.9808
Q16- I use AI tools to increase my knowledge of English and its culture.	I studied all levels	3.8958	.95674	3.7020	4.0897
	I skipped level 1	3.7976	.88875	3.6047	3.9905
	I skipped levels 1 and 2	3.7708	1.05668	3.4640	4.0777
	I skipped levels 1, 2, and 3	4.0000	1.30931	2.9054	5.0946
	Total	3.8390	.96289	3.7155	3.9625
Q17- I think AI tools offer me more options to learn vocabulary in English.	I studied all levels	3.8854	.84442	3.7143	4.0565
	I skipped level 1	3.6905	.91804	3.4912	3.8897
	I skipped levels 1 and 2	3.8542	.92229	3.5864	4.1220
	I skipped levels 1, 2, and 3	3.7500	.88641	3.0089	4.4911
	Total	3.8051	.88734	3.6913	3.9189
Q18- I think AI tools enhance my learning of new vocabulary in English.	I studied all levels	3.9375	.86830	3.7616	4.1134
	I skipped level 1	3.6310	1.02710	3.4081	3.8538
	I skipped levels 1 and 2	3.7083	.92157	3.4407	3.9759
	I skipped levels 1, 2, and 3	4.0000	.53452	3.5531	4.4469
	Total	3.7839	.93622	3.6638	3.9040
Q19- I think some answers of AI tools include wrong information.	I studied all levels	3.5833	.98051	3.3847	3.7820
	I skipped level 1	3.5000	.97561	3.2883	3.7117
	I skipped levels 1 and 2	3.4792	1.07168	3.1680	3.7903
	I skipped levels 1, 2, and 3	3.6250	.91613	2.8591	4.3909
	Total	3.5339	.99087	3.4068	3.6610
Q20- I think AI tools will solve the problem of learning new vocabulary in English.	I studied all levels	3.7917	.91671	3.6059	3.9774
	I skipped level 1	3.5952	.89334	3.4014	3.7891
	I skipped levels 1 and 2	3.7292	.89299	3.4699	3.9885
	I skipped levels 1, 2, and 3	3.6250	1.06066	2.7383	4.5117
	Total	3.7034	.90680	3.5871	3.8197

continued on following page

The dataset provides responses from EFL Omani students regarding their experiences with AI-based vocabulary learning. The data are categorized based on students who studied all levels, those who skipped level one, those who skipped levels one and two, and those who skipped levels one, two, and three. The analysis covers aspects, such as effectiveness, ease of use, trust, motivation, and recommendations for AI-based vocabulary learning tools.

EFFECTIVENESS AND BENEFITS OF AI-BASED VOCABULARY LEARNING

Students who studied all levels rated the effectiveness of AI-based vocabulary learning the highest (M=4.0521), whereas those who skipped levels one and two rated it the lowest (M=3.7708). However, students who skipped only level one and those who skipped all three levels provided similar ratings (M=3.8690 and M=3.8750, respectively). This suggests that skipping more levels does not necessarily correlate with a lower perception of effectiveness. Nonetheless, those who experienced the complete AI-based learning journey found it the most beneficial.

COMFORT IN USING AI TOOLS

Regarding comfort in using AI tools, those who skipped levels one and two showed the highest mean score (M=3.8333), indicating they were slightly more comfortable than those who studied all levels (M=3.7917). This contrasts with students who skipped only level one (M=3.7024) and those who skipped all three levels (M=3.8750). While comfort levels remain relatively high across groups, skipping early levels does not appear to significantly hinder ease of use.

PERCEIVED ADVANTAGES OF AI OVER TRADITIONAL METHODS

Students who skipped all three levels provided the highest mean score (M=4.0000) regarding the advantages of AI over traditional methods, whereas those who skipped level one rated it the lowest (M=3.6190). This suggests that students with less exposure to structured AI-based vocabulary learning may still recognize its benefits, potentially due to prior familiarity with AI tools or technology.

CHALLENGES IN USING AI TOOLS

The mean scores for the statement, "I have not encountered any challenges or difficulties when using AI for vocabulary learning," reveal that students who skipped levels one and two reported fewer difficulties (M=3.6875) than those who studied all levels (M=3.5417) or skipped only level one (M=3.4524). However, those who skipped all three levels reported the most challenges (M=3.3750). This suggests that some structured exposure to AI-based learning helps mitigate potential difficulties.

TRUST IN AI-RECOMMENDED VOCABULARY

Students who studied all levels showed moderate trust in AI recommendations (M=3.5625), whereas those who skipped levels one and two reported slightly lower trust (M=3.4583). Those who skipped only level one had the lowest trust levels (M=3.3095), whereas students who skipped all three levels had the highest trust (M=3.7500). This indicates that students with more structured learning may develop a more cautious approach toward AI-recommended vocabulary.

FREQUENCY OF AI TOOL USAGE

Students who studied all levels used AI tools more frequently (M=3.7396) than those who skipped levels (M=3.5714 for those who skipped one level, M=3.7083 for those who skipped two levels, and M=3.2500 for those who skipped three levels). This suggests that skipping more levels leads to a decrease in usage frequency, potentially due to a lack of familiarity or engagement with AI tools.

RECOMMENDATIONS TO PEERS

Students who studied all levels and those who skipped two levels were equally likely to recommend AI-based vocabulary learning to their peers (M=3.7083). However, those who skipped level one (M=3.4881) and those who skipped all three levels (M=3.5000) were less enthusiastic about recommending AI-based vocabulary tools. This could indicate that more structured exposure enhances perceived usefulness.

INTEREST AND MOTIVATION IN USING AI TOOLS

Students who studied all levels reported high interest in AI-based vocabulary learning (M=3.8958), whereas those who skipped two levels showed similar enthusiasm (M=3.8958). Those who skipped one level (M=3.6905) and three levels (M=3.6250) showed slightly lower motivation. This suggests that structured learning positively influences engagement and interest in AI-based vocabulary learning.

FUTURE USE OF AI-BASED VOCABULARY LEARNING

Students who studied all levels were the most inclined to use AI tools in the future (M=3.7708), followed closely by those who skipped levels one and two (M=3.7083) and those who skipped only level one (M=3.6548). Students who skipped all three levels also showed high interest (M=3.8750), indicating that despite limited exposure, they still recognize the potential benefits of AI-based learning. Overall, students who studied all levels generally rated AI-based vocabulary learning higher in terms of effectiveness, trust, and frequency of use. Those who skipped different levels demonstrated varying degrees of comfort and motivation, with some appearing to recognize AI's benefits even with limited exposure. Students who skipped more levels encountered more challenges, indicating that structured learning enhances familiarity and usability. While skipping levels did not drastically impact perceptions of AI's advantages, those with comprehensive exposure to AI-based learning were more consistent in recommending and using AI tools.

Table 4. Significant differences of the effect of English proficiency level on AI-integrated vocabulary learning

ANOVA						
		Sum of Squares	df	Mean Square	F	Sig.
Q1- Using AI for vocabulary learning is effective and beneficial for me.	Between Groups	2.974	3	.991	1.097	.351
	Within Groups	209.653	232	.904		
	Total	212.627	235			
Q2- I am completely comfortable with using AI-based tools or apps for vocabulary learning.	Between Groups	.710	3	.237	.246	.864
	Within Groups	222.935	232	.961		
	Total	223.644	235			
Q3- I believe the advantages of using AI for vocabulary learning over the traditional method are: faster learning, more personalized learning, better retention, fun and engaging methods, etc.	Between Groups	1.737	3	.579	.689	.560
	Within Groups	195.060	232	.841		
	Total	196.797	235			

continued on following page

Table 4. Continued

ANOVA						
		Sum of Squares	**df**	**Mean Square**	**F**	**Sig.**
Q4- I have not encountered any challenges or difficulties when using AI for vocabulary learning.	Between Groups	1.898	3	.633	.595	.619
	Within Groups	246.830	232	1.064		
	Total	248.729	235			
Q5- Especially compared to traditional vocabulary learning methods, I consider AI-based vocabulary learning more effective.	Between Groups	2.599	3	.866	.773	.510
	Within Groups	260.129	232	1.121		
	Total	262.729	235			
Q6- I completely trust the vocabulary words or phrases recommended by AI tools.	Between Groups	3.582	3	1.194	1.220	.303
	Within Groups	226.994	232	.978		
	Total	230.576	235			
Q7- I often use AI tools or applications for vocabulary learning.	Between Groups	2.721	3	.907	.955	.415
	Within Groups	220.478	232	.950		
	Total	223.199	235			
Q8- I would recommend AI-based vocabulary learning tools to my peers.	Between Groups	2.698	3	.899	.860	.463
	Within Groups	242.738	232	1.046		
	Total	245.436	235			
Q9- I would recommend AI-based vocabulary learning tools to my peers because of their ease of use.	Between Groups	3.298	3	1.099	1.108	.347
	Within Groups	230.244	232	.992		
	Total	233.542	235			
Q10- Using AI tools for vocabulary learning is interesting.	Between Groups	2.532	3	.844	1.046	.373
	Within Groups	187.265	232	.807		
	Total	189.797	235			
Q11- I easily understand the exercises of new vocabulary presented by AI tools.	Between Groups	2.759	3	.920	1.109	.346
	Within Groups	192.372	232	.829		
	Total	195.131	235			
Q12- I want to spend much time and effort using AI tools to learn new vocabulary in English.	Between Groups	6.005	3	2.002	1.993	.116
	Within Groups	232.978	232	1.004		
	Total	238.983	235			
Q13- I will use AI tools frequently in the future to learn new vocabulary in English.	Between Groups	.804	3	.268	.307	.820
	Within Groups	202.738	232	.874		
	Total	203.542	235			
Q14- I use AI tools because I am interested and motivated to learn new vocabulary in English.	Between Groups	.877	3	.292	.299	.826
	Within Groups	226.594	232	.977		
	Total	227.470	235			
Q15- I use AI tools to increase my vocabulary in English.	Between Groups	7.695	3	2.565	3.200	.024
	Within Groups	185.966	232	.802		
	Total	193.661	235			

continued on following page

Table 4. Continued

ANOVA						
		Sum of Squares	**df**	**Mean Square**	**F**	**Sig.**
Q16- I use AI tools to increase my knowledge of English and its culture.	Between Groups	.884	3	.295	.315	.814
	Within Groups	216.997	232	.935		
	Total	217.881	235			
Q17- I think AI tools offer me more options to learn vocabulary in English.	Between Groups	1.863	3	.621	.786	.503
	Within Groups	183.171	232	.790		
	Total	185.034	235			
Q18- I think AI tools enhance my learning of new vocabulary in English.	Between Groups	4.878	3	1.626	1.876	.134
	Within Groups	201.101	232	.867		
	Total	205.979	235			
Q19- I think some answers of AI tools include wrong information.	Between Groups	.541	3	.180	.182	.909
	Within Groups	230.188	232	.992		
	Total	230.729	235			
Q20- I think AI tools will solve the problem of learning new vocabulary in English.	Between Groups	1.812	3	.604	.732	.534
	Within Groups	191.426	232	.825		
	Total	193.237	235			

GENERAL TRENDS ACROSS RESPONSES

Overall, EFL Omani students perceive AI-integrated vocabulary learning as both effective and beneficial, with an average rating of 3.9237 on a 5-point scale. Notably, students who studied all proficiency levels reported the highest mean score (4.0521), indicating a more positive perception compared to those who skipped some levels. Regarding comfort with AI-based tools, the average score was 3.7712, with minor variations across proficiency groups. Additionally, students moderately agree that AI offers advantages over traditional vocabulary learning methods, reflected in a mean score of 3.6864. Despite these benefits, students also acknowledge challenges in using AI tools, with a mean rating of 3.5339, though the level of difficulty varies slightly across different proficiency groups.

Effectiveness Based on Proficiency Levels

The effectiveness of AI-integrated vocabulary learning appears to be influenced by proficiency levels. Students who studied all levels—presumably more proficient in English—consistently rated AI tools higher in terms of effectiveness, ease of use, and motivation. The overall mean for AI-integrated vocabulary learning was 3.6824, with students who completed all levels reporting the highest mean score (3.7568). This was followed by students who skipped levels 1 and 2 (3.7042), whereas the lowest mean was observed among those who skipped only level one (3.5780). This suggests that early-stage learners might struggle more with AI-based vocabulary tools, potentially due to weaker foundational skills.

STATISTICAL SIGNIFICANCE OF THE RELATIONSHIP

The ANOVA results suggest that most responses do not show statistically significant differences across proficiency levels, as most p-values exceed 0.05. This implies that proficiency level does not have a significant impact on students' overall perceptions of AI-based vocabulary learning. However, one exception is Q15, which examines AI's effectiveness in increasing vocabulary knowledge. This questionnaire item yielded a significant result ($p = 0.024$), indicating that students with different proficiency levels perceive AI's role in vocabulary expansion differently.

The findings suggest that students with higher proficiency levels tend to benefit more from AI-integrated vocabulary learning, likely because of their stronger foundational knowledge and ability to interact with AI tools more effectively. In contrast, lower proficiency students may encounter challenges in AI-based learning due to gaps in their foundational vocabulary and difficulties navigating AI tools. Although AI-based vocabulary learning is generally well-received, there is some scepticism regarding its trustworthiness and accuracy, particularly among less proficient students. Despite the observed variations in perceptions across different proficiency groups, statistical analysis indicates that proficiency levels do not significantly influence overall attitudes toward AI-assisted vocabulary learning, except in the area of perceived vocabulary expansion.

Table 5. Statistical analysis related to English proficiency level and AI-integrated vocabulary learning

	N	Mean	Std. Deviation	Std. Error	Lower Bound	Upper Bound
I studied all levels	96	3.7568	.58609	.05982	3.6380	3.8755
I skipped level 1	84	3.5780	.67665	.07383	3.4311	3.7248
I skipped levels 1 and 2	48	3.7042	.74853	.10804	3.4868	3.9215
I skipped levels 1, 2, and 3	8	3.7563	.86579	.30610	3.0324	4.4801
Total	236	3.6824	.66438	.04325	3.5972	3.7676

FURTHER STATISTICAL ANALYSIS OF THE EFFECT OF PROFICIENCY ON AI-INTEGRATED VOCABULARY LEARNING

To further investigate these differences, a Tukey's HSD post-hoc test was conducted. The results indicate that the difference between students who studied all proficiency levels and those who skipped only level one is statistically significant. However, the difference between students who completed all levels and those who skipped multiple levels appears to be less pronounced. This suggests that early-stage learners who skip foundational levels may experience more challenges with AI-based learning compared to those who gradually progress through all levels.

The effect size, measured using Eta squared, was found to be 14.76%, indicating a moderate to large effect. This suggests that proficiency level accounts for approximately 15% of the variance in students' perceptions of AI-integrated vocabulary learning. While other factors may also contribute to students' experiences, proficiency level remains a key determinant in how effectively they engage with AI tools.

The statistical findings reinforce that students with higher English proficiency levels tend to benefit more from AI-based vocabulary learning. They demonstrate greater confidence and ease in using AI tools, likely because of their stronger foundational knowledge. Conversely, lower proficiency students face more difficulties and express lower confidence in AI-assisted learning, possibly due to gaps in their vocabulary and digital learning skills. Given the statistically significant impact of proficiency level, these results highlight the importance of providing additional support to lower-level learners to help them maximize the benefits of AI-integrated vocabulary learning.

Part Two

The respondents (EFL Omani students) were categorized into three groups based on the academic performance related to their marks in the mid-term exam; group one included students who scored less than 10 marks out of 30, group two included those who achieved a score between 11 and 20 marks, whereas group three included students who got more than 20 marks.

Table 6. The effect of academic performance on AI-Integrated vocabulary learning among EFL Omani students

		N	Mean	Std. Deviation	Std. Error	95% Confidence Interval for Mean	
						Lower Bound	Upper Bound
Q1- Using AI for vocabulary learning is effective and beneficial for me.	Less than 10	20	3.7000	.86450	.19331	3.2954	4.1046
	11 to 20	160	3.9375	.96275	.07611	3.7872	4.0878
	21+	56	3.9643	.95278	.12732	3.7091	4.2194
	Total	236	3.9237	.95121	.06192	3.8017	4.0457
Q2- I am completely comfortable with using AI-based tools or apps for vocabulary learning.	Less than 10	20	3.5000	1.14708	.25649	2.9632	4.0368
	11 to 20	160	3.8188	.91715	.07251	3.6755	3.9620
	21+	56	3.7321	1.07011	.14300	3.4456	4.0187
	Total	236	3.7712	.97554	.06350	3.6461	3.8963
Q3- I believe the advantages of using AI for vocabulary learning over the traditional method are: faster learning, more personalized learning, better retention, fun and engaging methods, etc.	Less than 10	20	3.5000	1.10024	.24602	2.9851	4.0149
	11 to 20	160	3.7375	.86503	.06839	3.6024	3.8726
	21+	56	3.6071	.98495	.13162	3.3434	3.8709
	Total	236	3.6864	.91511	.05957	3.5691	3.8038
Q4- I have not encountered any challenges or difficulties when using AI for vocabulary learning.	Less than 10	20	3.1500	1.30888	.29267	2.5374	3.7626
	11 to 20	160	3.5125	.98407	.07780	3.3588	3.6662
	21+	56	3.7321	1.01786	.13602	3.4596	4.0047
	Total	236	3.5339	1.02880	.06697	3.4020	3.6658
Q5- Especially compared to traditional vocabulary learning methods, I consider AI-based vocabulary learning more effective.	Less than 10	20	3.3000	1.26074	.28191	2.7100	3.8900
	11 to 20	160	3.5813	1.00609	.07954	3.4242	3.7383
	21+	56	3.4821	1.12801	.15074	3.1801	3.7842
	Total	236	3.5339	1.05735	.06883	3.3983	3.6695
Q6- I completely trust the vocabulary words or phrases recommended by AI tools.	Less than 10	20	3.1500	1.08942	.24360	2.6401	3.6599
	11 to 20	160	3.5500	.93701	.07408	3.4037	3.6963
	21+	56	3.3036	1.07736	.14397	3.0151	3.5921
	Total	236	3.4576	.99054	.06448	3.3306	3.5847
Q7- I often use AI tools or applications for vocabulary learning.	Less than 10	20	3.6000	1.09545	.24495	3.0873	4.1127
	11 to 20	160	3.6188	.97046	.07672	3.4672	3.7703
	21+	56	3.7857	.94800	.12668	3.5318	4.0396
	Total	236	3.6568	.97457	.06344	3.5318	3.7818
Q8- I would recommend AI-based vocabulary learning tools to my peers.	Less than 10	20	3.7500	1.11803	.25000	3.2267	4.2733
	11 to 20	160	3.6375	1.06687	.08434	3.4709	3.8041
	21+	56	3.5357	.85204	.11386	3.3075	3.7639
	Total	236	3.6229	1.02196	.06652	3.4918	3.7539

continued on following page

Table 6. Continued

		N	Mean	Std. Deviation	Std. Error	95% Confidence Interval for Mean	
						Lower Bound	Upper Bound
Q9- I would recommend AI-based vocabulary learning tools to my peers because of their ease of use.	Less than 10	20	3.4500	.99868	.22331	2.9826	3.9174
	11 to 20	160	3.7688	.99193	.07842	3.6139	3.9236
	21+	56	3.6786	1.01098	.13510	3.4078	3.9493
	Total	236	3.7203	.99689	.06489	3.5925	3.8482
Q10- Using AI tools for vocabulary learning is interesting.	Less than 10	20	3.6500	.87509	.19568	3.2404	4.0596
	11 to 20	160	3.8125	.89855	.07104	3.6722	3.9528
	21+	56	3.8750	.91577	.12238	3.6298	4.1202
	Total	236	3.8136	.89869	.05850	3.6983	3.9288
Q11- I easily understand the exercises of new vocabulary presented by AI tools.	Less than 10	20	3.4500	1.35627	.30327	2.8152	4.0848
	11 to 20	160	3.5750	.87272	.06899	3.4387	3.7113
	21+	56	3.6786	.83355	.11139	3.4553	3.9018
	Total	236	3.5890	.91123	.05932	3.4721	3.7058
Q12- I want to spend much time and effort using AI tools to learn new vocabulary in English.	Less than 10	20	3.8000	.95145	.21275	3.3547	4.2453
	11 to 20	160	3.5125	1.01552	.08028	3.3539	3.6711
	21+	56	3.3929	1.00324	.13406	3.1242	3.6615
	Total	236	3.5085	1.00844	.06564	3.3791	3.6378
Q13- I will use AI tools frequently in the future to learn new vocabulary in English.	Less than 10	20	3.6500	1.03999	.23255	3.1633	4.1367
	11 to 20	160	3.7125	.89995	.07115	3.5720	3.8530
	21+	56	3.7679	.99070	.13239	3.5025	4.0332
	Total	236	3.7203	.93067	.06058	3.6010	3.8397
Q14- I use AI tools because I am interested and motivated to learn new vocabulary in English.	Less than 10	20	3.1500	1.22582	.27410	2.5763	3.7237
	11 to 20	160	3.6563	.89756	.07096	3.5161	3.7964
	21+	56	3.5179	1.09530	.14637	3.2245	3.8112
	Total	236	3.5805	.98385	.06404	3.4543	3.7067
Q15- I use AI tools to increase my vocabulary in English.	Less than 10	20	3.7000	1.12858	.25236	3.1718	4.2282
	11 to 20	160	3.8250	.90108	.07124	3.6843	3.9657
	21+	56	4.0357	.83043	.11097	3.8133	4.2581
	Total	236	3.8644	.90779	.05909	3.7480	3.9808
Q16- I use AI tools to increase my knowledge of English and its culture.	Less than 10	20	3.5500	1.53811	.34393	2.8301	4.2699
	11 to 20	160	3.8188	.89634	.07086	3.6788	3.9587
	21+	56	4.0000	.87386	.11677	3.7660	4.2340
	Total	236	3.8390	.96289	.06268	3.7155	3.9625
Q17- I think AI tools offer me more options to learn vocabulary in English.	Less than 10	20	3.5500	1.19097	.26631	2.9926	4.1074
	11 to 20	160	3.8125	.82559	.06527	3.6836	3.9414
	21+	56	3.8750	.93541	.12500	3.6245	4.1255
	Total	236	3.8051	.88734	.05776	3.6913	3.9189

continued on following page

Table 6. Continued

		N	Mean	Std. Deviation	Std. Error	95% Confidence Interval for Mean	
						Lower Bound	Upper Bound
Q18- I think AI tools enhance my learning of new vocabulary in English.	Less than 10	20	3.6500	1.18210	.26433	3.0968	4.2032
	11 to 20	160	3.7688	.92636	.07323	3.6241	3.9134
	21+	56	3.8750	.87516	.11695	3.6406	4.1094
	Total	236	3.7839	.93622	.06094	3.6638	3.9040
Q19- I think some answers of AI tools include wrong information.	Less than 10	20	3.4500	1.09904	.24575	2.9356	3.9644
	11 to 20	160	3.5438	.97029	.07671	3.3923	3.6952
	21+	56	3.5357	1.02628	.13714	3.2609	3.8106
	Total	236	3.5339	.99087	.06450	3.4068	3.6610
Q20- I think AI tools will solve the problem of learning new vocabulary in English.	Less than 10	20	3.8500	.87509	.19568	3.4404	4.2596
	11 to 20	160	3.6875	.92612	.07322	3.5429	3.8321
	21+	56	3.6964	.87219	.11655	3.4629	3.9300
	Total	236	3.7034	.90680	.05903	3.5871	3.8197

This study examines the relationship between students' academic performance and their perceptions of AI-integrated vocabulary learning. Students were categorized into three groups based on their scores: those scoring less than 10, those scoring between 11 and 20, and those scoring 21 or higher. The findings indicate that academic performance influences how students perceive the effectiveness, comfort, advantages, and challenges associated with AI-based vocabulary learning.

Table 7. Significance of academic performance in learning English vocabulary

		Sum of Squares	df	Mean Square	F	Sig.
Q1- Using AI for vocabulary learning is effective and beneficial for me.	Between Groups	1.124	2	.562	.619	.539
	Within Groups	211.504	233	.908		
	Total	212.627	235			
Q2- I am completely comfortable with using AI-based tools or apps for vocabulary learning.	Between Groups	1.918	2	.959	1.008	.367
	Within Groups	221.726	233	.952		
	Total	223.644	235			
Q3- I believe the advantages of using AI for vocabulary learning over the traditional method are: faster learning, more personalized learning, better retention, fun and engaging methods, etc.	Between Groups	1.464	2	.732	.873	.419
	Within Groups	195.332	233	.838		
	Total	196.797	235			
Q4- I have not encountered any challenges or difficulties when using AI for vocabulary learning.	Between Groups	5.222	2	2.611	2.498	.084
	Within Groups	243.507	233	1.045		
	Total	248.729	235			

continued on following page

Table 7. Continued

		Sum of Squares	df	Mean Square	F	Sig.
Q5- Especially compared to traditional vocabulary learning methods, I consider AI-based vocabulary learning more effective.	Between Groups	1.603	2	.801	.715	.490
	Within Groups	261.126	233	1.121		
	Total	262.729	235			
Q6- I completely trust the vocabulary words or phrases recommended by AI tools.	Between Groups	4.587	2	2.293	2.365	.096
	Within Groups	225.989	233	.970		
	Total	230.576	235			
Q7- I often use AI tools or applications for vocabulary learning.	Between Groups	1.227	2	.613	.644	.526
	Within Groups	221.972	233	.953		
	Total	223.199	235			
Q8- I would recommend AI-based vocabulary learning tools to my peers.	Between Groups	.783	2	.391	.373	.689
	Within Groups	244.654	233	1.050		
	Total	245.436	235			
Q9- I would recommend AI-based vocabulary learning tools to my peers because of their ease of use.	Between Groups	1.934	2	.967	.973	.379
	Within Groups	231.608	233	.994		
	Total	233.542	235			
Q10- Using AI tools for vocabulary learning is interesting.	Between Groups	.747	2	.373	.460	.632
	Within Groups	189.050	233	.811		
	Total	189.797	235			
Q11- I easily understand the exercises of new vocabulary presented by AI tools.	Between Groups	.867	2	.434	.520	.595
	Within Groups	194.264	233	.834		
	Total	195.131	235			
Q12- I want to spend much time and effort using AI tools to learn new vocabulary in English.	Between Groups	2.451	2	1.225	1.207	.301
	Within Groups	236.532	233	1.015		
	Total	238.983	235			
Q13- I will use AI tools frequently in the future to learn new vocabulary in English.	Between Groups	.235	2	.118	.135	.874
	Within Groups	203.307	233	.873		
	Total	203.542	235			
Q14- I use AI tools because I am interested and motivated to learn new vocabulary in English.	Between Groups	4.844	2	2.422	2.535	.081
	Within Groups	222.626	233	.955		
	Total	227.470	235			
Q15- I use AI tools to increase my vocabulary in English.	Between Groups	2.432	2	1.216	1.482	.229
	Within Groups	191.229	233	.821		
	Total	193.661	235			
Q16- I use AI tools to increase my knowledge of English and its culture.	Between Groups	3.188	2	1.594	1.730	.180
	Within Groups	214.694	233	.921		
	Total	217.881	235			

continued on following page

Table 7. Continued

		Sum of Squares	df	Mean Square	F	Sig.
Q17- I think AI tools offer me more options to learn vocabulary in English.	Between Groups	1.584	2	.792	1.006	.367
	Within Groups	183.450	233	.787		
	Total	185.034	235			
Q18- I think AI tools enhance my learning of new vocabulary in English	Between Groups	.860	2	.430	.488	.614
	Within Groups	205.119	233	.880		
	Total	205.979	235			
Q19- I think some answers of AI tools include wrong information.	Between Groups	.156	2	.078	.079	.924
	Within Groups	230.572	233	.990		
	Total	230.729	235			
Q20- I think AI tools will solve the problem of learning new vocabulary in English.	Between Groups	.473	2	.237	.286	.752
	Within Groups	192.764	233	.827		
	Total	193.237	235			

General Trends in AI Perceptions

Overall, students expressed generally positive perceptions of AI-assisted vocabulary learning, with a mean score of 3.6824. However, students with higher academic performance (21+) exhibited slightly more favorable views, with a mean score of 3.7036, compared to those in the lower performance range. Conversely, students scoring less than 10 had the lowest mean score (3.5275), suggesting that lower-performing students may struggle more with AI-based tools or perceive them as less beneficial.

Effectiveness of AI Vocabulary Learning

Students who scored 21 or higher rated AI-integrated learning as the most effective (mean = 3.9643), whereas those with the lowest academic performance had the lowest effectiveness rating (mean = 3.7000). This suggests that higher-achieving students may find AI tools more useful and engaging in expanding their vocabulary.

Comfort in Using AI Tools

Higher-scoring students (11–20 and 21+) reported greater comfort in using AI tools, with mean scores of 3.8188 and 3.7321, respectively. In contrast, students with lower scores (less than 10) expressed lower comfort levels (mean = 3.5000), indicating that they may require additional support in navigating AI-based learning platforms.

Perceived Advantages Over Traditional Methods

Interestingly, students in the mid-range performance category (11–20) reported the highest perceived advantages of AI over traditional learning methods (mean = 3.7375). Lower-performing students (less than 10) were less convinced of AI's superiority (mean = 3.5000), suggesting that they may struggle to recognize or utilize AI's potential benefits effectively.

Challenges with AI Learning

Lower-scoring students reported the most difficulties in using AI tools, with a mean score of 3.1500, whereas higher-performing students (21+) found AI easier to use (mean = 3.7321). This indicates that students with stronger academic abilities may adapt more quickly to AI-based learning environments, whereas struggling students may require more structured guidance and support.

Trust in AI Suggestions

Trust in AI-generated vocabulary suggestions varied among performance groups. Students scoring between 11 and 20 reported the highest trust levels (mean = 3.5500), whereas the lowest-performing students exhibited lower trust (mean = 3.1500). This suggests that academically weaker students may be more sceptical of AI recommendations or struggle to evaluate their accuracy.

Future Use and Motivation

Higher-performing students demonstrated greater motivation and willingness to continue using AI-based vocabulary learning tools. The lowest-performing students reported lower motivation (mean = 3.1500 in Q14), suggesting that they may require additional encouragement and structured learning approaches to engage effectively with AI resources.

Statistical Significance (ANOVA Results)

ANOVA tests for most questions yielded p-values > 0.05, meaning that academic performance does not significantly impact AI-integrated vocabulary learning.

DISCUSSION

This study examined the impact of AI-integrated vocabulary learning on Omani EFL students, particularly in relation to their academic performance and English proficiency. The findings indicate that students generally perceive AI tools as beneficial for vocabulary learning and acquisition, with higher proficiency learners and academically stronger students demonstrating greater ease of use, trust, and motivation in engaging with AI-driven learning. Those with lower proficiency and weaker academic performance reported encountering more challenges, including difficulties in navigating AI tools and scepticism about AI-generated vocabulary recommendations. Despite these trends, statistical analysis showed no significant effect of academic performance on AI-based vocabulary learning, suggesting that while AI tools are generally helpful, their effectiveness does not solely depend on a student's prior academic achievement. These findings highlight the potential of AI in language learning while underscoring the need for tailored strategies to support learners at different proficiency levels.

The results of this study align with previous research emphasizing the advantages of technology-enhanced language learning. For instance, a prior study by Wang, Teng, and Chen (2015) illustrated that mobile applications significantly improve student engagement in learning English. Similarly, research by Alharbi and Khalil (2023) reported that 80.6% of students had a positive attitude toward AI-based vocabulary learning, comparable to the findings in this study, where students generally acknowledged AI's effectiveness. However, some previous research has reported mixed findings regarding AI tools, particularly concerning their impact on different language skills. For example, Karataş et al. (2024) found that AI applications positively influenced writing skills but had limited effects on speaking and grammar acquisition. This study extends these findings by specifically examining vocabulary learning and identifying proficiency-related variations in AI tool adoption. Unlike studies that focused solely on engagement and motivation, the current study provides a more nuanced analysis of how different levels of academic performance and English proficiency shape students' experiences with AI-enhanced vocabulary learning.

The contribution of this study lies in its exploration of AI-integrated vocabulary learning within the specific context of EFL Omani students. By identifying the challenges faced by lower-proficiency students and highlighting the positive reception among higher-achieving learners, this study provides valuable insights for educators and policymakers seeking to implement AI-based learning tools more effectively. The findings suggest the need for structured AI training, personalized AI-assisted learning pathways, and gamification strategies to enhance vocabulary acquisition for all learners, regardless of proficiency level. Furthermore, the study's findings offer a more comprehensive understanding of students' attitudes toward AI-assisted learning, making it a useful reference for future studies aiming to optimize AI-driven educational interventions. Given the growing integration of AI in education, this study contributes to the broader discussion on technology-enhanced learning and provides a foundation for further investigations into AI's long-term impact on language acquisition.

CONCLUSIONS

This study examined the impact of AI-integrated vocabulary learning on Omani EFL students, focusing on the role of academic performance and English proficiency in shaping students' experiences with AI tools. The findings indicate that while students generally perceive AI tools as beneficial for vocabulary learning and acquisition, those with higher proficiency and stronger academic performance demonstrate greater trust, ease of use, and motivation. Conversely, lower-proficiency students and those with weaker academic backgrounds report more challenges in navigating AI tools and exhibit lower trust in AI-generated vocabulary recommendations.

The study's most significant findings reveal that proficiency level is a more influential factor than academic performance in determining students' engagement with AI-based vocabulary learning. While higher-proficiency students benefit more from AI integration, statistical analysis showed no significant impact of academic performance on AI-assisted vocabulary learning and acquisition. This suggests that AI tools, while widely appreciated, do not necessarily favor academically stronger students over weaker ones, making them accessible to learners at different levels.

Pedagogically, the findings highlight the importance of structured AI training and tailored learning approaches to support students with varying proficiency levels. Incorporating gamification, adaptive AI-based feedback, and interactive learning strategies can enhance vocabulary acquisition and engagement, particularly for lower-proficiency learners. Educators should also integrate AI tools into curriculum design to ensure a balanced approach that fosters digital literacy and independent learning skills.

However, the study has certain limitations. First, it relies on self-reported data, which may be subject to response bias. Additionally, the study is confined to a single institution in Oman, limiting the generalizability of its findings to broader EFL contexts. The study also focuses primarily on vocabulary learning, without examining AI's impact on other language skills, such as speaking, writing, or grammar learning and acquisition.

Future research should explore the long-term effects of AI-assisted vocabulary learning, incorporating longitudinal studies to assess retention and practical language application. Additionally, further investigations could examine the effectiveness of AI tools in enhancing other language skills and explore the role of different AI-powered learning strategies. Expanding research to diverse educational settings and including qualitative insights from teachers and learners can provide a more holistic understanding of AI's role in EFL education.

REFERENCES

Al-khresheh, M. H. (2024). Bridging technology and pedagogy from a global lens: Teachers' perspectives on integrating ChatGPT in English language teaching. *Computers and Education: Artificial Intelligence*, *6*(June), 1–12. DOI: 10.1016/j.caeai.2024.100218

Aldawsari, H. A. (2024). Evaluating Translation Tools: Google Translate, Bing Translator, and Bing AI on Arabic Colloquialisms. *Arab World English Journal (AWEJ)* Special Issue on ChatGPT (April, 2024) 237-251.DOI: https://dx.doi.org/ DOI: 10.24093/awej/ChatGPT.16

Alharbi, K., & Khalil, L. (2023). Artificial Intelligence (AI) In ESL Vocabulary Learning: An Exploratory Study On Students And Teachers' Perspectives. *Migration Letters : An International Journal of Migration Studies*, *20*(S12), 1030–1045.

Alsadoon, R. (2021). Chatting with AI Bot: Vocabulary learning assistant for Saudi EFL learners. *English Language Teaching*, *14*(6), 135–157. DOI: 10.5539/elt.v14n6p135

Alsahafi, M. (2023). The relationship between depth of academic English vocabulary knowledge and academic success of second language university students. *SAGE Open*, *13*(1), 1–9. DOI: 10.1177/21582440231153342

Alwahoub, H. M., Azmi, M. N. L., & Jomaa, N. J. (2020). Teachers' and Students' Perceptions of E-Learning Integration in the Primary Schools of Saudi Arabia. *International Journal of Advanced Research in Education and Society*, *2*(1), 116–126.

Amin, M. Y. M. (2023). AI and Chat GPT in Language Teaching: Enhancing EFL Classroom Support and Transforming Assessment Techniques. *International Journal of Higher Education Pedagogies*, *4*(4), 1–15. DOI: 10.33422/ijhep.v4i4.554

Aprizal, A. D., & Wachyudi, K. (2024). The Effectiveness of Memrise as a Vocabulary Learning Tool. *Jurnal Ilmiah Wahana Pendidikan*, *10*(4), 8–17.

Attamimi, R. A. (2025). AI and English Language Education: A New Era in the Arab World. In Jomaa, N. (Ed.), *Using AI Tools in Text Analysis, Simplification, Classification, and Synthesis* (pp. 113–130). IGI Global Scientific Publishing., DOI: 10.4018/979-8-3693-9511-0.ch004

Cloate, R. (2016). The relationship between international students' English test scores and their academic achievements. *Journal of pedagogic development*, *6*(2), 3-8.

Daller, M. H., & Phelan, D. (2013). Predicting international student study success. *Applied Linguistics Review*, *4*(1), 173–193. DOI: 10.1515/applirev-2013-0008

Elder, C., & Von Randow, J. (2008). Exploring the utility of a web-based English language screening tool. *Language Assessment Quarterly*, *5*(3), 173–194. DOI: 10.1080/15434300802229334

Eragamreddy, N. (2025). AI in ELT: ChatGPT's Role in English Language Teaching and Learning. In Jomaa, N. (Ed.), *Using AI Tools in Text Analysis, Simplification, Classification, and Synthesis* (pp. 159–196). IGI Global., DOI: 10.4018/979-8-3693-9511-0.ch006

Fajaruddin, S., Retnawati, H., Setiawan, C., Apino, E., Arlinwibowo, J., & Rachman, D. (2024). Technology's impact on language learning: Meta-analysis on variables and effectiveness. [EduLearn]. *Journal of Education and Learning*, *18*(2), 512–525.

Harrington, M., & Roche, T. (2014). Word recognition skill and academic success across disciplines in an ELF university setting. *Papers in Language Testing and Assessment*, *3*(2), 76–99. DOI: 10.58379/QPEW8104

Hasan, M. K., Fakih, A. H., & Seraj, P. M. I. (2022). The effect of technology-assisted language programme on vocabulary learning among EFL students at the tertiary level. *Heliyon*, *8*(8), 1–6. DOI: 10.1016/j.heliyon.2022.e10313 PMID: 36051275

Hendrawaty, N., Yuliati, Y., & Haryanti, R. P. (2024). EFL Students' Preferences on Vocabulary Learning. *Scope: Journal of English Language Teaching*, *8*(2), 541–550. DOI: 10.30998/scope.v8i2.21876

Jomaa, N., Attamimi, R., & Al Mahri, M. (2024). Utilising Artificial Intelligence (AI) in Vocabulary Learning by EFL Omani Students: The Effect of Age, Gender, and Level of Study. *Forum for Linguistic Studies*, *6*(5), 171–186. DOI: 10.30564/fls.v6i5.6968

Jomaa, N., Attamimi, R., & Al Mahri, M. (2025). The Use of Artificial Intelligence (AI) in Teaching English Vocabulary in Oman: Perspectives, Teaching Practices, and Challenges. *World Journal of English Language*, *15*(3), 1–13. DOI: 10.5430/wjel.v15n3p1

Jomaa, N., Attamimi, R., & Alghafri, K. (2025). Vocabulary Learning Strategies Utilised by EFL Omani Students in Oman: The Effect of Age, Gender, and Levels of Study. *Forum for Linguistic Studies*, *7*(2), 967–987. DOI: 10.30564/fls.v7i2.8450

Jomaa, N. J. (2025). Corrective Feedback of AI Tools in Writing and Translation. In Jomaa, N. (Ed.), *Using AI Tools in Text Analysis, Simplification, Classification, and Synthesis* (pp. 293–318). IGI Global Scientific Publishing., DOI: 10.4018/979-8-3693-9511-0.ch010

Jomaa, N. J., & Kamal, M. N. (2023). Perspectives of students and teachers towards developing speaking skills by using technology among EFL Iraqi students. In *Integrating TPACK and CALL in English Language Teaching* (pp. 153–173). IGI Global., DOI: 10.4018/978-1-6684-8546-0.ch007

Karataş, F., Abedi, F. Y., Gunyel, F. O., Karadeniz, D., & Kuzgun, Y. (2024). Incorporating AI in foreign language education: An investigation into ChatGPT's effect on foreign language learners. *Education and Information Technologies, 29*(15), 1–24. DOI: 10.1007/s10639-024-12574-6

Keerthiwansha, N. W. B. S. (2018). Artificial intelligence education (AIEd) in English as a second language (ESL) classroom in Sri Lanka. *Artificial Intelligence, 6*(1), 31–36.

Kheder, K. (2025). Using Artificial Intelligence in Learning Vocabulary by EFL Undergraduate Syrian Students. In Jomaa, N. (Ed.), *Using AI Tools in Text Analysis, Simplification, Classification, and Synthesis* (pp. 131–158). IGI Global Scientific Publishing., DOI: 10.4018/979-8-3693-9511-0.ch005

Lafleur, L. (2024). The effects of gamified daily awards on digital vocabulary flashcard learning: A case study. *Technology in Language Teaching & Learning, 6*(2), 1–20. DOI: 10.29140/tltl.v6n2.1195

Lim, Ch. P., & Chai, Ch. S. (2004). An activity-theoretical approach to research of ICT integration in Singapore schools: Orienting activities and learner autonomy. *Computers & Education, 43*(3), 215–236. DOI: 10.1016/j.compedu.2003.10.005

Lu, M. (2008). Effectiveness of vocabulary learning via mobile phone. *Journal of Computer Assisted Learning, 24*(6), 515–525. DOI: 10.1111/j.1365-2729.2008.00289.x

Mooij, T. (2007). Design of educational and ICT conditions to integrate differences in learning: Contextual learning theory and a first transformation step in early education. *Computers in Human Behavior, 23*(3), 1499–1530. DOI: 10.1016/j.chb.2005.07.004

Moxon, S. (2024). Computer-Assisted Vocabulary Learning for Thai Deaf Students: A Case Study of Sot Suksa School for the Deaf. *Asia Social Issues, 17*(1), 1–21.

Oktadela, R., Elida, Y., & Ismail, S. (2023). Improving English Vocabulary through Artificial Intelligence (AI) Chatbot Application. *Journal of English Language and Education, 8*(2), 63–67.

Özyildirim, İ., & Jomaa, N. J. (2023). Teaching and learning English online: The perspectives of English teachers and students at Karabuk University in Turkey. In *Shaping the Future of Online Learning: Education in the Metaverse* (pp. 220–249). IGI Global., DOI: 10.4018/978-1-6684-6513-4.ch012

Qasem, F., Ghaleb, M., Mahdi, H. S., Al Khateeb, A., & Al Fadda, H. (2023). Dialog chatbot as an interactive online tool in enhancing ESP vocabulary learning. *Saudi Journal of Language Studies, 3*(2), 76–86. DOI: 10.1108/SJLS-10-2022-0072

Rao, P. S. (2019). The Impact of Technological Innovations on English Language Teaching in The Modern Era. *International Journal of Engineering Research-Online, 7*(6), 58–67.

Rouabhia, R. (2025). Ethical Implications of AI: Examining Bias and Fairness in AI-Powered Education. In Jomaa, N. (Ed.), *Using AI Tools in Text Analysis, Simplification, Classification, and Synthesis* (pp. 409–436). IGI Global Scientific Publishing., DOI: 10.4018/979-8-3693-9511-0.ch014

Rusmiyanto, R., Huriati, N., Fitriani, N., Tyas, N. K., Rofi'i, A., & Sari, M. N. (2023). The role of artificial intelligence (AI) in developing English language learner's communication skills. *Journal of Education, 6*(1), 750–757.

Sumakul, D. T. Y. G., Hamied, F. A., & Sukyadi, D. (2022) 'Students' Perceptions of the Use of AI in a Writing Class:', in. 67th TEFLIN International Virtual Conference & the 9th ICOELT 2021 (TEFLIN ICOELT 2021), Padang, Indonesia. Available at: DOI: 10.2991/assehr.k.220201.009

Syahrin, S. & Akmal, N. (2024). Navigating the Artificial Intelligence Frontier: Perceptions of Instructors, Students, and Administrative Staff on the Role of Artificial Intelligence in Education in the Sultanate of Oman. *Arab World English Journal (AWEJ) Special Issue on ChatGPT*, (April, 2024) 73-89. DOI: DOI: 10.24093/awej/ChatGPT.4

Wang, B. T., Teng, C. W., & Chen, H. T. (2015). Using iPad to facilitate English vocabulary learning. *International Journal of Information and Education Technology (IJIET), 5*(2), 100–104. DOI: 10.7763/IJIET.2015.V5.484

Wang, Y., Liu, M., & Zhou, Z. (2024). Enhancing ESP Vocabulary Learning through ChatGPT: A Case Study. In J. Cohen & G. Solano (Eds.), *Proceedings of Society for Information Technology & Teacher Education International Conference* (pp. 907-913). Las Vegas, Nevada, United States: Association for the Advancement of Computing in Education (AACE). Retrieved May 29, 2024 from https://www.learntechlib.org/p/224061

Yu, A., & Trainin, G. (2022). A meta-analysis examining technology-assisted L2 vocabulary learning. *ReCALL, 34*(2), 235–252. DOI: 10.1017/S0958344021000239

ADDITIONAL READING

Al Matari, A. S., Mukit, A., Al Saadi, S., Balushi, W. A., & Al-Abri, J. S. (2023). Artificial intelligence and the future of teaching in higher education at A‘‘Sharqiyah University (ASU) in Oman. *Proceeding International Pelita Bangsa, 1*(01), 182–200.

Alhalangy, A., & AbdAlgane, M. (2023). Exploring the impact of AI on the EFL context: A case study of Saudi universities. *Journal of Intercultural Communication, 23*(2), 41–49. DOI: 10.36923/jicc.v23i2.125

Creswell, J. W. (2012). *Educational research: planning, conducting and evaluating quantitative and qualitative research* (4th ed.). Pearson Education.

Liu, P.-L., & Chen, C.-J. (2023). Using an AI-Based Object Detection Translation Application for English Vocabulary Learning. *Journal of Educational Technology & Society, 26*(3), 5–20. DOI: 10.30191/ETS.202307

Ma, Q., & Chiu, M. M. (2024). Self-regulated and collaborative personalised vocabulary learning approach in MALL. *Language Learning & Technology, 28*(1), 1–28.

Roschelle, J., Sharples, M., & Chan, T. W. (2005). Introduction to the special issue on wireless and mobile technologies in education. *Journal of Computer Assisted Learning, 21*(3), 159–161. DOI: 10.1111/j.1365-2729.2005.00123.x

KEY TERMS AND DEFINITIONS

Artificial Intelligence (AI): Computer systems designed to perform tasks that typically require human intelligence, such as understanding language, recognizing patterns, and providing feedback.

AI Tools: Software applications powered by artificial intelligence, used in educational settings to support language learning, such as chatbots, writing assistants, and translation tools.

ChatGPT: A conversational AI model developed by OpenAI that can generate human-like responses in real time. It is used to practice writing, expand vocabulary, and engage in interactive language tasks.

Chatbots: AI-powered virtual assistants that simulate conversation with users. In language learning, they offer practice opportunities and enhance vocabulary through interaction.

Adaptive Feedback: Real-time, personalized responses provided by AI tools based on a learner's input, helping them correct errors and improve language skills instantly.

AI-Assisted Learning: An educational approach that integrates AI technologies to support and enhance the teaching and learning process.

Personalized Learning: A method where AI tools adjust content and feedback based on individual learner needs, proficiency levels, and progress.

Gamification: The use of game elements (points, badges, leaderboards) in AI apps to make vocabulary learning more engaging and motivating.

AI-Based Language Apps: Mobile or desktop applications using AI to help users acquire a language through features like voice recognition, vocabulary games, and real-time translation.

Natural Language Processing (NLP): A field of AI focused on enabling machines to understand, interpret, and generate human language—essential for tools like ChatGPT and translation apps.

AI-Driven Translation Tools: Applications using AI to provide real-time translations and definitions, commonly used for vocabulary building and comprehension support.

Chapter 2
Using AI for Curriculum Development and Content Generation: Enhancing Diversity, Inclusion, and Adaptability in Language Education

Ridha Rouabhia
https://orcid.org/0000-0003-1930-4007
University Yahia Fares of Medea, Algeria

ABSTRACT

This chapter discusses the role of artificial intelligence in transforming curriculum development and content creation for language education. In fact, with institutions of learning under increased pressure to ensure that learners have more personalized, inclusive, and culturally sensitive learning experiences, AI emerges as a powerful tool in addressing such demands. The chapter examines how AI technologies enable adaptive learning pathways, in-class real-time feedback systems, and support for diverse learning styles using multimodal content delivery. It is intended to further examine such implementation of the use of AI-driven solutions for developing culturally responsive materials while maintaining the highest pedagogical standards. Discussions will involve key areas: personalization strategies, frameworks for the inclusivity of cultures, accommodation in terms of learning styles, and analytics for continuous improvement in real time.

DOI: 10.4018/979-8-3693-9606-3.ch002

1. INTRODUCTION

Contextual Background

The modern world that people live in today is characterized by globalization and the internet. This indicates that the need to speak more than one language has increased significantly. For instance, without a language barrier, one can look at the world in different ways, communicate with people from other cultures, and seek careers at the international level. However, conventional language instruction cannot address these issues. Most syllabuses implement common approaches that may not suit heterogeneous learners' differences due to their age, interest, or even level of learning and make language teaching in practice far from actual learners' lives.

The implementation of advanced technologies in teaching practices, particularly artificial intelligence (AI), is emerging as a revolutionary solution. Over the past two decades, these technologies have shifted from simple tools for process automation to systems that can create and adapt content in real-time. This transition is even more significant in language education, as learners can now engage with content embedded in and even created by technology. For reasons of effectiveness, this content is usually produced on a mass scale, contrary to effective practices. In most cases, the delivery mechanisms adopted for digital content tend to be AI solutions that efficiently carry out complex deliveries focused on the user's specific characteristics. The educational application of AI technologies begins with teaching people how to learn languages. However, this is not the ultimate goal. It is possible to develop learning materials that respect and represent the cultures of learners so that they can learn about their own and others' cultures as part of the educational process. This, in turn, helps create a classroom where the inclusion of diverse and prepared minds is embraced, fostering respect, understanding, and appreciation for differences and relationships beyond language. Learners can practice their language skills using technology in their classrooms. Busuu, an online language-learning platform, enables users to interact with native speakers and other learners in more than 90 countries across the globe. Learners who complete all levels of the program earn certificates issued by awarding institutions. Thus, technology can accomplish a great deal; however, it has certain limitations.

Purpose of the Chapter

The following chapter explores how AI catalyses the development of a language curriculum that is dynamic, adaptable and focused on personalisation while being heedful of cultural diversity. This chapter will demonstrate how AI tools can help educators develop curriculum content that reflects the rich cultural diversity around the globe, including inclusive practices that address different learning styles. Meanwhile, the chapter will elaborate on AI as a strong ally in contemporary educational processes, as there are no longer confines to what teachers can do or achieve, and because language education can be made to resonate on many levels with learners.

This chapter focuses on the following aspects:

1. Personalisation: How AI makes it possible to compose adaptive content for the precisely fitted needs of every individual learner, depending on their progress and allowing for multiple learning paths.
2. Diversity and Cultural Inclusivity: How can AI support the development of diverse content concerning linguistically and culturally relevant contexts that make language learning sensitive and inclusive?
3. Support for Varied Learning Styles: How does AI accommodate different learning preferences by creating all types of content—visual, auditory, and interactive—so that no learner is left behind in understanding the concepts?
4. Real-Time Feedback and Continuous Improvement: In what ways does AI provide direct feedback, steadily track learner performance, and revise the curriculum promptly based on data-driven insights?

This chapter describes how AI can be used as a tool to develop culturally sensitive, inclusive, and responsive language curricula that meet the needs of diverse learners today.

Thesis Statement

AI has the potential to ensure further adaptability of materials created at a multi-subjective level of language and culture, which is a variance that respects both cultural diversity and meets the needs of different learning styles. Artificial intelligence content creation, real-time adaptation, and building from diverse cultural perspectives are several ways in which AI can support language education that is both personalised and inclusive. By embedding AI in curriculum development, educators create an environment in which, besides language, learners develop an appreciation for different cultures and learning approaches for effective communication in a multicultural world.

2. THE ROLE OF AI IN CURRICULUM DEVELOPMENT

Overview of AI Tools in Education

AI technologies, such as adaptive learning platforms, natural language processing, and machine learning, have become crucial in educational settings for improving personalised learning experiences and access to education. Adaptive learning platforms apply machine learning to offer customised content via dynamic responses to learner performance. Technology is deployed to increase learner participation and consequently improve academic results. For example, tools such as Realizeit and Knewton use real-time analytics and adapt instructional materials to learner needs with measurable performance gains. Natural language processing (NLP) technologies hold the promise of disrupting education by automating grading feedback and interactions with learners via virtual teaching assistants (VTAs) that help create scalable and responsive learning environments (Sajja et al., 2024). Cognitive overload in higher education can be reduced with the help of AI-powered assistants, as their quiz generation and facilitation of knowledge assessments for just-in-time learning support are likely to have a significant impact on learner satisfaction and engagement (Shum & Ferguson, 2012). These tools simplify the learning processes and enhance educator time to better focus on learners' needs and strategic decision-making. Machine learning algorithms further support this by analysing complex datasets to predict and address the learning needs of learners through early intervention if they struggle academically (Hwang & Chen, 2023). AI-driven advancements are improving adaptive learning capabilities while unlocking new and efficient ways of delivering high-quality education across diverse learning environments.

Benefits of AI Integration in Curriculum Design.

The integration of artificial intelligence in curriculum development is beneficial in many ways, including the aspects of flexibility, content creation, and operational efficiency. The above constructs the notion of environments that are responsive to real-time analysis of activities by teachers improving student engagement and learning outcomes (Chen et al., 2020). This is what makes it possible to ensure that the educational materials will suit the different learning paces and needs of the students, thus supporting inclusive education. In addition, AI also aids in personalized content development by helping in the creation of instructional materials based on individual students. For instance, intelligent tutoring systems give students personalized, appropriate feedback and practice tutoring them about knowledge already learned (Luckin et al., 2016). Apart from this, curriculum design also becomes more efficient and cost-effective with the help of AI because routine tasks like assessment, lesson planning, and educational resource compilation are performed by machines instead of humans, which is time-consuming, improving the opportunities for active instruction which is more useful (Zawacki-Richter et al, 2019). Such automated systems, where administrative tasks are decreased, assist in streamlining educational activities, resulting in increased productivity and job satisfaction for the teachers. As a result of the integration of AI into educational technology, it is possible to create a curriculum for educational institutions that will be more dynamic, personalized and effective, contributing to a greater degree to the educational process.

3. PERSONALIZED AND ADAPTIVE CONTENT CREATION

AI enables personalised education by significantly improving the ability to analyse data on individual learning and adapt content to different proficiency levels, interests, and needs. Advanced algorithms used in AI platforms can track and interpret all data concerning learner performance, engagement, and learning patterns. This creates rich learner profiles that inform the real-time adjustment of instructional materials to learners' individual pace and competency levels (Zawacki-Richter et al., 2019). Such adaptive learning systems ensure that learners always confront challenges commensurate with their current abilities, which would certainly increase their level of engagement and deepen their learning processes (Woolf et al., 2013). In addition, at one refinement level, AI analysis reaches the sophisticated level, and the interests of learners can be identified by the assessment of interactions with various forms of content.

Indeed, the insight one may gain from this leads to personalized learning experiences that sustain motivation and foster deep cognitive processing (Luckin et al., 2016). Adaptive platforms can also provide differentiated feedback and additional resources for individual needs, thus providing scope for more learner-centred learning approaches (Holmes et al., 2019). This helps to create an inclusive environment wherein learning with the help of these AI-driven strategies is channeled to best meet the needs and achieve the ultimate goals of each learner.

Examples of Adaptive Content Generation

AI-powered platforms enable this through the adaptive generation of content for customized exercises, vocabulary lists, and reading materials that reinforce personalized learning. For instance, ALEKS assessment and LEARNING in Knowledge Spaces by McGraw Hill were designed to continuously assess learner knowledge in real-time and then offer customized exercises directly at the identified learning gaps. ALEKS generates problem sets that dynamically change in complexity and content through a constant assessment of learners' responses to nurture their mastery of subjects at an individualized pace (Falmagne et al., 2013).

Similarly, Duolingo uses AI to develop unique ways of learning languages. For example, it develops vocabulary lists and reading exercises, taking into account user engagement, historical results, and the problematic areas of the learners so that new content is based on what was previously mastered (Loewen et al., 2020). This ever-evolving mode of refreshing language content ensures that the learner remains focused on the activity and helps with language retention. Another platform associated with AI, Smart Sparrow, is celebrated for its ability to create complex learning environments. It encourages instructors to construct courses whereby the presence or absence of content depends on how the learners answer at that moment. This implies that when a learner does not understand one area, the system can provide more material or change the activities for that particular individual.

Such services show a possible way in which content creation may be automated as an educational tool, enabling the design of learning experiences for specific parameters and profiles of learners and averting distinct learning obligations. This strategy benefits learners and helps teachers as well – significant productive time is currently spent on lower-level and repetitive exercises.

Case Study

Duolingo is the perfect example of an educational platform that utilizes AI, which optimizes content based on a user's interaction history and feedback, especially when it comes to personalization of learning. The platform maintains an AI system that facilitates evaluating users' learning styles and training habits, mistakes, response time to questions, and overall improvement within a specified period. Data collected in this way are used to modify the lessons that follow in such a way that no learner is practising what they do not need to practice (Loewen et al., 2020). For example, if one does not seem to master a certain grammatical structure or type of vocabulary too well, the machine powered with intelligence from Duolingo would arrange such tasks more often and in many different situations. This aids learners in understanding their skills more comprehensively and encourages them to retain them for a longer period.

One more very notable feature of Duolingo is spaced repetition, a technique used to schedule the review of words and phrases based on the learner's memory retention. Hence, if a user is familiar with a word, the system delays its reappearance until the user has other new content to learn. For instance, if a user keeps forgetting a specific term, the AI ensures that the term is repeatedly reinforced until mastery is achieved. This personalized approach yields a better retention curve and avoids the rapid forgetting that is observed in traditional learning.

Duolingo also makes the lessons relevant for different learning paces by adjusting the difficulty of the tasks based on real-time data of performance. This makes learning seem more within reach and challenging without overwhelming users. Feedback mechanisms are a strong part of the platform, where immediate adaptive feedback allows users to correct mistakes and overcome learning obstacles. This improves the effectiveness of the learning process because users understand why an answer is incorrect and how to improve it.

Continuous adaptation goes beyond a simple review of hard topics to the integration of new relevant themes that match the interests of users. For users who enjoy considerable immersion in this course, Duolingo's AI would adapt by adding more contextual sentences and dialogues rather than isolated vocabulary drills. Such engagement would make the process even more interactive and enjoyable, thus enhancing user motivation and learning efficacy (Munday, 2016).

Duolingo's use of AI exemplifies how education technology can provide an individualized learning track that evolves with the learner. This adaptive model of content generation and feedback also considers diversity in learners' needs and levels while optimizing learning efficiency. Its success underlines the broader potential of AI in education; similar adaptive mechanisms may be applied in other educational fields and tools to support lifelong learning.

4. FOSTERING DIVERSITY AND INCLUSION IN CONTENT

Cultural Sensitivity and Representation

Coupled with the capability for multilingual and multicultural datasets, AI will be at the forefront of developing educational content imbued with cultural sensitivity and global representation. AI will use machine learning algorithms, trained on vast and various sources of data, to pinpoint and then integrate culturally specific knowledge, traditions, and languages into learning materials. This will ensure that content is not only linguistically appropriate but also resonates with the values and norms of different cultural groups; hence, it is inclusive (Floridi & Cowls, 2019). For instance, NLP technologies have their grounding in multilingual datasets that support AI systems in developing educational materials in many different languages and dialects. This will widen accessibility and support learners from non-dominant linguistic backgrounds, hence fostering a sense of belonging and engagement.

AI can also aggregate culturally relevant examples and scenarios in educational content that reflect the global diversity of the users. This will have special importance with subjects like Social Studies, Literature, and History, where the representation of multiple points of cultural view deepens the learners' experience with the subject matter and broadens their notion of perspective. With diverse cultures narrating their version of stories about historical contexts and examples, AI-generated content naturally avoids the chance of being biased or one-sided.

AI can detect and mitigate cultural biases through the active use of fairness algorithms and ethical guidelines. Such systems automatically flag words or misrepresentations that could be problematic, suggesting revisions by developers in the interest of inclusion (Bender et al., 2015). The dynamic nature of AI allows it to update continuously in light of evolving cultural norms and understanding, thus ensuring the continuously appropriate sensitivity of educational materials.

In practice, culturally sensitive language models that keep in mind context and cultural idioms are translated by platforms such as Google's AI translation services so that translations and adaptations are meaningful and appropriate. That is how AI's support for multilingual data bears on simple translation, but nuanced, culturally aware representation enables rich global educational content.

Multilingual Content Development

AI has revolutionized the development of multilingual educational materials; therefore, institutions are now in a better position to deal with diverse linguistic backgrounds. Advanced neural networks have made machine translation tools, such as Google Translate and DeepL, relatively more accurate for a wide range of educational content across multiple languages (Guerberof-Arenas & Moorkens, 2023). These intelligent technologies make the translation of content much easier because they automatically convert texts, audio, and videos into many other languages, thus saving the resources and effort required to enable manual translation. This technology democratizes information and allows learners to learn from materials in their preferred language, which may improve their comprehension and retention.

Moreover, NLP innovations make the personalisation of learning experiences possible, where the AI customises content to the linguistic and cultural contexts of the learner in relevance and access. AI further supports the creation of multilingual content that keeps its original educational intention intact and reduces the chances of misinterpretation, which is so common in traditional approaches to translation (Zou et al., 2022). This itself speaks to bridging language gaps, making AI a very valuable tool in fostering equity and inclusiveness within the many globalised classrooms, as educators can meet the unique needs of non-native-speaking learners better. Since AI tools are never in stasis, it is assumed that they would further refine multilingual content quality and ease, thereby making the educational environment inclusive for one and all.

Challenges and Solutions in Ensuring Cultural Accuracy

When it comes to materials focusing on multilingual content creation, inclusivity is of utmost importance. One aspect that should not be overlooked is attention to cultural sensitivities as this works in producing educational resources that are respectful to all religions and races. This is, however, easier said than done because of the stereotyping and biases associated with AI. Most AI language models today are trained on big internet sources and different modes of communication. Often, those sources reside in stereotypical viewpoints towards particular societies and cultural patterns. These models can inadvertently mirror and accentuate these biases, resulting in the reinforcement of gender, racial, and cultural stereotypes.

In response to these challenges, AI researchers have devised various fairness-sensitive algorithms and training methods to mitigate biases, including diversifying training data, using content filtering techniques to prevent discriminatory language from being produced and implemented, etc. Some of the methods include counterfactual data augmentation, whereby the training dataset is supplemented with images of people of different genders and ethnicities engaged in the same activity, thereby avoiding biased output (Lu et al., 2020). Furthermore, explainable AI (XAI) frameworks demonstrate to the developers and users the internal workings of algorithms and the presence of certain cultural biases in the models, which enables the refinement of algorithms in a more culturally inclusive manner (Gade et al., 2021). Hence, the importance of transparency in AI systems regarding their decision-making processes is particularly crucial for educators and content developers who wish to avoid creating content that is technically accurate but lacks cultural sensitivity.

Other developing areas include culturally adaptive algorithms for AI that interpret and apply regional dialects, idiomatic expressions, and culturally specific references in such a way as to preserve local context and meaning. These adaptive algorithms are critical in educational considerations where direct translations usually miss deeper cultural connotations that may affect comprehension. For example, AI models are trained on regional varieties of languages, such as Latin American versus Iberian Spanish vocabulary, so that learners are not alienated by a feeling of disconnection from the content, as it does not match their linguistic norms (Raji et al., 2021). Nonetheless, the complete removal of cultural stereotypes in AI systems would still necessitate the improvement of AI technologies and input from cultural and linguistic experts, who will help design appropriate AI systems. To achieve these objectives, many stakeholders, including universities, nonprofit organizations, and private enterprises, have worked together to formulate standards and strategies to mitigate AI prejudice and foster inclusiveness (Blodgett et al., 2020).

However, this is a challenge in making AI-driven multilingual content development culturally accurate rather than theoretical. This would require a multifactorial approach, with technical solutions interweaving ethical considerations. Integrating one system with fairness-aware algorithms, diverse datasets, mechanisms of transparency, and models that adapt to culture represents a forward-looking step toward the creation of AI tools that respect and celebrate rather than undermine cultural diversity. With further growth in AI technologies, interdisciplinary cooperation and the incorporation of various types of feedback from different user groups will lie at the heart of devising tools that can equally represent and serve a multicultural global audience (Johnson et al., 2023).

5. SUPPORTING VARIOUS LEARNING STYLES WITH AI

AI-generated Visual, Auditory, and Kinesthetic Resources

AI technologies have introduced new ways of generating different types of educational content for a wide range of learning preferences, thereby making learning more accessible. The visual type of learners will benefit significantly from the visuals presented through AI, such as built graphics, diagrams, and even AR application visualization of complex concepts. Examples include DALL-E and Midjourney, which generate specific images suitable for virtually any educational requirement. These tools will help instructors take abstract concepts and ideas and turn them into concrete visuals that learners can better retain and understand. For auditory learners, AI-powered speech synthesis and NLP tools create interactive auditory resources, including narrated texts, personalised audio summaries, and virtual lecture assistants that simulate live Q&A sessions. These are systems, such as WaveNet from Google or speech models generated by OpenAI, which are converted into natural-sounding audio with different accents and tonalities to meet the specific auditory needs of learner groups with diverse differences and provide visually impaired learners with access to content.

AI also has a greater potential for kinesthetic learners. In addition, AI allows movement and hands-on interactions through virtual reality (VR) and mixed reality (MR) tools for immersive experiences, whereby learners simulate or engage in simulated environments for practical or experiential learning. Such AI-powered tools offer reasonable learning flexibility to accommodate changing learner learning preferences, thereby fostering a better learning environment in the education sector. As the capabilities of AI increase, it is anticipated that systems will be able to create personalized education by delivering multiple types of content suited to an individual's taste.

Interactive Simulations and Virtual Scenarios

The accessibility of interactive simulations, virtual environments, and AI in language learning tools has made practical language applications and their benefits much more engaging. Such technologies are employed in conjunction with advanced computer vision techniques and natural language processing to develop user interfaces that include communication relevant to the learner in scenarios such as marketplaces, jobs, or travel. A prominent example of advanced AI technology is represented by virtual characters in language learning interfaces like Mondly or Duolingo, which respond to the learner while adapting to their proficiency level and the context of the conversation, making it more engaging for the learner. In VR systems, artificial intelligence enhances the experience by providing virtual tutors for learners to interact with and practice specific vocabulary, the pronunciation of which would be assessed during practice, or grammar through the use of mobile devices. Indeed, utilising VR goggles in applications like ENGAGE or ImmerseMe places learners in authentic scenarios such as visiting a restaurant to place an order or asking for directions in a foreign city, thus reinforcing language development through active practice (Huang et al., 2019). Such experiences tend to increase learners' language retention significantly and also boost their confidence towards making mistakes by placing them in a risk-free environment. In addition, the AI systems embedded in these language learning simulations can measure learners' input, language use, and progress and adjust the learning challenges so that the learner remains engaged throughout the experience. Interactive simulations and virtual scenarios, merging AI with VR and NLP, promise a highly engaging, context-rich platform that aligns with the very principles of experiential learning and is, therefore, effective for mastering language in real-life contexts. Furthermore, these tools not only support language acquisition but also foster cross-cultural understanding by exposing learners to diverse linguistic and social nuances, thus offering a comprehensive language learning experience often incomplete with traditional methods.

Case Study

Mondly VR is a state-of-the-art, artificially intelligent language-learning platform powered by VR to create an immersive skills-learning experience for a variety of learning styles. This makes Mondly VR the ultimate combination of language learning and chunking in terms of visual, auditory, and kinesthetic learning. For instance, in the app, visual learners can practise languages in real environments, such as restaurants, airports, or hotel receptions, in 3D. Such visually rich scenes help learners contextualise vocabulary and phrases, thus aiding memory retention through associations (Alnajjar & Park, 2020). Kinesthetic learners will also be able to practise the language in an active and practical form through simulated performance within the app. For example, a user ordering food from a virtual restaurant would have to get up and act out his or her actions in VR, thus engaging in muscle memory along with verbal and cognitive skills. This particular aspect of active engagement aligns with the principles of experiential learning and is especially helpful for learners whose learning style is hands-on. Furthermore, Mondly's adaptive learning technology ranks every user's performance and personalises the difficulty level of conversations and content, keeping the experience challenging yet attainable. Overall, Mondly VR shows how seamlessly AI and VR technologies can work together to create an extensive, flexible language learning atmosphere that supports most learning styles and proceeds incomparably towards becoming holistic and personalised in language acquisition.

6. REAL-TIME ANALYTICS AND CONTINUOUS IMPROVEMENT

AI-Powered Feedback and Analytics

AI-powered feedback and analytics systems provide transformative tools for monitoring learner progress, enabling educators to make evidence-based adjustments to their curriculum and instructional strategies. These systems can analyse the volume of learning data to uncover trends in learner performance and engagement, identifying points of struggle while delivering real-time insight to help teachers tailor their approaches to meet individual needs. For example, services such as DreamBox and Knewton leverage machine-learning algorithms that continually assess learner activities, from problem-solving strategies to response times, and translate these into tangible feedback for both learners and teachers. This kind of granular feedback helps educators understand not just where a learner may struggle but why, which in turn enables them to intervene with targeted support (Roschelle et al., 2016). Moreover, AI-powered analytics tools provide dashboards and progress reports that indicate overall class performance trends, allowing teachers to identify the common challenges their learners face and alter their instructional strategies. For instance, if analytics indicate underperformance by learners in a particular concept area, that concept may be revisited by the educator, resources may be added, or lesson pacing may be modified to ensure clear comprehension. With AI-powered tools, such as Carnegie Learning's MATHia and customised maths instruction, teachers can see learner proficiency levels in real time and know who needs more support and who is ready to move on to other, more advanced topics (Pane et al., 2014). This adaptive feedback fosters improvement not only in learning outcomes but also in decreasing teacher workload through the automation of time-consuming activities, including grading and progress tracking, enabling educators to free their time for more personalised engagement with learners. With AI for feedback and analytics, educators have a far more detailed view of learner learning trajectories. Equipped with such information-powered curricula, dynamic and responsive to the changing needs of learners can be created. Such data-driven approaches foster an adaptive learning environment in which individual growth matches the high standards of education in the entire classroom.

Personalization through Real-Time Updates

Real-time adaptation becomes possible with AI-powered learning platforms, which facilitate learning processes such as adapted content, adapted difficulty levels, and individual performance metrics per learner. Such intelligent, tailored learning platforms analyse a variety of data points that are characteristic of learners, from response accuracy to the time taken for completion and error patterns. This ability, harnessed by learning tools such as DreamBox for mathematics and Smart Sparrow for science, enables continuous updating of content. In instances where a learner demonstrates mastery of an underlying concept, the platform can build on this knowledge and further challenge the learner. In cases where a learner struggles with a specific concept, it may simplify explanations or provide additional resources to help the learner build foundational skills (Kulik & Fletcher, 2016). This practice has the added advantage of ensuring that every high-achieving, middle-range, and lower-performing learner works within the area of optimal challenge. An AI system can provide immediate personalised feedback that guides learners through misunderstandings to strengthen their grasp of deep concepts. For instance, Knewton platforms use machine learning algorithms to predict the next best learning path for each user, in effect scaffolding content to build on prior knowledge and address specific areas of need (Pane et al., 2014). Additionally, real-time adaptation helps sustain learner motivation and avoids the frustration commonly created by content that is well beyond learners' current skill level or the disengagement that occurs when the material is well below their current skill level. AI-powered learning systems react to pupil performance in real-time, changing the level of difficulty and complexity of what is learned. Thus, they provide a much more personalised learning journey that supports continuous growth by keeping learners within the so-called "zone of proximal development" and optimally aligning with individual learning trajectories.

Longitudinal Tracking of Learning Progress

AI is changing education; it provides lifelong data-based follow-up rather than creation or refinement. The function of this tracking capability reveals many performance indicators, such as mastery of concepts, levels of engagement, and rates of competency acquisition, enabling educators to keep track of emergent trends in strengths and gaps that learners evidence through their learning journeys. Consider curriculum learning models where the sophistication of objectives or tasks on the part of the AI algorithms adaptively manipulates the performance of the learners, for example, in reinforcement learning frameworks, with progression functions aimed at tailoring the learning path (Bassich et al., 2020). These findings hereby support moves toward an increasingly personalised and adaptive curriculum that could respond effectively to dynamic learner needs and relevance for individual learning trajectories. AI-based tools developed within the competence- or outcome-based curriculum can allow much greater detail in assessing the degree of attainment of specific educational objectives reached by learners. Advanced data analysis will highlight aspects where learners have problems and where they outperform; hence, executing targets for curriculum adjustment may result in an enhancement of learning efficacy (Pusporini & Nurdiyanto, 2024). Likewise, adaptive assessment technologies have the potential to provide teachers with immediate feedback and recommendations for adjustments in instruction, thereby maximising learners' levels of engagement and comprehension and keeping the curriculum relevant to the needs that emerge in modern times (Ejjami, 2024). This will be possible by embedding such AI-driven insights to help educators optimise content pacing, improve instructional strategies, and align learning with desired outcomes, thus rendering education agile and learner-centric. The position of AI in being capable of curriculum progression pathway analysis enhances its importance, at which point educators will be able to assess the progress of learning across cohorts and adjust programmes based on collective trends and statistical insights. Such data-driven refinement helps educators maintain an effective and scalable curriculum that supports diverse learning needs while continually aligning with both individual and institutional objectives (Haimowitz, 2014). A continuous feedback loop between AI-driven analytics and curriculum refinement creates a resilient, future-oriented approach to education that combines present learning challenges and future educational goals.

7. ADDRESSING CHALLENGES IN AI-DRIVEN CURRICULUM DEVELOPMENT

Ethical and Privacy Concerns

The integration of AI in educational contexts raises several serious ethical and privacy issues, especially regarding data security, algorithmic bias, and content development, in ways that are inclusive and ethical. Most AI-powered learning platforms require huge amounts of input data about learners as a first step toward personalisation. To handle all these issues, educators and technologists need robust frameworks that protect sensitive information and maintain data protection regulations, such as the General Data Protection Regulation (GDPR), to balance technological benefits with privacy rights. Further, AI systems can inherit some biases from the data sets with which they are trained, which can hit the very core of certain groups of learners. For example, biased algorithms in primary education inadvertently reinforce certain stereotypes that affect the delivery of education. This mitigation involves auditing algorithms, using diverse datasets, and promoting algorithmic transparency (Alawneh et al., 2024). The ethical impacts of AI extend to implications related to changes in educational dynamics, including autonomy and accountability when there is a need to make decisions. This has been a point of interest in studies; they highlighted how AI in education could be openly deployed in non-discriminatory ways to ensure that AI technologies complement rather than supplement human academic decisions in the classroom (Salloum, 2024). Ethical AI frameworks in education serve as an avenue to advance policies centred on learner privacy, algorithmic accountability, and fostering inclusivity within AI-enabled learning environments (Leta & Vancea, 2023). A balanced approach is needed: maximising the potential benefits of AI, with due care for responsible use toward an ethical and learner-centred future in education.

Bias Mitigation in AI-Generated Content

Various strategies and methods have been proposed to ensure that AI-generated content is unbiased and factually correct across cultural and linguistic contexts. Most AI models develop cultural biases owing to the lack of diversity within their training data, which may result in the misrepresentation or oversimplification of cultures other than those emanating from Western contexts. Various studies have shown that culturally sensitive topics visualised through AI, even text-to-image generators, are often burdened with exoticism or inaccuracies and therefore call for an inclusive design practice (Ghosh et al., 2024). This would allow for the nuanced expression of a particular cultural identity in a safe way and without stereotyping that can harm individuals within those cultural backgrounds. One of these methods is the incorporation of a community-centred approach: the development of the models should be guided by cultural insiders. Other biases involve different social norms that AI systems operating across diverse contexts must confront, particularly in sensitive areas that may relate to gender. AI responses designed to fit within a specific cultural or religious framework can find themselves uncontrollably shifting in terms of changing their stance and, therefore, demonstrate how contextual data would shift the output of AI responses generated. According to these researchers, embedding universal principles of human rights as generalised directions within AI responses will help AI stay consistent in ethical conduct across various contexts (Vicsek et al., 2024). The most important point is that expert reviews from diverse linguistic and cultural backgrounds should be provided at both training and assessment levels. Integrating bias-detection protocols and expertise in the training of AI will mean that culturally insensitive or linguistically biased content is highly unlikely; hence, this sets better avenues for AI to offer the desired fair and accurate representation (Zhang et al., 2022). These frameworks contribute to a Better Ethics and Inclusion-driven model for content creation that enables AI to serve cultural and contextual relevance to the broader audience of any part of the world.

Teacher and Learner Training on AI Tools

The speed at which AI is adopted within educational institutions places the training of teachers and learners on how best to employ these tools responsibly and effectively at the forefront. This is crucial because AI is an increasingly important shaper of learning experiences; therefore, time must be taken to equip educators with relevant skills and ethical awareness. Educators who understand the functionality and limitations of AI can integrate technologies in ways that enhance critical thinking, personalise learning, and build learners' digital literacy (Holmes et al., 2019). Professional development in AI also helps teachers meet the challenges of data privacy, algorithmic bias, and ethical consequences associated with automated decision-making in AI applications, both for building trust and transparency (Zawacki-Richter et al., 2019). While the training of learners in AI literacy turns them into enlightened consumers and future innovators who are ready to relate critically and ethically with AI, Long and Magerko (2020) add that placing greater emphasis on the responsible usage of AI within one's curriculum empowers the learners toward an understanding of AI's role in society and equips them with tools to question and assess information generated by AI. Therefore, success with AI in education lies in the direction of training programmes, which would contribute to both teachers and learners reaping the benefits of AI with minimal risks, developing a culture of ethical responsibility, and fostering a collaborative approach towards responsible AI adoption (Luckin, 2018).

8. FUTURE PROSPECTS OF AI IN LANGUAGE CURRICULUM

Emerging AI Trends in Education

The integration of AI into education continues to advance rapidly, reshaping the educational landscape through three key innovations: virtual tutors, augmented reality (AR), and AI-driven collaborative learning platforms. These technologies are transforming traditional teaching methods while creating more personalised and engaging learning experiences (Bai et al., 2023; Alam, 2023).

Virtual Tutors: Personalizing the Learning Experience

AI virtual tutors now represent a significant evolution in learning technology that integrates machine learning with natural language processing to offer personalised lessons. Intelligent virtual tutoring systems change their strategies of teaching according to the learner's learning styles, speed, and emotions, simultaneously offering immediate feedback and support (Holmes et al., 2019). The 24/7 availability of the systems means that learners can seek support and immediate feedback beyond class hours, thus enabling self-directed learning and helping bridge gaps in understanding. Virtual tutors are especially helpful for those learners who need additional equity, those with learning differences, or those who wish to accelerate their learning journey. Advanced systems involve the use of natural language processing and affective computing, enabling better communication and more empathetic support (Woolf et al., 2013). The more these systems continue to evolve with AI improvement, the better they understand learner queries and generate contextually relevant support. For educators, however, other challenges must first be resolved, such as algorithmic bias and data privacy concerns, since equity in implementation is still far from being achieved (Zawacki-Richter et al., 2019).

Augmented Reality (AR): Creating Immersive Learning Environments

This technology enhances learning by superimposing digital information onto the real world, which makes the experience more interactive and interesting (Radu, 2014). Such experiences include the hands-on handling of 3D models and simulations of abstract ideas, such as watching molecular structures in chemistry or exploring historical reconstructions in social studies. In science classes, learners can study complex systems and conduct numerous virtual experiments. History classes can utilise AR for the interactive reconstruction of historical events. Similarly, biology learners can perform virtual dissections and anatomical studies. Interactivity with AR tends to promote better comprehension and retention of the introduced material. According to previous studies, AR tools enhance learner motivation by transforming traditional learning content into interactive experiences that raise learners' curiosity (Cano & Troya, 2023; Kalyani, 2023). As more people use AR through smartphones and tablets, significant access to AR may be ensured for wider educational adoption. However, challenges are impending in terms of equipment costs, content development, teacher training, and technical infrastructure.

AI-Driven Collaborative Learning Platforms: Enhancing Learner Interaction

These intelligent features reinvent learner collaboration and interaction with instructors on these platforms. Through algorithms that analyse the profiles of learners, these platforms can match learners based on similar skills, learning styles, or shared academic interests and peer-to-peer interactions (Zhang et al., 2024). These platforms employ AI algorithms to form effective learning groups that spur peer-to-peer learning and knowledge co-construction. AI can support rich discussions by analysing individual learners' contributions, signalling where learners can learn from each other, and providing individualised feedback (Luckin et al., 2016). This allows for interactive activities within groups, thanks to the continuous monitoring of group dynamics and on-the-fly learner feedback about team performance. Instructors may take advantage of the generated information by modifying the groups or implementing other interventions to further enrich the teamwork experience and diversity of involvement. This AI-enhanced methodology focuses more on an interactive and supportive environment that emphasises active participation and promotes critical thinking, education, and career readiness (Hamdi, 2024; Trivedi, 2023).

Future Considerations and Challenges

Therefore, areas such as ethics, data protection measures regarding privacy, prevention of algorithmic bias, and transparency over the working of AI systems are paramount in building confidence and ensuring that AI is implemented responsibly.

The gathering and use of learner data must be dealt with accordingly, in light of ensuring privacy without losing system effectiveness.

Other challenges in implementation include equitability of access to technology, coupled with issues related to the digital divide. Surely, these issues are now of great importance when all educational institutions seek active learning engagement through an effective balance between AI support and human instruction. This prospect encourages passive learning, which should be carefully monitored and thoughtful strategies of integration applied appropriately.

Research priorities should focus on the creation of robust methodologies for evaluation that correctly measure the effectiveness of AI-driven educational interventions and investigate their long-term impacts on the development of learner learning. Moreover, this study will have to take into consideration the best design of the platform to achieve the most inclusive participation and to measure the overall effectiveness of an AI-driven intervention in the field of education.

New virtual tutors, augmented reality, and AI-driven collaborative platforms are developing at a rapid rate and represent a fundamental transformation in educational practice. While these technologies hold much promise for improving teaching methods and learner outcomes, there is a need to balance the momentum with prioritizing ethical considerations and addressing implementation challenges. With such innovations considered in their implementation, educators can create enriched, interactive, personalized learning environments that support learner engagement and foster lifelong learning. It is expected that, as these technologies progress, continuous research and informed judgment will be used to guide adequate implementations of the technologies in educational settings.

Potential for Broader Integration Across Disciplines

While impressive, the progress made in AI to help teach languages is found in its premises and principles, which provide the core for integration across disciplines. Adaptive learning, personalised feedback, and interactive engagement are just a few of the aspects AI provides to facilitate learners' experiences in diverse disciplines. This AI capability to analyse performance and create learning pathways in language learning easily translates to other subjects like mathematics, science, and history. By identifying strengths and weaknesses, AI can suggest suitable learning resources for individual learners while also adapting to the challenges of activities through actual progress (VanLehn, 2011). This kind of individual approach—which mirrors the personalised feedback loops now touted in so many language learning software programmes—allows for differences in styles and velocities of learning and makes learning outcomes optimum. AI-powered simulations and gamified learning utilised in reinforcing conversational aspects in language learning can be conducted in other disciplines. Learners study science disciplines through virtual labs, conducting experiments and examining complex phenomena in a secure but interactive environment, something very akin to the simulation aspect of learning a new language. In history, learners are given the capability to participate in simulated historical events by making choices and influential decisions toward developing skills in critical thinking and historical understanding (Johnson & Mayer, 2009). This also aligns with experiential learning, which in language acquisition is encouraged through interactive exercises. AI's capability for automated feedback on written and spoken language already applies to a wide range of other disciplines that require written assignments or oral presentations. For instance, writing-intensive courses can employ AI in the scoring of grammar, style, and content of essays, offering differential feedback, just as language learning platforms do (Shermis & Burstein, 2003). In the STEM disciplines, AI can automatically score problem-solving methods, offering individualised feedback on logical reasoning and analysis skills parallel to that provided on usage and pronunciation in language learning (Means et al., 2009). AI-powered language learning tools that specialise in real-time translation and transcription further create more accessible in-class learning opportunities for learners with disabilities across a wide range of disciplines. This accommodation shares many features with the assistive capabilities in language learning apps: captioning videos, translating text, and transcribing lectures make course material equally accessible to learners of different abilities (Burgstahler, 2015). Data collected by such AI systems during language learning serve to provide key information on the learning trends of learners, hence pointing out areas that require instructional modifications. The data-driven approach, applicable right across disciplines, will thus go on to inform curriculum design, teaching strategies, and assessment methods—to mention but a few—toward effective practices that yield improved learning outcomes as a matter of course (William & Burden, 2010). This is a re-echo of data analytics that are deployed in language learning platforms to monitor progress and adapt learning. AI can accelerate interdisciplinary relationships in a whole new dimension through the conceptual and skill links between disciplines. For example, the ability to carry out analytical procedures in mathematics is extended to problem-solving in science and critical analysis of literature. AI can emphasise these relationships and create avenues for applying knowledge in other contexts through holistic learning (Rhoten, 2004). This goes well with commonly integrated skills development in language learning, whereby vocabulary and grammar are applied to various communicative contexts. These adaptive AI-powered language-learning tools enable facilitators of learning to create more engaging, personalised, and widely accessible learning experiences across disciplines. The greater integration of AI into education has the potential to empower learners and instil in them a love of learning that may well last a lifetime.

Ethical considerations, data privacy, and what happens to the human educator in an AI-enhanced learning environment remain concerns that need consideration.

Long-Term Impact on Curriculum Design

The impact of AI on learning goes beyond classroom applications. It is set to engineer a radical long-term transformation in curriculum development and the entire education sector. The impending availability of various tools such as personalized learning pathways, intelligent tutoring systems and adaptive assessment solutions signals a transition to long-term and flexible learning ecosystems.

Personalised and Adaptive Curricula

The evolution of AI also assists in creating education models that consider the preferences, requirements and future career paths of each learner. This eliminates the conventional way of training where all the learners have to undergo the same training. This might include different learning paths and mastery of various concepts at different periods as well as topics that relate to individual objectives (Pane et al., 2015). Active learning environments could utilize curriculum intervention with AI algorithms in place, which would change the curriculum in real-time based on learners' performances.

Competency-Based Learning

Thanks to the potential of AI, it would be possible to transform the conventional education system that relies on time to one that is more based on the competencies attained by the learner. In this system of education, attendance is not of any importance as progression is made only after the learner has proven their ability to use certain skills or knowledge. There are AI assessment tools that can provide measured competencies on the learner's abilities, give them feedback and help them to master it. It allows for building more self-learning and personalized education.

Focus on 21st-Century Skills.

The use of AI can also enable the acquisition of definitional skills of the 21st century, such as critical thinking, problem-solving, creativity, and collaboration (Trilling & Fadel, 2009). For example, through detailed analysis of learners' work and interactions, AI can close the gaps where such competencies are lacking and suggest remediation learning opportunities. When used alongside training simulations and collaborative learning tools, the development of such competence can be further extended.

Lifelong Learning and Upskilling

AI can support lifelong learning and upskilling by providing personalized learning recommendations and resources throughout individuals' careers. As the job market evolves rapidly, AI can help individuals identify emerging skill gaps and access relevant training programs, enabling them to adapt to changing demands and remain competitive (World Economic Forum, 2020).

Reshaping the Role of Educators

As the world of AI introduces an increasing number of repetitive functions in the educational systems such as grading or delivering content to learners personally, the room for educators to implement higher-order activities such as mentoring, encouraging critical thinking among learners, and providing tailored learning opportunities to each learner increases (Holmes et al, 2019). As a result, teachers can turn into learning facilitators and coaches, supporting each learner in their learning process.

Decentralised and Democratized Education

Education and AI are two sides of the same coin as they can create a more dispersed and egalitarian education system where learning materials of the best quality will be offered to people irrespective of their physical location or economic status (Bates, 2019). AI-supported educational technologies can reach wherever there is the internet, even to the remotest of anthropological sites and address the impacts on the location of the pace and style of learning.

Nevertheless, there are salient issues that need to be taken into account about the extensive use of AI in designing curricula. The application of new technologies brings ethical challenges, issues concerning data protection and the possibility of biased algorithms. In addition, adequate access to the technology and availability of teacher preparation programs for effective use of the technology are important issues to address in the process. The curriculum design in the coming years will be underpinned by the strategic adoption and integration of AI in processes and practices towards curriculum design, although its benefits would be sought and its dangers contained.

9. CONCLUSION

The emphasis on AI in curriculum development and content generation has marked a sea change in the practice of education, particularly in language education. Through the course of this chapter, we have discussed how AI technologies are changing the educational landscape in terms of personalized learning experiences, cultural inclusivity, and real-time adaptation. The evidence attached suggests an unprecedented potential of AI in building dynamic learning environments that will respond to individual learner needs within a framework of high educational standards. Letting technology process and provide feedback in real-time on learning data has enabled curriculum adjustments that were simply impossible to have done previously and have fundamentally changed the way we think about educational content delivery.

One key insight arising from our literature review is the huge potential that exists for AI-based systems to help develop culturally sensitive content to pay respects to and represent diversified perspectives. Through using complex algorithms along with multi-diverse training grounds, AI will be able to create materials for learners from different parts of the world, thus making language learning more inclusive and highly applicable worldwide. In combination with AI, the support for the range of learning modalities- visual, auditory, and kinesthetic has created more engaging and effective learning experiences that address different learning preferences. The implementation of interactive simulations, virtual environments, and adaptive feedback mechanisms has been promising in their applications so far, with recorded improvement in learner engagement and consequent learning results.

This transformation extends into modes of delivery to assessment and improvement processes. Where continuous evaluation and modification are possible with AI, the way we assess and refine educational outcomes was completely remade, thus affording previously unattainable insights into learning patterns and allowing data-driven curricular refinements. This enables real-time analytics for educators to make informed decisions in terms of curriculum adjustments and interventional strategies, which tends to make the educational environment much more responsive and effective.

Considering the current pace of events, it is believed that the role of AI in language education will only get bigger. The interoperability of Virtual and Augmented Reality technologies with AI will provide more immersive and realistic experiences for language learners. More sophisticated natural language processing permits advanced features in language interaction, and further improved algorithms make learning pathways more personalized with a promise to maintain the highest standards of cultural sensitivity and inclusion. But this evolution has to be assiduously managed vis-à-vis remaining challenges, including the maintenance of the vital human contact in language teaching, the attainment of equity of access to AI-driven learning tools, the guarantee of privacy, and, of course, continued work on bias detection and curbing.

The future of AI in language education does not lie in taking over from human teachers but in enhancing the capability of teachers such that they can pay more attention to the higher-order aspects of education. As AI technology continues to mature, we will expect more sophisticated integrations across diverse educational contexts and disciplines, better support for lifelong learning and professional development, and improved capabilities in supporting special educational needs. Attention shall probably be given to the development of critical thinking and cultural competence associated with language acquisition to better prepare learners in an increasingly intermingled world.

However, the transformative potential of AI in language education extends beyond actual technological innovation. Rather, it has the potential to create more inclusive, engaging, and truly effective pedagogical experiences. As we go forward to further develop and refine these technologies, our focus should be on how AI capabilities can serve the very core of educational purposes: fostering understanding, enabling communication, and empowering learners in the pursuit of fulfilling their potential. The future directions will be done with full deliberation of ethical implications, further research on effectiveness, and continued collaboration among educators, technologists, and policymakers who will have the task of helping ensure AI integration serves the best interests of all learners.

REFERENCES

Alam, A. (2023). Harnessing the Power of AI to Create Intelligent Tutoring Systems for Enhanced Classroom Experience and Improved Learning Outcomes. In *Intelligent Communication Technologies and Virtual Mobile Networks* (pp. 571–591). Springer Nature Singapore. DOI: 10.1007/978-981-99-1767-9_42

Alawneh, Y. J. J., Radwan, E. N. Z., Salman, F. N., Makhlouf, S. I., Makhamreh, K., & Alawneh, M. S. (2024, April). Ethical Considerations in the Use of AI in Primary Education: Privacy, Bias, and Inclusivity. In *2024 International Conference on Knowledge Engineering and Communication Systems (ICKECS)* (Vol. 1, pp. 1-6). IEEE. DOI: 10.1109/ICKECS61492.2024.10616986

Bassich, A., Foglino, F., Leonetti, M., & Kudenko, D. (2020). Curriculum learning with a progression function. *arXiv preprint arXiv:2008.00511.*

Bates, A. W. (2015). *Teaching in a digital age: Guidelines for designing teaching and learning*. BCcampus.

Bender, E. M., Gebru, T., McMillan-Major, A., & Shmitchell, S. (2021, March). On the dangers of stochastic parrots: Can language models be too big? In *Proceedings of the 2021 ACM conference on fairness, accountability, and transparency* (pp. 610-623). DOI: 10.1145/3442188.3445922

Burden, R. L. (2010). *Psychology for language teachers: a social constructivist approach*. Cambridge University Press.

Burgstahler, S. E., & Cory, R. C. (Eds.). (2010). *Universal design in higher education: From principles to practice*. Harvard Education Press.

Cano, C. A. G., & Troya, A. L. C. (2023). AI is applied to teaching and learning processes. *LatIA*, *1*, 2–2. DOI: 10.62486/latia20232

Chen, L., Chen, P., & Lin, Z. (2020). AI in education: A review. *IEEE Access : Practical Innovations, Open Solutions*, *8*, 75264–75278. DOI: 10.1109/ACCESS.2020.2988510

Ejjami, R. (2024). The future of learning: AI-based curriculum development. *Int J Multidiscipline Res*, *6*(4).

Falmagne, J. C., Albert, D., Doble, C., Eppstein, D., & Hu, X. (Eds.). (2013). *Knowledge spaces: Applications in education*. Springer Science & Business Media. DOI: 10.1007/978-3-642-35329-1

Guerberof-Arenas, A., & Moorkens, J. (2023). Ethics and machine translation: The end user perspective. In *Towards Responsible Machine Translation: Ethical and Legal Considerations in Machine Translation* (pp. 113–133). Springer International Publishing. DOI: 10.1007/978-3-031-14689-3_7

Haimowitz, S. M. (2014). *U.S. Patent No. 8,666,300.* Washington, DC: U.S. Patent and Trademark Office.

Hamdi, M. (2024, July). How AI is Transforming and Shaping the Future of Education. In *2024 IEEE 28th International Conference on Intelligent Engineering Systems (INES)* (pp. 000115-000116). IEEE. DOI: 10.1109/INES63318.2024.10629089

Holmes, W., Bialik, M., & Fadel, C. (2019). *AI in education promises and implications for teaching and learning*. Center for Curriculum Redesign.

Huang, K. T., Ball, C., Francis, J., Ratan, R., Boumis, J., & Fordham, J. (2019). Augmented versus VR in education: An exploratory study examining science knowledge retention when using augmented reality/VR mobile applications. *Cyberpsychology, Behavior, and Social Networking*, *22*(2), 105–110. DOI: 10.1089/cyber.2018.0150 PMID: 30657334

Hwang, G. J., & Chen, N. S. (2023). Exploring the potential of generative AI in education: Applications, challenges, and future research directions. *Journal of Educational Technology & Society*, *26*(2).

Johnson, C. I., & Mayer, R. E. (2009). A testing effect with multimedia learning. *Journal of Educational Psychology*, *101*(3), 621–629. DOI: 10.1037/a0015183

Kalyani, L. K. (2023). Revolutionizing Education: AI's Pioneering Role in Shaping Tomorrow's Scholars. *International Journal of Multidisciplinary Research in Arts. Science and Technology*, *1*(2), 1–7.

Kulik, J. A., & Fletcher, J. D. (2016). Effectiveness of intelligent tutoring systems: A meta-analytic review. *Review of Educational Research*, *86*(1), 42–78. DOI: 10.3102/0034654315581420

Leta, F. M., & Vancea, D. P. C. (2023). Ethics in Education: Exploring the Ethical Implications of AI Implementation. *Ovidius University Annals. Economic Sciences Series*, *23*(1), 413–421.

Loewen, S., Isbell, D. R., & Sporn, Z. (2020). The effectiveness of app-based language instruction for developing receptive linguistic knowledge and oral communicative ability. *Foreign Language Annals*, *53*(2), 209–233. DOI: 10.1111/flan.12454

Long, D., & Magerko, B. (2020, April). What is AI literacy? Competencies and design considerations. In *Proceedings of the 2020 CHI conference on human factors in computing systems* (pp. 1-16). DOI: 10.1145/3313831.3376727

Luckin, R. (2018). *Machine Learning and Human Intelligence: The future of education for the 21st century*. UCL IOE Press. UCL Institute of Education, University of London, 20 Bedford Way, London WC1H 0AL.

Luckin, R., & Holmes, W. (2016). Intelligence Unleashed: An argument for AI in education.

Means, B., Toyama, Y., Murphy, R., Bakia, M., & Jones, K. (2009). Evaluation of evidence-based practices in online learning: A meta-analysis and review of online learning studies.

Munday, P. (2016). The case for using DUOLINGO as part of the language classroom experience (Duolingo como parte del curriculum de las clases de lengua extranjera).

Pane, J. F., Griffin, B. A., McCaffrey, D. F., & Karam, R. (2014). Effectiveness of cognitive tutor algebra I at scale. *Educational Evaluation and Policy Analysis*, *36*(2), 127–144. DOI: 10.3102/0162373713507480

Pane, J. F., Steiner, E. D., Baird, M. D., & Hamilton, L. S. (2015). *Continued Progress: Promising Evidence on Personalized Learning*. Rand Corporation. DOI: 10.7249/RR1365

Pusporini, W., & Nurdiyanto, H. (2024). Utilization of AI in Outcome-Based Curriculum Evaluation and Development. *Journal of Research in Social Science and Humanities*, *4*(1), 132–134. DOI: 10.47679/jrssh.v4i1.109

Radu, I. (2014). Augmented reality in education: A meta-review and cross-media analysis. *Personal and Ubiquitous Computing*, *18*(6), 1533–1543. DOI: 10.1007/s00779-013-0747-y

Rhoten, D. (2004). Interdisciplinary research: Trend or transition. *Items & Issues*, *5*(1-2), 6–11.

Roschelle, J., Feng, M., Murphy, R. F., & Mason, C. A. (2016). Online mathematics homework increases learner achievement. *AERA Open*, *2*(4), 2332858416673968. DOI: 10.1177/2332858416673968

Sajja, R., Sermet, Y., Cikmaz, M., Cwiertny, D., & Demir, I. (2024). AI-enabled intelligent assistant for personalized and adaptive learning in higher education. *Information (Basel)*, *15*(10), 596. DOI: 10.3390/info15100596

Salloum, S. A. (2024). AI Perils in Education: Exploring Ethical Concerns. *AI in Education: The Power and Dangers of ChatGPT in the Classroom*, 669-675.

Shermis, M. D. (2003). *Automated essay scoring: A cross-disciplinary perspective*. Inc., Publishers. Mahawah. DOI: 10.4324/9781410606860

Shum, S. B., & Ferguson, R. (2012). Social learning analytics. *Journal of Educational Technology & Society*, *15*(3), 3–26.

Trilling, B., & Fadel, C. (2009). *21st-century skills: Learning for life in our times*. John Wiley & Sons.

Trivedi, N. B. (2023, November). AI in Education Transformative Force. In *2023 1st DMIHER International Conference on AI in Education and Industry 4.0 (IDICAIEI)* (Vol. 1, pp. 1-4). IEEE. DOI: 10.1109/IDICAIEI58380.2023.10406541

VanLehn, K. (2011). The relative effectiveness of human tutoring, intelligent tutoring systems, and other tutoring systems. *Educational Psychologist*, *46*(4), 197–221. DOI: 10.1080/00461520.2011.611369

Vicsek, L., Vancsó, A., Zajko, M., & Takacs, J. (2024). Exploring LGBTQ+ Bias in Generative AI Answers across Different Countries and Religious Contexts. *arXiv preprint arXiv:2407.03473*.

Woolf, B. P., Lane, H. C., Chaudhri, V. K., & Kolodner, J. L. (2013). AI grand challenges for education. *AI Magazine*, *34*(4), 66–84. DOI: 10.1609/aimag.v34i4.2490

World Economic Forum. (2020). *The Future of Jobs Report 2020*. World Economic Forum. https://www.weforum.org/publications/the-future-of-jobs-report-2020/

Zawacki-Richter, O., Marín, V. I., Bond, M., & Gouverneur, F. (2019). A systematic review of research on AI applications in higher education–where are the educators? *International Journal of Educational Technology in Higher Education*, *16*(1), 1–27. DOI: 10.1186/s41239-019-0171-0

Zhang, Z., Li, J., Stork, D. G., Mansfield, E., Russell, J., Adams, C., & Wang, J. Z. (2022). Reducing bias in AI-based analysis of visual artworks. *IEEE BITS the Information Theory Magazine*, *2*(1), 36–48. DOI: 10.1109/MBITS.2022.3197102

ADDITIONAL READING

Alier, M., Pereira, J., García-Peñalvo, F. J., Casañ, M. J., & Cabré, J. (2025). LAMB: An open-source software framework to create artificial intelligence assistants deployed and integrated into learning management systems. *Computer Standards & Interfaces*, *92*, 103940. Advance online publication. DOI: 10.1016/j.csi.2024.103940

Dickey, E. (2024). GAIDE: A Framework for Using Generative AI to Assist in Course Content Development. In *Proceedings - Frontiers in Education Conference, FIE*. https://doi.org/DOI: 10.1109/FIE61694.2024.10893132

Doyle, A., Sridhar, P., Agarwal, A., Savelka, J., & Sakr, M. (2025). A comparative study of AI-generated and human-crafted learning objectives in computing education. *Journal of Computer Assisted Learning*, *41*(1), e13092. Advance online publication. DOI: 10.1111/jcal.13092

Hoffman, E. R. (2024). Leveraging AI for Educational Content Consistency: An Evaluation of Text-to-Text and Image-to-Text Metadata Generation for Online Course Development. In *2024 IEEE Digital Education and MOOCS Conference, Proceedings*. https://doi.org/DOI: 10.1109/DEMOcon63027.2024.10747877

Lee, J., Cimová, T., Foster, E. J., France, D., Krajňáková, L., Moorman, L., Rewhorn, S., & Zhang, J. (2025). Transforming geography education: The role of generative AI in curriculum, pedagogy, assessment, and fieldwork. *International Research in Geographical and Environmental Education*, 1–17. Advance online publication. DOI: 10.1080/10382046.2025.2459780

Li, D., Xia, S., & Guo, K. (2025). Investigating L2 learners' text-to-video resemiotisation in AI-enhanced digital multimodal composing. *Computer Assisted Language Learning*, 1–32. Advance online publication. DOI: 10.1080/09588221.2025.2481402

Mehta, N., Agrawal, A., Benjamin, J., Mehta, S., MacNeill, H., & Masters, K. (2024). Pedagogy and generative artificial intelligence: Applying the PICRAT model to Google NotebookLM. *Medical Teacher*, 1–3. Advance online publication. DOI: 10.1080/0142159X.2024.2418937 PMID: 39460933

Pesovski, I., Santos, R., Henriques, R., & Trajkovik, V. (2024). Generative AI for Customizable Learning Experiences. *Sustainability (Basel)*, *16*(7), 3034. Advance online publication. DOI: 10.3390/su16073034

Schutte, S. (2025). Optimizing content for educational curricula with Large Language Models (LLMs). In *Generative Artificial Intelligence Applications* (pp. 205–226). Holistic Reflections From The Educational Landscape.

Wilby, R. L., & Esson, J. (2024). AI literacy in geographic education and research: Capabilities, caveats, and criticality. *The Geographical Journal, 190*(1), e12548. Advance online publication. DOI: 10.1111/geoj.12548

KEY TERMS AND DEFINITIONS

Adaptive Learning: An educational method that relies on AI algorithms to sort and analyse performance metrics, modifying instruction in real-time to suit a learner's needs and maximize learning outcomes.

Natural Language Processing (NLP): A subset of AI that enables machines to read, interpret, and generate human language for applications such as automated grading, feedback mechanisms, and conversational software for language learning and practice.

Cultural Inclusivity: In AI-based curriculum development, the practice of including a variety of cultural lenses or lenses (including traditions and languages), to ensure representation and relevance to students from varying cultural orientations or backgrounds.

Competency-Based Learning: An education model enabled by AI (also known as mastery learning) that allows students to master skills rather than the amount of time spent learning, leaving the progression to the demonstrated skill acquisition.

Virtual Teaching Assistants (VTAs): AI-based chatbots that provide instant feedback, answer questions, or provide support for learners pursuing their studies outside of the traditional class schedule by providing real-time learning environments.

Personalized Learning Pathways: A learning sequence generated by AI that is individualized and adapts to proficiency, style, interest, and pace to best serve the learner.

Explainable Artificial Intelligence (XAI): AI systems that are transparent in the decision-making process of their recommendations and adaptations, enabling educators to better understand why the AI made decisions.

Chapter 3
The Role of Teachers in an AI-Driven Language Learning Environment

Rohit Yadav
https://orcid.org/0000-0002-7573-8005
IILM University, Greater Noida, India

Mohit Yadav
https://orcid.org/0000-0002-9341-2527
O. P. Jindal Global University, India

Xuan-Hoa Nghiem
https://orcid.org/0000-0003-2292-0257
Vietnam National University, Hanoi, Vietnam

Ali Najeeb
https://orcid.org/0000-0003-4663-9347
Qasim Ibrahim School of Business, Villa College, Maldives

Asanga Ranasinghe
https://orcid.org/0009-0005-2846-0732
University of Sri Jayewardenepura, Sri Lanka

ABSTRACT

This chapter explores the evolving role of teachers in an AI-driven language learning environment. With the rapid advancement of AI, traditional methods of language education are undergoing significant transformation. AI tools offer personalized learning experiences, real-time feedback, and adaptive assessments, enhancing the efficiency and accessibility of language instruction. However, the role of the teacher

DOI: 10.4018/979-8-3693-9606-3.ch003

remains essential in guiding, supporting, and interpreting AI-generated data to ensure a holistic and human-centered learning experience. This chapter discusses the shifting roles of teachers as facilitators, mentors, and ethical leaders in an AI-enhanced classroom. It emphasizes the need for teachers to develop AI literacy, adapt pedagogical strategies, and foster emotional connections with students. The integration of AI in education also raises ethical considerations related to equity, privacy, and bias. Ultimately, the future of language education lies in the synergy between AI tools and human expertise, ensuring effective and inclusive language learning.

1. INTRODUCTION

Use of AI in education has significantly transformed how both knowledge is passed on and acquired through language learning. Technologies, for instance, are machine learning, natural language processing, and adaptive learning systems. It has enabled powerful tools, allowing for more personal and adaptive instructions of languages, with automatic feedbacks and continuing support during learning. This shift poses both opportunities and challenges for educators, especially in language teaching, where the dynamics of student engagement and individualized support are crucial. Teachers are now not only required to deliver content but also to meaningfully integrate AI tools into their pedagogical practices. While AI can make language learning more efficient and accessible (Guszcza et al., 2017), the role of the teacher is still crucial in guiding students, developing emotional intelligence, and ensuring that technology supports rather than replaces human interaction (Huang et al., 2020).

The role of the teacher is changing with the changing model of the traditional classroom. Teachers are not only distributors of information but also learning facilitators who, as a need of the task, are to collaborate with AI in designing personal and adaptive experiences for learning by learners. AI will be capable of adapting the learner's pace to respond instantly to any learner, but human teachers will bridge in to make the learners motivated, attentive, and cognitively and emotionally equipped for performance (Luckin et al., 2016). The landscape is shifting, but demand for teaching and learning knowledge-compassionate, responsive education is still forming the backbone of such learning. Hence, the following chapter will look keenly into the multiple roles a teacher can assume within the new environment of language learning AI: up to what point does AI aid a teacher, how it challenges it, and in what ways do they have synergies toward optimising outcomes.

2. AI AND LANGUAGE LEARNING: A PARADIGM SHIFT

AI will change the paradigms in which language learning is achieved and how teaching and the tools that learners use are done. Traditionally, language learning is approached through structured class teaching, focusing on grammar and vocabulary and conversational practice in a classroom setting. Today, adaptive learning systems, chatbots, and speech recognition technology and other AI-powered technologies are changing the way language skills are learned. These AI systems give learners the chance to experience personalized, self-paced learning, which caters to their unique needs and pace. These tools, by using big data and machine learning algorithms, adjust to the student's strengths, weaknesses, and learning style to facilitate a more customized approach to language acquisition (Heffernan, 2019).

In particular, AI-driven tools are revolutionizing vocabulary acquisition, pronunciation, and grammar correction-all with immediate feedback (Vogel et al., 2019). Thus, for example, natural language processing algorithms allow students to interact in real time with the AI, being corrected and supported as they engage in practice exercises. More than this, applications such as Duolingo and Babbel bring language lessons straight into the student's laps and allow learning at any point, shattering the traditional constraints of the physical classroom environment (Fitzpatrick et al., 2021). Technology also helps students overcome fears, like fear of mistakes around their peers, by providing practice and experimenting in non-judgmental space.

Although AI proved to be an incredibly powerful tool in improving language learning, it also requires rethinking the role of the teacher. Today, the teacher is expected to combine old pedagogical methods with new AI tools by producing a hybrid learning space that allows technology and human teaching to support each other in terms of learning. AI can offer the possibility of personalized learning, but it cannot replace the empathy, encouragement, and context-sensitive guidance that teachers provide (Godwin-Jones, 2019). This is a transition from the traditional model of language teaching to a more dynamic and interactive system, one that is more responsive to the needs of the learner while also presenting new challenges for educators in their teaching methods and interactions with students.

3. TEACHERS AS FACILITATORS IN AI-POWERED CLASSROOMS

In an AI-powered classroom, the role of the teacher changes dramatically from that of a traditional instructor to that of a facilitator. While AI technologies provide the tools and resources to support individualized learning, the teacher remains central in guiding and managing the learning process. In this new paradigm, educators need to adapt to a dynamic learning environment in which AI tools assist with personalized learning, but the teachers are the ones who can still be critical in fostering critical thinking, engagement, and motivation in students. The teacher is no longer a source of knowledge but the designer of a learning ecosystem where AI supplements human interaction and helps the students navigate their educational journey (Dabbagh & Kitsantas, 2012).

With AI-based platforms, educators can create differentiated learning experiences for every student; lessons are customized to fit each child's progress, strength, and challenges. For example, ITS makes use of data-driven insights to recognize when students have trouble and provides the right intervention (VanLehn, 2011). In this regard, teachers play the role of facilitators, making sure that these AI interventions are in line with the educational objectives and maintaining a balance between the automation of AI and human-directed learning. Although AI can provide real-time feedback, teachers are still responsible for the classroom environment, group dynamics, and emotional and motivational support, all of which are essential to the success of students (Huang et al., 2020).

The teacher in an AI-powered classroom helps students develop their metacognitive skills, like self-reflection and goal setting, which are far beyond the reach of AI. They can enable learners to think critically over the feedback AI systems provide and question assumptions so that they use knowledge creatively (Luckin et al., 2016). For example, should AI recommend using vocabulary or to correct grammatical usage, the instructor can take his students through knowing why the changes are necessary and how they can best apply them for different contexts. This will encourage students to exercise deeper language skills that promote autonomy as they learn since AI is incorporated as a resource rather than a method of replacing valuable teacher involvement in the learning.

Teachers should also be able to select and apply appropriate AI tools for their pedagogical purposes. With the many applications of AI in language learning, teachers need to critically evaluate which technologies are best suited for their students' needs and the specific learning objectives of their curriculum (Godwin-Jones, 2019). They also have to be flexible and responsive to the changing needs of students by adjusting the use of AI tools to ensure that technology complements, rather than overpowers, traditional learning methods. Thus, the teacher as a facilitator becomes strategic in decision-making where the teacher has to integrate AI in their teaching practice so that it adds to, rather than supersedes, their pedagogical skills.

The teacher in an AI-powered classroom would act as a facilitator, meshing the technical tools with their own expertise to foster better engagement, critical thinking, and individualized learning. The role of an educator changes such that AI can only be seen as an assistant and not as a replacement to the human bonds and support systems necessary for a good language learner.

4. AI AS SUPPORT TECHNOLOGY: FACILITATING TEACHER EFFECTIVENESS

The language learning context now reveals AI as an effective support tool that can facilitate the work of a teacher by automatically performing administrative work, providing real-time feedback, and offering data-driven insights into students' performance. One of the most significant benefits of AI in language education is its ability to automate repetitive tasks such as grading and assessment, freeing up valuable time for teachers to focus on more personalized aspects of teaching, such as addressing individual students' needs and fostering meaningful interactions. AI tools can evaluate the written and spoken language of students very rapidly, providing instant feedback that allows students to know their mistakes without having to wait for teacher intervention (Chen et al., 2021). This automation can help teachers focus more time on the interactive, creative, and human aspects of teaching and improve teaching in general.

Furthermore, AI-based learning platforms can track the progress of students over time and provide real-time insights to teachers about the performance of an individual and trends at the class level. Intelligent LMS, for instance, integrated with AI, gather large amounts of data on how students interact with learning materials, how fast they are moving through lessons, and where they get stuck. The data analysis creates reports from the AI system that reflect where students are succeeding or failing, enabling the teacher to intervene in better ways and modify instruction according to such information. Data-driven methods help teachers understand the pattern of learning behaviors and specific areas where more support is needed to make them improve their adaptability of instruction for varied student needs (Hwang et al., 2020).

AI also aids in differentiated learning since it offers a student-tailored learning path according to the student's strengths, weaknesses, and interests. For instance, many language learning apps and platforms, such as Duolingo and Rosetta Stone, alter the difficulty of exercises and lessons based on the learner's progress. For example, if a student is having difficulty with verb conjugation, more exercises and reminders on the topic can be provided, whereas a student who demonstrates mastery can be advanced to more complex grammatical structures. Teachers can use these insights to guide students through tailored learning experiences and even offer additional exercises or real-world applications that complement AI-generated activities (Fitzpatrick et al., 2021). This approach allows teachers to reach across a broader range of abilities within the classroom without needing to have individualized lesson plans to every student, greatly improving classroom efficiency.

Moreover, AI-powered language tools support teachers in maintaining an environment fostering continuous, formative assessment; traditional assessments, on the other hand, typically occur at set intervals. AI tools provide the means for ongoing monitoring of a student's language development. For instance, speech recognition technology, which is integrated into most language learning platforms, can assess a student's pronunciation and fluency in real-time, giving immediate feedback on errors and suggesting improvements. This constant assessment enables teachers to monitor the minute changes in language acquisition over time and intervene before misunderstandings or mistakes become ingrained, helping students improve more efficiently and effectively (Vogel et al., 2019).

Despite these merits, it's crucial to identify that AI is really best used alongside a teacher's expertise. Sure, AI can be helpful in analyzing things and automating routine tasks; however, only the teacher's role is decisive in interpreting feedback from AI systems, providing emotional support, and giving context-dependent guidance that can never be rendered by machines. Teachers can use AI-based tools in an appropriate and ethical manner to create an environment that balances technology with human-centered pedagogy. Using AI to automate tasks, track student progress, and personalize learning experiences, teachers can be more effective in creating a responsive, engaging, and supportive language learning environment.

5. ALIGNING TEACHING STRATEGIES WITH AI POTENTIAL

This means there should be a shift in traditional teaching methods if AI technologies are to be included into language learning and their potentials are to be completely exploited without impeding effective pedagogical practices. Adjusting the teachers' teaching strategy to include the AI capabilities makes sure that it does not take the place but instead supports them. One key shift in transformation is from the teacher-centered approach to a learner-centered teaching method. AI can offer personalized learning experiences, meaning that teachers can adapt content and lessons to meet the needs of each student. However, this would require teachers to rethink their role in the classroom and develop new strategies for delivering instruction, monitoring progress, and supporting learners in more interactive and dynamic ways.

The first teaching adaptation is using AI to promote more individualized and differentiated instruction. Traditional classrooms usually practice a "one-size-fits-all" practice, teaching otherwise abled children the same kind of content within the same schedule. However, an AI-based tool for learning adapts the exercises and learning content according to the output of the child, allowing that child to learn on his or her own pace. Thus, these revelations can help teachers set up lessons a little more sharply, giving individual practice or adding challenges to students at their discretion. For example, a non-ed-tech application like Duolingo and Babbel will track the performance of learners as well as have exercises continue to gradually become harder when learners show increased proficiency; this ensures that they neither remain challenged nor under-challenged (Fitzpatrick et al., 2021). Thus, teachers can forget all about content delivery and focus more on how to create experiences that cater to the different needs of their learners.

This goes further, as AI can also help to implement flipped-classroom models, a combination in which students learn at their own pace, usually through AI-based applications outside of the classroom. A flipped classroom lets teachers free up classroom time with more interactive and collaborative activities by providing students with language exercises or lessons that use AI-powered tools outside of the classroom. A teacher can use data generated by AI tools to monitor student's progress before class. For example, if the AI platform shows that a student is failing to grasp a particular grammatical concept, this can be discussed before class during the in-class session. The appropriate instruction and extra practice can be furnished by the teacher. This fosters an active student and maximizes the use of time in the class by taking greater control of the learning from out of the classroom (Bergmann & Sams, 2012).

This also fosters creating more interactive experiences of learning through applications which have included gamification, speech recognition, and virtual reality by AI for language learning. For instance, AI-based chatbots and virtual assistants allow students the opportunity to try speaking and writing in real-life settings without the apprehension of dealing with a real audience. Such tools can mimic natural conversations, assess pronunciation, and give immediate correction, which language learners may be shy to speak for fear of mistakes in front of others. These AI tools can be used by teachers to facilitate learning among their students. In this way, students are made to use them as part of a comprehensive learning experience that will include both the traditional language teaching and interactive practice with AI (Vogel et al., 2019). By embracing such new approaches, teachers can make learning more interesting, motivational, and effective for students.

Moreover, the change in teaching approaches toward AI requires that students develop a critical awareness of technology. Although AI tools are a great strength for language acquisition, the teacher is also required to help the learner become a discerning user of these technologies. The ability to use an AI tool proficiently goes along with the development of a mind to critically think about the information given by those systems. Teachers can teach their students that AI cannot be understood in all the cultural nuances or even the context of meanings; therefore, they should apply the knowledge learned to real-life scenarios where human interaction remains paramount. The critical approach would ensure that students are reminded of the limits of AI and use it as an augmentation tool instead of a substitute for human expertise (Godwin-Jones, 2019).

The third requirement is that educators should be ready to continuously review the effectiveness of AI tools and to modify their teaching skills. Since the AI technologies change, new applications and platforms start to emerge and thus, educationists need to be updated regarding the latest discoveries and best practices in AI-based learning. Teachers can update themselves on professional development opportunities as well as read the scholarly literature on AI in education and share experiences with colleagues to get a better insight into the subject. Such continuous evolution makes teachers' teaching methodology always current, relevant, and responsive to the growing needs of students as well as the abiding dynamism in educational technology (Huang et al., 2020).

To summarize, what is required in order to communicate with AI capabilities is an adaptable and innovative teaching approach. Teachers need to find the balance between pedagogical practices and tools embedded in AI to make learning as attractive and engaging as possible for their students, catering to different needs. Teaching will be enabled to support AI as a tool by promoting more autonomy, collaboration, and critical thinking in the language learning environment.

6. ETHICAL ISSUES AND CHALLENGES

However, integrating AI into the language learning context raises several ethical questions and dilemmas that teachers, developers, and policymakers should handle sensitively. On one hand, AI has tremendous potential for learning experience but poses questions over the data protection of users, bias in the algorithm, and the issue of access, balancing the role between man and machine. These issues call for continuous discussion and thoughtful action to ensure that AI tools are used responsibly and ethically without compromising the very basis of equitable and inclusive education.

1. **Data Privacy and Security:** One of the major ethical concerns related to AI in education is the collection, storage, and use of student data. AI systems heavily depend on large datasets to personalize learning experiences, track progress, and provide targeted feedback. Such data often contains sensitive information, such as the level of language proficiency, personal learning habits, and sometimes behavioral patterns among students. This raises significant privacy issues, especially when the information about students is collected and processed without adequate safeguards in place or used for unintended purposes. Schools and educational institutions must ensure that AI tools comply with data protection

regulations, such as the General Data Protection Regulation (GDPR) in Europe or similar laws elsewhere, to protect students' privacy and maintain trust in these technologies (Sundar, 2019).

There is also a risk of data misuse or unauthorized access to private information, which could result in serious consequences for students. It involves transparent communication on data collection and usage, assuring students as well as families in connection with those details regarding the student records how and where their information is processed. Institutions of education must commit themselves to protect information from accessing people who want it for unlawful reasons. All those involved-in creating ethical AI -must uphold students' confidentiality to create that trusted and fair atmosphere in these language learning with AI environments.

2. **Algorithmic Bias and Fairness:** Another ethical issue is the possibility of algorithmic bias in AI-based learning tools. AI learns from the data it is trained on, and if the data used to train these systems is biased or unrepresentative, the AI's recommendations and feedback can reflect those biases. For example, language learning algorithms are learned mainly from the data of native English speakers, and less efficient or culturally inappropriate pedagogy emerges when teaching students whose first languages or linguistic cultures differ. This sort of bias only perpetuates stereotyping, discrimination, and exclusion of learners for certain populations. According to O'Neil, 2016

AI also creates biases, possibly favoring a particular mode of teaching or speaking or certain types of cultural norms in which the variety in the learner's background will suffer. There is a need to have inclusive data that mirror linguistic, cultural, and educational backgrounds when developing and validating AI tools. It will be the responsibility of teachers to scrutinize some recommendations made by AI in case these possess bias so these resources work equitably in helping all kinds of learners from any background in any context. The only way to avoid the reinforcement of existing inequalities in language education is through promoting diversity and fairness in AI design.

3. **Accessibility and the Digital Divide:** Another key concern is accessibility with regard to the digital divide in AI-based language learning tools. AI technologies might make language learning more accessible for a wider population, but a significant digital divide exists with respect to necessary hardware, software, and reliable internet connectivity. In low-income communities, rural areas, or developing countries, students may lack the resources to fully benefit from AI-driven language learning platforms (González, 2019). As AI becomes more

integrated into educational systems, the gap between students with access to advanced technologies and those without could widen, exacerbating existing educational inequalities.

Policymakers and educators need to ensure AI tools are available for all students from any socio-economic background. They could provide cheap devices and internet connectivity, or come up with an offline version of AI tools, or a mobile-based platform which is not a bandwidth-intensive system. Finally, there could be AI solutions compatible with disabled pupils, providing inclusions with adequate opportunities to every learner to become disabled with impairing physical, cognition, or sensing parts, sharing all learning prospects as other people of normal mental.

4. **Instructor Autonomy with the aid of AI in teaching:** Another major dilemma is that these AI systems pose a possibility where teaching autonomy gets destroyed. While AI tools, therefore increase teaching effectiveness by automating tasks and providing learners with personalized learning experiences, there lies a concern that over-reliance on AI may undermine the role of teachers, reducing professional agency and influence inside the classroom (Selwyn, 2019). Teachers may be coerced into embracing AI tools just to stay in pace with technological development, or their professional judgment is constrained by their inability to meet the diverse needs of students.

The third concern is that AI systems might perpetuate more standardized and algorithm-driven approaches to education, potentially at the expense of the nuanced contextual understanding brought by human teachers. Teachers must be kept at the center of the learning process, with AI used as a support tool and not as a replacement for the teacher's own expertise. It is crucial that teachers be able to adapt and make decisions based on their own knowledge and experience so that the use of AI enriches rather than dictates the educational experience.

5. **Teacher Preparation and Responsible AI Use:** As more advanced AI tools become increasingly prevalent, in-service and preservice teacher education must ensure that educators obtain strong training to use such technologies knowledgeably and responsibly. Teachers have to be supported with relevant ability: critically reviewing AI tools; their functioning and limitations; and how to harness the latter appropriately for more democratic learning outcomes. Training should also be conducted on the ethical aspects of AI, such as bias potential, data privacy, and the need for inclusive and accessible technologies. This will enable educators to become AI literate, thus allowing teachers to be

equipped with the knowledge to make informed decisions about how AI can be responsibly integrated into teaching practices.

In summary, even though AI presents immense potential in enhancing language learning, ethical issues regarding AI have to be thoughtfully considered. Issues such as data privacy, algorithmic bias, accessibility, and teacher autonomy must be addressed through careful policies, inclusive design, and professional development. With these challenges, AI will be a powerful tool in language education that will help bring fairness, equity, and the best interest of students.

7. BUILDING TEACHER COMPETENCE IN AI INTEGRATION

Building teacher competence on AI integration will be a determinant for effective and ethical use of AI technologies within language learning. While AI can bring immense improvements to educational practice, teachers also need to acquire the knowledge, skills, and confidence to implement these tools effectively in their teaching. Teacher competence in the integration of AI is not only about understanding the technology tools themselves but also being critical and adapting solutions to fit different needs among the students. Thorough professional development, support, and collaboration, therefore, have to be an important component of achieving successful AI adoption in the classroom.

The first way of building competence among teachers is by providing them with targeted professional development programs that focus on AI literacy. These programs should be designed in a way to help familiarize educators with the basic principles of AI and different types of AI applications in education settings, their benefits, and their limitations. This way, teachers will be better positioned to evaluate which tools are best suited for their educational goals and student populations by gaining a foundational understanding of AI technologies. Professional development should also include hands-on training with AI tools and platforms, enabling teachers to gain practical experience and integrate these technologies into their existing teaching practices (Luckin et al., 2016).

At a deeper level, AI literacy surpasses the technical approach to AI devices and includes reflections on ethical implications, such as considerations about data privacy, algorithmic biases, or ensuring that each student has access to learning. Concomitantly, teachers also have to learn how AI functions, what kinds of data each collects, and how these resources can be maximally utilized toward creating an environment of inclusiveness and equity for all learners. Professional development programs should address such ethical concerns and prepare educators to make informed decisions about the use of AI in the classroom and ensure AI integration does not impact inequities or reproduce bias (O'Neil, 2016).

Teachers also need continuous support as they transition into using AI in the classroom. Actually, teachers should have adequate access to professional updated learning on the new tools and best practice as updated platforms in using AI productively in class. The school and education authorities should set networks of support, for example, mentorship, peer collaboration, and online access, which will allow teachers to share experiences, troubleshoot the identified challenges, and exchange strategies for the effective integration of AI. The collaborative learning environment will also ease teachers' nerves as they experiment with new technologies while simultaneously enjoying a sense of community as they cope with the changes AI brings into their classrooms (Dabbagh & Kitsantas, 2012).

Teachers must be able to shift the teaching style according to the personalized and data-driven nature of AI tools. For example, if the teacher is trained on how to interpret insights and feedbacks generated from AI systems, then this information would be brought into instructional practices. Commonly, the data of student progress, strength, and weakness from AI systems require the teachers to understand how this applied information influences altering a lesson plan, personal support, and an individualized approach towards learning. This shift makes the teacher take a much more fluid and responsive teaching role, where the learning automation is weighed against the human, emotional, and creative and critical thinking dimensions of education (Hwang et al., 2020).

Further, competence development for AI integration must be facilitated by a culture of experimentation and adaptation. Educators should be empowered to try new AI tools and share their perceptions about applicability with the team. Development of a growth mindset allows educators to explore new technologies in AI with more confidence and develop informed judgment and decision-making skills in this field of knowledge. This further helps to refine teaching. Schools should provide opportunities where teachers interact with AI both in the classroom and in their professional learning journey, so they understand AI as an enabler not as a threat but increases their capacity to teach and support more effectively.

Teacher competence to harness AI is a collective responsibility. Policymakers, educational institutions, and technology developers must collaborate to provide teachers with the resources, training, and support they need to succeed in an AI-enhanced educational landscape. Collaborative efforts should focus on making AI tools accessible and user-friendly, developing comprehensive teacher training programs, and ensuring that AI technologies are aligned with curriculum standards and pedagogical goals. By investing in the professional growth of educators and fostering a culture of continuous learning, we can ensure that AI becomes a positive force in language education, supporting teachers in their mission to provide the best possible learning experiences for their students.

8. STUDENT-TEACHER RELATIONSHIPS IN AN AI-ENHANCED LEARNING ENVIRONMENT

The student-teacher relationship is altered in the presence of AI in the learning environment. Technology becomes accommodated while the very basic human element of teaching and learning remains intact. All classroom dynamics can change with AI tools, providing numerous possibilities for more personalized learning; however, this also comes with the challenge of ensuring a supportive, empathetic, and truly human teacher-student relationship. The role of the teacher shifts from being the sole provider of knowledge to a facilitator, guiding students through a learning journey augmented by AI-powered tools. In this context, fostering positive and meaningful student-teacher relationships is critical to ensuring that AI contributes to, rather than detracts from, students' emotional and academic growth.

1. **Emotional Connection and Support:** Some of the significant challenges AI offers in the classroom is how to maintain an emotional connection or a bond between the students and teachers. Although an AI system can offer personalized feedback, tailoring a learning experience according to individual needs, there is no human way of understanding the emotional and social issues that a classroom offers. However, teachers are best at recognizing what their students may need emotionally, and they respond that way. Teachers provide support and encouragement and motivation for which AI lacks. Students have to feel protected, understood, and motivated, and that they can only be gotten from a teacher in the process of learning (Zhao, 2020).

Teachers, though AI is on the scene, still play an important role concerning the emotional needs of learners by establishing a friendly and open classroom (Zhao, 2020). Teachers can use AI data to gain insights into a student's progress and areas of struggle, but it is their empathetic and individualized responses to this data that help students build resilience and self-confidence. For instance, when a student does not understand a particular concept, AI may suggest a remedial activity, but it is the motivation and individualized support from the teacher that can make all the difference in how the student feels about himself or herself. Teachers who are more concerned with students' emotional and social needs ensure that AI becomes a means of empowerment and not alienation or stress for them (Tegmark, 2017).

2. **Personalized feedback and guidance:** AI systems are excellent for immediate, personalized feedback on student progress. Machine learning tools can analyze individual performance in real-time to provide students with recommendations and corrective feedback. However, teachers have an ability to contextualize feedback within a larger educational framework that AI systems lack. Teachers can interpret the AI-generated data through a broader lens by understanding the specific learning styles, cultural contexts, and personal motivations of the students. Blending insights from AI into human understanding can enable teachers to provide feedback that is academically helpful yet emotionally resonating and motivating for the students. Hwang et al., 2020.

In an AI-enhanced learning environment, students may be getting more frequent customized feedback, but this would still depend on good teachers' interpretations of AI-generated data on how to create action from data. Teachers have the opportunity and ability to get insights from AI into their students' activities that they will not be seeing otherwise, such as students who consist of struggling with the exact same part in language learning to those who never fully engage with content. With this information, the teacher can provide more focused intervention, suggest specific change, or alter teaching practices in order to see that all children are supported in the classroom.

3. **Collaboration and Social Learning:** AI can encourage collaboration and peer learning, but it is only the teacher who can make the experience meaningful in building strong relationships with others. Because although AI is capable of delivering individualized learning paths to students, it cannot provide the social interaction and collaborative problem-solving of a teacher. Collaborative learning opportunities-which include such practices as group discussions, peer reviews, and shared projects-remain important in education, and the role of the teacher is paramount to constructing and enacting such an activity. In a classroom that is AI-enriched, the teacher can make use of AI applications that are designed to enhance collaboration, for instance, language learning apps that allow students to practice using language with each other, or working together on AI-generated challenges; thus, the core focus remains on communication, social skills, and teamwork (Vogel et al., 2019).

The human presence of a teacher in collaborative activities fulfills the emotional and social needs of students. Teachers can observe group dynamics, intervene when necessary, and guide a lot of ways on how to negotiate conflicts or differences in opinion. Social learning is essential in helping students develop such critical interpersonal skills, from empathy to negotiation and effective communication-something which AI cannot replace.

4. **Trust and Autonomy:** AI technologies will allow students to learn on their own time, giving them the autonomy to explore content and receive feedback that is unique to their learning needs. This enables students to have a sense of independence and be empowered. Yet, for all of this to occur, students need to trust not only the technology but also their teachers. Teachers can build such trust by making sure that the AI systems used are ethical and transparent, and then explaining to students how the tools work and what they will gain from them. Teachers should model positive behaviors in regard to technology use, demonstrating that AI is a resource to supplement their learning and not a replacement for human guidance and support (Luckin et al., 2016).

The challenges students face in learning with AI would be well-known to the teacher, who can handle them effectively to foster trust, especially those less familiar with technology or afraid of it. Thus, giving clear instructions, providing emotional reassurance, and offering alternative methods of support are very crucial strategies that make sure all the students are confident in their learning journey. A teacher can create balance between autonomy, trust, and human connection so that the students can be positive towards AI and their whole learning experience.

5. **Teacher as a Role Model and Facilitator:** Even as AI continues to find its place in education, it is the teacher who is central to the role of guiding the student through their learning journey. Facilitation, mentorship, and mentoring are crucial elements a teacher in the AI-augmented class is expected to do. To use technology efficiently, teachers and the students ought to make them ethically. Educators should assist learners to harness tools of artificial intelligence not for an easy route into learning, but as supplementary aides that develop autonomous and assertive learners. This is how the teacher will play a mentoring role by being morally and academically sound while establishing a mutually respectful and collaborative relationship with his student (Selwyn, 2019).

In addition, the teachers must foster critical thinking of AI and its impact on society. Encouraging the students to think critically about the role of AI in their education, how it affects their learning, and its broader societal implications helps students develop a more nuanced understanding of technology. This approach ensures that the student-teacher relationship remains grounded in trust, respect, and shared goals, as opposed to the idea that AI is replacing human interaction.

In summary, while AI will undoubtedly advance the field of language learning, teaching professionals need to take special care not to forget those elements related to human development. Human touch, specific feedback, social learning, trust, and mentorship are aspects that, even in the technologically enhanced environment, make the relationship between the teacher and student very necessary. If teachers keep these basic foundations intact, then AI technologies would not replace meaningful interaction in the classroom, but enhance it.

9. THE FUTURE OF LANGUAGE EDUCATION: TEACHERS IN THE AI ERA

With AI changing the game in each and every sector, it's now all set to change the teaching practice in schools and redefine the role of the educator in unprecedented ways. The integration of AI technologies into the language classroom does not signal a decrease in the need for teachers but rather demands a reevaluation of their role as facilitators, mentors, and decision-makers within an increasingly AI-driven environment. The future of language education depends on how educators adapt to such technological changes in a manner that ensures AI acts to complement human instruction, not replace it. As technologies and traditional teaching continue to blur together, teachers need to prepare themselves for the opportunities as well as challenges presented by AI, keep sight of human-centered pedagogy, and at the same time take advantage of AI tools.

1. **Teachers as Designers of Personalized Learning Experience:** In the AI era, teachers will no longer be the sole source of knowledge, but rather the designers of personalized learning experiences. This allows AI to offer real-time insights into students' learning behaviors, track progress, and offer feedback tailored to the needs of individual students. But teachers are in a unique position to interpret such data and apply it within a broader pedagogical framework that takes into account not only the students' academic needs but also their emotional and social well-being. With AI systems providing learning pathways that are personalized, the teachers will be expected to curate, modify, and refine the content for learning so that it aligns with the curriculum as well as the different learning needs of students.

Teachers will also have the role of selecting and integrating the best AI tools that suit their pedagogical approach and that encourage creativity, collaboration, and critical thinking within the learning environment. While AI brings tailor-made learning to the classroom, it is this very expertise with understanding the motivations, cultural backgrounds, and individual challenges of the students that will allow teachers to mold and shape the learning experience accordingly (Chen et al., 2020). In these, teachers will have to continuously assess whether the AI tools in the classroom are meeting the changing needs of students.

2. **Teacher-Student Collaboration in AI-Enhanced Classrooms:** The future of the teacher-student relationship will shift from a hierarchical structure to a more collaborative partnership in the AI-enhanced classroom. AI systems can automate certain tasks, such as grading, feedback, and administrative duties, freeing up time for teachers to engage in more meaningful interactions with students. Teachers will have more time to focus on creativity, guide students through problem-solving, and help them navigate complex concepts in language learning. This shift enables a more student-centered learning environment, where students actively participate in their own learning journey with the support and mentorship of their teacher.

Students will then be more responsible for their active use of AI tools in facilitating their learning processes, while the teachers will then act as facilitators who direct students on the proper use of AI for the acquisition of language. Teachers will be giving them feedback not only over progress but also developing the attributes and, consequently, the skills needed to interact critically with these tools, including evaluating the effectiveness of AI-generated feedback and making decisions about their learning trajectory. This collaboration between AI, teachers, and students will, therefore, start a more dynamic, interactive, and engaging learning process (Baker et al., 2020).

3. **AI-Based Assessment and Teacher Insights:** AI can help transform the use of assessments by checking language; it provides real-time, personalized feedback, detailed analytics, and learning suggestions. They track the real-time progress of the student and gauge areas where improvement is necessary, all around the skill level of the students for their assessments. However, while AI-driven assessments can efficiently evaluate language skills, teachers will still play a crucial role in interpreting these results, contextualizing them within the broader curriculum, and making instructional decisions based on these insights.

The future of language education will see a hybrid approach to assessment, where AI provides objective data on student performance, but teachers apply their professional judgment to interpret and respond to that data. For instance, AI can track the accuracy of pronunciation, grammatical correctness and vocabulary usage of a student. However, it is only the teacher who is at the liberty to evaluate the communicative intent, contextual accuracy, and many other linguistic details that AI cannot pick up. AI and human judgment will combine together to ensure that assessment is complete both in terms of linguistic and communicative competencies (Jisc, 2020).

4. **Teacher Professional Development and Lifelong Learning:** As AI in language learning gains more prominence, teachers need continuous professional development. Such training will keep teachers up-to-date with the emergent technologies, AI trends, and pedagogies evolving. In such a fast rate of AI innovation, teachers are lifelong learners seeking skills and knowledge to make them effective practitioners. Professional development programs must not only address how to use AI tools but also help teachers understand the underlying AI technologies, ethical considerations, and best practices for integrating AI into their teaching practices.

Teachers will need to develop AI literacy, not just for using tools in the classroom but also for critically assessing the impact on student learning, ethics, and privacy. The future of language education will make teachers leaders in technology integration; they will mentor their peers and students on how to navigate an increasingly AI-centric educational landscape. With this shift toward lifelong learning, teacher education programs also need to shift toward incorporating AI literacy from the start, ensuring that future educators are equipped with AI technologies as part of the pedagogical toolkit from the very start (Schmid et al., 2019).

5. **Human Factor:** Compassion, Incentive, and Innovation. As much as AI provides a lot in terms of possibilities for optimizing the learning process, it is highly unlikely to make human qualities such as empathy, motivation, and creativity less relevant. In the future of language education, both AI capabilities and the irreplaceable human factors that teachers introduce into the classroom must be balanced. AI cannot replace the emotional support, encouragement, or personalized mentorship that a teacher provides. Teachers will still be the most important motivators for students in overcoming learning difficulties and creating a safe learning environment in which students can feel valued, respected, and inspired.

In the AI era, language education will require teachers to tap into their creativity and emotional intelligence, qualities that AI cannot replicate. Teachers will still need to develop interesting, interactive lesson plans, facilitate student collaboration and argumentation, and drive students to be thoughtful about their learning. The most effective AI-enabled classrooms will be those in which teachers employ AI as a tool to enrich human-centered teaching rather than replace the very elements of humanity that inspire and energize their students (Baker et al., 2020).

6. **Ethical Leadership and Advocacy:** Teachers will be tasked with the responsibility of becoming leaders in advocating for the ethical use of AI in education. As AI continues to evolve, concerns like data privacy, algorithmic bias, and the digital divide will come to the forefront. Teachers should advocate for responsible AI practice that places central values on the safety of students regarding privacy, inclusion, and fairness. They will be very instrumental in ensuring that AI is used in ways that positively impact the issue of educational equity, where each child whatever his or her background or ability gets to learn equally.

Teachers should keep themselves updated about AI ethics, data protection regulations, and the possible influence of AI on students' lives. This way, they will be in a position to contribute to responsible use of AI, ensuring that these technologies enhance the learning experience without sacrificing equity, justice, and well-being for students (O'Neil, 2016).

The future of language education remains a one with teachers at the center. However, there may be new roles as breakthroughs in technology are seen to occur. Teachers would remain facilitators, designers of learning experiences, and critical interpreters of data produced by artificial intelligence. Empathy, creativity, and mentorship as human qualities would continue to become important aspects where AI would simply be used to enhance, rather than replace the teacher-student relationship. Education would thus not only have integrated AI but required teachers to focus on continuous professional development, ethical leadership, and responsibility for creating an inclusive and balanced learning environment to ensure that education in language continues to be human-centric and empowering to all learners.

10. CONCLUSION

The introduction of AI in language education is an opportunity to deeply alter the ways of teaching and learning, opening a new field with great challenges as well as tremendous opportunities. In the course of this chapter, we have illustrated how AI may be a helpful tool in support of language learning, including its capacity for tailored instruction, more effective assessment, and easier access to learning material. While AI promises to revolutionize education, the teacher remains central to meaningful, human-centered learning. The role of a teacher will change in this AI-enhanced environment; it will not get replaced. Instead, teachers will continue to act as facilitators, mentors, and interpreters of data generated by AI to ensure that technology will complement and amplify rather than undermine traditional pedagogical practices.

As AI usage in the classroom continues to grow, it is important to understand that the balanced use of technology and human aspects of teaching has to be embraced to keep up with growth. Teachers must learn to change their strategies as designers of student-centered learning experiences that include using AI tools but remain emotionally and relationally positioned in the class. Their experience in the field of human development, sensitivity to culture, and social-emotional learning will be the core of this potential in order to ensure that AI can contribute to greater student engagement, well-being, and academic growth holistically.

Lastly, the language education of the future means teachers must build new competencies, among which deeper knowledge of AI technologies and their implications regarding ethics. For effective engagement in this new landscape, there will be a need for continued collaboration with peers, development of AI literacy among teachers, and focus on the development of critical thinking skills and creativity among students. While instant feedback and multiple approaches to learning might seem to argue for automation, human contact will remain important: building emotional resilience among students, fostering social interaction, and encouraging collaborations-all factors central to language learning.

It is still the ethics that will determine future AI in education. The teacher will become an advocate for the proper use of AI in the learning process-to guarantee that all technologies used in the classroom reflect values of equity, privacy, and fairness. As AI continues improving, teachers will also be that key force ensuring that the human in education will never lose its soul and that AI will always find its way of helping everyone regardless of his background and ability.

Finally, if educators, policymakers, and developers of technology could work together toward integrating AI that emphasizes both innovation in technology and human connection, the future for language education promises a great deal toward enhancing teaching and learning experiences in this AI era. In the future, the role of the teacher will not be a competition against AI but will utilize AI to improve the teacher's practice and ensure that the students get an all-rounded, engaging, and personalized education that develops linguistic proficiency but also fosters critical thinking, creativity, and empathy. As AI continues to evolve, so will the significance of the teacher as the heart of the educational experience, assisting students through an ever more complex and technological world. Henceforth, the future of language education belongs to the successful merge of AI capabilities and human expertise at once intellectually enriching and emotionally supportive.

REFERENCES

Baker, R. S.. (2020). Designing personalized learning experiences with AI: A framework for language education. *Educational Psychologist, 55*(3), 121–136.

Bergmann, J., & Sams, A. (2012). *Flip your classroom: Reach every student in every class every day*. International Society for Technology in Education.

Chen, W., Li, J., & Zha, D. (2021). Artificial intelligence in language education: A review of applications and effects. *Journal of Educational Computing Research, 59*(3), 507–525.

Chen, X.. (2020). AI in education: The role of teachers in the future classroom. *Journal of Educational Technology & Society, 23*(2), 40–52.

Dabbagh, N., & Kitsantas, A. (2012). Using technology to enhance learning and teaching in the 21st century: The role of teachers as facilitators. *Computers in Human Behavior, 28*(4), 1167–1175.

Fitzpatrick, T., Alvarado, P., & Tolk, A. (2021). Personalized language learning with AI-powered apps: A case study of Duolingo and Babbel. *International Journal of Education Technology, 22*(3), 245–259.

Godwin-Jones, R. (2019). Language learning and technology: A new paradigm. *CALICO Journal, 36*(1), 1–13.

González, C. (2019). The digital divide and its impact on education: Bridging the gap with technology in language learning. *Journal of Educational Technology & Society, 22*(3), 156–167.

Guszcza, J., Chui, M., & Patel, S. (2017). *The future of work: How AI will change the way we learn*. McKinsey Global Institute.

Heffernan, N. (2019). The evolution of adaptive learning systems in language education. *Educational Technology Review, 45*(2), 76–88.

Huang, R. H., Spector, J. M., & Yang, J. (2020). Educational technology and the transformation of the classroom: The role of AI in personalized learning. *Journal of Educational Technology & Society, 23*(4), 1–10.

Hwang, G. J., Chen, P. H., & Huang, Y. M. (2020). Integrating AI-based technologies for personalized language learning. *Educational Technology Research and Development, 68*(4), 2203–2224.

Luckin, R., Holmes, W., Griffiths, M., & Forcier, L. B. (2016). *Intelligence unleashed: An argument for AI in education*. Pearson Education.

O'Neil, C. (2016). *Weapons of math destruction: How big data increases inequality and threatens democracy*. Crown Publishing Group.

Schmid, K.. (2019). Teacher education in the age of AI: Preparing educators for the future classroom. *International Journal of Educational Development*, *67*, 44–53.

Selwyn, N. (2019). Should robots replace teachers? AI in education. *International Journal of Educational Technology in Higher Education*, *16*(1), 5–15.

Sundar, S. S. (2019). Data privacy in AI: Challenges and opportunities for education. *International Journal of Educational Policy*, *24*(2), 143–155.

Tegmark, M. (2017). *Life 3.0: Being human in the age of artificial intelligence*. Alfred A. Knopf.

VanLehn, K. (2011). The relative effectiveness of human tutoring, intelligent tutoring systems, and other tutoring systems. *Educational Psychologist*, *46*(4), 197–221. DOI: 10.1080/00461520.2011.611369

Vogel, D., Stetson, H., & Patel, S. (2019). Advancements in AI for language learning: The promise and potential. *Journal of Computer Assisted Learning*, *35*(5), 488–497.

Zhao, Y. (2020). The future of education: The impact of AI on teaching and learning. *Journal of Educational Technology & Society*, *23*(4), 130–142.

ADDITIONAL READING

Alia, M., & Aliia, A. M. (2025). How AI Tools Affect Discourse Markers When Paraphrased. In Jomaa, N. (Ed.), *Using AI Tools in Text Analysis, Simplification, Classification, and Synthesis* (pp. 319–348). IGI Global Scientific Publishing., DOI: 10.4018/979-8-3693-9511-0.ch011

Attamimi, R. A. (2025). AI and English Language Education: A New Era in the Arab World. In Jomaa, N. (Ed.), *Using AI Tools in Text Analysis, Simplification, Classification, and Synthesis* (pp. 113–130). IGI Global Scientific Publishing., DOI: 10.4018/979-8-3693-9511-0.ch004

Mohammadkarimi, E., Omar, J. A., & Rashid, A. S. (2025). Advancements and Challenges in Automated Evaluation of Spoken Language Proficiency Using AI. In Jomaa, N. (Ed.), *Using AI Tools in Text Analysis, Simplification, Classification, and Synthesis* (pp. 225–256). IGI Global Scientific Publishing., DOI: 10.4018/979-8-3693-9511-0.ch008

Owais, A. K. (2025). AI in English Teaching With ChatGPT: Does It Really Work? In Jomaa, N. (Ed.), *Using AI Tools in Text Analysis, Simplification, Classification, and Synthesis* (pp. 197–224). IGI Global Scientific Publishing., DOI: 10.4018/979-8-3693-9511-0.ch007

KEY TERMS AND DEFINITIONS

AI-driven language learning environment: A setting for language education where artificial intelligence tools are integrated to personalize learning, provide real-time feedback, and adapt assessments to individual learner needs.

Personalized learning experiences: Tailored educational approaches that use AI to meet the specific needs, pace, and interests of each learner.

AI-generated data: Information produced by AI systems (e.g., learner analytics or performance metrics) used to inform instruction and support learning.

Pedagogical strategies: Teaching methods and approaches adapted to incorporate AI tools effectively in the classroom.

Emotional connections: The bonds teachers form with students to support motivation, empathy, and a humanized learning experience.

Ethical considerations: Moral questions and challenges related to the implementation of AI in education, including issues of equity, privacy, and bias.

Equity: Ensuring fair and inclusive access to AI tools and learning opportunities.

Privacy: Protecting student data and personal information in AI systems.

Bias: Preventing discrimination or unfair treatment stemming from AI algorithms.

Chapter 4
The Key Obstacles to using Emerging Artificial Intelligence Tools in Foreign Language Learning: A Systematic Review

Joelle Danielle Ngo Ndjama
https://orcid.org/0000-0002-2472-2329
Department of Human Resource Management, Faculty of Management Sciences, Vaal University of Technology, Vanderbijlpark, South Africa

ABSTRACT

The advent and integration of artificial intelligence (AI) in higher education have become invaluable. The pursuit of learning foreign languages has been a continuous and significant human effort, motivated by the desire to enhance cross-cultural interaction, enhance job prospects, and promote cognitive growth; there has been a growing focus on integrating artificial intelligence technologies into different educational domains, including language learning recently. Nevertheless, the utilisation of these technologies also presents obstacles and possible drawbacks. Grounded in the theory of constructivism, this study aims to identify and analyse the key barriers that hinder the effective use of artificial intelligence tools in foreign language education. A systematic literature review was conducted as the research method to achieve the research objectives. The results revealed several obstacles, which include lack of accessibility and affordability to technology, and limited understanding of how to effectively integrate artificial intelligence into language instruction.

DOI: 10.4018/979-8-3693-9606-3.ch004

1. INTRODUCTION

The Fourth Industrial Revolution (4IR or Industry 4.0) signifies the swift technological progress of the 21st century, characterised by enhanced interconnectivity, automation, sophisticated manufacturing technologies and machine learning (Dugošija, 2024). A prominent feature of the 4IR is Artificial Intelligence (AI), which has been integrated into nearly every facet of human endeavour (Dugošija, 2024). Moulieswaran and Kumar (2022) posit that the 4IR, alongside the integration of AI technologies, is transforming both the business and industrial sectors, as well as the educational landscape, which is experiencing an evolution and is now termed Education 4.0. These innovations offer educators in the field of foreign language instruction a valuable resource to enhance their pedagogical approaches, thereby facilitating improved academic performance among students (Alshaikhi & Khasawneh, 2024). Within the dynamic realm of education, educators find themselves at a distinct crossroads, where conventional teaching beliefs intersect with state-of-the-art technology, for instructional delivery (Grubaugh, Levitt & Deever, 2023). The incorporation of AI into the teaching and learning of foreign language education is not a novel concept. According to Pokrivcakova (2019), the concept was first introduced by McCarthy (1956), who convened a workshop at Dartmouth College, stating that the exploration of AI would be grounded in the hypothesis that all elements of learning and other characteristics of intelligence can be accurately delineated. The delineation enables the creation of machines capable of simulating these processes. AI denotes the capacity of computer systems to perform tasks typically associated with human intelligence, such as learning and reasoning (Sadiku, Ashaolu, Ajayi-Majebi & Musa, 2021). Since the 1970s, the domain of AI in education has emerged, significantly impacting the integration of technology in teaching and learning, aimed at enhancing educational processes and fostering student success (Dimitriadou & Lanitis, 2023). The utilisation of digital technologies is essential in foreign language instruction, yet to maximise their effectiveness and enhance foreign language learning, they must offer additional pedagogical benefits in the classroom. Hence, Alshaikhi and Khasawneh (2024) explain that the integration of AI-driven technologies holds the promise of transforming the methodologies employed in the teaching and learning of foreign languages.

A language is deemed foreign when primarily obtained in an educational setting and not commonly used in the surrounding community (Moeller & Catalano, 2015). Moeller and Catalano (2015) argue that the learning of a non-native language, known as foreign language learning, occurs in a setting where the language is not commonly spoken. Hubackova (2016) posits that individuals are required to become proficient in a foreign language at some point in their lives. According to Murphy et al. (2020), English is the preferred foreign language in many countries, driven by the desire for non-native English speakers to gain proficiency to access more educational and employment prospects. In the Czech school system, children are mandated to start learning a foreign language during elementary school, with education in this area continuing throughout their academic journey. Additionally, adults frequently need to pursue foreign language studies as part of their professional development (Hubackova, 2016). Therefore, Suman and Suman (2023) assert that the pursuit of learning foreign languages has been a continuous and significant effort by humans, motivated by the desire to enhance cross-cultural interaction, enhance job prospects, and promote cognitive growth. Learning a foreign language is a crucial link in the interconnected relationships of the upcoming era (Gbollie & Gong, 2013). In addition, Moeller and Catalano (2015) point out that proficiency in a foreign language enables individuals to communicate proficiently and creatively, engaging in real-world scenarios within the culture's authentic linguistic framework.

In recent years, researchers have shown significant interest in the utilisation of information technology in language learning and teaching (Shadiev, Wen, Uosaki, Song, 2023; Lai, Saab & Admiraal, 2022; Lei, Fathi, Noorbakhsh & Rahimi, 2022; Soleimani et al., 2022; Shadiev & Yang, 2020; Ahmadi, 2018). Hence, recently, there has been a growing focus on integrating AI technologies into different educational domains, including language learning (Suman & Suman, 2023). Chemnad and Othman (2024) define AI as the capacity of a machine or computer system to simulate and perform tasks that typically require human intelligence, such as logical reasoning, learning, and problem resolution. As noted by Schwendicke, Samek and Krois (2020), AI was first coined in the 1950s to describe the development of machines capable of mimicking human cognitive functions. Despite differing opinions on Technology-enhanced language learning (TELL), research has indicated that technology plays a significant role in shaping educational processes and outcomes, leading many countries to invest in technological resources to support teaching and learning (Paiva & Bittencourt, 2020). De la Vall and Araya (2022) state that the popularity of AI in language learning has grown significantly because of its effectiveness and convenience. With the widespread use of smart devices and the Internet, individuals now have access to various methods of language learning. AI tools designed for language learning can assist learners by completing specific tasks on their behalf, ultimately saving them time. Additionally, these tools offer a personalised learning experience tailored to the individual's requirements and progress (De la Vall & Araya, 2022). The integration of information technology in language education has the potential to improve the learning journey for learners through the facilitation of customised, engaging, and collaborative learning methods (Rahimi & Fathi, 2022; Shatri, 2020). Moreover, Ilkka (2018) explains that AI has the potential to revolutionise the field of education by introducing innovative methods of learning, teaching, and education. Foreign language learning enhanced by

AI presents opportunities for a more tailored, adaptable, inclusive, and stimulating learning experience (Pokrivcakova, 2019). Pokrivcakova (2019) adds that it equips both educators and students with resources to address not only the content being taught but also the methods of learning and the emotional states of learners. Moreover, its impact on society cannot be overlooked, as it brings forth new challenges for educational institutions to address (Ilkka, 2018).

2. PROBLEM STATEMENT

Conventional methods of teaching foreign languages have often been characterised by rigid curricula, uniform teaching methods, and minimal customisation (Suman & Suman, 2023). McCarthy's (1956) initial predictions concerning AI, suggested that computers would emulate human cognitive processes and that AI systems would possess human-like thinking abilities, raising concerns about potential dominance over human control. However, these expectations have not materialised as anticipated (Pokrivcakova, 2019). This view is underscored by Suman & Suman, 2023) stating that learners encounter challenges with tailored progression, practice chances, and prompt feedback, all essential for successful language learning (Suman & Suman, 2023). On the other hand, the rapid advancement of emerging technologies and the accompanying digital changes pose substantial challenges for society as a whole and across all tiers of the educational sector (Schmidt & Strasser, 2022). Moreover, Schmidt and Strasser (2022) and Grimm et al. (2015) posit that the debate surrounding technology-enhanced language learning (TELL) has been a topic of international discussion, with varying viewpoints ranging from optimistic views to concerns about the risks associated with digital media. Furthermore, foreign language learning classrooms are prevalent in many high schools and even in some primary schools; however, despite foreign language becoming a standard in education, educators face challenges due to limited research and resources available for teaching the subject (Kuhlman, 2017). Additionally, the utilisation of AI technology in higher education has been extensively debated, yet there remain research deficiencies in examining the obstacles to using emerging AI tools in foreign language learning. These limitations have spurred an exploration of novel strategies that harness AI technology to deliver customised learning experiences. Schmidt and Strasser (2022) add that the complexity of the educational systems means that the development of AI-driven foreign language learning environments that cater to diverse learners and facilitate advanced subject learning is still in its early stages. In addition, the persistent issue of delayed practical application of theory arises from various factors such as delayed pedagogical recommendations for campus learning spaces, conceptual challenges in utilising AI tools, and the need to find innovative methods to engage learners in foreign language learning.

3. SIGNIFICANCE OF THE STUDY

The primary challenges in implementing AI technologies for foreign language learning are multifaceted and complex. These obstacles hinder the effective integration of AI tools into language learning environments, impacting the potential benefits that these technologies could offer to learners. This study is vital, as it not only informs the development of more effective pedagogical strategies but also guides the design of AI tools that are better aligned with the needs of language learners. Furthermore, the study's findings are relevant to the Sustainable Development Goals (SDGs), particularly in promoting quality education and fostering inclusive and equitable learning opportunities.

4. THEORETICAL FRAMEWORK

This study is grounded in the theory of constructivism. The theoretical roots of constructivism can be traced back to the early 20th century, with Vygotsky's (1984) framework being the most commonly referenced constructivist perspective (Amineh & Asl, 2015). According to Jonassen and Rohrer-Murphy (1999), constructivism serves as a theoretical framework for designing a constructivist learning environment. Language is considered fundamental to human thought processes, personal identity formation, and individual growth (Sa'd & Hatam, 2017). Grubaugh et al. (2023) emphasise that constructivism, a long-standing educational philosophy, stipulates that learning is not simply the transmission of facts, but a process of active engagement by learners drawing upon their existing knowledge and experiences. Sa'd and Hatam (2017) explain that learning a new language is a comprehensive experience that engages the individual on physical, cognitive, and emotional levels. In the teaching-learning process, both instructors and learners collaboratively engage with materials to facilitate knowledge construction (Tanjung, 2018). During this process, language learners navigate their self-perception as speakers of their native language (L1) while simultaneously recognising their roles as learners of a second language (L2), influencing their sense of identity (Sa'd & Hatam, 2017). Consequently, the formation of identity through language interaction is viewed as a perpetual, evolving, and dynamic journey. Hence, constructivists posit that learners actively build knowledge instead of simply absorbing information (University at Buffalo, 2024). However, Tanjung (2018) states that the effectiveness of this knowledge construction is compromised if instructors are the only ones making efforts to involve learners in the learning process. Therefore, it is essential for learners to actively participate by employing various strategies to engage with the content presented by their instructors (Tanjung, 2018).

With the advent of AI, a revolutionary technology capable of customising, adjusting, and improving instructional approaches and the learning process in alignment with constructivist ideals, a new era has dawned (Grubaugh et al., 2023). Roll and Wylie (2016) report that AI systems can develop knowledge from datasets through machine learning techniques. AI educators utilise interactive simulations, personalised feedback loops, and open-ended environments to involve learners in active discovery (Roll & Wylie, 2016). Hence, educators frequently utilise AI tools that are embedded in common software, including Microsoft Word, for tasks such as information retrieval (Grubaugh et al., 2023). In addition to these tools, educators can now purposefully incorporate AI tools like ChatGPT, BARD, Microsoft Bing, and others into constructivist pedagogy. This integration can enhance student engagement, metacognition, and conceptual change, while still maintaining the humanistic principles of education (Grubaugh et al., 2023). From this theoretical perspective, Huang, Mao and Zhang (2024) conclude that learning is seen as a self-regulated process that involves grappling with the tension between one's current personal worldview and novel ideas. It entails constructing fresh and realistic representations and models using cultural tools and symbols of development (Huang et al., 2024).

5. LITERATURE REVIEW

5.1 Foreign language learning

As described by Mitchell and Myles (1998), foreign language pertains to a form of communication that is seldom utilised in an individual's home country. Foreign language learning is distinguished from second language learning, which occurs when the learner is in an environment where the language being learned is spoken (Moeller & Catalano, 2015). For example, Hubackova (2016) comments that the linguistic environment of different countries may influence language learning, such as Canadian children learning French as a second language due to its status as one of Canada's official languages. While foreign language according to Gbollie and Gong (2013), typically lacks practical applications within one's immediate surroundings. It is believed that there are approximately 6,000 to 7,000 different languages spoken worldwide (Gbollie & Gong, 2013). Language learning in educational settings can be facilitated through various programs, with one common scenario being foreign language instruction where learners dedicate a portion of their weekly schedule to studying a new language in school (Murphy et al., 2020). Another educational context for language learning involves minority language learners in majority language environments, where learners from ethnic minority backgrounds are taught in the majority language, which may differ from their home language (Murphy et al., 2020).

Lantolf and Sunderman (2001) identified four primary objectives for language studies, which encompass reading foreign literature to gain insight into different cultures, practical aims such as employability and business utility, intellectual and linguistic growth through language learning, and the enhancement of personal enjoyment and cultural appreciation through travel and exploration. Moeller and Catalano (2015) add that learning a new language offers a unique perspective beyond one's own, enhancing the capacity to draw connections across various subjects and fostering an interdisciplinary outlook while fostering intercultural awareness. Language serves as a vital tool for effective interpersonal communication, facilitating a deeper comprehension of one's native language and heritage (National Standards in Foreign Language Education Project (NSFLEP), 2014). Language studies afford learners the chance to acquire linguistic and social insights, guiding them on when, how, and why to communicate with others (NSFLEP, 2014). For Gbollie and Gong (2013), the advantages associated with learning a foreign language are communication, mobility, economics, and employment. Communication is a crucial aspect of using foreign languages, especially in educational settings where learning occurs in a different language environment. The competitive job market today requires individuals to possess optimal skills and talents, making effective communication in foreign languages a valuable asset for employers. Economic interdependence in today's world necessitates understandable communication in business dealings, where foreign languages play a significant role in facilitating collaboration and cooperation.

5.2 Emerging AI tools

Schmidt and Strasser (2022) contend that AI is a rapidly advancing technological field that has garnered increasing attention to various inquiries. Jain and Jain (2019) refer AI to as the replication of human cognitive processes such as speech and visual recognition, language interpretation, and virtual decision-making by machines and robots. AI (AI) refers to machines, computers, or computer systems that replicate cognitive abilities typically linked to human intelligence, including learning and problem-solving (Pokrivcakova, 2019). It encompasses a distinct array of capabilities within computers, characterising AI as systems that execute cognitive functions generally associated with human thought processes, especially in the realms of learning and problem-solving (Baker & Smith, 2019). The ability of machines to mimic human thinking and behaviour has made AI highly significant across various domains (Jain & Jain, 2019).

In the realm of language learning, Pokrivcakova (2019) argues that digital platforms are progressively establishing themselves as standard tools. AI language learning tools are computer programs or software apps that assist users in learning and honing their foreign language skills through the use of AI algorithms (Alshaikhi & Khasawneh, 2024). These cloud-based systems, which integrate natural language processing (NLP), crowdsourcing, gamification features, automatic speech recognition, automatic speech generation, and AI writing assistance, are among the most favoured resources among younger learners (Pokrivcakova, 2019). Healey (2020) is of the view that while there exist numerous interpretations of AI, there appears to be a shared fundamental understanding: AI encompasses a range of technologies capable of problem-solving and task execution to attain specific objectives without direct human intervention. De la Vall and Araya (2022) assert that various AI language learning tools are available in the market, each offering unique features and capabilities and the popular examples include Duolingo, Elsa Speak, and Google Translate. Alharbi (2023) states that AI is used in language learning applications such as Babbel and Duolingo, highlighting its role in delivering tailored feedback to users regarding their educational advancement. Dugošija (2024) mentions Tutor AI, Conversly, Speak, Talkio AI, Lingostar, Duolingo, ELSA Speak, HelloTalk, and Speechling as platforms that function as virtual tutors, offering tailored instruction, focused exercises, and realistic practice situations, while evaluating students' spoken language by measuring their pronunciation and intonation against native speakers, delivering immediate feedback and improvement recommendations. These tools are software applications utilising AI algorithms to assist individuals in enhancing their proficiency in a foreign language, offering advantages like time efficiency, personalised learning experiences, and cultural insights (de la Vall & Araya, 2022).

5.2.1 AI listening and speaking tools

Sussmann (2024) posits that Speechify offers the feature of reading text aloud with customisable listening speed and a selection of voices. Otter.ai utilises AI technology to provide transcription services, enabling educators to generate written versions of audio material for improved listening skills practice (Sussmann, 2024). Educators can select specific segments from podcasts or conversations for learners to read and enhance their understanding. Moreover, Liu (2023) explains that speech recognition technology allows learners to enhance their speaking and listening abilities by receiving precise feedback.

According to Liu (2023), the utilisation of speech recognition technology allows learners to promptly receive feedback on their pronunciation and intonation, both of which are crucial components in enhancing their oral expression abilities. Consequently, learners can boost their confidence when communicating in a foreign language, leading to a higher likelihood of actively participating in conversations with native speakers (Liu, 2023). In addition, Flow Speak enables learners to enhance their confidence and fluency by offering unlimited speaking practice sessions. With the assistance of AI, learners receive feedback on their pronunciation, speed, fluency, and grammar. Speaking skills are often a priority for learners, but due to time constraints in the classroom, they may not get enough practice (Sussmann, 2024).

5.2.2 AI reading and comprehension tools

The enhancement of students' reading comprehension and vocabulary can be achieved through various functionalities provided by AI-assisted tools (Lestari et al., 2022). Dugošija, (2024) argues that these tools utilise adaptive learning algorithms to deliver personalised instruction tailored to individual students' needs, interests, and levels of English proficiency. They facilitate targeted reading activities, such as gap-fill tasks, comprehension assessments, flashcard generation, and interactive reading games, while also automating grading processes and offering constructive feedback and improvement suggestions (Dugošija, 2024). Sussmann (2024) argues that Readlang supports language learners in comprehending foreign texts through immediate word translations and AI-generated vocabulary explanations tailored to the context. Resource technologies like online dictionaries, translators, and grammar checkers play a crucial role in enhancing linguistic knowledge by aiding in vocabulary learning and improving language use through the provision of contextual information, translations, synonyms, and pronunciation models (OECD, 2024). Furthermore, Bahari and Gholami (2022) and Bikowski (2018) highlight that text analysis technologies enable learners to identify specific words, patterns, and vocabulary lists, allowing them to understand how words are utilised in various contexts.

5.2.3 AI writing tools

Recent advancements in AI have facilitated the development of innovative electronic writing tools, enhancing existing capabilities and introducing entirely new systems (Alharbi, 2023). Schmidt and Strasser (2022) opine that over the past few years, there has been a significant improvement in the built-in spell-checkers found in text processing software. Initially, these spell-checkers only focused on identifying spelling mistakes made by users. However, as time went on, these software applications expanded their capabilities by incorporating grammar-checking tools (Schmidt & Strasser, 2022). Alharbi (2023) notes that these writing support mechanisms assist in the writing process, proving essential for many writers, especially students, who benefit from human-like sentence completion suggestions and text generation. According to Sussmann (2024), practical AI tools such as Grammarly, ProWritingAid, Slick Write, QuillBot, and AI Email Writer can be utilised to enhance writing skills. A useful method of utilising these tools is by assigning learners the task of creating sample email responses to sample messages (Sussmann, 2024). According to Dale and Viethen (2021), one of the most significant advancements in writing attributed to AI is the implementation of AI-driven sentence and phrase auto-completion, along with alternative wording suggestions. These innovations have emerged and will persist in evolving due to AI applications and systems that aggregate extensive data sets and analyse them through artificial neural networks and machine learning techniques (Dale & Viethen, 2021).

The discussion surrounding the utilisation of AI-driven tools for aiding students in their writing endeavours remains contentious (Gayed, Carlon, Oriola & Cross, 2022; Fitria, 2021). Perkins (2023) argues that a distinct class of AI-driven software utilised by students to enhance their writing comprises Automated Paraphrasing Tools (APTs). These applications employ machine translation techniques to convert existing texts into new forms (Rogerson & McCarthy, 2017). Numerous scholars promote the usage of AI-driven platforms or applications to support students in their writing endeavours (Rukiati, Wicaksono, Taufan & Suharsono, 2023; Fyfe, 2022; Gayed et al., 2022; Godwin-Jones, 2022; Fitria, 2021). Indeed, a significant number of students and professionals leverage these tools to enhance the quality of their writing and guarantee its accuracy (Rukiati et al., 2023). Since its debut in the community on November 30, 2022, ChatGPT has captivated global attention with its remarkable capacity to execute highly intricate tasks (Baidoo-Anu & Ansah, 2023). Ma, Da and Hanh (2024) argue that it can produce coherent, somewhat accurate, systematic, and informative responses that maintain the topic and context of the discussion. Rather than depending on conventional internet searches, many learners might consider utilising ChatGPT for various text-related activities (Ma et al., 2024).

Nonetheless, Dugošija (2024) notes that the capacity of these tools to produce written content rapidly based solely on keywords or phrases raises significant concerns about the potential for increased academic dishonesty.

5.2.4 Machine translation technology

Alhaj (2023) posits that the advent of the digital era has significantly transformed teaching and learning methodologies, especially in the realm of translation education, due to the extensive use of the Internet and various network technologies. Schmidt and Strasser (2022) note that machine translation involves the automatic translation of text from one language to another through the utilisation of a vast linguistic database and sophisticated algorithms for the automatic translation of written content. Liu (2023) points out that mastering a foreign language involves grappling with the complexities of comprehending and translating text written in that language. However, the advent of machine translation technology has provided a valuable tool for learners to surmount these challenges and enhance the effectiveness of their language learning endeavours (Liu, 2023). De la Vall and Araya (2022) explain that machine translation tools utilise AI algorithms to automatically convert text or speech from one language to another in real-time. Liu (2023) observes that machine translation technology grants instant entry to foreign language resources and promotes interaction among learners speaking different languages. These tools are frequently employed for swift translations of brief phrases or sentences and are commonly integrated into mobile applications or online platforms. Prominent examples of machine translation tools encompass Google Translate and Bing Translator (Ducar & Schocket, 2018). Nevertheless, Schmidt and Strasser (2022) are of the view that DeepL is currently one of the leading AI-powered translation platforms, utilising deep learning technology rooted in neural network technology.

A diverse array of AI-driven tools is available for both foreign language learners and educators, aimed at facilitating their educational endeavours (Pokrivcakova, 2019). Dimitriadou and Lanitis (2023) assert that AI is widely implemented in educational settings through various mediums, including software applications, humanoid robots, web-based chatbots, and online platforms. Pokrivcakova (2019) states that the integration of AI in language education offers students prompt and tailored feedback, serving as a crucial foundation for personalised learning, which is a key principle of modern pedagogical practices. Alshaikhi and Khasawneh (2024) further explain that various AI feedback mechanisms, such as programmable writing evaluation tools, intelligent tutoring systems, and language learning applications, which leverage machine learning algorithms alongside NLP to offer learners insights into their language proficiency are employed in foreign language instruction.

6. METHOD AND MATERIALS

Various extant studies have been conducted on AI, especially its integration into higher education (Alshaikhi & Khasawneh, 2024) and foreign language learning (Shadiev et al., 2023; Lai et al., 2022; Lei et al., 2022; Soleimani et al., 2022; Shadiev & Yang, 2020; Ahmadi, 2018). This study employed a systematic literature review approach to explore relevant studies, across the globe, to provide in-depth information. The method used in this study involved conducting a comprehensive literature review to identify the key obstacles to using emerging AI tools in foreign language learning. Xiao and Watson (2019) describe a literature review as an analytical assessment of prior research and academic publications that establishes a basis for the research study, guides the research methodology, and enhances the theoretical comprehension of the subject matter. The researchers utilised literature search and keywords (obstacles, challenges, issues, AI, AI technologies, emerging AI tools, foreign language learning, and education) to identify relevant studies and articles. In addition, inclusion and exclusion criteria were established to ensure that only the most relevant and high-quality sources were included in the review. The inclusion criteria for the study involved selecting articles and studies that specifically addressed the challenges and obstacles related to the use of emerging AI tools in the context of learning a foreign language. The exclusion criteria for this study encompassed various teaching factors that act as obstacles to the effective implementation of AI tools in foreign language learning. These factors were carefully selected to ensure that the focus remained on the learners and their experiences, rather than on the educators or other external influences. Hence, this method allowed the researchers to gather a wide range of perspectives and insights from existing literature, providing a solid foundation for their analysis and discussion of the obstacles to integrating AI tools in foreign language learning.

Thus, a systematic approach was followed to identify relevant studies, using keywords such as 'AI', 'foreign language', 'teaching and learning' and 'higher education', from Scopus and Google Scholar databases. The search resulted in the identification of many studies, which were further screened. Screening was based on studies peer-reviewed and published in English, for higher education. Thus, the first exclusion and inclusion criteria narrowed down literature sources to 12680 publications. Access to full publications of 18600 articles, resulted in the final 39 articles, appropriate for the study as shown in Figure 1.

Figure 1. Flow diagram of the systematic search process

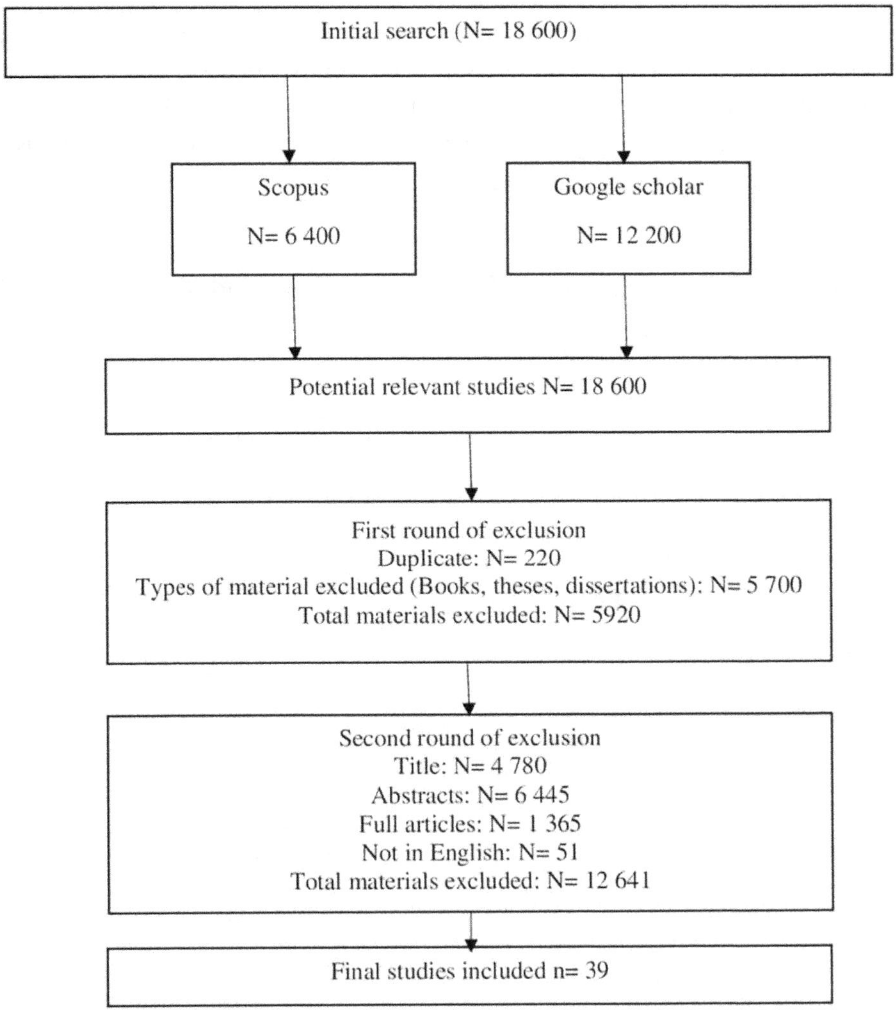

Hence, Braun and Clarke's (2006) procedures for thematic analysis were applied to data analysis of the final articles, using the research objectives as a guide. This systematic literature analysis procedure, as indicated below, resulted in themes (as presented and discussed in the next section).

7. FINDINGS

As explained in the methodology, the systematic procedure for this study resulted in themes, to cluster ideas from various scholars, from various studies. The studies among other things highlighted key obstacles (Dugošija, 2024; Tahir, Hassan & Shagoo, 2024; Zucchet, 2023). The key obstacles to using emerging AI tools in foreign language learning are presented in Table 1.

Table 1. Key obstacles to using emerging AI tools in foreign language learning

Key obstacles	Authors	Findings
1. **Accessibility and affordability constraints**	Dugošija (2024) Golovatska and Tereshchuk (2024) Tahir et al. (2024) Ade-Ibijola & Okonkwo (2023) Hubert, Elisha and Kaledi (2023) Zucchet (2023) De la Vall and Araya (2022) Rebolledo and González (2022) Pylypchuk (2021) Garcia and Kelly (2015)	• Insufficient infrastructure • Limited network affordability • Lack of equal access to technology • Lack of high-speed internet • Expenses related to acquiring and maintaining software programs
2. **Pedagogical concerns**	Al-Batineha and Tenaijya (2024) Dugošija (2024) Tahir et al. (2024) Alghamdy (2023) Alhaj (2023) Ramírez-Polo and Vargas-Sierra (2023) Chounta, Bardone, Raudsep and Pedaste (2022) Erton (2022) Schmidt and Strasser (2022) Alharbi (2021) Seufert, Guggemos and Tarantini (2018) Fu (2013)	• The swift growth of AI technologies and their applications • Concerns regarding the knowledge levels of learners • Blurred lines between formal school settings and informal learning opportunities • The integration of digital writing tools • "Inconvenient" ethical considerations • Neglect of the socio-cultural dimensions and the interdisciplinary aspects inherent in translation and interpretation • The integration of a pragma-semiotic perspective
3. **Ethical concerns**	Dugošija (2024) Allam, Dempere, Akre and Flores (2023) Alghamdy (2023) Grubaugh et al. (2023) Liu (2023)	• Misuse of information • Cyber security risks • Privacy concerns • Violations in terms of data access • Concerns regarding the security and privacy of sensitive information

8. DISCUSSION OF THE FINDINGS

The primary challenges hindering the utilisation of emerging AI tools in the context of foreign language learning are multifaceted and include issues such as lack of accessibility, pedagogical concerns, technological limitations, and reduced human interactions.

8.1 Accessibility and affordability constraints

Insufficient infrastructure and limited network affordability represent significant obstacles to the adoption of AI, especially in Africa (Ade-Ibijola & Okonkwo, 2023). Garcia and Kelly (2015) complement that the advancement of infrastructure and mobile technology connectivity across the continent is progressing at a sluggish pace. Relatedly, Dugošija, et al. (2024) commented that the availability of the internet and modern technology is not uniform among students. De la Vall and Araya (2022) revealed that disparities in technology and internet access among learners impact their utilisation of AI language learning tools. Additionally, Hubert et al. (2023) found that the lack of equal access to technology and high-speed internet creates obstacles in obtaining AI-powered tools, thereby hindering equitable access. Educational inequalities may be further exacerbated by disparities in access to technology and high-quality resources, potentially leading to a digital divide among learners, despite the vast potential offered by AI-driven language learning tools (Zucchet, 2023). Likewise, Tahir et al. (2024) argue that numerous people lack equitable access to technology, placing them at a disadvantage. Hubert et al. (2023) observe that this issue is particularly evident in underserved areas where schools often face financial constraints and limited resources, making it challenging to incorporate AI technologies into their educational systems. For instance, numerous learners in developing nations lack smartphones or internet connectivity, putting them at a disadvantage compared to their peers who have access to such resources (Tahir et al., 2024). Therefore, it is imperative to take into account the diverse needs and resources of all learners to ensure equitable access to AI language learning tools (Rebolledo & González, 2022).

The growing availability of AI-driven language learning tools presents a significant challenge for language educators, who must stay abreast of emerging trends and technologies while mastering their application to create innovative and engaging educational resources (Dugošija, 2024). Golovatska and Tereshchuk (2024) mention that aspiring translators are encountering new challenges as traditional linguistic education, understanding of translation theory, and practical experience no longer suffice in light of rapid advancements in information and computer technologies, alongside evolving labour market demands. Pylypchuk (2021) asserts that contemporary translators must be proficient in various computer applications, particularly text editors, spell-check tools, email, and internet resources. Therefore, professionals in this field need to acquire skills in computer-assisted translation (CAT) tools, which significantly enhance the efficiency and accuracy of the translation process (Golovatska & Tereshchuk, 2024). An important obstacle lies in the lack of readiness among educators and learners in general. Training a significant number of tutors and educational administrators to effectively utilise AI can be a complex endeavour. The educational system in numerous countries is not sufficiently modernised to seamlessly integrate this technological shift, presenting a persistent challenge (Tahir et al., 2024). Furthermore, educational systems face significant financial burdens when it comes to providing the necessary funds for software and cloud support (Tahir et al., 2024). The initial expenses alone can be quite costly, and this is further compounded by the high costs associated with continuous employee training. The cost of implementing AI in educational settings involves expenses related to acquiring and maintaining software programs, as well as ensuring adequate cloud support for data storage and processing. These financial burdens can arise from the initial investment required to purchase AI technologies, as well as the ongoing costs associated with software updates, technical support, and cloud infrastructure maintenance. Furthermore, educational institutions may need to allocate additional funds for training staff members to effectively utilise AI tools and integrate them into the curriculum, further adding to the overall cost of implementing AI in education. Additionally, if there are any changes in organisational processes, the ongoing training of the AI system would also incur additional expenses (Tahir et al., 2024). The resulting resource allocation disparities in institutions further exacerbate the digital divide, preventing learners in these areas from benefiting from the advancements and opportunities offered (Hubert et al., 2023).

8.2 Pedagogical concerns: limited understanding of how to effectively integrate AI into language instruction

Dugošija (2024) states that AI's innovative approach to teaching and learning seeks to fundamentally reshape education for the future by utilising advanced technology and automation in its pedagogical practices. Similarly, educators today possess a wealth of contemporary technology and automated communication tools that are deemed essential for organisational transformation and play a crucial role in fostering new educational paradigms and resources (Fu, 2013; Chounta et al., 2022). However, the swift growth of AI technologies and their applications presents a significant challenge for educators, who struggle to effectively integrate these tools into the creation of innovative learning resources (Dugošija, 2024). Alhaj (2023) confirms that current educators, researchers, and academics express concerns regarding the knowledge levels of learners. Seufert et al. (2018) argue that new technologies have a significant impact on the educational system beyond surface-level didactic structures by blurring the lines between formal school settings and informal learning opportunities at home or during leisure time. This shift challenges both learners and educators to embrace a fresh perspective on digitally enhanced educational spaces (Schmidt & Strasser, 2022). When it comes to integrating AI in education and language learning, some pedagogical limitations need to be considered. For example, Alharbi (2021) points out that the integration of digital writing tools in various every day and academic settings has been met with controversy in language education. As AI-driven writing assistance evolves to offer advanced, human-like support that extends beyond basic vocabulary and grammar, language educators and researchers express valid concerns regarding the authenticity of students' submissions. According to Alharbi (2021), these apprehensions are justified, as such intelligent tools enable users to access near-human translations, rephrased sentences, and substantial text segments effortlessly, facilitating a process where learners may simply copy and paste these suggestions into their work, thereby hindering genuine learning.

In 2021, the global market for translation and language services was valued at approximately US$ 62.6 billion and is projected to experience ongoing growth in the forthcoming years (Al-Batineha & Tenaijya, 2024). The authors add that the market is continuously adapting and expanding to cater to the demands of a progressively diverse clientele and a variety of tasks. Thus, Alhaj (2023) states that the essential competencies required for translators have evolved significantly due to the increasing integration of technology in translation education. Historically, translators primarily focused on the act of translation itself, accumulating their knowledge and skills through this singular role (Erton, 2022). Ramírez-Polo and Vargas-Sierra (2023) state that contemporary translation practices are deeply intertwined with technological advancements, which significantly shape the conceptual framework of learning in this field, as technology permeates all aspects of training. However, advancements in technology have introduced a diverse array of new skills, leading to the emergence of additional responsibilities for translators, including application and software programming (Alhaj (2023). As a result, an increasing number of scholars are expressing apprehensions regarding the ethical implications associated with the integration of technology and AI systems (Ramírez-Polo & Vargas-Sierra, 2023). Attitudes towards these new technologies have varied, with some recognising their benefits while others deem them "inconvenient" due to the ethical considerations surrounding technological use, which have been a topic of concern since the early 2000s, and even before that (Ramírez-Polo & Vargas-Sierra, 2023).

Furthermore, in the current decade, the instruction of translation and interpretation skills within university settings appears to be treated as a purely linguistic endeavour, neglecting the socio-cultural dimensions and the interdisciplinary aspects inherent in translation and interpretation studies (Erton, 2022). The interplay between utterances and their intended meanings necessitates analyses that extend beyond mere semantics. While discourse analysis provides insights into meaning within specific contexts, it falls short of fully capturing the communicative significance of spoken exchanges, as context merely offers information about participants, locations, and temporal factors. A comprehensive understanding of the cognitive mechanisms involved in language production requires a pragma-semiotic perspective (Erton, 2022). In the realm of translation, the integration of a pragma-semiotic perspective by AI remains a complex issue. While AI systems are increasingly adept at processing and translating language, their ability to fully grasp the nuances of context, intention, and the semiotic dimensions of communication is still limited. This limitation raises questions about the effectiveness of AI in capturing the richness of human discourse

8.3 Ethical concerns: privacy issues and data security

AI tools gather data regarding the interactions between students and educators on various platforms, raising concerns about the potential misuse of this information (Dugošija, 2024). In the digital era, the rapid increase in data and cyber security risks have made data privacy a significant issue (Sharma et al., 2023). Therefore, the protection of privacy is a significant consideration in the utilisation of AI tools within the educational sector (Allam et al., 2023). Privacy concerns typically emerge when individuals disclose an excessive amount of personal information on online platforms. Despite the presence of regulations and standards aimed at safeguarding sensitive data, violations by AI-driven technology companies in terms of data access and security contribute to heightened privacy concerns among the public. (Akgun & Greenhow, 2022). Additionally, Zucchet (2023) explains that language learning platforms powered by AI gather extensive user data, raising significant concerns regarding the security and privacy of sensitive information. This encompasses details such as language proficiency levels, learning styles, and progress, which should not be disclosed without their explicit consent (De la Vall & Araya, 2022). Liu (2023) points out that AI technology's trustworthiness and precision can be compromised, resulting in incorrect feedback and deceptive information. As a result, the potential risks associated with data privacy might discourage certain educational institutions from adopting AI within their educational framework. These concerns arise from the need to protect sensitive student information and ensure that it is not misused or accessed by unauthorised individuals. The fear of data breaches or unauthorised data sharing can hinder the integration of AI technologies, as institutions prioritise safeguarding student privacy and maintaining trust within their educational systems. These concerns may act as a barrier to the widespread adoption of AI in education. Consequently, it is crucial to prioritise safeguarding user privacy and preventing potential breaches or misuse of data (Zucchet, 2023). Similarly, De la Vall and Araya (2022) contend that safeguarding the personal information of language learners is crucial to respect their privacy and ensure confidentiality. Emphasising student data privacy and consent, along with inclusive designs catering to diverse needs, is crucial in educational settings (Bennett & Foltz, 2019).

8.4 Reduced human interactions: the absence of student engagement

According to Allam et al. (2023), while AI may have its benefits in terms of efficiency and data analysis; however, it cannot truly understand and connect with learners on a personal level. One major concern in the integration and use of AI in language learning is the lack of emotional intelligence and empathy in AI systems, which are crucial for effective communication and understanding in educational settings. AI may struggle to provide personalised feedback and support that human educators can offer, leading to a more impersonal learning experience for learners. However, the challenge of comprehending and reproducing linguistic nuances, including idiomatic and colloquial expressions or regional accents, can lead to inaccuracies and unnatural phrasing (Rebolledo & González, 2023). Furthermore, Dugosija (2024) highlights that the limited capacity of AI tools to detect errors and offer explanations with the same precision as human educators may cause students to persist in their mistakes or cultivate poor language learning practices.

Allam et al. (2023) note that educators bring a unique perspective and experience to the table, which cannot be replicated by machines as their guidance, mentorship, and encouragement are invaluable in shaping the minds and hearts of the next generation. Despite the advanced analytical capabilities of AI robots, they are unable to foster the growth of a student's mind with the same level of flexibility as an educator (Allam et al., 2023). This is because educators possess the ability to provide a diverse range of problem-solving strategies, whereas AI cannot offer various teaching approaches (Allam et al., 2023). Therefore, the educator's role holds significance not just in imparting education, but also in moulding the learners' career paths. Consequently, the emergence of AI poses a challenge as reduced reliance on educators may result in a diminished emphasis on the moral and personality growth of learners (Tahir et al. 2024).

Sorgner (2019) comments that the advancements in new digital technologies, such as AI, machine learning algorithms, cloud computing, and dexterous robotics, have the potential to significantly alter the current labour markets. The significance of social and emotional bonds in the learning process cannot be overlooked, as they play a crucial role in the overall development of learners. Sussmann (2024) emphasises that merely supplying learners with the necessary tools will not be enough to achieve the desired outcomes. Thus, the human touch and empathy that educators provide are essential in creating a supportive and nurturing environment for learners to thrive. Liu (2023) is of the view that AI may not have the capacity to completely substitute human educators, particularly in domains like language proficiency and interpersonal interaction. The rigid and uniform instructional approach of AI could also be deficient in the emotional connection and tailored teaching methods that certain learners necessitate (Liu, 2023). In addition, the study of Suman and Suman (2023) revealed that learners expressed worry over the possible decline of genuine human connection because of excessive dependence on AI feedback. The absence of emotional subtleties in AI interactions has been recognised as a drawback, especially in contexts that demand cultural sensitivity and compassion (Suman & Suman, 2023).

8.5 Academic dishonesty: the prevalence of transformer AI applications

While learning nowadays does not inherently lead to greater instances of academic misconduct among students, research indicates that assessments are linked to heightened risks to academic integrity (St-Onge et al., 2022; Miller & Young-Jones, 2012), resulting in a higher number of cases. Makelenia et al. (2023) add that the rise of AI has facilitated a surge in automated academic dishonesty. The increasing prevalence of Transformer AI applications like ChatGPT for academic writing has raised significant concerns. Sharples (2022) reported that students are leveraging these tools to produce essays rapidly, often eluding detection by plagiarism software since the content is generated rather than copied. Fyfe (2022) underscores that AI has significantly advanced the challenge of plagiarism detection, rendering traditional methods such as searching for phrases on Google or comparing documents to established databases like Turnitin less effective. Hence, students increasingly utilise AI-driven essay-writing applications capable of producing texts that closely resemble human writing, with some of these tools adept at evading plagiarism detection through techniques that rephrase sentences (Cotton et al., 2023; Mutongoza & Olawale, 2022). Perkins (2023) comments that the advent of tools leveraging AI for generating original text has gained momentum in recent years, particularly through the development of LLMs that can produce substantial amounts of novel text from brief input prompts. This represents a departure from the previously discussed Algorithm Publication Tool (APT) and Data Warehouse Automation (DWA) tools, which are primarily concerned with modifying existing text such as through paraphrasing, suggesting revisions, or offering predictions for completing sentences (Perkins, 2023). Consequently, educators are challenged with evaluating work that may not reflect the students' efforts (Sharples, 2022). Dugošija (2024) adds that this practice constitutes a serious breach of academic integrity and poses risks to students' educational development, as these AI systems can fabricate details, including citations and research findings, or disseminate misleading information. Despite notable advancements in these AI tools, they remain prone to inaccuracies, occasionally yielding awkward or illogical outputs (Afram et al., 2022). Rudolph et al. (2023) contend that students can submit high-quality assignments with minimal effort, leading language instructors to occasionally encounter submissions containing errors typical of AI-generated content. Fyfe (2022) posits that the definition of "plagiarism" requires greater nuance, especially as it becomes increasingly ambiguous in the context of AI usage.

Zucchet (2023) concludes that the overreliance on AI-powered language learning platforms may undermine the significance of human interaction, potentially resulting in decreased social engagement during language practice. Consequently, this could hurt conversational abilities and cultural comprehension (Zucchet, 2023). Alghamdy (2023) observes that the challenge involves achieving a balance between technological innovation, the interpersonal relationships between educators and learners, and the welfare of society. The successful implementation of the integration process is vital for the effective utilisation of AI tools within English language classrooms (Sussmann, 2024). These obstacles pose significant barriers to the widespread adoption and successful implementation of AI technologies in language education.

9. IMPLICATIONS OF THE FINDINGS

From the findings of this study, various complex obstacles impede the effective integration of AI technologies in the realm of learning foreign languages, encompassing factors like limited availability of resources, pedagogical dilemmas, technological constraints, and diminished opportunities for human interaction. The implications of these findings are significant as they underscore the need for addressing these challenges to fully harness the potential benefits of AI tools in language learning. Overcoming issues related to resource accessibility, pedagogical strategies, technological advancements, and interpersonal communication can lead to more efficient and engaging language learning experiences for learners. By recognising and tackling these barriers, educators and app and tools developers can work towards creating a more conducive environment for the successful implementation of AI in foreign language instruction.

10. CONCLUSION

In conclusion, the integration of AI tools in foreign language learning is impeded by a variety of intricate obstacles. Overcoming these challenges will require a comprehensive approach that addresses issues related to resource accessibility, pedagogical strategies, technological advancements, and the preservation of human interaction.

11. RECOMMENDATIONS

To overcome learners' lack of accessibility to AI technologies, firstly, educators should ensure that learners with limited digital literacy skills can readily access and receive assistance is crucial for the successful implementation of new AI tools. One suggestion for introducing an AI tool or application is to demonstrate to learners during class how to set it up and use it. Secondly, in communities where learners do not have access to AI technologies, it is crucial to explore alternative methods and resources that can be utilised offline. This may involve incorporating traditional language learning materials such as textbooks, workbooks, and flashcards into the curriculum to supplement the lack of online resources. Thirdly, educators can also leverage other forms of technology that do not require internet connectivity, such as language learning apps that can be downloaded and used offline. These apps can provide interactive exercises, quizzes, and vocabulary drills to enhance learners' language proficiency without the need for constant internet access. Lastly, establishing language learning centres or resource hubs within communities can also help bridge the gap for learners who do not have access to AI technologies at home. These centres can provide learners with computers, tablets, and other devices equipped with AI language learning tools, allowing them to benefit from the advantages of technology-assisted language education.

Dugošija (2024) recommends that when incorporating AI language learning tools into language education, it is essential to guarantee that these resources are readily accessible to both educators and all learners. To overcome the affordability of AI technology, educators or institutions can explore alternative options for obtaining the necessary resources. This may involve seeking out free or low-cost AI tools that are available online, collaborating with other educators or institutions to share resources, or applying for grants or funding to acquire the needed technology.

In the digital era, the rapid increase in data and cybersecurity risks have made data privacy a significant issue. Consequently, Dugošija (2024) states that it is crucial to implement robust privacy protections to safeguard personal data and ensure that it is not disclosed without the explicit consent of the users. Sharma et al. (2023)

contend that with its distinctive attributes, blockchain, the underlying technology of cryptocurrencies, presents itself as an optimal solution for safeguarding data privacy. Consequently, educational institutions should consider integrating this technology into their systems to ensure the protection of learners' privacy.

Dugošija (2024) points out that it is essential for educational professionals today to develop a more profound comprehension of contemporary, AI-driven pedagogical advancements. It is therefore recommended that educational institutions invest in comprehensive training programs for educators, enabling them to harness AI tools proficiently and adapt their teaching methodologies accordingly. This approach will not only enhance the learning experience for students but also ensure that educators remain at the forefront of technological advancements in language instruction.

The use of AI was reported to reduce human interactions. This can be seen in the potential destruction of human labour when digital technologies replace it (Sorgner, 2019). However, Frey and Osborne (2017) as well as Brynjolfsson and McAfee (2014) observe that these tools can have transformative effects by complementing human labour rather than replacing it. The constructivist philosophy emphasizes learner agency, dignity, and interpersonal relationships, placing humans at the centre of the learning process (Grubaugh et al., 2023). Despite this, the integration of AI poses risks such as dehumanisation, data exploitation, and ethical concerns. To address these challenges, constructivist AI integration should focus on designing sociotechnical systems that prioritise humanistic values (Makridakis, 2017). Furthermore, educators should have a comprehensive understanding of both the advantages and limitations of AI technologies in language learning. However, it is equally important to maintain a harmonious equilibrium between AI and human teaching methods. This balanced approach, according to Liu (2023), ensures that learners receive the best of both worlds, benefiting from the efficiency and accuracy of AI technology while also benefiting from the empathy, creativity, and adaptability that human educators bring to the table.

REFERENCES

Afram, G. K., Benjamin, A. W., & Adebayo, A. F. (2022). Twieng: A multi-domain Twi-English parallel corpus for machine translation of the Twi language, A low-resource African language. *Journal of Mathematical Techniques & Computational Mathematics, 1*(1), 48–57. DOI: 10.20944/preprints202203.0303.v1

Ahmadi, D. M. R. (2018). The use of technology in English language learning: A literature review. *International Journal of Research in English Education, 3*(2), 115–125. DOI: 10.29252/ijree.3.2.115

Akgun, S., & Greenhow, C. (2022). Artificial intelligence in education: Addressing ethical challenges in K-12 settings. *AI and Ethics, 2*(3), 431–440. DOI: 10.1007/s43681-021-00096-7 PMID: 34790956

Al-Batineha, M., & Tenaijya, M. (2024). Adapting to technological change: An investigation of translator training and the translation market in the Arab world. *Heliyon, 10*(7), 1–12. PMID: 38560143

Alghamdy, R. Z. (2023). Pedagogical and Ethical Implications of Artificial Intelligence in EFL Context: A Review Study. *English Language Teaching, 16*(10), 87–98. DOI: 10.5539/elt.v16n10p87

Alhaj, A. A. M. (2023). Exploring the Challenges and Obstacles Encountered in Utilizing Artificial Intelligence Tools (AITs) in Translation Teaching from the Perspectives of Faculty Members at Saudi Universities. *Migration Letters : An International Journal of Migration Studies, 21*(3), 398–412.

Alharbi, W. (2023). AI in the Foreign Language Classroom: A Pedagogical Overview of Automated Writing Assistance Tools. *Education Research International, 2023*, 1–15. DOI: 10.1155/2023/4253331

Allam, H., Dempere, J., Akre, H., & Flores, P. (2023). Artificial Intelligence in Education (AIED): Implications and Challenges. *Atlantis Highlights in Social Sciences, Education and Humanities, 13*, 126–140. DOI: 10.2991/978-94-6463-286-6_10

Alshaikhi, T., & Khasawneh, M. A. S. (2024). Investigating the benefits and drawbacks of selected AI-powered instruments employed for foreign language education. *Kurdish Studies, 12*(2), 2156–2169.

Amineh, R. J., & Asl, H. D. (2015). Review of constructivism and social constructivism. *Journal of Social Sciences, Literature, and Languages, 1*(1), 9–16.

Bahari, A., & Gholami, J. (2022). A Systematic review of current research on affordances and challenges of technology-assisted grammar learning. *Computer Assisted Language Learning, 32*(1), 125–148.

Baidoo-Anu, D., & Ansah, O. L. (2023). Education in the era of generative Artificial Intelligence (AI): Understanding the potential benefits of ChatGPT in promoting teaching and learning. *Journal of Artificial Intelligence, 7*, 52–62.

Baker, T., & Smith, L. (2019), Educ-AI-tion rebooted? Exploring the future of artificial intelligence in schools and colleges, Available at: https://media.nesta.org.uk/documents/Future_of_AI_and_education_v5_WEB.Pdf. (Accessed 20 August 2024)

Bennett, E., & Foltz, P. W. (2019). The constructivist ethics algorithm: Value sensitive design for ethical mediation between humans and systems. *Journal of Human-Computer Studies, 132*, 110–124.

Bikowski, D. (2018). *Technology for Teaching Grammar*. Wiley. DOI: 10.1002/9781118784235.eelt0441

Brynjolfsson, E., & McAfee, A. (2014). *The second machine age: Work, progress, and prosperity in a time of brilliant technologies*. WW Norton & Company.

Chemnad, K., & Othman, A. (2024). Digital accessibility in the era of artificial intelligence—Bibliometric analysis and systematic review. *Frontiers in Artificial Intelligence, 7*, 1–17. DOI: 10.3389/frai.2024.1349668 PMID: 38435800

Chounta, I. A., Bardone, E., Raudsep, A., & Pedaste, M. (2022). Exploring teachers' perceptions of artificial intelligence as a tool to support their practice in Estonian K-12 education. *International Journal of Artificial Intelligence in Education, 32*(3), 725–755. DOI: 10.1007/s40593-021-00243-5

Cotton, D. R., Cotton, P. A., & Shipway, J. R. (2023). Chatting and Cheating: Ensuring academic integrity in the era of ChatGPT. *Innovations in Education and Teaching International*, •••, 1–12.

Dale, R., & Viethen, J. (2021). The automated writing assistance landscape in 2021. *Natural Language Engineering, 27*(4), 511–518. DOI: 10.1017/S1351324921000164

De la Vall, R. R. F., & Araya, F. G. (2022). Exploring the Benefits and Challenges of AI-Language Learning Tools. *The International Journal of Social Sciences and Humanities Invention, 10*(1), 7569–7576. DOI: 10.18535/ijsshi/v10i01.02

Dimitriadou, E., & Lanitis, A. (2023). A critical evaluation, challenges, and future perspectives of using artificial intelligence and emerging technologies in smart classrooms. *Smart Learning Environments*, *10*(12), 1–26. DOI: 10.1186/s40561-023-00231-3

Ducar, C., & Schocket, D. H. (2018). Machine translation and the L2 classroom: Pedagogical solutions for making peace with Google translate. *Foreign Language Annals*, *51*(4), 779–795. DOI: 10.1111/flan.12366

Dugošija, T. (2024). Benefits and challenges of artificial intelligence in English language teaching. *Knowledge International Journal*, *62*(2), 275–280.

Erton, I. (2022). Pragmatic issues in teaching translation and interpretation: A curricular perspective at university level. *Eurasian Journal of Language Teaching and Linguistic Studies*, *2*(2), 237–244.

Fitria, T. N. (2021). Grammarly as AI-powered English writing assistant: Students' alternative for writing English.Metathesis. *Journal of English Language, Literature, and Teaching*, *1*(5), 65–78. DOI: 10.31002/metathesis.v5i1.3519

Frey, C. B., & Osborne, M. A. (2017). The Future of Employment: How Susceptible are Jobs to Computerization? *Technological Forecasting and Social Change*, *114*, 254–280. DOI: 10.1016/j.techfore.2016.08.019

Fu, J. (2013), "Complexity of ICT in education: A critical literature review and its implications", *International Journal of Education and Development using ICT*, Vol. 9 No. 1, pp. 112-125.

Fyfe, P. (2022). How to cheat on your final paper: Assigning AI for student writing. *AI & Society*, *38*(4), 1395–1405. DOI: 10.1007/s00146-022-01397-z

Garcia, J. M., & Kelly, T. (2015). *The economics and policy implications of infrastructure sharing and mutualisation in Africa*. World Bank.

Gayed, J. M., Carlon, M. K. J., Oriola, A. M., & Cross, J. S. (2022). Exploring an AI-based writing assistant's impact on English language learners. *Computers and Education: Artificial Intelligence*, *3*, 1–8. DOI: 10.1016/j.caeai.2022.100055

Gbollie, C., & Gong, S. (2013). The Essence of Foreign Language Learning in Today's Globalizing World: Benefits and Hindrances. *New Media and Mass Communication*, *9*, 35–44.

Godwin-Jones, R. (2022). Partnering with AI: Intelligent writing assistance and instructed language learning. *Language Learning & Technology*, *26*(2), 5–24.

Golovatska, I., & Tereshchuk, G. (2024). The use of digital technologies to prepare future translators for the modern requirements of the linguistic services market. *Journal of Educational Technology Development and Exchange*, *17*(1), 175–187. DOI: 10.18785/jetde.1701.10

Grimm, N., Meyer, M., & Volkmann, L. (2015). *Teaching English*. Narr Francke Attempto.

Grubaugh, S., Levitt, G., & Deever, D. (2023). Harnessing AI to Power Constructivist Learning: An Evolution in Educational Methodology [JETM]. *Journal of Effective Teaching Methods*, *1*(3), 81–83. DOI: 10.59652/jetm.v1i3.43

Healey, J. (2020). [). Thirroul: The Spinney Press.]. *Artificial Intelligence*, *450*, •••.

Huang, Z., Mao, Y., & Zhang, J. (2024). The Influence of Artificial Intelligence Technology on College Learners' Learning Effectiveness from the Perspective of Constructivism — Taking ChatGPT as an Example. *Journal of Education, Humanities and Social Sciences*, *30*, 40–46. DOI: 10.54097/y1x3jj43

Hubackova, S. (2016). The importance of foreign language education. *New Trends and Issues Proceedings on Humanities and Social Sciences*, *5*, 98–101.

Hubert, K, Elisha B. and Kaledio, P. (2023), Address the potential disparity in access to AI-powered education, Available at: (1) (PDF) Address the potential disparity in access to AI (researchgate.net) (Accessed 05 June 2024).

Ilkka, T. (2018). *The Impact of Artificial Intelligence on Learning, Teaching, and Education*. European Union.

Jain, S., & Jain, R. (2019). "Role of artificial intelligence in higher education- an empirical investigation", *IJRAR-*. *International Journal of Research and Analytical Reviews*, *6*(2), 144–150.

Jonassen, D. H., & Rohrer-Murphy, L. (1999). Activity theory as a framework for designing constructivist learning environments. *Educational Technology Research and Development*, *47*(1), 61–79. DOI: 10.1007/BF02299477

Klein, W. (2001), "Second Language Acquisition", *International Encyclopedia of the Social & Behavioral Sciences*, No. 2001, pp. 13768-13771.

Kuhlman, K. (2017), Best Practices in Foreign Language Learning. Master's thesis. Northwestern College, Iowa. Orange City.

Lai, Y., Saab, N., & Admiraal, W. (2022). University students' use of mobile technology in self-directed language learning: Using the integrative model of behaviour prediction. *Computers & Education*, *179*, 1–13. DOI: 10.1016/j.compedu.2021.104413

Lantolf, J. P., & Sunderman, G. (2001). The struggle for a place in the sun: Rationalizing foreign language study in the twentieth century. *Modern Language Journal*, *85*(1), 5–25. DOI: 10.1111/0026-7902.00094

Lei, X., Fathi, J., Noorbakhsh, S., & Rahimi, M. (2022). The impact of mobile-assisted language learning on English as a foreign language learners' vocabulary learning attitudes and self-regulatory capacity. *Frontiers in Psychology*, *13*, 1–14. DOI: 10.3389/fpsyg.2022.872922 PMID: 35800918

Lestari, S., Usadiati, W., & Misrita, M. (2022). The correlation between students' artificial intelligence and theirEnglish reading skills achievement. *Bahasa: Jurnal Keilmuan Pendidikan Bahasa Dan Sastra Indonesia*, *3*(2), 103–111. DOI: 10.26499/bahasa.v3i2.110

Liu, M. Y. (2023), "Exploring the Application of Artificial Intelligence in Foreign Language Teaching: Challenges and Future Development", *SHS Web of Conferences*, Vol.168, pp. 1-4. DOI: 10.1051/shsconf/202316803025

Ma, D. T. T., Da, C. V., & Hanh, N. V. (2024). The use of ChatGPT in teaching and learning: A systematic review through SWOT analysis approach. *Frontiers in Education*, *9*, 1–17. DOI: 10.3389/feduc.2024.1328769

Makelenia, S., Mutongoza, B. H., & Linake, M. A. (2023). Language Education and Artificial Intelligence: An Exploration of Challenges Confronting Academics in Global South Universities. *Journal of Culture and Values in Education*, *6*(2), 158–171. DOI: 10.46303/jcve.2023.14

Makridakis, S. (2017). The forthcoming Artificial Intelligence (AI) revolution: Its impact on society and firms. *Futures*, *90*, 46–60. DOI: 10.1016/j.futures.2017.03.006

Miller, A., & Young-Jones, A. D. (2012). Academic integrity: Online classes compared to face-to-face classes. *Journal of Instructional Psychology*, *39*(3), 1–8.

Mitchell, R., & Myles, F. (1998). *Second language learning theories*. Oxford Press, Inc.

Moeller, A. J., & Catalano, T. (2015). *Foreign Language Teaching and Learning* (2nd ed.). International Encyclopedia of the Social & Behavioral Sciences. DOI: 10.1016/B978-0-08-097086-8.92082-8

Moulieswaran, N., & Kumar, P. N. S. (2022). Education 4.0 – An artificial intelligence technology driven second language learning and teaching. In Karthikeyan, J., & Jin, N. Y. (Eds.), *Neophytes of ELT Research*. Royal Book Publishing.

Murphy, V. A., Arndt, H., Baffoe-Djan, J. B., Chalmers, H., Macaro, E., Rose, H., Vanderplank, R., & Woore, R. (2020). *Foreign language learning and its impact on wider academic outcomes: A rapid evidence assessment*. University of Oxford.

Mutongoza, B. H., & Olawale, B. E. (2022). Safeguarding academic integrity in the face of emergency remote teaching and learning in developing countries. *Perspectives in Education*, *40*(1), 234–249. DOI: 10.18820/2519593X/pie.v40.i1.14

National Standards in Foreign Language Education Project (NSFLEP). (2014), World Readiness Standards for Learning Languages (WRSLL), Alexandria. VA, Available at: http://actfl/org/publications/all/world-readiness-standards-learninglanguages (Accessed 10 July 2024).

Paiva, R., & Bittencourt, I. I. (2020). *Helping Teachers Help Their students: A Human-AI Hybrid Approach*. Springer Switzerland International Publishing.

Perkins, M. (2023). Academic integrity considerations of AI large language models in the post-pandemic era: ChatGPT and beyond. *Journal of University Teaching & Learning Practice*, *20*(2), 7–24. DOI: 10.53761/1.20.02.07

Pokrivcakova, S. (2019). *Preparing teachers for the application of AI-powered technologies in foreign language education*. Sciendo. DOI: 10.2478/jolace-2019-0025

Pylypchuk, M. L. (2021). Structure of professional readiness of future translators for innovative activities. *Professional and Artistic Translation*, *1*, 371–378.

, R. and Yang M. (2020), "Review of studies on technology-enhanced language learning and teaching", *Sustainability*, Vol. 12, pp. 524.

Rahimi, M., & Fathi, J. (2022). Exploring the impact of wiki-mediated collaborative writing on EFL students' writing performance, writing self-regulation, and writing self-efficacy: A mixed methods study. *Computer Assisted Language Learning*, *35*(9), 2627–2674. DOI: 10.1080/09588221.2021.1888753

Ramírez-Polo, L., & Vargas-Sierra, C. (2023). Translation Technology and Ethical Competence: An Analysis and Proposal for Translators' Training. *Languages (Basel, Switzerland)*, *8*(2), 1–22. DOI: 10.3390/languages8020093

Rebolledo, F. D. L. V., & González, A. F. (2023). Exploring the benefits and challenges of AI-language learning tools. *International Journal of Social Sciences and Humanities Invention*, *10*(1), 7569–7576. DOI: 10.18535/ijsshi/v10i01.02

Rogerson, A. M., & McCarthy, G. (2017). Using internet-based paraphrasing tools: Original work, patchwriting or facilitated plagiarism? *International Journal for Educational Integrity*, *13*(1), 1–15. DOI: 10.1007/s40979-016-0013-y

Roll, I., & Wylie, R. (2016). Evolution and revolution in artificial intelligence in education. *International Journal of Artificial Intelligence in Education*, *26*(2), 582–599. DOI: 10.1007/s40593-016-0110-3

Rudolph, J., Tan, S., & Tan, S. (2023). ChatGPT: Bullshit spewer or the end of traditional assessments in higher education? *Journal of Applied Learning and Teaching*, *6*(1), 1–22.

Rukiati, E., Wicaksono, J. A., Taufan, G. T., & Suharsono, D. D. (2023). AI on Learning English: Application, Benefit, and Threat. *Journal of Language, Communication, and Tourism*, *2*(1), 32–40. DOI: 10.25047/jlct.v1i2.3967

Sa'd, T., & Hatam, S. (2017). Foreign language learning and identity reconstruction: Learners' understanding of the intersections of the self, the other and power. *CEPS Journal*, *7*(4), 13–36.

Sadiku, M. N., Ashaolu, T. J., Ajayi-Majebi, A., & Musa, S. M. (2021). Artifcial intelligence in education. *International Journal of Scientifc Advances*, *2*(1), 5–11.

Schmidt, T., & Strasser, T. (2022). Artificial intelligence in foreign language learning and teaching: A CALL for intelligent practice. *Anglistik*, *33*(1), 165–184. DOI: 10.33675/ANGL/2022/1/14

Schwendicke, F., Samek, W., & Krois, J. (2020). Artificial intelligence in dentistry: Chances and challenges. *Journal of Dental Research*, *99*(7), 769–774. DOI: 10.1177/0022034520915714 PMID: 32315260

Seufert, S., Guggemos, J. and Tarantini, E. (2018), "Digital transformation in schools. Competency requirements for teachers", *Contributions to teacher training*, Vol. 36 No. 2, pp. 175-193.

Shadiev, R., Wen, Y., Uosaki, N., & Song, Y. (2023). Future language learning with emerging technologies. *Journal of Computers in Education*, *10*(3), 463–467. DOI: 10.1007/s40692-023-00285-9

Sharples, M. (2022). Automated essay writing: An AIED opinion. *International Journal of Artificial Intelligence in Education*, *32*(4), 1119–1126. DOI: 10.1007/s40593-022-00300-7

Shatri, Z. G. (2020). Advantages and disadvantages of using information technology in learning process of students. *Journal of Turkish Science Education*, *17*, 420–428. DOI: 10.36681/tused.2020.36

Soleimani, H., Mohammaddokht, F., & Fathi, J. (2022). Exploring the effect of assisted repeated reading on incidental vocabulary learning and vocabulary learning self-efficacy in an EFL context. *Frontiers in Psychology*, *13*, 1–11. DOI: 10.3389/fpsyg.2022.851812 PMID: 35250786

St-Onge, C., Ouellet, K., Lakhal, S., Dubé, T., & Marceau, M. (2022). COVID-19 as the tipping point for integrating e-assessment in higher education practices. *British Journal of Educational Technology*, *53*(2), 349–366. DOI: 10.1111/bjet.13169 PMID: 34898680

Suman, C. and Suman, S. (2023), "Using Artificial Intelligence for Foreign Language Learning", *A Peer Review Research Journal of Language and Human Development*, Vol. 1 No. 1, pp. 57-64.

Sussmann, M. (2024). *AI Tools for the Four Skills in English Language Learning*. Tesol Connections.

Tahir, M., & Hassan, F. D. (2024). Role of artificial intelligence in education: A conceptual review. *World Journal of Advanced Research and Reviews*, *22*(1), 1469–1475. DOI: 10.30574/wjarr.2024.22.1.1217

Turaeva, S. (2024), Language, learning and teaching. *Development and Innovations in Science: International scientific-online conference*, pp. 1-4.

University at Buffalo. (2024). *Constructivism: Creating experiences that facilitate the construction of knowledge. North Campus*. University at Buffalo.

Vygotsky, L. S. (1984), "The problem of age" in *The collected works of L. S. Vygotsky. Vol. 5. Child psychology*. ed. Rieber R. W. Plenum, New York, NY.

Xiao, Y., & Watson, M. (2019). Guidance on Conducting a Systematic Literature Review. *Journal of Planning Education and Research*, *39*(1), 93–112. DOI: 10.1177/0739456X17723971

Zucchet, E. (2023), How artificial intelligence is revolutionizing language learning, Available at: https://www.berlitz.com/blog/artificial-intelligence-ai-language-learning (Accessed 14 July 2024).

ADDITIONAL READING

Abdalgane, M., & Othman, K. A. (2023). Utilizing artificial intelligence technologies in Saudi EFL tertiary level classrooms. *Journal of Intercultural Communication*, *23*(1), 92–99. DOI: 10.36923/jicc.v23i1.124

Alhusaiyan, E. (2025). A systematic review of current trends in artificial intelligence in foreign language learning. *Saudi Journal of Language Studies*, *5*(1), 1–16. DOI: 10.1108/SJLS-07-2024-0039

Dai, K., & Liu, Q. (2024). Leveraging artificial intelligence (AI) in English as a foreign language (EFL) classes: Challenges and opportunities in the spotlight. *Computers in Human Behavior*, *159*, 108354. DOI: 10.1016/j.chb.2024.108354

Hapsari, I. P., & Wu, T. T. (2022). AI chatbots learning model in English speaking skill: Alleviating speaking anxiety, boosting enjoyment, and fostering critical thinking. *Lecture Notes in Computer Science*, *13449*, 444–453. DOI: 10.1007/978-3-031-15273-3_49

Khanzode, K. C. A., & Sarode, R. D. (2020). Advantages and Disadvantages of Artificial Intelligence and Machine Learning: A Literature Review [IJLIS]. *International Journal of Library and Information Science*, *9*(1), 3.

Lisovets, V. (2017), Essentials of Artificial Intelligence for Language Learning."Intellias – Intelligent Software Engineering, Available at: https://www.intellias.com/how-ai-helps-crack-a-new-language/ (Accessed 29 May 2024).

Panagiotidis, P., Krystalli, P., & Arvanitis, P. (2023). Technology as a motivational factor in foreign language learning. *European Journal of Education*, *6*(1), 69–84. DOI: 10.2478/ejed-2023-0007

Schmidt, T. and Strasser, T. (2022), Artificial Intelligence in Foreign Language Learning and Teaching: A CALL for Intelligent Practice, *Anglistik: International Journal of English Studies,* Vol. 33 No. 2022, pp. 165-184.

Seda, K. (2022). *Applications of machine learning and artificial intelligence in education*. IGI Global.

Zhou, J. (2020), Design of AI-based self-learning platform for college English listening. Proceedings of 2020 2nd International Conference on Machine Learning, Big Data and Business Intelligence (MLBDBI).

KEY TERMS AND DEFINITIONS

AI language learning tools: are computer programs or software applications that assist users in learning and honing their foreign language skills through the use of AI algorithms (Alshaikhi & Khasawneh, 2024).

Artificial Intelligence (AI): is the capacity of a machine or computer system to simulate and perform tasks that typically require human intelligence, such as logical reasoning, learning, and problem resolution (Chemnad & Othman, 2024).

Constructivism: is a long-standing educational philosophy, that stipulates that learning is not simply the transmission of facts, but a process of active engagement by learners drawing upon their existing knowledge and experiences (Grubaugh et al., 2023).

Digital technologies: are electronic tools, devices, systems, and resources which generate, store or process data. Digital tools include social media, mobile phones, online games, and multimedia (Haleem, Javaid, Qadri & Suman, 2022).

Foreign language: is the learning of a non-native language that occurs in a setting where the language is not commonly spoken (Moeller & Catalano, 2015)

Fourth Industrial Revolution: means the swift technological progress of the 21st century, characterised by enhanced interconnectivity, automation, sophisticated manufacturing technologies and machine learning (Dugošija, 2024).

language learner: is someone who is learning a foreign language, or developing their ability to communicate in a second language (Klein, 2001).

Language learning: refers to the active process of acquiring the ability to understand and use a language, encompassing the development of skills in listening, speaking, reading, and writing, typically through conscious study and practice, allowing individuals to communicate effectively in a new language, whether in a formal learning setting or through immersion and natural exposure (Turaeva, 2024).

Second language learning: occurs when the learner is in an environment where the language being learned is spoken (Moeller & Catalano, 2015).

Chapter 5
Evolution and Future Trends in Artificial Intelligence in Education (AIEd)

Anandharajah Sagadevan
https://orcid.org/0009-0005-4354-2680
Marwadi University, Rajkot, India

T. Premavathi
https://orcid.org/0009-0003-0172-2021
Marwadi University, Rajkot, India

Damodharan Palaniappan
https://orcid.org/0009-0003-0721-3068
Marwadi University, Rajkot, India

ABSTRACT

AIEd has widely facilitated the transformation of practices in teaching and learning environment as well as the organizational administrative functioning in the education system. Growing from rule-and-coded programs in instruction applications and early types of instructional software, AIEd is an improved system that consists of ITS, EDM, and adaptive learning. These innovations have enabled the emergence of the learning map to meet the learner needs with different learning approaches which are cognition, behaviour and emotion learning styles. Many of such issues are not only explained with reference to examples and existing experiences and lessons of AIEd at its current stage, but also discussed further opportunities and trends for AIEd, including the further applications and developments of the immersive

DOI: 10.4018/979-8-3693-9606-3.ch005

learning technologies like AR/VR; the advanced paradigms of AI + X Education integrated with cognitive science theories and insights from other disciplines; and the use cases of lifelong learning solutions pertinent to the rapidly changing global work environment.

1.INTRODUCTION

AI in education has developed rapidly over the last decade, and changed the education process and learning experience globally. AIEd merges computer science, cognitive psychology, education, big data and data mining to deliver superior solutions that merge the virtual classroom and the physical classroom. Cognitive systems in AIEd learning environments improve or supplement teaching approaches, strategies, programs, curricula, and administrative systems. This assists in availing itself to prospects that influence education for example granting equity and participation. Refer the Figure.1for transformative impact of AI on global education systems.

In the early stages of development of AIEd it was characterized by rule-based Tutoring systems in the 1970's. These systems employed computer technologies to deliver sequenced training but were slightly rigid and not as engaging as computer-base Technologies now offer several training systems with restrictions of flexibility and interaction in their application. However, these ideas prepared the ground for Intelligent Tutoring Systems that appeared in the 1990s. ITS use machine learning to adaptively teach and also gives timely feedback to the learner in instructional systems such as ASSISTments and Cognitive Tutor. These advancements enable learners to rehearse and remember better; (Zawacki-Richter et al., 2019)

The latest forms of AIEd incorporate deep learning, natural language processing, and affective computing into enhanced forms of virtual teaching assistants, learning analytics, adaptive curriculum, and others. Modern applications of AIEd are wider than ITS, since refer to them tools that can cover different stages of learning process. Learning Analytics and Educational Data Mining are the processes of helping the educators in analyzing big data, course audition, and identification of students at risk for developing methodologies for interventions. Further, evolution in natural language processing is redefining language learning and language skills using automated essay grader, conversational partner, and multilinguality learning. More so, application of Kahoot! and other learning platforms adapt components of play and project based learning using Augmented Reality and Virtual Reality and its applicability is mirrored for fields including medicine, engineering among others.

However, many challenges are recently being realized interfering with the execution of AIEd in the following manner. Questions concerning data confidentiality and algorithmic bias remain a challenge despite the fact that students' data is most often employed for prediction or decision making purposes. For instance, there is some literature on the bias in the models for identifying at-risk students that are excluded from the population. Thirdly, the possibility of the digital divide is also an obvious issue: there are many regions and localities around the world that cannot afford to procure advanced AI systems and solutions. So, endorsement from the educators is still scarce, which mostly stems from the received lack of preparedness or de-evaluation worries; creating teacher-first AI and PD interventions, therefore, underlines the relevance of the subject.

Figure 1. Transformative impact of AI on global education systems

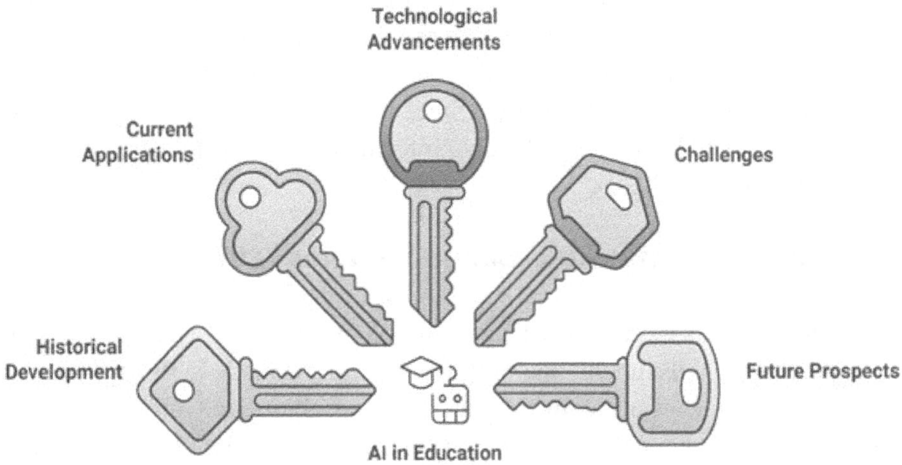

From the trends highlighted in this literature review the future of AIEd seems bright. When combined with augmented reality and virtual reality learning setting, AI enhances learners of all ages to apply what he/she has learnt without restriction of the real-life environment. Moreover, there is a quite popular concept of "AI + X", where X is a certain field, such as humanities and law, that means AI integrated into individual courses, helping to develop new ideas, thinking patterns and different models. In addition, the shifting of workforce demands that AI has identified has been instrumental in designing solutions for continuous learning and training. At the same time, the eXplainable AI frameworks studies, also, known as post hoc accountability, are being conducted in order to guarantee the AIEd systems' credibility and responsibility (Mäkelä & Stephany, 2024).

This Chapter offers a review of the experiences of AIEd discussing its development and prospects in detail. This chapter explores the history of AIEd development, presents current and future applications and issues, and examines the pertinent prospects. Using previous developments to future trends, this study endeavours to prescribe possibilities of how AIEd can unlock equitable, inclusive, and efficient learning environments in global contexts.

2. HISTORICAL OVERVIEW OF AIED

Extending from this study, it is possible to state that AIEd is the best transitional and technological integration of practical and theoretical approaches to education. For the Evolution of Artificial Intelligence in Education refer the Figure.2. AIEd has advanced from rule-based systems existing in prior decades but has moved into modern systems that are capable of delivering learning across multi-faceted levels. This section explores the historical milestones that have shaped the field, tracing its evolution through three pivotal phases: Since the increasing of Intelligent Tutoring Systems in mid-1990s, the post-ITS data informed and post-ITS data adaptive approaches (Luan et al., 2020).

Early Developments: Rule-Based Systems (1970s–1990s)

AIEd has its roots in the '70s when the notion of rule-based systems was applied to CAI in school environment, one of the first tries was made in this sphere. These systems referred to working algorithms and program charts, and offered information through sequential channel descends. SCHOLAR developed by Jaime Carbonell in 1970 and used semantic networks was an attempt towards teaching Geography by asking questions and answering the same from the learner. SCHOLAR was unique in its way to represent knowledge relationships; however, the system was not scalable and could not deal with the other types of concern except a set of questions (Chen et al., 2021).

At this time the instructional software is best described as behaviourist, in that practice and reward are the dominant learning strategies. Such programs as PLATO aimed at providing teaching of structured lessons for students at basic literacy and mathematic level. However, these systems act rather inappropriately as they do not consider the learner differences and the vary market of educational learning requirements.

Thus, knowledge-based systems installed understanding of how rule-based computer learning systems work, although they were not as memorable or easily scalable as the next generation of learning systems. Continuing this development, scholars started to consider the possibility to apply the concept of AI in the sphere of education in order to enhance the process even further (Al-Abdallat & Mansour, 2020).

Figure 2. Evolution of artificial intelligence in education

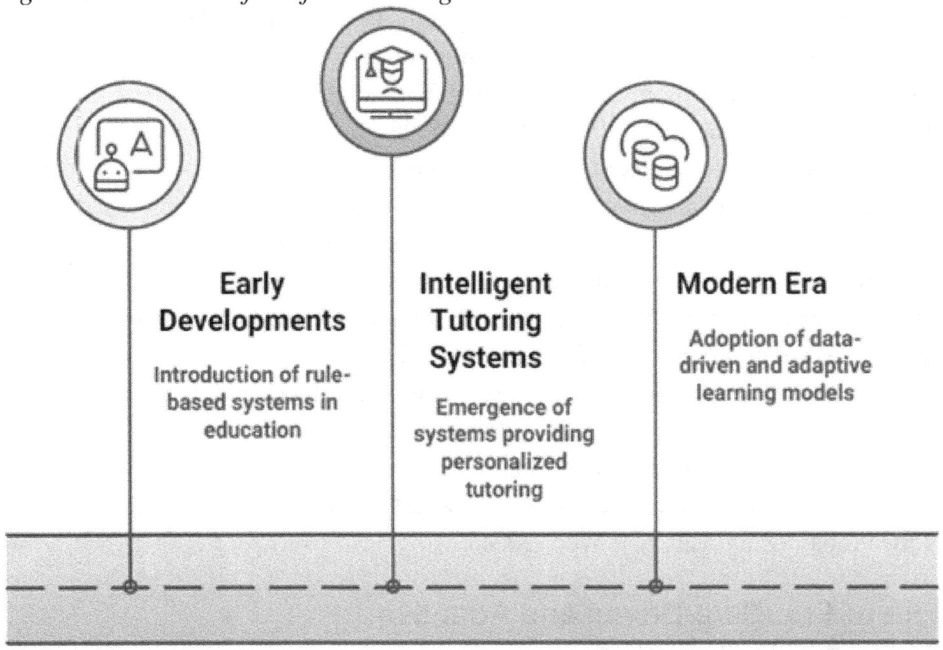

Emergence of Intelligent Tutoring Systems (ITS) (1990s–2000s)

Intelligent Tutoring Systems ushered in a new era of AIEd in the 1990s, as advancements in cognitive science increased the reliance on artificial intelligence. While ITS built upon rule-based systems, they operated at a more sophisticated level, employing computational models to provide personalized tutoring to each student. These systems implemented teaching techniques that dynamically adjusted based on the student's performance (Zawacki-Richter et al., 2019).

In one of the pioneering ITS, Cognitive Tutor was recognized to be one of the most effective. Based on a cognitive tutoring model, Cognitive Tutor identified the level of a student's mastery of particular content and skills via the Bayesian Knowledge Tracing algorithm. The assessments taken at the end of each learning module in the Cognitive Tutor offered information on the learner's weak mastery areas, making the results learning based on mastery to improve performance in mathematics and science. When implemented, ITS could decide on the best sequence of actions an individual could take when solving problems and give precisely the kind of feedback that supports learning. Another well-known ITS was ASSISTments, that provided instantaneous feedback to students but also monitored students' activity data, which was then made available to teachers and researchers. Specifically, ASSISTments illustrated how ITS could promote learning gains for students and teachers because instruction is aligned to instructional learning targets.

ITS was employed more actively in STEM disciplines because their problem-solving paradigms and the ability to adjust the learning process to a task are beneficial in these disciplines. Joshi & Pillay also proposed other factors which can be included in ITS for example use of computer simulations and graphics. However, the implementations of these solutions proved to be useful for ITS, or at least to be largely unproblematic; it was also found that the organisation lacked the means and resources to optimise its solutions, and did not have the technology which was perceived as necessary for their full execution. Such systems were computationally extensive involving much knowledge-based expert interfaces and therefore were not quite suitable for actual working environments let alone sub-saharan Africa which experiences high resource constrainment. However, through ITS the foundation was set out for the principles of adaptivity and basically all of the AIEd that is in practice today (Zhai, Lin, and Wen, 2021).

Modern Era: Data-Driven and Adaptive Learning (2010s–Present)

Over the last ten years, there has been an emphasis on utilisations of big data insights and AI approaches to development of more data and dynamic learning models in the sphere of Artificial Intelligence in Education. Educational Data Mining and Learning Analytics have become popular modes of analyzing data on students' behavior with the aim of helping educators and researchers fathom out interventions, redesign instructions and get models of at-risk learners (Heilala et al., 2020).

Drawing on these developments, collection wise adaptive learning platforms like ALEKS as well as DreamBox learning have incorporatedFigure3: Active Data Gathering and Reporting processes the application of learning models to observe learner performance, and consequently address content and delivery frequency in line with the learners' needs. For example, ALEKS uses Knowledge Space Theory to assess the learner state and provides an exercise to fill the gaps that were discovered.

Moreover, with the aid of new technologies in Natural Language Processing, new areas in AIEd have emerged, for example, in the automatic writing assessment and scoring methods that are used to support and offer instant feedback on the students' writing tasks, other than intelligent conversational agents as tutors such as AutoTutor used in language learning. Also, a new wave of spare AIEd possibilities was discovered with the integration of gamification and VR/AR. Kahoot! as well as Classcraft use game aspects to improve learner engagement and Augmented

Reality and Virtual Reality technologies to popularize learning in several subjects (Zhao et al., 2021).

AIEd is best understood when viewed as a progression of advancements in technology-supported learning starting from the use of analytical rule based systems of early 1970 right up to self-adaptive and fully automotive systems of the present time. These advancements help to overcome not only the discontinuity of learning processes but also continuing education at the same time on fair, large-scale, and individualized basis. Applying historical analysis to AIEd's ongoing growth will help shape future development to meet new opportunities while hurdling future ethical, access, and sustainability concerns.

3. CURRENT TRENDS IN ARTIFICIAL INTELLIGENCE IN EDUCATION (AIED)

AIEd has transformed education systems because it offers learners smart systems that can solve some of the issues and enhance learning. These systems make it possible for an instruction to be arranged in reference to the learner and to make interest as well as to yield outcomes that come make education even better and efficient. In this particular section, common trends in AIEd are highlighted and how they are deployed, areas they have been applied, and challenges that accompany them. (Lai et al., 2023)

3.1. Personalized and Adaptive Learning

To the second stream, we have to also relate another important contribution of AIEd to the realm of learning, namely the so called adaptive and intelligent approaches to learning with contents adapted to learners and learning processes and sequences. Since adaptive learning systems are developed based on ML algorithms, the system would have the ability to assess the student performance, detect the misconceptions and present the related content at the same time.

Some of these are examples are DreamBox Learning and ALEKS. ALEKS, following the KST concept and based on its principles, continuously monitors a learner's knowledge state and defines the meaning of the term weaknesses in order to provide problems that help to enhance it. Like with Knewton, DreamBox Learning too personalizes the kind of problem it offers in relation to difficulty level for math and it is always engaging yet not hard for a specific learner. Student Modeling within Cognitive Tutor the other landmark system is achieved with the help of Bayesian Knowledge Tracing to keep track and facilitate the mastery of the student in mathematical fields. These tools are more effective in STEM classes as content in this learning area is cumulative and cannot be presented until a certain area has been developed (Donnelly-Hermosillo et al., 2019).

Figure 3. Adaptive learning systems in transform of education

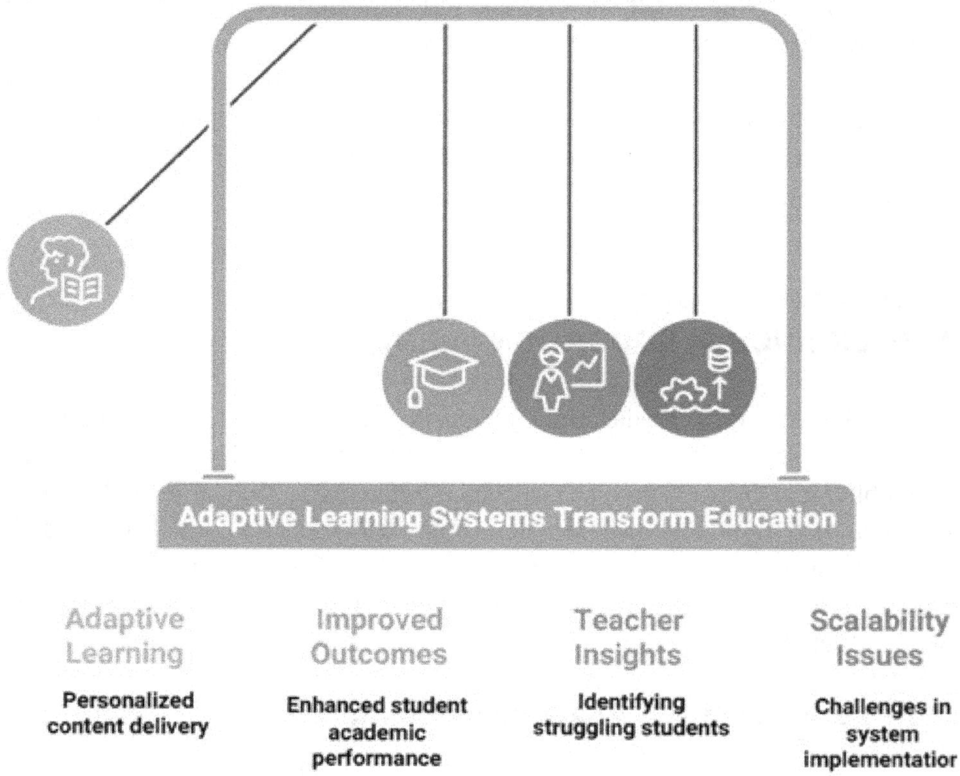

In addition to altering student's academic performance, personalized learning platforms assist educators through providing details of the results of the performance. All these insights assist teachers in the realization of which students might be struggling and ways of responding to learning needs of such pupils. Though, it is equally important to realise some of the difficulties that may encountered when putting into practice such systems. Virtual lessons rely on data and because problems associated with data ownership and protection. But in order to make these systems sustainable particularly in the different pre-industrial or industrially developing zones there is a major issue of scalability because of restrictions in infrastructure.

3.2 Gamification and Engagement

Gamification has emerged as the approach of enhancing students' interest and motivation and applying the game elements into education. By applying such items as points, badges, ranks, and virtual prizes for the learners to accomplish the learning activities makes the students to be more involved in their targets.

In today's world, almost all classes employ Kahoot!, Classcraft, and Quizizz or their counterparts to create competitive or cooperative contexts in learning. For instance, Kahoot! enables teachers to develop live quizzes in which students act to answer questions successfully and provided that, quickly. Similarly, Classcraft transforms behavioral lessons into adventure in which students and their group members gather points for positive behavior and other accomplishments within the class. Computer simulations, also a type of gamification in STEM education enables students to practice the real-life experiments or problems, view in addition to navigating the concepts essentially literally (Ishak et al., 2020).

The beauty of the concept of gamification can be viewed in its ability to keep interest high and the self-executive motivation. When they are learnt in the form of tasks or challenges, the learners naturally put pressure on themselves to attempt to solve what they regard as tasks or challenges. However, there are concerns with learning retention that results from gamification that needs other research. Moreover, critics carry on the conversation about potential adverse repercussions of excessive usage of extrinsic motivation, such as points and badges, and restart the topic about the successful balance in design.

3.3 Affective Computing and Emotional Intelligence

Intelligent affective computing that recognizes learners' intelligence of emotions as it formulates technologies is revolutionizing how AIEd systems interact with learners. These systems are designed to deliver personal and caring teaching-learning environments since the systems themselves accommodate the identification of students' emotional states. One of the key aspects of affective computing is based on the systems that can identify and recognize – through faces, voice, and other body indices – frustrations or boredom or confusion and subsequent changes (Zhao et. al., 2021).

AutoTutor is a well-developed system of affective computing applied for learning and possesses one of the functions of the assessment of students' emotions as well as affective computing in work with learning tasks. For instance, if a student appears unmotivated, the system will issue motivational instructions, or the system will present content in an easier manner should it wish to attract the attention of that student. This capability is very useful when an Instructor is in and online or remote learning scenario where there will be very few, if any physical cues for her to "pick up' with her eyes that the learner is feeling a particular way (Gu et al, 2024).

Besides engagement, affective computing has a significant contribution to other forms of interventions. For instances, if students exhibiting some symptoms of exitus while solving a difficult numeracy one or a problem orientated question, further complexities or other ways of handling the same topic are explained. In notion of affective computing the prospect is open ended However, it has an ethical concern. Controversies related to efficiency of the ER, purposes and consequences of employing and misusing the emotional data, or sameness or differences in the emotional experience of subjects indicate that better ethical norms and decision making paradigms are required.

3.4 Educational Data Mining (EDM) and Learning Analytics (LA)

Educational Data Mining (EDM) and Learning Analytics (LA) are two sub-fields of AIEd that have provided the tools with which educators can extract useful knowledge from massive educational data. These methodologies identify patterns throughout the students' behavior, the possible outcomes a student may have in the future and the most efficient strategy to use in teaching, all these being supported by statistical and measurable approaches to teaching(Heilala et al., 2020).

Examples of these learning analytics dashboards being implemented are Canvas, moodle, and other customized platforms used by institutions that will show student activity, attendance, engagement, and performance. These tools help the educators to know who is behind in his class work so as to intervene early enough to help the learner. For instance, the involvement models can predict that a student is likely to drop out based on some of his/her interaction characteristics this will help schools to develop a good dropout intervention plan (Matz et al., 2023).

It concerns the education sector and organizational or institutional decision-making EDM. Using retention, enrollment, and program-based data enables the administrator to allocate scarce resources better and design contingency methods for enhancing performance. Nevertheless, the application of these findings into practical instructional interventions within the classroom is an area that continues to present tremendous difficulty, both in everyday practice and for teachers who are relatively new to the data analysis concept. In addition, issues and fears regarding data protection and discrimination of EDM and LA also argue for the responsible behaviour in the domains.

3.5 AI for Equity in Education

AI can as well be used to address the issue of how equity in education will be attained since it avails solution that is cheap to scale up. The relevancy of location and language use in the adoption of the learning tools, as well as the economic barrier to education can all be countered by applying AI in an effort to open up education to all. Refer the Figure.4 AI in Education Equity.

For instance, an online application called Duolingo is offering the mass free and personalized education in as many languages as people want throughout the world using high quality in order that people could study in good school if people do not have money for that. Here in the rural areas of India, attempts have been made to implement short term endeavors through dependency on Artificially Intelligent based systems of adaptive learning, through which learners are provided better resources than what they could prepare with, in the past. The ideas highlighted in this paper demonstrate that AI can overcome the challenges in learning and delivering quality education.

Figure 4. AI in education equity

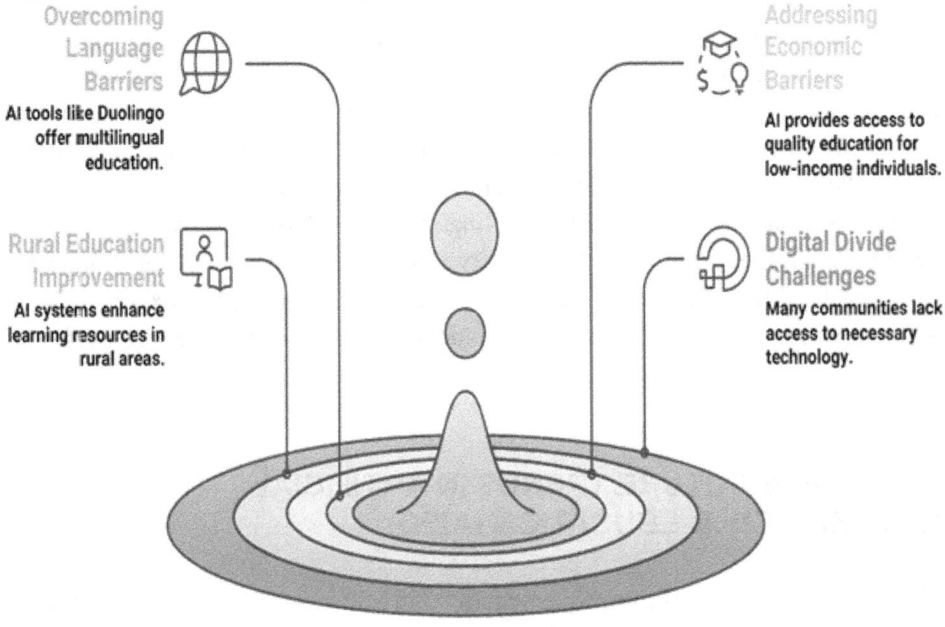

Of course, the opportunities of a digital divide remain an enormous obstacle on the way to educational equity. There are many communities that are not connected, many communities do not have sufficient hardware, and often many communities do not even have the proper tools to harness the full potential of today's advanced AI solutions. The strength of utilizing AI systems is in the capability to provide information, and this reemphasizes the need for the systems to be affordable, accessible and culturally bounded.

3.6 Ethics and Privacy in AIEd

Another new concept is the ethical objective which has been brought by the recent developments in AIEd systems as well. Just as important is the fact that issues, which are linked to protection of data and algorithms, freedom and responsibility, are necessary for the use of AI as the approach to addressing the challenges rather than the root of the problem.

There has been effort such as the UNESCO Beijing Consensus on AI and Education that has acted as a call for ethic framework that will be governing the creation and use of AIEd systems. Details of the type of openness of the implemented AI recommendation systems are disclosed by employing XAI frameworks with an aim of enabling educators and learners to understand how specific forms were developed. In addition, new norms are being establishing for masking the identity of the students and protecting their data (Kamalov & Gurrib, 2023).

Thus, the question of how it is possible to fully appreciate the opportunities offered by user customization and at the same time meet the need for discretion has remained an open one. These guarantees for trust in the AIEd transcend the technical safeguard level and embrace the exchange and true conversation where educators, policymakers, developers, and the community are engaged. However, the question of how to choose the best of having the application tailored to the individual user and needing certain measures of confidentiality has not been answered. The guarantee of trust in the AIEd is not only technical protection proven by the exchanges and the conversation but also to engage the educators, policymakers, developers, and the community (Lüthi et al., 2020).

4. EMERGING FUTURE TRENDS IN ARTIFICIAL INTELLIGENCE IN EDUCATION (AIED)

The opportunities for the improvement of AI in Education (AIEd) remain nascent as new technologies and innovative ideas can improve schooling. Such development is to address existing needs, enhance the quality of benefits, and increase the range of subjects and learners that are served by education in those countries. These trends concerning future development of AIEd are considered in this section with regard to possible applications, benefits and risks (Chen et al., 2020).

4.1 Immersive Learning Environments with AR/VR and AI

The incorporation of Artificial Intelligence with Augmented Reality (AR) and Virtual Reality (VR) is making the creation of annotations of concept and skills in situations which attract the learners towards the environment of learning which has been set. When integrated with AI, such technologies can provide personalized content; timely and personalized feedback; and differing forms of learning case types in addition to what is taught in the classroom (Zhai et al., 2021). Refer the Figure.5 for integrating technology for effective education.

For instance, the medical education training paradigm of developing VR surgical simulation systems allow students to perform typical complicated surgical operations and when performing on actual patients, reduced risk is felt. Similarly, engineering students to let using AR applications for the interaction with the focuses in terms of 3D models of machinery, and let get the touch-driven feel of some systems and their parts devoid of all the required physical cues. For example, AI supplements these experiences with the capability to monitor and scrutinize a learner in real-time, and modify the nature of tasks that a learner has to solve and even guide the learner while doing so.

Figure 5. Integrating technology for effective education

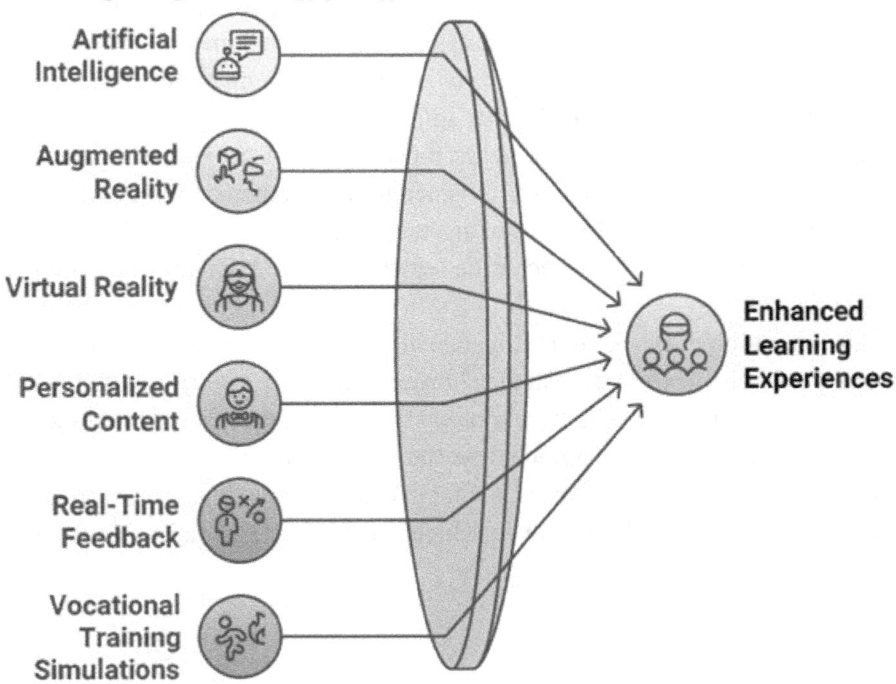

In vocational training it has become very possible to use full environment in training people in welding, car mechanics, firefighting among other. For instance, VR working with Artificial Intelligence is capable of creating real life threats such as firefighting or chemical leakage and educates learners on how best to handle such mishaps. As much as these tools are very useful they remain expensive and can only be afford by very few schools teachers who have access to hardware equipment and the training of teachers would definitely take a lot of time. Also, special efforts will be needed to avoid aggravation of the digital divide while making these technologies available.

4.2 Interdisciplinary Education and the "AI + X" Model

The appreciation of the future education is hoped to be interdisciplinary and profession inclusive especially with the support of artificial intelligence and other overseas disciplines. The "AI+X" approach which incorporates the use of artificial intelligence in humanities, arts, law and social sciences, is gradually becoming popular since it develops qualities such as creativity, critical thinking and ethical characteristics (Wang & Lester, 2023).

For example, where there are social relations, such as history students learning and comparing different cultures and traditions. In legal education, there are emerging personalized learning interfaces that are being designed to assists the students in case solutions, legal writings and analysis of precedents, making it more practical for the learners all through the intake of an artificial companion interface.

In arts, DeepArt and AIVA apps implant artificial intelligence technologies enabling learners to learn and develop music, art, and stories with great style. In the examples where students want to generate music, they can train AI systems in various types of music, or in terms of art, they can build it utilizing the help of some algorithms that are characteristic of the selected artists, as Zhao et al. demonstrated in 2024.

Incorporation of artificial intelligence in teaching in context to interdisciplinary learning is likely to be of an advantage however, effective synergy has to be achieved so as to avoid a situation where technology takes over the teaching learning process. Moreover, it becomes relevant to stress the need to effective teaching of corporate ethics since ethical consciousness is vital in corporations. In addition, the audience must always aware of the extent to which AI can go, especially in places where creativity is vital.

4.3 Lifelong Learning and Workforce Development

Learning in today's society is a dynamic process because of changes arising from technology and the society. To address this, the formation of U-shaped learning model and self-pace, modular lifelong learning platforms powered by AI technology has been developed. These platforms are intended to offer learners the best learning solutions depending on their needs and learning levels they encounter while practicing their careers.

These future learning platforms such as Coursera or edX are also gradually using AI for recommending courses, for monitoring learner progress and for providing official certifications. Likewise, in the workplace, the sophisticated usage of Artificial Intelligence is to offer the exact kind of training required and required by the employee to meet the new innovative flow of technology and demands of the work arena. For instance, it can keep track of an employee's performance in order to recommend topics for training where the employee has been found wanting (Gligorea et al., 2023).

For instance, the upcoming industry like renewable energy industry can enhance the production of AI focus skill development for practices like solar panel fixing and wind turbine repair. Similarly, the healthcare industry can use Artificial intelligence in tele-consultation, diagnosis through digital means and understand the patient needs at a personal level.

Following the growth of institutional lifelong learning platforms, another challenge lies in funding the target group that cannot be considered as traditional students or members of vulnerable organizations. These areas will include consideration of culture, both in regard to content and latent inabilities of learners to understand content delivered in a format different from the one they are familiar with. It is concerning that AI has been integrated into learning systems; trustworthiness and ethically questionable AI technologies (Hockly, 2023).

4.4 Explainable AI (XAI) and Ethical Frameworks

As the continual development of AIEd systems enhances, there is also an equivalent increase in the demand for ex- AI as well as ethical consideration. The use of XAI is to explain and make artificial intelligence more explainable so that users who interact with it can trust AI's outputs. We also found that XAI can assist educators and learners to understand the rationale behind the determination of the personalized recommendations in an educational context. For example, if an AI system detects that a learner is at risk of dropping out from the course, then XAI frameworks can explicate details such as attendance, interaction, and performance metrics, that allows instructors to assist, meaningfully. Also, present days ethical objectives are enumerated, such as UNESCO guidelines concerning AI usage in education in 2017, where the main problems associated with satisfying goals for applying AI are described, including the problems of officers' biased perspective, data protection, and other essential concerns (Bulut cbssBeiting-Parrish, 2024).

For incorporating XAI in to education the development of new algorithms for a shift in focus from building applications to the end users is necessary. Promoting ethical consideration will also require its endorsement by all the societies for enhanced policy consistency across different educational levels.

4.5 AI for Global Education and Inclusivity

Possibly one of the most significant ideas that can be achieved with the help of AI in context with the education system is the fulfilment of the mission to provide education to the students with varying geographical, economic, as well as language barriers. Heterogeneous learning requirements can be addressed by effective and economical AIEd-powered platforms. For example, language translation applications like the Google Translate AND Microsoft Translator will help students from different language backgrounds for equal contribution on certain tasks. In addition, through its adaptive learning platforms such as the EdTech Hub, developed countries are extending capability in literacy and numeracy for the less developing nations. For instance, schools in the rural areas of India are applying AI systems to work alongside conventional teaching learning approaches like using virtual laboratories in the teaching of Science, Technology, Engineering and Mathematics subjects.

However, a key issue that hinders commitment on the use of AI Ed on a bigger scale at the international level is the digital divide. To overcome this challenge, more funds will be needed for developing the physical infrastructure and connectivity, and for preparing teachers for embracing equitable uses of AI.

4.6 AI-Driven Sustainability in Education

As sustainability is emerging as a significant factor AI is being incorporated to serve sustainability in learning processes and support the initiatives of the Global Sustainable Development Goals (SDGs). It is going toward sustainable status as it raises resource utilization and creates avenues to lessen one's carbon footprint.

For instance, the teaching through online learning resources reduces the depletion of paper and travel reducing the effects of school on the environment. AI grounds technologies in which energy is used in schools and consults them on how to optimally reduce consumption of energy through smart lighting and conditioning. Moreover, the provisions of different education training in the sector of renewable energy and the concerns of circular economy are useful for developing learners equipped with adequate competencies to address environmental issues (Hipogrosso & Nesmachnow, 2020).

Thus, arguing this chapter, the author has pointed out that sustainability in education means that attempts at implementing innovations in use of technology has to be supported side by side with environmentalism and economism. Optimization of concern AI systems for their reduced computational and energy inquiries for the systems will also be a goal. The new trends in AIEd can be studied in terms of innovation, diversity and ethics that are destined to condition the web of learning. Evaluating the examples of immersive technologies and interdisciplinary approaches, learning throughout life, and sustainability, the developments outline the integrated value of AI for solving global educational challenges. If achieved, all these trends present educators, policymakes, and technologists with a vision of what learning can be in the future, now – inclusive, effective, and flexible (Mello et al., 2023).

5. CHALLENGES AND OPPORTUNITIES IN ARTIFICIAL INTELLIGENCE IN EDUCATION (AIED)

When it reaches technological development and spreads educational systems around the globe, there are critical barriers to encountering during its application. However, on the positive side, AIEd also has strong opportunities to redesign learning processes, diversify them and improve learning systems. This section revisits the main challenges and opportunities of AIEd based on the available literature (Pérez-Ortiz et al., 2021).

Ethical Concerns and Algorithmic Bias

In learning environments specifics of AIEd the ethical factors arise as particularly significant, and there is algorithmic bias amongst them. In other cases, the growth of the algorithms to identify vulnerable students for decision-making needs to be biased by the training data. For instance, performance data analysis on students may result in preference of a certain minority or low income student for remedial action based on historical tendencies in data, ethical issues in the use of Artificial Intelligence in educational prediction. Moreover, many AI algorithms are 'black box,' it difficult for educators amd administrators to understand how decisions have been made. This lack of explainability might prevent educationists from relying on AIEd systems for decision making due to a lack of trust in technology that they cannot understand. In an attempt to overcome some of these challenges some frames for AI has been recommended for instance the one that states that the AI must be transparent, educative, fair, and accountable (Tan & Subramonyam, 2023).

Digital Divide and Infrastructure Gaps

According to the principles of AIEd mentioned above, the accessibility of education is improved, however, the digital divide issue remains an issue. A major concern that low income and rural school face in terms of use of AI is access to supporting structures because development of structures such as internet, electricity, and devices to support program like AI require lots of resources. For instance, a study on distribution of adaptive learning system in sub Saharan Africa on coverage pointed to advantages of the urban schools as compared to their rural counterparts, a subject of discussion by Murgatroyd. Here too however, if infrastructure has been developed, costs of AIEd solutions remain prohibitive and therefore AIEd solutions are unlikely to be feasible in faculties and facilities located in low income settings (Zhu & Li, 2020). This concern raises the need for reasonably priced and openly accessible AI-based technologies for a setting like the limited-resource one outlined herein through relief-informal education supply projects such as EdTech Hub, which employs the adaptive learning approach in low income countries.

Teacher Resistance and Skill Gaps

Teacher resistance to AIEd is typical, and the main concern is, as always, professionalisation and job loss. AI threatens to replace the teacher since many teachers assume that in light of different systems implemented, the authority of the teacher will be diminished or that the role of the teacher's judgment will be taken away. For example, a quantitative survey that was cascaded in one study of the use of AI tools in European schools was rejected by educators who did not feel they possessed competency in the effective use of AI. Additionally, a small number of faculty members are ready to apply AI enable technologies in their practice regarding how to analyze the data or integrate a learning analytics dashboard or an adaptive learning system into the curriculum plan. Perhaps other scientific interventions such as job training activities which have been integrated in Singapore improvement of teacher education based on AI might be long in filling these gaps by imparting educators with adequate knowledge and attitude, and emphatic orientation towards incorporation as well as management of AI systems.

Scalability and Localization

The challenges arise primarily when applying AIEd solutions in environment encompassing more students' learning-teaching processes, including the questions of culture, linguistic and curricula differences. For example, a study done on Personalized Learning Tools in use in the world adoption in Learning Management

Systems showed that, this was the reason why systems do not integrate to the corresponding syllabi and languages in the nations that are non-English speaking. Promises to localization entail great extent of resource to translate content, algorithms, and interfaces to the people. Moreover, discussing AI scaling itself raises concerns about the computational environment because extensive models entail extensive resources. Some solutions to these problems are discussed by exploration of approaches to obtain energy-efficient AI solutions such as lightweight algorithms for machine learning systems.

Global Access and Inclusivity

The challenges arise primarily when applying AIEd solutions in environment encompassing more students' learning-teaching processes, including the questions of culture, linguistic and curricula differences. For example, a study done on Personalized Learning Tools in use in the world adoption in Learning Management Systems showed that, this was the reason why systems do not integrate to the corresponding syllabi and languages in the nations that are non-English speaking. Promises to localization entail great extent of resource to translate content, algorithms, and interfaces to the people. Moreover, discussing AI scaling itself raises concerns about the computational environment because extensive models entail extensive resources. Some solutions to these problems are discussed by exploration of approaches to obtain energy-efficient AI solutions such as lightweight algorithms for machine learning systems.

Empowering Educators

As such, Falkenberg and Mattis' constructs indicate that, rather than displacing educational decision makers, AIEd is potentially tied to improving upon currently representative educators through such time liberation through schedule and data analysis tasks and useful findings on student achievements. For instance, Intelligent Tutoring Systems such as ASSISTments help teachers in how exactly student performers are doing and entails enhanced assessment that can aid in creating favorable learning atmosphere as well as capacitance better performance. Additionally, the activities that might take machines hours to complete like marking or monitoring the students' attendance reduces a vast amount of time that could have been used by a teacher coming up with more and better challenging lessons, as well as addressing each student. Such tools function together with teachers, enhance and supplement the work of teachers, and remain the means utilized in the educational process at the same time.

Data-Driven Decision Making

EDM and LA are paving the way in the rapid change in decision-making within FE via AIEd. These contain vast amount of data within them to be used by the AI systems to help in determining their patterns of behaviors and performances of students as well as conduct their academic performances, and then recommend course of action that have to be taken regarding them. For example, Siemens and Baker in their study found that; efficient analytics can be created with models of student characteristic or behaviour to identify students inclined to drop out to reach them before so as to retain them. At an organisational level, it provides administration an analytical insight of structural, trend of learningprocess, effectiveness, enrollment and programme performance to enable decision making. These improvements do in fact increase the flexibility, muability and capability of instructional structures.

Interdisciplinary and Lifelong Learning

AI is integrated with all sectors in education and is following the "AI + X" model for shifting the learning pattern. For instance in the field of arts, into are creative AI technologies including AIVA (Artificial Intelligence Virtual Artist) that assists students in writing music as well as design digital arts through blending computation potency with creativity. In the same way with legal education help for analyzing local laws and scrip arguments-learning difficulties are made more interesting and practical in the usage of AI. Lifelong learning also supplements workforce development by providing the carrying out of customized, flexible training according to the market. That shall offer the solutions to the growing need for training and development across workplace in regarding new sectors such as; renewable energy, and digitization.

Sustainability and Environmental Impact

AIEd systems are capable of supporting sustainability since it sustains resources or even support recycling. This also reduces the use of papers and transport that results in a minimal emission of carbon and hence computer based learning methods. That is why, controlling the usage rate, AI-powered energy efficient systems in schools on such resource as electricity can help to achieve the goals related to sustainability. In addition, capacities developed in training programs in areas like renewable energy equip the learners with adverse elements to respond to environmental challenges challenging the globe making education responsive to sustainable development goals. They aid in showing how AIEd can be used to support change across and within education and the environmental sectors.

The points outlined within the challenges and opportunities of AIEd establish and emphasise the context of dual (contradictory) technology investment in education in the discussion. While it might be necessary to persist with ethical concerns, infrastructure deficiency and size issues in AIEd, the strong affirmative call for social equity, participation and efficiency that the rationale offered was unmistakable. When done in synergy, including by drawing upon innovation and the cross-country cooperation, such policy strategies would significantly tap into the possibilities of AIEd to build the long-term variety, strength, and equity of the learning systems in the global context.

6. ENSURING EQUITABLE ACCESS AND INCLUSIVITY

AIEd results in having positive impacts that bring a new concept that serves as an enabler of education to the marginalised. Some of AI examples include Duo-lingo and Khan academy which are capable of educating millions of students irrespective of their; origin, language used or status of their families' wealth. In contexts where resources are scarce, as an example KitKit School AI enabled tools have been adopted to help introduce literacy and numeracy services for children in remote areas, and therefore reflects the ability of AIEd in making educational services a reality. In addition, apart from language translation technologies for example Google Translate in a learning platform, learners who speak different languages can enroll and engage with other learners from different global regions in their online classes, these create cultural intercommunication.

Let me also note that at the same time the AI application in learning context shall be regarded not as a problem-free solution, but as the one that may deepen the pre-existing gaps or even create new ones. Poor nations and minority groups may lack suitable technology, training, and other assets essential for engaging AI-supported learning applications (Bulathwela et al., 2021). Therefore, equal distribution of the systems, design, development and deployment should be done thoroughly to avoid any risk that may lead to a wider gap between the students.

, it should be noted that in the implementation of AIEd, increasing access to technology and narrowing the digital divide should be high on the list of priorities. It will be important for the governments, policymakers, and stakeholders to step up investment in enhancing the technological foundation, offering ICT skills development, and bearing the cost for providing technological tools and applications to less privileged groups. It thus imperative that with the stakeholder support Public-Private-Partnership, international organizations, able to amplify the usage of

AIEd in a way that will address existing inequalities in the education systems and make learning more inclusive across the world.

7. EMERGING TRENDS AND INNOVATIONS

Another new frontier in future AIEd is the creation of intelligent and learning models that are tailored to the style or type of learner of each individual learner (Bulathwela et al., 2021). These systems incorporate AI heuristics for examining data about the student and the data comprises of performance data, interaction data, and prior knowledge of a particular content. Research has found that this approach leads to raised achievement, enhanced motivation and enhanced growth mind-sets.

Another practice existent in AIEd is the use of multimodal interfaces, which enables the learners use more than one modes while engaging with the learning resources including voice, gesture, and touch, among others. This will compliment the characteristics that make learning the more engaging and interactive by allowing for greater visualization and even kinesthetic learning especially for complex topics such as STEM.

There are lots of more advanced Generative AI products that are coming in the near future for educational content creation including large language models and text-to-image generators. Teachers can use these models for producing content similar to customized pedagogical content, computer-simulated instruction, and even automated instruction that can greatly decrease the learning curve in terms of preparing effective educational content. (Mello et al., 2023)

8. PROMISING FUTURE OF AIED: BALANCING OPPORTUNITIES AND CHALLENGES

The application of artificial intelligence in the education industry has a bright future toward changes within the teaching-learning process. If the challenges are met and the opportunities are grasped AIEd has the potential to be applied as a solution for increased equity, effectively and efficiently personalized and thus generally more engaging teaching and learning facilitated for all students irrespective of their context and geographical location (Ojha et al., 2023). Making use of AIEd can facilitate creation of learning environments flexibility, individual differences in the learning process may also be addressed. Such systems can provide teachers with students' information to identify the content, sequence, and instructional approaches for the content to achieve positive results, enhance learners' interest, and promote a growth mindset.

Additionally, the adoption of multimodal interfaces into AIEd can improve the richness and interactivity of the learning elements specifically in learning domains such as STEM where a combination of visual and tactile learning is desirable. Similar to Generative AI creating large language models and text-to-image generators there is the potential to use it in creating educational content rapidly developed by educators which in turn could reduce substantially the time taken to produce quality, relevant learning materials and can include such creations as intelligent simulation & tutors.

With the current increased use of AIEd it is still important to be moderate in the practice and ensure it enhances the actions of educators and learners and not act in place of them. By bringing together AI scientists, practitioners, and policymakers and engaging with various community stakeholders we can realise the benefits of AI for education, learning, and general societal and sustainable wellbeing.

CONCLUSION

The use of AI in education is undergoing a redefinition of the education sector. Just as with other technologies, this one offers prospects for addressing the chronic issues and creating new valuable approaches to learning for all people. It has evolved into a complex solution for learners, educators, and various institutions simultaneously. Based on the positive outcomes of these technologies, the learners' interest has been induced, learning enhanced and useful data collected by the educationists through intelligent tutoring systems, Educational Data Mining, Gamification, and Affective Computing. They also illustrate that the use of AI in education is also in the process of reinvention, which became clear with the recent advancements. Instructions can be recorded to the learner's needs and motivational systems can enhance retention of learners. Learner's emotion can be addressed without stressing them through affective computing for effective educational practices. New learning analytics and adaptive technologies help educators and administrators to modify the context of learning.

However, there are very important challenges that AI in education have to solve so to be used successfully. Problems such as the presence of algorithmic bias, data privacy, and the absence of the prerequisite infrastructure must be addressed through openly addressable methods, which are progressive and adequately indefinite in capacity. Teachers' reluctance and inability hinder the implementation of AI in class, so, professional development should assist them to engage AI. Digital divide must be closed as the communities require both affordable user devices and connection to networks.

REFERENCES

Al-Abdallat, M., & Mansour, A. (2020). The Effect of Teaching Using Artificial Intelligence Software's on the Academic Achievement of the 10th Grade Students in Computer Science Subject and Their Attitudes Towards It in Jordan. In Journal of Education and Practice. DOI: 10.7176/JEP/11-7-10

Bulathwela, S., Pérez-Ortiz, M., Holloway, C., & Shawe-Taylor, J. (2021). Could AI Democratise Education? Socio-Technical Imaginaries of an EdTech Revolution. In arXiv (Cornell University). Cornell University. https://doi.org//arxiv.2112.02034DOI: 10.48550

Bulut, O., & Beiting-Parrish, M. (2024). The Rise of Artificial Intelligence in Educational Measurement: Opportunities and Ethical Challenges. In Chinese/English Journal of Educational Measurement and Evaluation (Vol. 5, Issue 3). DOI: 10.59863/MIQL7785

Cai, M., Akçayır, G., & Epp, C. D. (2021). Exploring Augmented Reality Games in Accessible Learning: A Systematic Review [Review of Exploring Augmented Reality Games in Accessible Learning: A Systematic Review]. arXiv (Cornell University). Cornell University. https://doi.org//arxiv.2111.08214DOI: 10.48550

Chen, C.-H., Shiu, M.-F., & Chen, S. (2021). Use Learnable Knowledge Graph in Dialogue System for Visually Impaired Macro Navigation. In Applied Sciences (Vol. 11, Issue 13, p. 6057). Multidisciplinary Digital Publishing Institute. DOI: 10.3390/app11136057

Chen, X., Xie, H., & Hwang, G. (2020). A multi-perspective study on Artificial Intelligence in Education: grants, conferences, journals, software tools, institutions, and researchers. In *Computers and Education Artificial Intelligence* (Vol. 1, p. 100005). Elsevier BV., DOI: 10.1016/j.caeai.2020.100005

Donnelly-Hermosillo, D., Gerard, L., & Linn, M. C. (2019). Impact of graph technologies in K-12 science and mathematics education. In *Computers & Education* (Vol. 146, p. 103748). Elsevier BV., DOI: 10.1016/j.compedu.2019.103748

Gligorea, I., Cioca, M., Oancea, R., Gorski, A.-T., Gorski, H., & Tudorache, P. (2023). Adaptive Learning Using Artificial Intelligence in e-Learning: A Literature Review. Education Sciences, 13(12), 1216. Multidisciplinary Digital Publishing Institute. DOI: 10.3390/educsci13121216

Gu, C., Peng, Y., Nastase, S. A., Mayer, R. E., & Li, P. (2024). Onscreen presence of instructors in video lectures affects learners' neural synchrony and visual attention during multimedia learning. In Proceedings of the National Academy of Sciences (Vol. 121, Issue 12). National Academy of Sciences. DOI: 10.1073/pnas.2309054121

Heilala, V., Jääskelä, P., Kärkkäinen, T., & Saarela, M. (2020). Understanding the Study Experiences of Students in Low Agency Profile: Towards a Smart Education Approach. In Lecture notes in electrical engineering (p. 498). Springer Science+Business Media. DOI: 10.1007/978-3-030-53187-4_54

Hipogrosso, S., & Nesmachnow, S. (2020). Analysis of Sustainable Public Transportation and Mobility Recommendations for Montevideo and Parque Rodó Neighborhood. In Smart Cities (Vol. 3, Issue 2, p. 479). Multidisciplinary Digital Publishing Institute. DOI: 10.3390/smartcities3020026

Hockly, N. (2023). Artificial Intelligence in English Language Teaching: The Good, the Bad and the Ugly. In Journal, R. E. L. C. (Ed.), *Issue 2* (Vol. 54, p. 445). SAGE Publishing., DOI: 10.1177/00336882231168504

Ishak, S. A., Din, R., & Hasran, U. A. (2020). Defining Digital Game-Based Learning for Science, Technology, Engineering, and Mathematics: A New Perspective on Design and Developmental Research. In Journal of Medical Internet Research (Vol. 23, Issue 2). JMIR Publications. DOI: 10.2196/20537

Kamalov, F., & Gurrib, I. (2023). New Era of Artificial Intelligence in Education: Towards a Sustainable Multifaceted Revolution. In arXiv (Cornell University). Cornell University. https://doi.org//arxiv.2305.18303DOI: 10.48550

Lai, T., Xie, C., Ruan, M., Wang, Z., Lu, H., & Fu, S. (2023). Influence of artificial intelligence in education on adolescents' social adaptability: The mediatory role of social support. In PLoS ONE (Vol. 18, Issue 3). Public Library of Science. DOI: 10.1371/journal.pone.0283170

Luan, H., Géczy, P., Lai, H., Gobert, J. D., Yang, S. J. H., Ogata, H., Baltes, J., Guerra, R. da S., Li, P., & Tsai, C. (2020). Challenges and Future Directions of Big Data and Artificial Intelligence in Education [Review of Challenges and Future Directions of Big Data and Artificial Intelligence in Education]. Frontiers in Psychology, 11. Frontiers Media. DOI: 10.3389/fpsyg.2020.580820

Lüthi, P., Gagnaux, T., & Gygli, M. (2020). Distributed Ledger for Provenance Tracking of Artificial Intelligence Assets. In arXiv (Cornell University). Cornell University. https://doi.org//arxiv.2002.11000DOI: 10.48550

Mäkelä, E., & Stephany, F. (2024). Complement or substitute? How AI increases the demand for human skills. In arXiv (Cornell University). Cornell University. https://doi.org//arxiv.2412.19754DOI: 10.48550

Matz, S., Bukow, C. S., Peters, H., Deacons, C., Dinu, A., & Stachl, C. (2023). Using machine learning to predict student retention from socio-demographic characteristics and app-based engagement metrics. In Scientific Reports (Vol. 13, Issue 1). Nature Portfolio. DOI: 10.1038/s41598-023-32484-w

Mello, R. F., Freitas, E., Pereira, F. D., Cabral, L., Tedesco, P., & Ramalho, G. (2023). Education in the age of Generative AI: Context and Recent Developments. In arXiv (Cornell University). Cornell University. https://doi.org//arxiv.2309.12332DOI: 10.48550

Ojha, S., Narendra, A., Mohapatra, S., & Misra, I. (2023). From Robots to Books: An Introduction to Smart Applications of AI in Education (AIEd). In arXiv (Cornell University). Cornell University. https://doi.org//arxiv.2301.10026DOI: 10.48550

Pérez-Ortiz, M., Novak, E., Bulathwela, S., & Shawe-Taylor, J. (2021). An AI-based Learning Companion Promoting Lifelong Learning Opportunities for All. In arXiv (Cornell University). Cornell University. https://doi.org//arxiv.2112.01242DOI: 10.48550

Tan, M., & Subramonyam, H. (2023). More than Model Documentation: Uncovering Teachers' Bespoke Information Needs for Informed Classroom Integration of ChatGPT. In arXiv (Cornell University). Cornell University. https://doi.org//arxiv.2309.14458DOI: 10.48550

Wang, N., & Lester, J. C. (2023). K-12 Education in the Age of AI: A Call to Action for K-12 AI Literacy. In International Journal of Artificial Intelligence in Education (Vol. 33, Issue 2, p. 228). Springer Science+Business Media. DOI: 10.1007/s40593-023-00358-x

Zawacki-Richter, O., Marín, V. I., Bond, M., & Gouverneur, F. (2019). Systematic review of research on artificial intelligence applications in higher education – where are the educators? In International Journal of Educational Technology in Higher Education (Vol. 16, Issue 1). Springer Nature. DOI: 10.1186/s41239-019-0171-0

Zhai, X., Chu, X., Chai, C. S., Jong, M. S., Starčič, A. I., Spector, M., Liu, J., Jing, Y., & Li, Y. (2021). A Review of Artificial Intelligence (AI) in Education from 2010 to 2020 [Review of A Review of Artificial Intelligence (AI) in Education from 2010 to 2020]. Complexity, 2021(1). Hindawi Publishing Corporation. DOI: 10.1155/2021/8812542

Zhao, D., Playfoot, J., Nicola, C. D., Guarino, G., Bratu, M., Salvadore, F. D., & Muntean, G. (2021). An Innovative Multi-Layer Gamification Framework for Improved STEM Learning Experience. In Access, I. E. E. E. (Ed.), Vol. 10, p. 3879). Institute of Electrical and Electronics Engineers., DOI: 10.1109/ACCESS.2021.3139729

Zhao, S., Jia, G., Yang, J., Ding, G., & Keutzer, K. (2021). Emotion Recognition From Multiple Modalities: Fundamentals and methodologies. In IEEE Signal Processing Magazine (Vol. 38, Issue 6, p. 59). Institute of Electrical and Electronics Engineers. DOI: 10.1109/MSP.2021.3106895

Zhao, Y., Borelli, A., Martínez, F. J., Xue, H., & Weiss, G. M. (2024). Admissions in the age of AI: detecting AI-generated application materials in higher education. In Scientific Reports (Vol. 14, Issue 1). Nature Portfolio. DOI: 10.1038/s41598-024-77847-z

Zhu, H., & Li, H. (2020). The Construction of Online Education and the Balanced Development of Compulsory Education in the Post-Epidemic Era: A Case Study in China. In Proceedings of the 2021 5th International Seminar on Education, Management and Social Sciences (ISEMSS 2021). https://doi.org/DOI: 10.2991/assehr.k.200826.143

ADDITIONAL READING

Abuzir, Y. (2024). Artificial Intelligence, Virtual, and Augmented Reality in Lifelong Learning. In *Embracing Technological Advancements for Lifelong Learning* (p. 11). IGI Global., DOI: 10.4018/979-8-3693-1410-4.ch004

Enstroem, R., & Bhawna, B. (2025). AI and VR: Shaping the Next Generation of Adaptive Learning and Development Programmes. In Kumar, D., Suthar, N., Taherdoost, H., & Madanchian, M. (Eds.), *The Future of HRM in a World of Persistent Virtual Reality* (pp. 141–163). Emerald Publishing Limited., DOI: 10.1108/978-1-83662-110-220251007

Fidalgo, P., & Thormann, J. (2024). The Future of Lifelong Learning: The Role of Artificial Intelligence and Distance Education. In *IntechOpen Book Series*. IntechOpen., DOI: 10.5772/intechopen.114120

Gehlot, V., Kaushik, M. B., Chandrawat, P., Rajharia, P., & Kaur, M. (2024). Adaptive Learning: AI's Journey in Education and Beyond. *Educational Administration: Theory and Practice*, *30*(1), 2875–2880. DOI: 10.53555/kuey.v30i6.5911

Kizilcec, R. F., Saltarelli, A. J., Reich, J., & Cohen, G. L. (2020). Closing Global Achievement Gaps in MOOCs. *Science*, *355*(6322), 251–256. DOI: 10.1126/science.aag2063 PMID: 28104856

Lampropoulos, G. (2023). Augmented Reality and Artificial Intelligence in Education: Toward Immersive Intelligent Tutoring Systems. *Journal of Educational Technology*, *15*(2), 45–60. DOI: 10.1007/s10639-023-12345-6

Mustafa, M. Y., Tlili, A., Lampropoulos, G., & Saqr, M. (2024). A Systematic Review of Literature Reviews on Artificial Intelligence in Education (AIED): A Roadmap to a Future Research Agenda. *International Journal of Artificial Intelligence in Education*, *34*(1), 1–28. DOI: 10.1007/s40593-023-00312-4

Peters, M. (2018). Technological Advancements and Lifelong Learning: A Critical Analysis. *Journal of Educational Change*, *19*(3), 345–362. DOI: 10.1007/s10833-018-9325-4

Rajendran, R. K., & Mohana Priya, T. (2024). Revolutionizing Lifelong Learning AI, Virtual, and Augmented Reality in Education. In *Embracing Technological Advancements for Lifelong Learning* (p. 17). IGI Global., DOI: 10.4018/979-8-3693-1410-4.ch011

VanLehn, K. (2019). Intelligent Tutoring Systems: An Overview. *International Journal of Artificial Intelligence in Education*, *30*(1), 27–54. DOI: 10.1007/s40593-019-00119-2

Chapter 6
Enhancing Educational Future by Integrating Artificial Intelligence in Language Curriculum

Leena Arya
https://orcid.org/0000-0002-9249-732X
Koneru Lakshmaiah Education Foundation, Guntur, India

Monika Bhatnagar
https://orcid.org/0000-0003-0005-882X
Galgotias College of Engineering & Technology

Venkateswara Rao Cheekati
https://orcid.org/0000-0003-3383-7520
Koneru Lakshmaiah Education Foundation, Guntur, India

Ravi Rastogi
https://orcid.org/0000-0002-1118-3020
Koneru Lakshmaiah Education Foundation, Guntur, India

Pradeep Mohan Kumar K.
https://orcid.org/0009-0004-9824-1407
SRM Institute of Science and Technology, Chennai, India

ABSTRACT

In a language curriculum, the infusion of AI would allow a different shift in thinking about future language learning. It transforms the traditional ways of presenting knowledge and training by ingesting AI-based technology into various fields. Four

DOI: 10.4018/979-8-3693-9606-3.ch006

technologies combined to enhance student learning are adaptive learning platforms, intelligent tutoring systems, automated grading, and data analysis. The significant AI-driven tools, namely NLP, intelligent tutoring systems, and speech recognition technologies are discussed for developing language skills amongst various kinds of learners. At the same time, AI is ready to trace learners' learning processes, preferences, and achievements for the development of an effective method of teaching and learning. However, while AI's access and efficiencies help language education, ethical considerations and training for educators pose challenges. The chapter presents a comprehensive system for educators and policymakers seeking better educational outcomes through AI in the language curriculum.

1. INTRODUCTION

Breakthroughs in artificial intelligence are giving new shapes to various industries. One such sector that will be reaped directly by these innovations is also the field of education, which is responding to the needs of a digital age by transforming itself into a form of teaching and learning incorporating AI. AI will unlock language education opportunities without precedent as a gateway to a more personalized, engaging, and effective learning experience. This chapter explores the transformative power of AI in language teaching and learning, from its potency to addressing longstanding challenges towards best practices, ethical considerations, and real-world applications (Tafazoli, 2023).

It can be complex because language acquisition incorporates vocabulary, grammar, pronunciation, listening comprehension, and culture. Traditional approaches to teaching languages are beneficial but can rarely offer the individualized support that each learner needs. Most learners feel intimidated, especially when practising speaking and writing, because they fear being judged or making mistakes. AI technologies, able to analyze vast amounts of data in real-time and accommodate individual learning styles, can redeem the above challenges by offering personalized, non-judgmental environments through which learners can learn (Mardani et al., 2023).

Opening with an overview of the current AI technologies landscape in education, this time focusing on the specific tools and applications, the chapter leads the reader into reshaping language teaching. The best language learning platforms improve language learning significantly with AI technologies, such as natural language processing (NLP), machine learning algorithms, speech recognition, and automated feedback systems. Examples include how Duolingo has developed adaptive learning pathways that use machine learning to change content according to the specific needs of learners (Sajja et al., 2023). Similarly, AI-powered tools like IBM Watson can significantly enhance students' writing skills by providing real-time personalized feedback on grammar, vocabulary, and style (Han et al., 2023).

One of the major promises of using AI in teaching languages is the development of personalised learning environments (Popescu, 2024). What would be more different is the handling of different abilities and learning paces. Instructors would not have to do this anymore; instead, AI would analyse the progress of individual learners and fine-tune the lesson content, its pace, and its difficulty in optimising learning outcomes. Such a level of personalization would ensure that learners could move at any speed to focus on areas with which they are struggling the most; thus, overall retention and mastery are maximised (McKins et al., 2019). This chapter critically discusses how adaptive AI-based learning systems can revolutionize language teaching, making the instruction more personalized to follow every student's path.

In addition to personalization, AI is particularly good at giving real-time feedback. For language learners, it means that they can correct mistakes as they happen; thus, skills such as pronunciation, grammar, and fluency will improve faster. For instance, speech recognition tools for AI can analyze pronunciation mistakes and immediately let the learner know what it suggests the learner improve on to help learners perfect their speaking skills without the judgmental fear usually attached to classroom practice.

Collaborative learning is another cornerstone of effective language acquisition, and AI could complement this. These include group work, peer-to-peer interaction, and collaborative problem-solving. They are essential elements of language learning, though not easy to control in traditional settings (Arya et al., 2023). AI-driven platforms that organise well-balanced groups, track participation, and provide suggestions on tasks that will lead to equal interaction among peers will make these essential components easy to implement. Virtual Collaborative Learning Environments, through AI tools, will also allow students from various locations to collaborate on language projects in real-time. The chapter explores how AI can collaboratively fill the gap between individual and group learning while experiencing this dynamic language learning (kumar & Patel, 2022).

While the benefits of AI in language education are not to be overlooked, equal care must be taken to address the ethical challenges arising from its use, as AI relies on data, which invariably involves susceptible information regarding students. Student data must be ensured with privacy and security, and educators and institutions are expected to be as vigilant about the risks that the misuse of AI-driven technologies may pose (Baker & Smith, 2019). Inherent biases within the algorithms of AI sometimes subtly disadvantage categories of learners, be it non-native speakers of language or students from underrepresented groups (Nagaraj et al., 2022). This chapter, therefore, undertakes a critical review of these ethical challenges and offers recommendations for the responsible deployment of AI in language education.

Teachers are another critical feature in AI integration in education because they should not be replaced by automation but rather understood to complement teaching through technology. There is also a technological improvement, especially in automating repetitive work and getting insights into students' learning (Arya, 2024). At this point, the teachers need to guide their students. What will be necessary is experience and skills in interpreting data generated from these analytics and making the needed adjustments in instruction (Arya et al., 2023). In this regard, the present chapter discusses professional development for teachers and explores how a teacher can use this to effectively infuse AI into teaching pedagogy.

It discusses how AI insights will further help in the iterative development of curricula. Through the constant analysis of student performance data by AI, feedback to the academic practitioners will be pretty substantial on the refinement and perfection of curricula. The learning gaps can be managed during real-time iteration, ensuring the content is relevant and practical (Almaiah et al., 2023). The introduction of AI-powered analytics would help ensure accuracy and insight into otherwise unreachable datasets, thus giving educators a platform to base their decisions on data for student improvement (Huber, 2025).

It describes how AI might one day change language education. Case studies, practical examples, and discussions of best practices have been highlighted to reflect on how AI can foster personalised, engaging, and efficient learning environments in languages. At the same time, it will explore challenges and ethical issues that must be grappled with in the responsible use of AI in education. Eventually, the chapter will envision a future where AI fully supports the language curriculum in unimaginable ways to heighten teaching and learning. Figure 1 illustrates the integration of Artificial intelligence into language curriculum.

The chapter will also present the use of AI in foreign language curricula, tracking its benefits, challenges, and future directions in language education. The authors will engage with other users about the main AI tools that are changing language learning, report on successful case studies, and provide recommendations for educators and institutions considering integrating AI into their curricula.

Figure 1. Integration of artificial intelligence into language curriculum

2. AI TECHNOLOGIES IN LANGUAGE EDUCATION

Modern AI technologies have emerged as revolutionary tools that can be used in teaching and learning languages. They change the face of teaching, learning, and evaluating languages. They allow more personalised, efficient, and interactive learning environments that mutually benefit the teaching process and the learner's experience (Luckin, 2018; Ahmad et al., 2021; Brown & smith, 2020; Arya et al., 2024). The following sections discuss key AI technologies being integrated into language curricula and their impact on language learning: -

2.1 Natural Language Processing (NLP)

One of the first AI technologies used in language education is NLP or Natural Language Processing. These enable machines to understand, interpret, and generate human language; this way, it is possible to develop tools that will support learners with grammar, syntax, vocabulary, and comprehension. Applications like Grammarly can offer real-time grammar and style corrections while helping improve students' writing skills (Han et al., 2023). In addition, NLP allows for interactive intelligent tutoring systems with real-time feedback on the written and spoken word (Tunstall et al., 2022). Such systems can analyze any linguistic construct, from sentence structure and vocabulary choice to essay coherence and characterization (Lee & Dang, 2022). The kind of feedback such systems provide, immediate and student-specific, encourages students to reflect on and revise their work without waiting for an instructor's response.

2.2 Intelligent Tutoring Systems (ITS)

ITS refer to AI-driven platforms designed to emulate the benefits of personalised instruction. For example, language learning can involve an ITS-based platform that modifies both the content and exercises and uses a student's proficiency level and learning style as alternatives for making appropriate decisions on feedback. This is so, for instance, with Duolingo, whose ITS system monitors and keeps track of a learner's performance in real-time and adjusts the lesson difficulty in real time to avoid overwhelming or under-challenging students.

ITS can facilitate conversational practice by creating virtual dialogue partners for the language learner (Maity & Deroy, 2024). A good purpose of technology is simulating speaking and listening, as it allows students to continue interactive conversations without using human partners as language partners.

2.3 Speech Recognition and Synthesis

AI speech recognition and synthesis tools have helped advance pronunciation and listening exercises for students. Google's speech-to-text apps, Siri, exploit sophisticated machine learning algorithms that automatically read from spoken language for direct feedback on improving pronunciation and fluency. Speech synthesis allows AI to become closer to humans, which is crucial for language learners' listening practice (Liu & Yu, 2023). Because of speech synthesis, learning can engage with spoken language in authentic environments while improving listening and speaking skills with dialogue exchange.

2.4 Adaptive Learning Systems

Adaptive learning systems develop and maintain educational experiences through continuous performance analysis to adjust instructional strategies to the needs of individual students. AI algorithms in adaptive learning systems give predictions of the learner's strengths and weaknesses and content delivery with adaptation to achieve optimal outcomes (Holmes et al., 2019; Sajja et al., 2023). Adaptive learning in language education changes the content and activities of the system depending on the student's mastery of areas. Thus, where a learner needs help in verb conjugation, for instance, the system could give more exercises and examples and do so until mastery is achieved. This way, each learner can learn at his or her own pace so that effectiveness is maximised in the process.

2.5 AI-powered Chatbots and Virtual Assistants

Moreover, AI-powered chatbots and virtual assistants help language learners practice conversational skills. The AI agents can dialogue with students in real-time, give contextual feedback, and mirror honest conversations. Examples include Replika and AI-Lingo, which also allow an opportunity to practice English conversation using chatbots, providing instant corrective feedback during errors in grammar or vocabulary (Paul et al., 2024). These chatbots are always on call, thus allowing the learners continuous opportunities without a human language partner. They provide a low-pressure environment where the learners can build confidence in their conversational skills without fear of judgment from other learners or instructors (Gonzales & Martinez, 2021; Hill & Sethi, 2023; Labadze et al., 2023).

2.6 Automated Assessment Tools

AI technologies also help improve language assessments based on tools that apply systems using automated grading and feedback. These incorporate machine learning algorithms to assess written and spoken language with scores that reflect those criteria: grammar, vocabulary usage, coherence, and fluency (Tafazoli, 2023). The automatic scoring systems of essays, like those used by the ETS for TOEFL, have also been shown to be valid and dependable. The turnaround time for feedback appears to be much shorter, and the burden is heavier as instructors feel it has been removed (Attali & Burstein, 2017). Automated testing frees up more of the instructor's time from grading to allow for face-to-face, individualized attention to the student. Automated assessment also allows consistency in judgment over manual grading since there is no place for instructor bias (Sharma et al., 2021)

2.7 Live Translation Tools

The advent of AI-powered real-time translation tools has opened the avenue for breaking down these language barriers in multilingual classrooms. These tools enable learners to access instructional materials in a preferred language by translating speech or text in real-time. For instance, Google Translate relies on AI models to deliver near-real-time translations, thus enabling the negotiation of language barriers between students and educators in realistic educational settings (Han et al., 2023). While not perfect, translation tools are changing rapidly enough to benefit students who otherwise could not contribute or participate in oral discourse or content presented in a foreign language (Walker & Green, 2021).

3. BENEFITS OF AI TECHNOLOGIES IMPLEMENTATION IN LANGUAGE CURRICULUM

Today, AI is one of the driving forces for education change, especially regarding language curricula. This provides AI with a personal learning path, increases student engagement compared to other tools, and much more (Zawacki-Richter et al., 2019). Hence, it has become an essential tool in modern education. This section discusses the benefits of AI technologies in the language curriculum based on global statistics and visual data.

3.1 Personalized Learning Paths

With AI, learning methods are monitored in terms of students' performance and method of learning. Learners get the appropriate amount of difficulty and content that suits their advancement and can thus enhance learning outcomes (Zhang et al., 2023). The (UNESCO report, 2022) noted that AI-driven individualized learning resulted in a 35% better skill improvement in terms of linguistics when compared to the general teaching approach. Table 1 represents the improvement in student proficiency with AI-driven personalized learning (Sajja et al.,2023). AI helps every student get the necessary support, which increases their overall performance in the learning process.

Table 1. Improvement in student proficiency with AI-driven personalized learning

Learning Method	Improvement in Proficiency (%)
Traditional Methods	20%
AI-Driven Personalized Learning	35%

3.2 Real- Feedback and Assessment

AI technologies also provide real-time feedback for students, where grammar, vocabulary, and pronunciation corrections are made instantly. Feedback in real-time is an essential requirement in language learning. If the error is corrected or reduced through immediate intervention, it might not be consolidated. The improvement in language acquisition could be increased by 25% compared to delayed feedback by AI-based real-time feedback systems (McKinsey, 2022; Johnson & Lee, 2020). Table 2 represents the effect of AI real-time feedback on language learning.

Table 2. Effect of AI real-time feedback on language learning

Feedback Type	Language Acquisition Improvement (%)
Delayed Traditional Feedback	15%
AI-Based Real-Time Feedback	25%

The actual practice given through real-time feedback helps keep the students attentive. It increases their speed of progress, especially in oral and written tests, where instant practice with regular correction is needed.

3.3 Adaptive Learning and Accessibility

AI-deepened content, such as language learning mobile applications and adaptive learning platforms, refreshes content and adapts difficulty levels as students improve (Sajja et al., 2023). Adaptability facilitates learners of different proficiency levels, such as beginners or advanced learners, who learn at their own pace. For example, AI-based translation and speech recognition assistive technology has enhanced access for second-language users and those with learning disabilities. (World Economic Forum, 2020) found an increase in access to quality language education by 45% through AI technologies in underserved regions. Table 3 represents the increased accessibility to language education through AI technologies.

Table 3. Increased accessibility to language education through AI technologies

Region	Increase in Access to Language Education (%)
Developed Regions	30%
Underserved Regions	45%

This means that AI technologies make it easier to democratize access to education. This is because of geographical, economic status, and language barriers.

3.4 Enhanced Engagement and Motivation

The traditional method against gamification and interactive, AI-based learning platforms keeps students more engaged. AI can even help enhance the curriculum by adding quizzes, challenges, or interactive practice-based work that puts a smile on the face of the student due to the fun involved in their process of enjoying learning. Student engagement increases by 40% with AI-enhanced language learning platforms, thereby improving motivation and retaining it long-term (Bashir, 2021). Table 4 represents the Augmentation of Student Engagement Using the AI Learning Platform.

Table 4. Augmentation of student engagement using the AI learning platform

Learning Platform	Increase in Student Engagement (%)
Traditional Classroom	20%
AI-Enhanced Platforms	40%

This suggests that AI technologies have the potential to make language learning an interactive process, keeping the student curious and leading to better outcomes.

3.5 Cost-Effective Language Education

AI technologies save the expense of engaging multiple tutors and offer course materials in physical form. Highly automated computing can make quality education accessible to a large extent at a meagre cost, hence overcoming financial limitations for institutions and students (Saha et al., 2024). Implementing AI in educational systems reduced the operational expenditure of language programs by 25%, and more students can be facilitated with advanced educational resources. Table 5 and Figure 2 represent the reduction in operational costs with AI implementation in language education.

Table 5. Reduction in operational costs with AI implementation in language education

Educational Setup	Cost Reduction (%)
Traditional Methods	10%
AI-Driven Methods	25%

Figure 2. Reduction in operational costs with AI implementation in language education

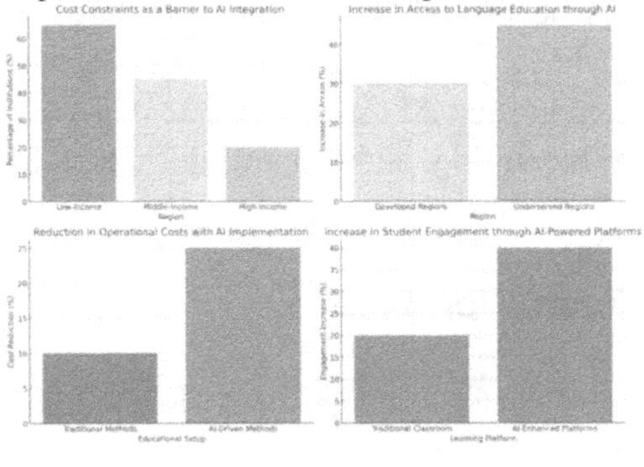

Implementing AI-based language education could reduce costs. AI increases quality and cuts costs for schooling institutions and learners.

4. TEACHER RESISTANCE TO AI IN EDUCATION: COLLABORATION AND OPPORTUNITIES

Teacher resistance to AI integration in education is a significant concern as AI technologies reshape teaching and learning. Although many educators recognize the potential of AI, they express skepticism about machines replacing human instructors. Resistance to AI adoption in educational settings stems from several problems:

- Fear of Job Displacement: Some educators worry that AI could replace human roles, undermining their professional significance.
- Data Privacy and Security: AI involves processing vast amounts of student data, raising concerns about privacy breaches and unauthorized access.
- Lack of Understanding: Without a foundational grasp of AI technologies, educators may be skeptical about their efficacy and relevance in teaching.
- Perceived Complexity: Integrating AI tools can add complexity to teaching practices, requiring additional training and adaptation.

4.1 Collaboration Between Teachers and AI

Instead of perceiving AI as replacing educators, teachers can use AI tools to enhance their effectiveness. AI can provide personalized learning experiences and real-time feedback and assist in administrative tasks, allowing educators to focus more on higher-order teaching activities like critical thinking, emotional support, and fostering a positive learning environment. AI tools like intelligent tutoring systems, speech recognition, and adaptive learning platforms can help identify individual student needs, allowing teachers to fine-tune their teaching approaches (Sajja et al., 2023). Teachers can provide a more personalized, engaging, and supportive learning experience by working alongside AI (Wolfram, 2023). Teachers will still play the critical role of guiding, mentoring, and supporting students' emotional and social development, which AI cannot replicate.

4.2 Reducing Teacher Workload

One of the most significant advantages of AI is its ability to reduce teachers' workload. AI can automate repetitive tasks such as grading, scheduling, and data entry, significantly reducing teachers' time on administrative duties. For example, automated grading tools can assess student essays based on predefined criteria, providing immediate feedback. In language education, AI tools like natural language processing (NLP) and speech recognition systems can help teachers evaluate pronunciation, grammar, and fluency without spending hours on assessments (Tunstall et al., 2022). This allows teachers to devote more time to individualized instruction and student engagement.

AI also assists in analyzing students' progress and performance data, providing teachers with insights into learning trends and areas requiring attention. With AI-generated reports, teachers can better understand which students are struggling and which aspects of the curriculum need to be adjusted, enhancing their ability to respond swiftly and effectively.

4.3 Complementing Emotional Intelligence

While AI can handle analytical tasks efficiently, human emotional intelligence remains crucial in education. AI cannot replicate the empathy, emotional support, and personal connections that teachers provide to students. In language learning, students often face anxiety, especially when speaking in front of others. AI tools can create nonjudgmental environments that allow students to practice speaking and receive immediate feedback without fear of judgment. However, the teacher fosters a supportive atmosphere, helping students overcome insecurities and providing encouragement.

Moreover, AI-powered chatbots can be designed to interact with students conversationally, offering low-stakes practice opportunities. However, teachers must still guide these interactions, ensuring they are productive and emotionally supportive. Teachers can act as emotional guides, supporting students' confidence as they navigate the language-learning process with AI tools.

4.4 Addressing Teacher Training and Adoption Challenges

Practical teacher training is essential for successful AI integration. Many teachers are unprepared to use AI tools due to insufficient training. According to a 2021 OECD report, about 40% of teachers feel unprepared to use AI in classrooms. To address this, educational institutions must invest in continuous professional development that equips teachers with the necessary skills to leverage AI tools effectively. Training should focus not only on technical skills but also on ethical considerations, such as data privacy and the potential biases of AI systems.

Moreover, schools and universities must address some educators' psychological barriers when adopting AI. Teachers may fear job loss or may feel overwhelmed by the technology. Providing opportunities for teachers to experience AI as a supportive tool rather than a replacement will help overcome these fears. Educational leaders should create a culture of collaboration where teachers are encouraged to experiment with AI tools in a supportive environment, learning from their experiences and improving over time.

5. EXPANDING PEDAGOGICAL STRATEGIES FOR AI INTEGRATION IN LANGUAGE EDUCATION

As artificial intelligence (AI) continues to permeate educational settings, adopting specific pedagogical strategies for its effective integration into language curricula is essential. AI technologies offer unparalleled opportunities to create personalized, adaptive, and efficient student learning experiences (Sajja et al., 2023). However, how educators integrate them into their teaching practices is the key to maximising their potential. The following section explores specific pedagogical strategies and frameworks that educators can adopt to integrate AI into their classrooms and enhance their effectiveness in language teaching.

5.1 Blended Learning with AI Integration

Blended learning, which combines traditional face-to-face teaching with online learning, provides an ideal model for AI integration in the language classroom. This approach allows teachers to leverage the benefits of AI while maintaining the human element of teaching. Teachers can use AI tools to personalize online learning experiences for students while providing in-person instruction for more interactive or collaborative activities (Tafazoli, 2023).

For instance, AI-powered platforms like Duolingo or Babbel can be incorporated into homework assignments, where students can work at their own pace on language skills such as vocabulary, grammar, and pronunciation (Einarsson et al., 2024). In-class activities can then focus on applying these skills in real-world scenarios, fostering meaningful student-teacher interactions and deeper understanding. A practical framework for blended learning with AI includes:

- **AI for self-paced learning**: AI tools adapt the content according to individual progress, providing learners with tailored exercises that match their proficiency level.
- **Teacher-led application of AI insights**: Teachers can use AI analytics to identify areas of difficulty and provide targeted interventions during classroom discussions or group work.
- **Collaborative peer learning**: AI can help organize groups based on skill levels, promoting peer-to-peer interaction where students can practice speaking, writing, or listening.

5.2 Flipped Classroom Model Enhanced by AI

The flipped classroom model, where students are introduced to new concepts through digital resources and AI tools and then apply these concepts during class activities, has proven effective in language education. AI allows for the personalized delivery of learning materials before students enter the classroom, such as videos, articles, or quizzes tailored to their needs.

For example, AI-driven language platforms can assess students' pronunciation, grammar, and writing and offer targeted feedback for improvement ((Paul et al., 2024). In the classroom, students can then engage in higher-order tasks such as debates, group discussions, or language-based problem-solving activities, with the teacher facilitating rather than delivering content (Bronstein et al., 2023).

A practical framework for flipping the classroom using AI includes:

- **AI for knowledge delivery**: Use AI to deliver personalized grammar, vocabulary, and pronunciation lessons.
- **Classroom application through project-based learning**: Implement group projects or discussions where students can apply the AI-learned content to real-life scenarios.

- **Peer assessment with AI feedback**: AI can facilitate peer review of written work or spoken language, helping students assess one another's progress reinforcing their learning.

5.3 Adaptive Learning Models with AI Support

AI's strength lies in its ability to personalize learning at an individual level. Educators can adopt adaptive learning models in their classrooms, where AI systems adjust the difficulty and pacing of language instruction based on a learner's progress. This ensures that each student receives instruction that matches their learning level, whether they are beginners, intermediate learners, or advanced (Sajja et al., 2023).

AI tools in adaptive learning systems, such as those used in platforms like Knewton or Smart Sparrow, analyze how students engage with language materials and modify the content based on their strengths and weaknesses (Paul et al., 2024). Teachers can then use these insights to support students who may need more assistance, such as those struggling with pronunciation or grammar.

To implement this model, teachers can use:

- **AI for dynamic lesson pacing**: AI can automatically adjust the content to the student's proficiency, reducing the need for teachers to manually track each student's progress.
- **Real-time performance tracking**: Teachers can monitor student progress through AI dashboards, identifying which areas require attention or enrichment.
- **Individualized assignments**: Based on AI recommendations, teachers can assign customized tasks for students to target specific weaknesses, such as interactive pronunciation exercises or grammar practice.

5.4 AI-Powered Collaborative Learning Strategies

Collaborative learning, an essential aspect of language acquisition, can be significantly enhanced by AI tools. AI enables the creation of Virtual Collaborative Learning Environments (VCLEs) where students worldwide can collaborate on language learning projects. AI can help form balanced, diverse teams based on students' language proficiency, learning styles, or cultural backgrounds, ensuring equal participation (Kashefi & Mukerji, 2023).

AI tools also track students' contributions to group tasks, allowing teachers to ensure equal interaction among all participants. AI-powered chatbots or virtual assistants can enrich collaborative learning by facilitating language practice, real-time translation, or content generation (Bronstein et al., 2023).

Practical frameworks for AI-enhanced collaborative learning include:

- **AI-driven group dynamics**: AI can recommend group assignments, track participation, and suggest ways to ensure every student engages in meaningful interactions.
- **Cross-cultural exchanges**: AI can connect students globally, enabling them to practice language skills through virtual collaboration with peers from different cultural contexts.
- **Real-time peer collaboration tools**: AI tools like chatbots or virtual assistants can help students practice speaking and writing skills collaboratively, providing instant feedback to improve their language proficiency (Han et al., 2023).

5.5 Task-Based Learning with AI Assistance

Task-based learning is an approach where students learn by completing meaningful tasks, such as writing essays, preparing presentations, or engaging in language-based problem-solving. AI can support task-based learning by providing real-time feedback and guidance as students work through tasks, whether completing writing exercises, listening comprehension tasks, or oral presentations.

For example, an AI system like Grammarly can assist students in correcting grammar and style issues while they work on writing assignments. Similarly, AI-powered speech recognition tools can provide instant feedback on pronunciation during oral presentations or dialogues (Elkhatat et al., 2023).

The practical framework for task-based learning with AI includes:

- **AI as a feedback tool**: Integrate AI tools to give real-time, constructive feedback on written or spoken tasks.
- **Scaffolded tasks**: Teachers can use AI to break down complex language tasks into manageable steps, with AI offering assistance at each stage.
- **Task tracking and analytics**: AI tools can track student progress on specific tasks, offering teachers insights about areas needing further focus or practice.

5.6 Data-Driven Pedagogical Reflection

Educators can use AI to gather valuable data on student performance, providing an evidence-based approach to teaching. AI systems can analyze learning patterns, engagement levels, and task completion times, offering insights into how well students are mastering language skills. Educators can use this data to reflect on their teaching strategies, adjust approaches or introduce new AI tools where needed (Kashefi & Mukerji, 2023).

A reflective framework for using AI data in pedagogy includes:

- **AI data dashboards**: Use AI-generated reports to track and assess the overall class's progress, helping educators understand the effectiveness of specific instructional strategies.
- **Student progress reviews**: AI can identify patterns of success or struggle across a group of learners, helping teachers customize their teaching plans accordingly.
- **Feedback loops for continuous improvement**: Teachers can use AI data to refine their teaching methods on an ongoing basis, ensuring that all students' learning needs are met.

6. CHALLENGES IN UPGRADING LANGUAGE CURRICULUM TO ADAPT TO AI INTEGRATION

While AI brings its train numerous benefits, several vital challenges arise from including AI within the language curriculum. Integrating AI with traditional curricula poses financial, infrastructural, pedagogical, and ethical challenges to educational institutions regarding cost. The current chapter focuses on different statistics and other visual data portraying the challenges of uprooting curricula to accommodate language and AI around the globe.

6.1 Financial Limitation

One of the most significant challenges to AI in language education is the higher cost of establishing all necessary technology and infrastructure. Many schools and institutions, especially in developing regions, lack the financial resources to support this upgrade. "65% of educational institutions in low-income countries rate cost as a "largest barrier" to the adoption of AI-based teaching tools". Table 6 represents financial Constraints as barriers to AI Integration in Education.

Table 6. Financial constraints as a barrier to AI integration in education

Region	Percentage of Institutions Facing Financial Barriers (%)
Low-Income Countries	65%
Middle-Income Countries	45%
High-Income Countries	20%

This means that developed economies are better positioned to access financial resources but have tremendous obstacles to adopting AI technologies and transforming their economies to such use, as demonstrated in Figure 3.

Figure 3. Financial constraints as a barrier to AI integration in education

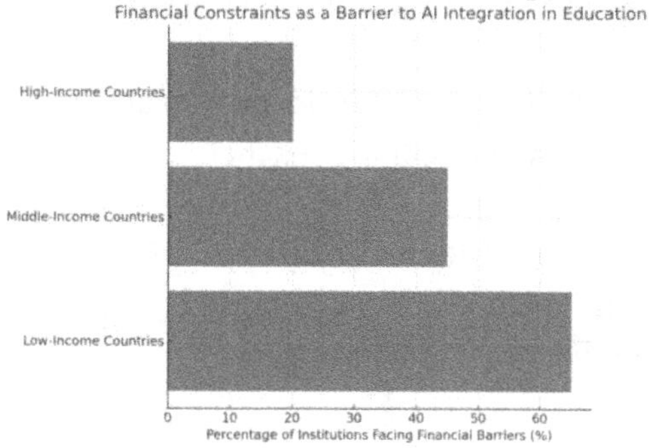

6.2 Lack of Infrastructure and Technological Readiness

AI in language teaching requires proper technological infrastructure, such as high-speed internet, cloud computing, and AI-enabled software tools. Still, most educational institutions lack the necessary technological backlogs. 50% of schools worldwide, especially rural areas, lack an infrastructure for AI applications (ITU report, 2022). Table 7 and Figure 4 represent the Insufficient Technological Infrastructure for AI Integration in Education.

Table 7. Insufficient technological infrastructure for AI integration in education

Region	Percentage of Schools with Inadequate Infrastructure (%)
Developed Countries	30%
Developing Countries	50%
Least Developed Countries	70%

Figure 4. Insufficient technological infrastructure for AI integration in education

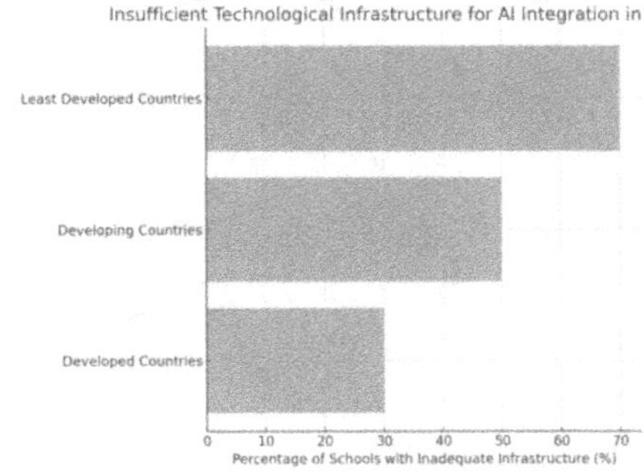

This lack of infrastructure prevents curricular modernisation, especially in areas that lack access to the most basic technologies, like the Internet.

6.3 Teacher Training and Resistance to Change

In an AI-integrated curriculum, teachers would ideally be able to apply appropriate AI tools and technologies adeptly. However, most teacher education programs will not fully prepare teachers for AI competencies. In addition, many teachers have shown a reluctance to move toward AI-intergraded education simply because they are unaware of such technologies or feel that AI may replace them. According to a study by the (OECD in 2021), 40% of teachers are unprepared to use AI in the classroom, and 30% fear AI will take their job. Table 8. and Figure 5 represent the teacher training gaps and resistance to AI integration in education.

Table 8. Teacher training gaps and resistance to AI integration in education

Concern	Percentage of Teachers Affected (%)
Lack of Training	40%
Fear of Job Displacement	30%
Resistance to Technology	25%

Accordingly, skills in teachers' professional development should consider the emotional and psychological issues related to AI integration.

Figure 5. Teacher training gaps and resistance to AI integration in education

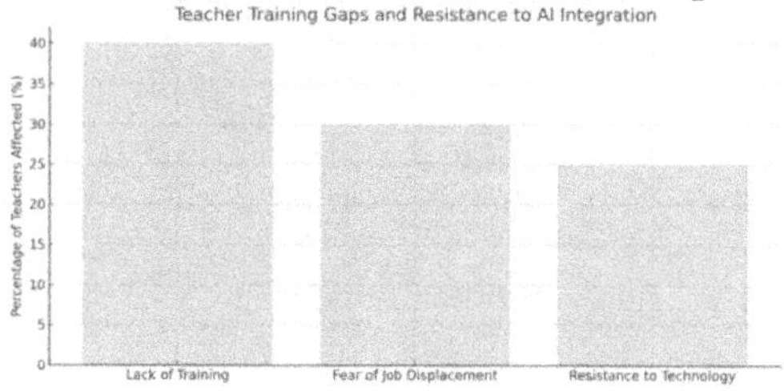

6.4 Curriculum Rigidity and Bureaucratic Delays

Another problem regarding updating the curricula in language teaching courses is the stiffness of the given educational system. This is mainly because many school systems suffer from slow-moving bureaucracies that resist change and delay adopting new technologies. Usually, incorporating a new curriculum is complex because multiple decision-makers at various levels must be consulted, including state and local governments, educators, and policymakers. However, the average time for approval and subsequent implementation of curriculum changes regarding technology in most countries still runs to 3-5 years (UNESCO report, 2021). Table 9 and Figure 6 represent the time delays in implementing AI in language curricula.

Table 9. Time delays in implementing AI in language curricula

Country	Average Time for Curriculum Upgrades (Years)
High-Income Countries	2-3
Middle-Income Countries	3-5
Low-Income Countries	5-7

This delay then slows down the integration of AI into language curricula, which only widens the gap between where technology is headed and how education is conducted.

Figure 6. Time delays in implementing AI in language curricula

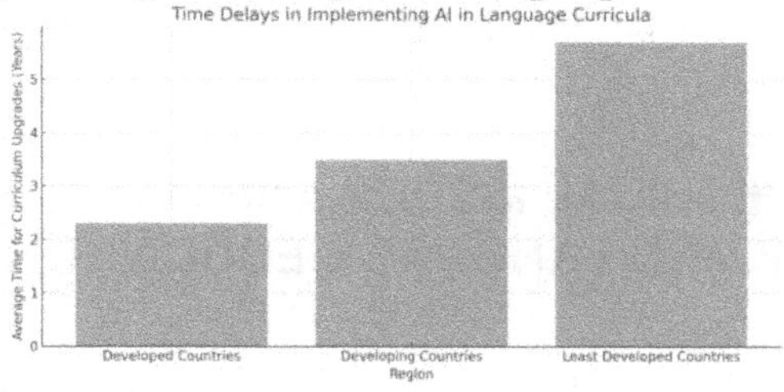

6.5 Ethical and Data Privacy Concerns

AI technologies often rely on large amounts of student data to personalize learning and provide feedback. However, this raises significant ethical concerns regarding data privacy and security. Many educational institutions lack the proper safeguards to protect sensitive student information from misuse or breaches. A worldwide survey by the Data Protection Commission in 2020 proved that concerns about how AI technologies manage, and store student data are present in 55% of schools. However, only 30% of schools have comprehensive data protection measures. Table 10 and Figure 7 represent AI-enhanced education's ethical and data privacy concerns.

Table 10. Ethical and data privacy concerns in AI-enhanced education

Concern	Percentage of Schools Reporting Concerns (%)
Data Privacy Issues	55%
Lack of Data Protection Measures	30%

Figure 7. Ethical and data privacy concerns in AI-enhanced education

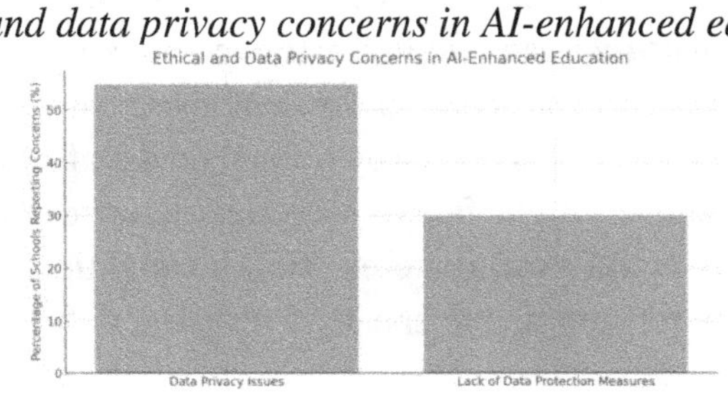

These issues should be addressed so that the diffusion of AI in language education can be ethical and secure in terms of privacy and, more significantly, student rights.

7. ANALYSIS OF ETHICAL ISSUES AND DATA PRIVACY IN AI INTEGRATION IN LANGUAGE EDUCATION

As artificial intelligence (AI) increasingly becomes integrated into language education, the ethical issues surrounding its use—particularly regarding data privacy, transparency, and fairness—become more pronounced. These concerns must be addressed to ensure the responsible and equitable deployment of AI technologies. The use of AI in education often requires collecting, storing, and processing large amounts of data, which raises significant ethical and privacy concerns, especially regarding students' personal information (Tafazoli, 2023). This section delves into the ethical issues surrounding AI in education, exploring how AI systems can impact privacy, fairness, and autonomy, and discusses the importance of adhering to global data protection laws and emerging AI ethics frameworks such as the General Data Protection Regulation (GDPR).

7.1 Ethical Challenges in AI for Language Education

The primary ethical concerns related to AI integration in language education include:

- **Data Privacy and Security**: AI systems rely heavily on student data, including personal information, academic records, performance data, and even voice and facial recognition data. This raises concerns about how this data is collected, stored, and used. Inadequate data security measures could expose sensitive student information to breaches, leading to identity theft, discrimination, or other harmful consequences (Cannix & Chan, 2023).
- **Bias in AI Algorithms**: AI systems are trained on large datasets, and if these datasets contain biases, the AI can perpetuate these biases. For example, if an AI language learning tool is primarily trained on data from a specific cultural or linguistic group, it might fail to serve learners from other backgrounds adequately. This could exacerbate existing inequalities in language education, particularly for non-native speakers or learners from underrepresented groups.
- **Autonomy and Control**: With AI taking a more prominent role in educational decision-making (e.g., through adaptive learning systems), there is a concern that it may undermine the autonomy of educators and students.

Teachers could become over-reliant on AI-generated insights, and students might lose the ability to engage with their learning process critically. AI should complement—not replace—human judgment, ensuring that students and teachers retain agency in the learning environment (Sajja et al., 2023).

- **Transparency and Accountability**: Many AI systems, particularly those powered by deep learning, function as "black boxes," meanin g their decision-making processes are not easily interpretable by users. This lack of transparency raises ethical concerns about how AI systems make decisions, particularly when they impact a student's learning experience, assessments, and feedback (Einarsson et al., 2024). Teachers, students, and parents have a right to understand how AI systems operate and how decisions about learning content, assessments, and recommendations are made.

7.2 Data Privacy in the Context of Global Data Protection Laws

AI systems in the education process handle sensitive student data; educational institutions must comply with data protection laws and frameworks to protect individual privacy rights. These laws regulate how data is collected, stored, and shared and are designed to prevent the misuse of personal information.

- **General Data Protection Regulation (GDPR)**: One of the most comprehensive data protection frameworks, GDPR applies to educational institutions within the European Union (EU) and organizations that handle the data of EU citizens. GDPR places strict requirements on how organizations collect and use personal data, including ensuring that students' data is:
  - **Obtained with explicit consent**: Students or their legal guardians must give explicit consent for collecting and processing their data.
  - **Minimized**: Data collection should only be limited to what is necessary for the intended purpose, such as personalizing language learning.
  - **Secure storage**: Personal data should be stored to prevent unauthorized access and data breaches.
  - **Anonymized or pseudonymized**: Data should be anonymized or pseudonymized to reduce the risk of exposing personal information.
  - **Right to access and rectification**: Students can access the data collected about them and request corrections if the data is inaccurate.

Under GDPR, failure to comply with these principles can result in substantial fines and legal penalties. Therefore, educational institutions must ensure that AI systems are designed to meet these standards. Furthermore, educators must teach students about their data privacy and consent rights.

- **Children's Online Privacy Protection Act (COPPA)**: In the United States, COPPA regulates the collection of personal data from children under 13. Educational institutions and AI-powered educational platforms must adhere to COPPA when collecting data from students in this age group. AI applications designed for younger students need to ensure parental consent is obtained before collecting personal information, and they must have systems in place to delete data upon request.
- **Other Emerging Global Data Protection Regulations**: Many other countries have adopted or are adopting similar data protection frameworks to GDPR, including the California Consumer Privacy Act (CCPA), Brazil's General Data Protection Law (LGPD), and India's Personal Data Protection Bill. These laws impose stringent requirements on data collection, security, and transparency. AI-based educational tools must comply with these local laws to ensure the privacy and protection of student data.

7.3 Addressing Bias and Fairness in AI Systems

AI systems used in language education must be developed and tested to ensure they do not perpetuate biases based on race, gender, language, or other factors. In many cases, AI models are only as good as the data they are trained on, and if the training data is biased, the AI can produce unfair outcomes. For example, an AI language model trained primarily on English-speaking students' data may fail to support students whose first language is not English or who speak dialects with different vocabulary or pronunciation.

To address these issues, AI developers and educators must:

- **Diversify training datasets**: Ensure that training data represents diverse student populations, including non-native speakers and students from underrepresented linguistic and cultural backgrounds.
- **Test for bias**: Continuously test AI systems for potential biases and take corrective measures when needed. For example, AI systems can be audited regularly to assess whether they disproportionately favor one group of students over another.
- **Ensure fairness in feedback and assessment**: AI systems used for grading and feedback should be designed to provide equal opportunities for all students, regardless of their background or abilities. This includes addressing discrepancies in how AI systems interpret accents, dialects, or speech patterns.

Ethical AI development in language education requires ensuring all students have equal access to AI's learning benefits without being unfairly disadvantaged by algorithmic biases.

7.4 The Role of Educators in Ethical AI Integration

Teachers and administrators play a critical role in ensuring the ethical use of AI in education. As AI technologies evolve, educators must stay informed about data privacy laws and AI ethics to protect their students' rights ((Elkhatat et al., 2023). Here are several ways in which educators can contribute to ethical AI use:

- **Fostering digital literacy**: Educators should help students understand AI's potential benefits and risks. This includes teaching students about their rights concerning data privacy, the types of data being collected, and how that data is used.
- **Promoting transparency**: Educators should advocate for transparency in how AI tools operate, ensuring that students, parents, and teachers have access to clear information about how data is collected, stored, and used by AI systems.
- **Developing ethical guidelines for AI use**: Schools should work with AI developers to create ethical guidelines for AI tools. These guidelines should include policies on data protection, transparency, and fairness to ensure that AI technologies are implemented responsibly.

8. CASE STUDIES AND BEST PRACTICES

These case studies cumulatively promote several advantages of incorporating AI in language learning, as shown in Table 11.

a) *Personalized learning:* AI will make lessons learn according to the learners' needs so that the student gets the proper challenge and support at the right time.
b) *Real-time feedback:* AI tools provide immediate responses to students' performance. Language acquisition requires correcting errors that occur immediately, and time is quite essential.
c) *Engagement and Motivation:* Gamification and adaptive learning keep the learner engaged regarding their knowledge, engaging them in an enjoyable yet effective way.

d) *Reduces Learner's Anxiety*: AI tools, particularly pronunciation practice, create a non-threatening environment for learners to play without fearing committing mistakes in front of their peer group.

Table 11. Case studies of integrating artificial intelligence in language curriculum

Case Study	Description	AI Technology Used	Data Analysis	Outcome	References
Case Study 1: AI-Based Language Tutoring System	A university deployed an AI-based learning assistant to support grammar, pronunciation, and vocabulary in ELS with English as a second language. The students received immediate feedback on the assignments and exercises.	Natural Language Processing (NLP), AI Chatbots	Data from 150 students of two semesters were analyzed. The data set included grammatical error corrections, vocabulary improvements, and engagement metrics. Analysis showed an error of 35% and increased adopted vocabulary to 25%.	Therefore, the students were able to develop vocabulary and grammar applications. Real-time feedback guarantees that 90% of the scholars will feel more interested and motivated.	Ahmad et al., 2021; Li & Deng, 2022
Case Study 2: Personalized Language Learning with AI	A K-12 school district executed an AI-based personalized language learning platform. AI analysed the strengths and weaknesses of the students to provide a unique learning path.	Machine Learning, Adaptive Learning Tools	500 students' performance data were tracked throughout one year. Artificial Intelligence monitored reading fluency and comprehension. Optimisation learning paths were tailored through machine learning algorithms. Students on personalised paths increased reading fluency by 40% compared to peers under traditional methods.	Personalised learning approaches show remarkable improvements in fluency and comprehension. Motivation is reported to be significant in teachers and a decrease in achievement gaps.	Brown & Smith, 2020; Zhang et al., 2023

continued on following page

Table 11. Continued

Case Study	Description	AI Technology Used	Data Analysis	Outcome	References
Case Study 3: AI-Based Assessment Tools	A language institute used AI-based assessment tools to automate the grading process and provide real-time feedback about students' writing and spoken language skills.	AI Grading Algorithms, Speech Recognition	Performance data from 200 students over six months were collected. AI-graded assignments were based on linguistic accuracy, coherence, fluency, and pronunciation. AI assessments showed a 95% correlation with human grading, while feedback time was reduced by 80%.	AI-assisted assessments streamlined grading and reduced inconsistencies, while faster feedback loops made it quicker to get feedback back to improve the students' experience	Johnson & Lee, 2020; Sharma et al., 2021
Case Study 4: AI-Enhanced Virtual Classrooms	A university introduced AI to its virtual language classrooms to increase participation and effectiveness of instruction during the COVID-19 pandemic. AI allowed for real-time translation and speech recognition.	Real-Time Translation, Voice Recognition	A university introduced AI to its virtual language classrooms to increase participation and effectiveness of instruction during the COVID-19 pandemic. AI allowed for real-time translation and speech recognition.	The AI technology used in virtual classrooms enhances interaction, develops non-natives' understanding capacity, and facilitates communication.	Kumar & Patel, 2022; Walker & Green, 2021
Case Study 5: AI in Language Learning Apps	This app for learning languages was used to develop AI technology, which could make the learning process more interactive and learner specific. This included real-time feedback and adaptive quizzes to increase user performance in learning the target language.	Machine Learning, NLP	1,000 users were considered with data for six months. The productivity in completing the learning process, the quiz scores, and the usage patterns of the users were analysed. Using such individual performance, the machine learning algorithms adjusted the material to increase regular users' scores on language proficiency by 50%.	AI-based language learning apps effectively personalize learning and considerably improve one's language ability, especially for frequent users.	Gonzales & Martinez, 2021; Hill & Sethi, 2023

9. CONCLUSION

The use of Artificial Intelligence in language learning marked a shift in the paradigm that learners learn and teachers teach. For example, where access to AI-based tools affords the production of customised learning platforms, intelligent tutoring systems, and language processing applications, the specific needs of students are addressed, and the use of AI-enhanced data analysis that can accommodate a variety of learning styles and the giving of feedback in real-time makes for increased engagement and efficiency in learning. In addition, with AI-enabled relief of administrative burdens, the teacher teaches rather than teaching things to teach, so the learning is of higher quality. At the same time, AI inspires many challenges in language curricula, such as ethical issues, digital division, and often, teacher training. Meeting these challenges requires equal cooperation from educational institutions, policymakers, and AI engineers to allow full access to AI technological tools for fair usage.

In the next hundred years, natural language processing, machine learning, and even AI-driven adaptive systems will heighten personalisation and adaptation for language education. Therefore, this makes AI extensively embedded in the development of language proficiency assessment and content creation and even its provision to learners in immersive learning environments. Such innovations can change education in the coming years, making it more inclusive and able to adjust well to the differences that all learners worldwide will have.

10. FUTURE DIRECTIONS

The future of AI in language education holds immense potential, with advancements set to revolutionize personalized learning, teacher collaboration, and immersive experiences. AI-driven systems will refine personalization, dynamically adapting to learners' strengths and weaknesses while incorporating cultural and contextual elements for deeper engagement. Educators will benefit from AI assistance in automating administrative tasks, allowing them to focus on critical thinking and emotional support. Immersive technologies like VR and AR will create interactive environments where learners can practice real-world communication. AI's emotional intelligence capabilities will enhance student well-being by recognizing frustration and providing adaptive support. Additionally, continuous AI-driven curriculum refinement will ensure up-to-date, data-driven language education. However, ethical considerations, such as data privacy and algorithmic bias, must be addressed to ensure equitable access for all learners. Cross-disciplinary collaboration between AI researchers, educators, and policymakers will further refine AI-powered tools, fostering global connections and multilingual learning opportunities. As AI evolves, it will transform language education into a dynamic, personalized, and inclusive experience.

REFERENCES

Ahmad, M., Khalid, A., & Khan, R. (2021). AI-driven tools for language learning: A comprehensive review. *Journal of Educational Technology*, *12*(4), 342–360.

Ahsan, M., Nygard, K. E., Gomes, R., Chowdhury, M. M., Rifat, N., & Connolly, J. F. (2022). Cybersecurity threats and their mitigation approaches using machine learning—A review. *Journal of Cybersecurity and Privacy*, *2*(3), 527–555. DOI: 10.3390/jcp2030027

Almaiah, M. A., Yelisetti, S., Arya, L., Christopher, N. K. B., Kaliappan, K., Vellaisamy, P., Hajjej, F., & Alkdour, T. (2023). A novel approach for improving the security of IoT–medical data systems using an enhanced dynamic Bayesian network. *Electronics (Basel)*, *12*(20), 1–15. DOI: 10.3390/electronics12204316

Aoun, J. E. (2017). *Robot-proof: Higher education in the age of artificial intelligence*. MIT Press. DOI: 10.7551/mitpress/11456.001.0001

Arya, L. (2024). Securing healthcare data and cybersecurity innovations in the era of Industry 5.0. In *Cybersecurity and data management innovations for revolutionizing healthcare* (pp. 132–147). IGI Global., DOI: 10.4018/979-8-3693-7457-3.ch006

Arya, L., & Rastogi, R. (2024). Study on aerial monitoring system in agriculture, forestry, defense, and border protection using artificial intelligence (AI). In *Agriculture and aquaculture applications of biosensors and bioelectronics* (pp. 392–407). Scopus Indexed. DOI: 10.4018/979-8-3693-2069-3.ch021

Arya, L., Sharma, Y. K., & Kumar, R. (2023). Towards a greener tomorrow: IoT-enabled smart environment monitoring systems. *2023 International Conference on Advances in Computation, Communication and Information Technology (ICAICCIT)*, Faridabad, India, 1112-1117. DOI: 10.1109/ICAICCIT60255.2023.10465894

Arya, L., Sharma, Y. K., Kumar, R., Padmanaban, H., Devi, S., & Tyagi, L. K. (2023). Maximizing IoT security: An examination of cryptographic algorithms. *2023 International Conference on Power, Energy, Environment & Intelligent Control (PEEIC)*, Greater Noida, India, 1548-1552. https://doi.org/DOI: 10.1109/PEEIC59336.2023.10451210

Attali, Y., & Burstein, J. (2017). Automated essay scoring with e-rater® V.2. Journal of Language Testing and Assessment.

Baker, T., & Smith, L. (2019). *Education rebooted? Exploring the future of AI in schools and colleges*. NESTA.

Bashir, N. (2021). Impact on student engagement and learning outcomes. EdTechBooks. https://edtechbooks.org/ai_in_education/exploring_the_impact_of_ai_integration_on_student_engagement_and_learning_outcomes

Bronstein, B., Wolfe, Z. M., & Ciampa, K. (2023). Transforming digital literacy practices: ChatGPT in education. *International Journal of Educational Technology in Higher Education*, *20*(1).

Brown, P., & Smith, J. (2020). Personalized learning and AI: Impacts on K-12 education. *Journal of the Learning Sciences*, *18*(2), 123–135.

Cannix Yau, K., & Chan, K. (2023). *University of Hong Kong temporarily bans students from using ChatGPT*. China News Service.

Denny, P., Gulwani, S., Heffernan, N. T., Käser, T., Moore, S., Rafferty, A. N., & Singla, A. (2024). Generative AI for education (GAIED): Advances, opportunities, and challenges. arXiv preprint arXiv:2402.01580.

Einarsson, H., Lund, S. H., & Jónsdóttir, A. H. (2024). Application of ChatGPT for automated problem reframing across academic domains. *Computers and Education: Artificial Intelligence*, *6*, 100194. DOI: 10.1016/j.caeai.2023.100194

Elkhatat, A. M., Elsaid, K., & Almeer, S. (2023). Evaluating the efficacy of AI content detection tools in differentiating between human and AI-generated text. *International Journal for Educational Integrity*, *19*(1), 17. DOI: 10.1007/s40979-023-00140-5

Gonzales, L., & Martinez, P. (2021). Language learning apps and AI: Tailoring education for better outcomes. *Educational Technology Review*, *9*(3), 245–260.

Han, J., Yoo, H., Kim, Y., Myung, J., Kim, M., Lim, H., Kim, J., Lee, T. Y., Hong, H., Ahn, S.-Y., & Oh, A. (2023). RECIPE: How to Integrate ChatGPT into EFL Writing Education. arXiv preprint arXiv:2305.11583. DOI: 10.1145/3573051.3596200

Hill, R., & Sethi, D. (2023). AI-powered language learning apps: A review of effectiveness. *International Conference of Language Learning*, 15(1), 57-72.

Huber, M. (2025). *AI for language education: Project developments 2024. European Centre for Modern Languages*. ECML.

International Telecommunication Union (ITU). (2022). Global connectivity and infrastructure for education. https://www.itu.int/dms_pub/itu-d/opb/ind/d-ind-global.01-2022-pdf-e.pdf

Johnson, M., & Lee, W. (2020). AI in language education: Applications in assessment and evaluation. *Educational Assessment Review*, *24*(3), 198–210.

Kashefi, A., & Mukerji, T. (2023). ChatGPT for Programming Numerical Methods. ArXiv, abs/2303.12093.

Kumar, V., & Patel, N. (2022). Virtual classrooms with AI: Enhancing engagement during the pandemic. *Journal of Online Education*, *19*(1), 89–104.

Labadze, L., Grigolia, M., & Machaidze, L. (2023). Role of AI chatbots in education: Systematic literature review. *International Journal of Educational Technology in Higher Education*, *20*(1), 56. DOI: 10.1186/s41239-023-00426-1

Li, X., & Deng, Z. (2022). NLP in language tutoring systems: Enhancing feedback and learning outcomes. *Applied Linguistics Research Journal*, *30*(5), 401–417.

Liu, M., & Yu, D. (2023). Towards intelligent e-learning systems. *Education and Information Technologies*, *28*(7), 7845–7876. DOI: 10.1007/s10639-022-11479-6 PMID: 36532790

Luckin, R. (2018). *Machine learning and human intelligence: The future of education for the 21st century*. UCL Institute of Education Press.

Maity, S., & Deroy, A. (2024). Generative AI and Its Impact on Personalized Intelligent Tutoring Systems. arXiv preprint arXiv:2410.10650.

Mardani, A., Devi, S., Alrasheedi, M., Arya, L., Singh, M. P., & Pandey, K. (2023). Hybrid intuitionistic fuzzy entropy-SWARA-COPRAS method for multi-criteria sustainable biomass crop type selection. *Sustainability (Basel)*, *15*(10), 7765. Advance online publication. DOI: 10.3390/su15107765

McKins, W., Bialik, M., & Fadel, C. (2019). *Artificial intelligence in education: Promises and implications for teaching and learning*. Centre for Curriculum Redesign.

McKinsey. (2022). How technology is shaping learning in higher education. https://www.mckinsey.com/industries/education/our-insights/how-technology-is-shaping-learning-in-higher-education

McKinsey & Company. (2020). How artificial intelligence will impact K-12 teachers.

Nagaraj, S., Kathole, A. B., Arya, L., Tyagi, N., Goyal, S. B., Rajawat, A. S., Raboaca, M. S., Mihaltan, T. C., Verma, C., & Suciu, G. (2022). Improved secure encryption with energy optimization using random permutation pseudo algorithm based on Internet of Thing in wireless sensor networks. *Energies*, *16*(8), 1–16. DOI: 10.3390/en16010008

OECD. (2021). Artificial intelligence and education and skills. https://www.oecd.org/en/topics/sub-issues/artificial-intelligence-and-education-and-skills.html

Popescu, A. (2024). AI's secret weapon in education: ChatGPT—the future of personalized learning. *Bulletin of the Transilvania University of Brasov. Series V, Economic Sciences, 16*(65), 2. DOI: 10.31926/but.es.2023.16.65.2.5

Saha, A., Senapati, T., Akram, M., Kahraman, C., Mesiar, R., & Arya, L. (2024). Dual probabilistic linguistic consensus reaching method for group decision-making. *Granular Computing, 9*(1), 35. Advance online publication. DOI: 10.1007/s41066-024-00458-6

Sajja, R., Sermet, Y., Cikmaz, M., Cwiertny, D., & Demir, I. (2023). Artificial Intelligence-Enabled Intelligent Assistant for Personalized and Adaptive Learning in Higher Education. arXiv preprint arXiv:2309.10892.

Sharma, S., Gupta, P., & Rao, K. (2021). AI in automated assessment: Transforming language learning. *Journal of Educational AI, 13*(2), 158–169.

Tafazoli, D. (2023). Critical Appraisal of Artificial Intelligence-Mediated Communication.

Tunstall, L., Von Werra, L., & Wolf, T. (2022). *Natural language processing with transformers*. O'Reilly Media.

UNESCO. (2021). UNESCO strategy on technological innovation in education (2021-2025). https://unesdoc.unesco.org/ark:/48223/pf0000375776

UNESCO. (2022). AI for education: Personalized learning systems report.

Walker, T., & Green, J. (2021). Real-time translation and voice recognition: AI in virtual classrooms. *International Journal of Digital Education, 8*(4), 299–315.

Wolfram, S. (2023). What is ChatGPT doing . . . and why does it work? http://tinyurl.com/43anvwyb

World Economic Forum. (2024). The future of learning: How AI is revolutionizing education 4.0. https://www.weforum.org/agenda/2024/04/future-learning-ai-revolutionizing-education-4-0

Zawacki-Richter, O., Marín, V. I., Bond, M., & Gouverneur, F. (2019). Systematic review of research on artificial intelligence applications in higher education. *International Journal of Educational Technology in Higher Education, 16*(1), 39. DOI: 10.1186/s41239-019-0171-0

Zhang, H., Liu, F., & Wang, Y. (2023). Machine learning in K-12 education: A study on personalized learning paths. *The Journal of Educational Research, 20*(3), 185–201.

KEY TERMS AND DEFINITIONS

Natural Language Processing (NLP): A field of AI that enables computers to understand, interpret, and generate human language, used in language education for grammar correction, translation, and speech recognition.

Machine Learning (ML): A subset of AI that enables computers to learn from data and improve their performance over time without explicit programming, essential for adaptive learning systems.

Intelligent Tutoring Systems (ITS): AI-driven platforms that provide personalized instruction and feedback, simulating the role of a human tutor in language learning.

Virtual Reality (VR): A simulated digital environment where learners can practice real-life language interactions, enhancing immersion and engagement.

Augmented Reality (AR): A technology that overlays digital content in the real world, offering interactive language learning experiences.

Chatbots: AI-powered virtual assistants that engage in conversations with learners, providing practice opportunities in spoken and written language.

AI-Powered Analytics: The use of AI to analyze student learning data, providing insights for curriculum improvement and personalized instruction.

Teacher-AI Collaboration: The partnership between human educators and AI tools to enhance teaching effectiveness without replacing the instructor's role.

Live Translation Tools: AI applications that provide instant spoken or written language translations, aiding multilingual communication.

Algorithmic Bias: Unintended discrimination in AI decision-making due to imbalanced training data can impact diverse learners' language learning outcomes.

Chapter 7
Developing AI-Enhanced Task-Based Language Learning (TBLL) Activities

Rohit Yadav
https://orcid.org/0000-0002-7573-8005
IILM University, Greater Noida, India

Xuan-Hoa Nghiem
https://orcid.org/0000-0003-2292-0257
Vietnam National University, Hanoi, Vietnam

Mohit Yadav
https://orcid.org/0000-0002-9341-2527
O. P. Jindal Global University, India

Damith Sanjaya Kumara Gangodawilage
https://orcid.org/0000-0001-7968-6284
Qasim Ibrahim School of Business, Villa College, Male, Maldives

ABSTRACT

This chapter explores the integration of Artificial Intelligence (AI) into Task-Based Language Learning (TBLL) to create innovative, learner-centered language education experiences. It examines the theoretical foundations of TBLL and AI's transformative potential in language instruction, highlighting technologies such as adaptive learning platforms, natural language processing, and immersive virtual environments. By leveraging AI, educators can design dynamic, personalized tasks that foster meaningful communication, real-time feedback, and cultural relevance. The chapter also addresses challenges, including ethical considerations, algorithmic biases, and the digital divide, emphasizing the need for balanced implementation to

DOI: 10.4018/979-8-3693-9606-3.ch007

maintain TBLL's communicative focus. Future directions include advanced personalization, multimodal interaction, and the incorporation of emerging technologies like augmented reality (AR) and virtual reality (VR).

1. INTRODUCTION

Task-Based Language Learning (TBLL) has emerged as a leading approach in language education, which focuses on the use of authentic, goal-oriented tasks to foster communicative competence and linguistic development (Ellis, 2003). TBLL differs from traditional grammar-focused methods in that it situates learning within meaningful contexts, allowing learners to engage in real-world activities that mirror everyday language use. This focus on task authenticity is in line with the growing recognition that language acquisition is most effective when learners are actively involved in purposeful communication (Nunan, 2004).

Recent developments in artificial intelligence have opened new frontiers in education, especially in language learning. AI technologies like NLP, adaptive learning systems, and virtual assistants have demonstrated the potential to personalize instruction, provide instantaneous feedback, and simulate immersive conversational environments (Luckin et al., 2016). Such tools not only complement the principles of TBLL but also respond to some of its intrinsic challenges, like real-life interaction and individualized support.

While the integration of AI into TBLL is a paradigm shift, educators can now create activities that are at once both learner-centered and technology-enriched. With the added powers of AI, language tasks can be adjusted to the proficiency levels, learning preference, and cultural contexts of the learners. In addition, AI analytics allow detail on learners' progress to emerge, thus helping interventions be more specific and improving overall effectiveness (Kukulska-Hulme & Traxler, 2019).

This chapter explores the intersection of AI and TBLL to provide a framework for designing AI-enhanced language learning activities that are at once pedagogically sound and technologically innovative. It first establishes the theoretical underpinnings of TBLL, followed by the examination of the role of AI in language education. It is followed by useful tips on developing TBLL activities using AI and illustration, respectively. Lastly, it discusses themes of challenge, ethics, and future prospects in view of how AI may soon revolutionize the face of language instruction.

2. PRINCIPLES OF TBLL

Task-Based Language Learning is one approach that is learner-oriented, where activities undertaken would be authentic in nature to enhance language acquisition. At its core, TBLL is based on the idea that language is learned best when it is used as a tool for meaningful communication rather than an abstract system to be memorized (Ellis, 2003). This approach encourages learners to engage with real-world challenges that mimic the contexts in which they might use the target language, such as planning a trip, solving a problem, or discussing a social issue. The emphasis on authentic tasks sets TBLL apart from traditional language teaching methods, which often prioritize explicit grammar instruction and vocabulary memorization (Skehan, 1998).

TBLL is underpinned by several theoretical frameworks. The interaction hypothesis, proposed by Long (1996), posits that meaningful interaction in the target language facilitates language acquisition through processes such as negotiation of meaning and corrective feedback. On the other side, the sociocultural theory of Vygotsky (1978) reveals how the social interaction and talk develop language as well as thinking capability. These approaches unite at TBLL during which learners collaborate on performing a task with support from their peers and scaffolding in order to achieve a result; Willis & Willis, 2007) Task design is the other most critical aspect of the approach in TBLL. Nunan (2004) classifies tasks into two broad categories: pedagogical tasks, which are specifically designed for language learning, and real-world tasks, which mimic activities that learners are likely to experience outside the classroom. Effective TBLL tasks have a clear purpose, a focus on meaning, and opportunities for learners to use the target language creatively and collaboratively. Skehan (1998) adds that tasks must also be balanced in terms of accuracy, fluency, and complexity for adequate language development.

In application, TBLL has several benefits. It enhances learner autonomy by encouraging individuals to assume control over their learning and increases motivation by making the use of language relevant and interesting for learners (Ellis, 2009). Additionally, since it is communicative, the learner acquires pragmatic and sociolinguistic competence, which is rarely attained in traditional methods. However, TBLL only works if activities are well prepared with the need of learners in mind and classroom management is properly done to retain a communicative focus of activities, according to Willis (1996).

The following challenges can be met by embedding AI in the foundations of TBLL: immediate feedback for all learners, differentiation of tasks to accommodate individual learners, and immersion within an interactive environment conducive to meaningful language use. These possibilities are discussed in the following sections as a precursor to integrating technology into the TBLL framework.

3. ROLE OF AI IN LANGUAGE LEARNING

Artificial intelligence has emerged as a transformative force in education, particularly in the realm of language learning. The introduction of new technologies such as natural language processing, machine learning, and adaptive systems has significantly improved the experiences associated with language learning. AI has the capability to process vast amounts of data in real time and adapt to the needs of individual learners by giving personalized instruction, feedback, and support, which would be hard for educators to do in a traditional classroom setting. This is according to Luckin et al. (2016).

AI has made one of the most critical contributions toward language learning through personalized instruction. Adaptive learning platforms apply AI algorithms that conceptualize learners' proficiency levels and, accordingly, find their weak points and strengths to personalize the content. Other tools, such as Duolingo and Babbel, have integrated machine learning into observing users' progress and proposing a customized exercise type that goes with users' learning speed and goals. This flexibility fosters learner autonomy and desirably keeps the challenge for the tasks, which is vital to the maintenance of motivation and engagement. In this regard, Kukulska-Hulme & Traxler (2019) comment that

Another very prominent use of AI in language learning is conversational agents and chatbots. Based on NLP, these technologies simulate human-like interactions with users, thus allowing learners to have opportunities for speaking and writing in real-time. For example, AI-driven chatbots like ChatGPT can engage learners in contextual dialogues, answer language-related questions, and even do some role plays to develop communicative competence. These interactions provide a safe, non-judgmental space for learners to try out the language and develop their confidence and fluency. Zawacki-Richter et al., 2019

AI also enhances feedback mechanisms while learning languages. While traditional methods often delay the process of feedback, AI-powered systems offer immediate, detailed responses on learners' performance. Integrated speech recognition technologies in platforms like Google Translate and Rosetta Stone analyze pronunciation and intonation to provide corrective feedback that helps refine speaking skills. Similarly, AI systems can assess written language for grammatical, vocabulary, and coherence errors, with suggestions for improvement. This immediate feedback accelerates the learning process and helps learners internalize corrections more effectively (Heil et al., 2020).

Additionally, AI supports the development of immersive learning experiences using technologies like virtual reality (VR) and augmented reality (AR). These technologies allow learners to experience real environments with realistic interactive conditions, thereby practicing language skills in contextually rich settings. For example, a VR platform can simulate a scenario like ordering food in a restaurant or navigating a foreign city, enabling learners to apply language in authentic contexts without geographical boundaries (Luo et al., 2021).

But with its innumerable merits, the addition of AI into language learning isn't all sail and smooth riding. Algorithmic bias, data privacy, and the digital divide are some problems that need to be addressed if use of AI in education is to be used equitably and ethically. Furthermore, AI can support teaching but never wholly replace nuanced understanding and emotional support given by a human educator. Integrate AI in education settings effectively as well as balance technological innovation with pedagogical expertise (Holmes et al., 2019).

AI aligns perfectly with TBLL principles, such as automation of routine activities, personalized pathways, and spaces for meaningful interaction that allow an extension of effectiveness and the diversification of learners. The following sections will show how such technologies can be integrated purposefully within TBLL activities to make their pedagogical potentials most realistic.

4. DESIGNING AI-ENHANCED TBLL ACTIVITIES

Designing AI-enhanced TBLL activities integrates the principles of TBLL with the advanced capabilities of AI to create personalized, interactive, and effective language learning experiences. This section presents a systematic approach toward developing such activities, focusing on needs analysis, task design, delivery, and assessment while leveraging AI affordances to maximum pedagogical impact.

4.1 Needs Analysis

Effective TBLL activities start with a clear understanding of learners' needs, goals, and contexts. Needs analysis, the heart of task-based instruction, is even more potent when used in conjunction with AI. AI tools can analyze large volumes of learner data, such as language proficiency, past performance, and learning preferences, to identify individual strengths and weaknesses (Holmes et al., 2019). Adaptive learning platforms, for instance, apply machine learning algorithms to track the progress of learners and suggest areas of improvement, thus allowing educators to design tasks that align with specific linguistic and cognitive requirements.

Moreover, AI applications such as sentiment analysis and speech recognition provide learners' emotional status and their communication skills about the specific tasks. For example, AI can be able to notice hesitation patterns or pronunciation issues in real-time, thus providing feedback for intervention towards specific areas.

This data-based approach ensures that the tasks designed are relevant, challenging, and appropriately tailored to the learners' needs.

4.2 Task Selection and Design

The design of AI-enhanced TBLL activities involves selecting tasks that are authentic and mirror real-life language use while incorporating AI functionalities to enhance the learning experience. According to Nunan (2004), tasks should be authentic, goal-oriented, and involve meaningful interaction. AI can enhance these tasks by introducing dynamic elements such as virtual scenarios, gamification, and real-time adaptability.

For instance:

- Interactive Scenarios: Virtual reality, made possible by AI, can simulate the scenario of booking a hotel room or a job interview. An immersive environment can allow learners to practice language in the context of very rich environments without leaving the classroom (Luo et al., 2021).
- Problem-Solving Tasks: AI chatbots can support collaborative problem-solving by acting as either a conversational partner or a mediator. For example, learners might collaborate on negotiating a journey plan with an AI-powered virtual travel assistant.
- Role-Playing Activities: AI systems can dynamically adapt dialogue scripts based on learners' input and thus offer personalized role-playing exercises. For example, an AI tutor might play the role of either a customer or a shopkeeper, changing the level of difficulty according to learner performance.

In the design of such tasks, educators must assure that AI tools do not take over the communicative focus of TBLL but play an enabling role in meaningful interaction.

4.3. AI in Task Delivery

AI enhances task delivery through real-time support, scaffolding, and interactivity. Conversational AI, either in the form of chatbots or voice assistants, can play the role of virtual tutors that engage learners in dialogue and simultaneously offer instant feedback. For example, tools like ChatGPT are able to simulate interactive discussions where learners practice asking and answering questions, receive corrections, and explore alternative expressions.

AI also facilitates scaffolding through gradual task complexity. Adaptive systems continuously monitor learners' performance while engaging in activities and then modify the task difficulty accordingly, so that learners are always challenged yet not overwhelmed. This dynamic adjustment of difficulty also fits into the TBLL principle of balancing accuracy, fluency, and complexity (Skehan, 1998).

Further, AI-powered tools can infuse game-based elements into the delivery of tasks. Leaderboards, badges, and points systems, in an integration with AI-driven platforms, engage learners in efforts toward task completion and skill performance improvement. For instance, a learner engaging in a vocabulary practice through a game-like task might get immediate feedback and encouragement from the AI system, sustaining engagement (Zawacki-Richter et al., 2019).

4.4 Assessment and Reflection

Assessment is a crucial ingredient of TBLL, which shows progress and weaknesses about the learners. AI helps make formative as well as summative assessment very detailed and available in real-time. For example,

- Speech Recognition: AI systems, such as Google Speech-to-Text, analyze pronunciation, fluency, and intonation so that speaking activities can be done with proper correction.
- Text Analysis: NLP tools evaluate a written task, such as coherence, grammar usage, and vocabularies in use, show errors, and suggest corrections for the same.
- Analytics Dashboards: AI platforms collate performance data into visual reports that allow learners and educators to track progress over time.

Apart from assessment, AI also encourages learner reflection through the availability of individual feedback and suggestions that pertain to further practice. An AI platform could suggest other activities or resources to focus on, based on the kind of errors a learner commits during the completion of an activity. Reflection activities that are supported by AI make learners reflect deeply on performance, ensuring much more autonomous and engaged learning. Heil et al., 2020.

5. EXAMPLES OF AI-ENHANCED TBLL ACTIVITIES

AI-enhanced TBLL activities synthesize the very best of the task-based pedagogies and the AI in the sense that such activities are always engaging, learner-centered, and interactive. AI-driven tools and applications, among others, will include chatbots, speech recognition systems, virtual reality, and adaptive platforms, which support learners in accomplishing authentic uses of the target language while providing feedback and dynamic support. Examples of AI-enhanced TBLL activities are given as follows to present how technology could enhance this method:

5.1 Role Plays Using AI Chatbots

One excellent example of AI-supported TBLL is when the learner uses any conversational AI-a ChatGPT or the Duolingo's AI chatbot, for instance-to engage in simulated role-playing. As examples, they may practice ordering something in a restaurant, thereby 'talking' with a waiter in that setting or with someone when discussing consumer services. Contextual responses in variable language complexity-the chatbot does just that when interacting with learners. For example, if a learner is having difficulty in framing a question, the interaction can be suggested, wherein the chatbot will paraphrase the responses to guide the learner. This interaction emulates real-life communication from a supportive learning environment.

The role plays are congenial to TBLL by their very design that centers around meaning-oriented use of language, with plenty of space for meaning negotiation. Furthermore, learners instantly get feedback on errors pertaining to grammar, vocabulary, and pronunciation; thus, they can rectify their language skills then and there (Heil et al., 2020).

5.2 Collaborative Problem-Solving in Virtual Environments

AI-powered VR puts users together in virtual environments in which to jointly solve problems using the target language. This can include learners preparing a travel plan, finding hidden treasures, or even solving logistical issues while preparing a meeting event-all in a virtual environment. Simultaneously, the AI system, embedded in the VR environment, might act as a facilitator by providing contextual cues, managing task complexity, and giving hints or corrections when needed.

These tasks can foster communicative competence, whereby learners are called to use the language collaboratively to achieve shared goals. Immersion by VR increases authenticity, while AI provides the adaptation of tasks according to the proficiency level of the learners and their scaffolded support (Luo et al., 2021).

5.3 AI-Facilitated Debate and Discussion

Debate and discussion activities may be adapted as AI-assisted formats to investigate the learner's input to better understand their use of language. For instance, a formal debate on an issue of interest would involve the learner, and it would be used with an AI which would track the fluency, coherence, and lexical range of the utterances. The AI tool would provide alternative phrases or would highlight the creative use of emotive language while conversing.

For example, learners might participate in a debate on environmental policies, during which AI provides immediate feedback regarding the validity and effectiveness of their arguments. Following the activity, learners can reflect on AI-generated reports containing analytics related to speaking time, error patterns, and engagement with opposing views, thus encouraging reflection and focused improvement (Zawacki-Richter et al., 2019).

5.4 Individualised Writing and Editing Tasks

AI-powered writing tools, such as Grammarly or Google's NLP systems, can enhance TBLL writing tasks with on-the-spot feedback on grammar, coherence, and even style. Examples of activities may involve having learners collaboratively draft a business email, create a travel itinerary, or write a story. AI tools not only fix mistakes but also suggest sentence restructuring, vocabulary enhancement, and stylistic appropriateness.

For instance, students writing a travel brochure could get AI-recommended ideas for more vivid adjectives or other ways to rephrase sentences to make the document more readable. Such systems also allow for reflective examination of their own writing process by comparing their original drafts with AI-imbued versions so that the students experience autonomy and self-criticism (Holmes et al., 2019).

5.5 Gamified Language Challenges

AI-based gamification injects an element of competition and fun into the TBLL activity. Learners can engage in language challenges by solving riddles, decoding messages, or answering trivia questions in the target language for points, badges, or rewards. The AI ensures these challenges are suited to the skill level of the learner and will immediately provide instant feedback to the learner to consolidate the learning process.

For instance, with AI-enhanced games, learners explore a virtual city to collect clues by engaging in dialogues with AI-powered virtual characters. Based on the students' performance as they progress through the game, the AI automatically adjusts the degree of difficulty or tasks to maintain that balance between the challenge and skills (Kukulska-Hulme & Traxler, 2019).

Through the use of AI in the development of these TBLL activities, educators can create an engaging and effective way of language learning relevant to a range of learner needs. These examples thus show how AI is able not only to enhance the authenticity and interactivity of tasks but also to provide the personalized feedback and scaffolding necessary for meaningful language development.

6. CHALLENGES AND ETHICAL CONSIDERATIONS

The introduction of AI into TBLL offers several benefits but, simultaneously, introduces substantial challenges and ethical considerations educators and developers must deal with to make sure that the technology is implemented fairly, efficiently, and ethically. From technical limitations, to pedagogical challenges and more extensive ethical questions on privacy, bias, and accessibility, it has all aspects covered.

6.1 Technical Challenges

One of the primary challenges for AI-enabled TBLL activities is the reliability and accuracy assurance of AI systems. NLP and speech recognition, two of the most prominent AI technologies, have matured much but are very far from flawless. For example, speech recognition systems can easily be challenged by non-standard accents or speech patterns, leading to misinterpretation and frustration from the learners (Heil et al., 2020). For instance, the corrections by NLP systems on complex grammatical errors or pragmatic language use are less nuanced, thus may be ineffective for the sophisticated use of the language.

Another technical challenge relates to the need for robust computational infrastructure. Most AI-enhanced tools rely on fast internet and powerful hardware, which may not be readily available in all learning environments. This results in a technological divide that impedes the implementation of AI-enhanced TBLL activities, especially in under-resourced schools or distant locations.

6.2 Pedagogical Challenges

Although AI tools carry huge potential, integrating them into TBLL poses considerable demands regarding pedagogic preparation. Ensuring that the AI tools will not outbalance the communicative core of the TBLL class remains one of the critical challenges: overuse for the purposes of either correcting mistakes or task implementation risks making class interactions and peer human interaction more rare-the key in TBLL according to Ellis (2003). Any adoption has, therefore, always to seek an excellent balance between full utilization of the opportunities of AI yet keeping intact a strong, individual-focused flavor.

In addition, the dynamic and adaptive capabilities of AI systems can intimidate educators who, themselves, might not be able to design and develop these enhanced AI activities. This requires professional training or opportunities that will prepare teachers for meaningful integration of AI tools into their TBLL practices.

6.3 Ethical Considerations

There are several ethical concerns pertaining to the use of AI in language learning; among them, data privacy and security come first. AI systems usually need a lot of learner data, including performance metrics, audio recordings, and written texts, to work efficiently. This calls for questions about how the data of learners is collected, stored, processed, and shared. The mishandling of such data may lead to privacy breaches or unauthorized use, thereby undermining learners' trust in AI tools (Holmes et al., 2019).

Another important issue is algorithmic bias: AI systems are trained on datasets that could either mirror biases from the creators themselves or limitations of the training data. For instance, some NLP tools may favor specific dialects, accents, or linguistic conventions over others, thus disadvantageing learners with diverse linguistic or cultural backgrounds. According to Zawacki-Richter et al., 2019, addressing issues of this kind would require increasing transparency in the process of developing AI and ensuring the diversification of data sources included in training datasets.

Another significant ethical issue is the digital divide. AI-boosted TBLL activities often depend on high-quality technology and stable internet connectivity, which is not accessible to everyone. This gap may exacerbate existing educational inequalities, especially for learners from low-income regions or marginalized communities. In this regard, stakeholders should develop low-resource AI tools and support inclusive policies that bridge the digital gap (Luckin et al., 2016).

6.4 Overuse of AI

One of the major issues with AI- enhanced TBLL is overreliance on technology. AI can enable many meaningful experiences of learning, but AI is never able to interpret nicely what being human means, such as understanding empathy and cultural sensitivity. Overrelating to AI may result in a transactional approach to language learning, where learners are inclined to merely complete all their tasks and then receive feedback rather than exploring deeper, human-centered interactions (Ellis, 2009).

Trainers and trainees must treat AI as a supplement and not a substitute for age-old pedagogic approaches. Human guidance is essential in making sure that tasks do not lose their communicative sense and are in harmony with general learning aims.

6.5 Overcoming Problems and Ethical Considerations

These are challenges that should be mitigated with a multi-method approach. Developers must ensure that transparency is manifest in the design of AI systems; the uses of data should be clearly elaborated to ensure that algorithms are trained on diverse datasets. The educational institution must apply strict data protection policies to protect the privacy of learners and align with legal frameworks like the General Data Protection Regulation.

Educators should be subjected to professional development to make them well aware of the responsible and effective use of AI in TBLL contexts. The trainings may include task design, ethical considerations, and strategies on how to integrate AI without losing the pedagogical integrity of TBLL.

Finally, stakeholders must collaborate in making AI tools more accessible and inclusive, especially for under-resourced communities. Open-source AI solutions, partnerships with non-profit organizations, and government funding initiatives can help ensure that the benefits of AI-enhanced TBLL are equitably distributed.

Tackling these challenges and ethical considerations on the design, development, and implementation of educational technology can also be unlocked in TBLL which is equitable, inclusive, and learner-centered through the use of AI. This will lead to a meaningful step toward holistically and ethically integrating technology in language teaching.

7. FUTURE DIRECTIONS

The integration of AI into TBLL is still in its infancy, holding promise for large amounts of innovation and expansion. With evolutionary advancements, future projects can change the face of language learning as never before, making learning more personalized, accessible, and engaging. This section discusses main future directions for research, development, and implementation of AI-enhanced TBLL, focusing on emerging technologies, pedagogical innovations, and ethical considerations.

7.1 Advanced Personalization with AI

A promising direction is the elaboration of more sophisticated personalization systems. Although already existing AI solutions can adapt assignments to learners' proficiency levels, future systems might be able to make use of deep learning and user modeling advances in order to further enhance customization. These systems would analyze a wider array of data-cognitive style, emotional state, and cultural context-to create very individualized learning paths.

For example, adaptive AI can create sequences of tasks that may engage with the learner's real-time progress; such elements include motivational strategies, cultural appropriateness, and many more. These in their development will ensure that activities under TBLL are both linguistically apt and psychologically engaging as well as contextually meaningful and instrumental (Holmes et al., 2019).

7.2. Integration of Emerging Technologies

The future of AI-enhanced TBLL will be further evidenced by the integration of augmented reality, virtual reality, and the Internet of Things. AR and VR, for example, will let the users experience more realistic immersion into the language learning environment through interacting with AI-driven characters or objects in real-life settings. Think of a virtual marketplace where learners bargain over prices with an AI shopkeeper or go on an AR-enhanced museum tour conducted by an AI curator.

Similarly, IoT devices could make language learning ubiquitous in that TBLL activities can be embedded into contexts of everyday life. For example, smart home devices could remind a learner to finish some language activity while cooking, cleaning, or even commuting, blending learning into life (Luo et al., 2021).

7.3 Multimodal AI Systems

Future AI systems may support more complex, multimodal learning interactions that make use of spoken language, texts, gestures, and even face expressions. For instance, in the future, such systems would allow for rich and natural communication forms that simulate true conversational behaviors. For example, AI can analyze a student's tone when speaking, how they express through facial expressions or body language, all of which aspects can be factored into evaluation not only regarding linguistic features but also pragmatic as well as nonverbal communication ability (Zawacki-Richter et al., 2019).

This multimodal capability would also improve the collaborative TBLL activities so that learners can interact with AI and their peers more naturally in virtual or hybrid environments.

7.4 Cross-Linguistic and Multicultural Applications

With advanced AI, they may give more support to multilingual and multicultural contexts of language learning. Future TBLL platforms may enhance cross-linguistic transfer by the AI system being able to recognize and address particular challenges that a learner may face when changing from their first language to the target language. For instance, AI can recognize common patterns of interference or errors among first language speakers and give feedback according to that.

In addition, AI could expand on the use of culturally authentic materials and interactions in TBLL tasks, which would not only enhance linguistic competence but also intercultural awareness. Such features would be highly useful in internationalized learning contexts where learners from a variety of linguistic and cultural backgrounds work together.

7.5 AI in Teacher Training and Professional Development

AI could be a potential tool in training teachers to use TBLL and AI technologies appropriately. Future AI-based platforms could give teachers individualized training by mimicking classroom scenarios, providing feedback on task design, implementation, and assessment. For instance, AI could analyze lesson plans or recorded teaching sessions and give suggestions for improvement based on TBLL principles and best practices (Luckin et al., 2016).

These systems also assist professional learning communities in connecting people from around the globe to share resources, insights, and experiences concerning AI-enhanced TBLL.

7.6 Ethical and Inclusive AI Development

As AI becomes the core of TBLL, future efforts should be placed on ethical development and inclusivity of the AI. In this regard, researchers and developers need to focus their attention on creating AI systems free from bias and accessible to all learners, irrespective of their socioeconomic status or geographical location.

This may also involve low-resource AI development that can function well under offline or low-bandwidth settings.

Also, policy makers and other stakeholders will be required to collectively set guiding ethics of AI deployment in education focusing on issues related to data protection, algorithm transparency, and equality. All these ensure equitable and fair resource distribution by deploying AI-facilitated TBLL benefits responsibly (Holmes et al., 2019).

7.7 Interdisciplinary Research and Collaboration

The future of AI-enhanced TBLL will be based on interdisciplinarity, in which linguists, educators, computer scientists, and policymakers work together to answer such complex questions as how AI best supports cognitive and sociocultural aspects of language learning or how to design tasks for TBLL that exploit the strengths of AI without compromising pedagogical principles.

Other longitudinal aspects that could be observed, for research purposes, with regards to AI-improved TBLL are effects on the users' language competencies, engagement, and general results. Such a research-based resource will contribute to an increased effectiveness of sustainability within more successful AI applications in language learning.

7.8 Lifelong Learning and AI

Finally, AI-enhanced TBLL can extend far beyond formal education to support lifelong language learning. AI systems could provide flexible, on-demand learning opportunities for individuals at any stage of life-from young learners to professionals and retirees. For instance, mobile AI applications could deliver short, task-based lessons tailored to users' immediate needs, such as preparing for a business meeting or learning basic phrases for travel.

This lifelong learning approach resonates with the increased call for flexible, self-directed language learning opportunities in this increasingly globalized world.

The future directions are embraced by educators, developers, and researchers to fully tap into AI-enhanced TBLL, transforming language education into a more personalized, inclusive, and impactful experience. Further innovation and collaboration will be key to the challenge and opportunities ahead.

CONCLUSION

The integration of AI into TBLL is a sea change in modern language education. This chapter has underlined the synergies between what AI can do and the core principles of TBLL, highlighting how technologies such as adaptive systems, natural language processing, and immersive tools can enrich task design, delivery, and assessment. AI, by addressing individual learner needs and facilitating authentic, meaningful interactions, enhances the learner-centered and communicative focus central to TBLL.

However, it brings its own set of challenges in this new and innovative approach: technical limitations, ethical considerations, and balanced implementation so that the humanistic elements of education are not overshadowed. These will require joint efforts by educators, technologists, and policymakers to ensure accessibility, equity, and pedagogical soundness in AI tools.

Looking ahead, the potential for AI-enhanced TBLL lies in its capacity to foster personalization, inclusivity, and lifelong learning. By leveraging emerging technologies and embracing ethical innovation, the field can unlock new possibilities for learners across diverse contexts. Ultimately, the successful fusion of AI and TBLL promises to reshape language education into a dynamic, adaptive, and empowering experience for all.

REFERENCES

Ellis, R. (2009). The differential effects of three types of task planning on the fluency, complexity, and accuracy in L2 oral production. *Applied Linguistics, 30*(4), 474–509.

Heil, C., Wu, J. S., Lee, J. H., & Schmidt, T. (2020). A review of mobile language learning applications: Trends, challenges, and opportunities. *The EuroCALL Review, 28*(1), 20–50.

Holmes, W., Bialik, M., & Fadel, C. (2019). *Artificial intelligence in education: Promises and implications for teaching and learning*. Center for Curriculum Redesign.

Kukulska-Hulme, A., & Traxler, J. (2019). *Mobile learning: The next generation.* Routledge.

Long, M. H. (1996). The role of the linguistic environment in second language acquisition. In Ritchie, W., & Bhatia, T. (Eds.), *Handbook of second language acquisition* (pp. 413–468). Academic Press.

Luckin, R., Holmes, W., Griffiths, M., & Forcier, L. B. (2016). *Intelligence unleashed: An argument for AI in education.* Pearson Education.

Luo, H., Yang, C., & Li, L. (2021). Immersive virtual reality in foreign language education: A meta-analysis. *Educational Technology Research and Development, 69*(3), 705–729.

Nunan, D. (2004). *Task-based language teaching*. Cambridge University Press.

Skehan, P. (1998). *A cognitive approach to language learning*. Oxford University Press.

Vygotsky, L. S. (1978). *Mind in society: The development of higher psychological processes*. Harvard University Press.

Willis, D., & Willis, J. (2007). *Doing task-based teaching*. Oxford University Press.

Zawacki-Richter, O., Marín, V. I., Bond, M., & Gouverneur, F. (2019). Systematic review of research on artificial intelligence applications in higher education: The state of the art and future research directions. *International Journal of Educational Technology in Higher Education, 16*(1), 1–27.

ADDITIONAL READING

Hasan, M. K., Fakih, A. H., & Seraj, P. M. I. & Hasmirati. (2022). The effect of technology-assisted language programme on vocabulary learning among EFL students at the tertiary level. *Heliyon, 8*(8), 1–6.

Hendrawaty, N., Yuliati, Y., & Haryanti, R. P. (2024). EFL Students' Preferences on Vocabulary Learning. Scope. *Journal of English Language Teaching*, *8*(2), 541–550.

Jomaa, N. J. (2025). Corrective Feedback of AI Tools in Writing and Translation. In Jomaa, N. (Ed.), *Using AI Tools in Text Analysis, Simplification, Classification, and Synthesis* (pp. 293–318). IGI Global Scientific Publishing., DOI: 10.4018/979-8-3693-9511-0.ch010

Jomaa, N. J., & Kamal, M. N. (2023). Perspectives of students and teachers towards developing speaking skills by using technology among EFL Iraqi students. In *Integrating TPACK and CALL in English Language Teaching* (pp. 153–173). IGI Global., DOI: 10.4018/978-1-6684-8546-0.ch007

Rouabhia, R. (2025). Ethical Implications of AI: Examining Bias and Fairness in AI-Powered Education. In Jomaa, N. (Ed.), *Using AI Tools in Text Analysis, Simplification, Classification, and Synthesis* (pp. 409–436). IGI Global Scientific Publishing., DOI: 10.4018/979-8-3693-9511-0.ch014

Vettriselvan, R., Deepan, A., Garg, P. K., Suresh, N. V., & Velmurugan, P. R. (2025). Advanced Text Analysis, Simplification, Classification, and Synthesis Techniques: Leveraging AI for Enhanced Medical Education. In Jomaa, N. (Ed.), *Using AI Tools in Text Analysis, Simplification, Classification, and Synthesis* (pp. 37–66). IGI Global Scientific Publishing., DOI: 10.4018/979-8-3693-9511-0.ch002

KEY TERMS AND DEFINITIONS

Artificial Intelligence (AI): A branch of computer science focused on creating machines and software that can perform tasks typically requiring human intelligence—such as learning, problem-solving, decision-making, and language understanding.

Task-Based Language Learning (TBLL): A language teaching method centered on meaningful tasks—such as giving directions, writing emails, or solving problems—that promote authentic language use and focus on communication over grammar drills.

Natural Language Processing (NLP): A field of AI that enables computers to understand, interpret, and generate human language, used in applications like chatbots, language translation, and speech recognition.

Communicative Competence: The ability to effectively and appropriately use a language in various social and cultural contexts, including grammar, vocabulary, and the pragmatics of interaction.

Virtual Reality (VR): A computer-generated simulation of a three-dimensional environment that users can interact with in a seemingly real way using special equipment (like headsets), often used in immersive learning experiences.

Chapter 8
Challenges of Integrating Artificial Intelligence With Language Curriculum:
Addressing Pedagogical, Technological, and Ethical Barriers

M. R. Ramesh
https://orcid.org/0000-0002-1648-9387
Indira Gandhi Centre for Atomic Research, India

ABSTRACT

This chapter explores the multifaceted challenges of integrating Artificial Intelligence (AI) into language curricula, focusing on pedagogical, technological, and ethical barriers. It begins by examining the theoretical foundations of AI in education and its potential to enhance language learning through personalized and adaptive teaching methods. However, the integration is complicated by pedagogical challenges such as alignment with curriculum objectives, teacher preparedness, and the need for effective assessment strategies. Technological hurdles include access disparities, infrastructure limitations, and the necessity for adaptable AI tools. Ethical concerns, particularly regarding data privacy, algorithmic bias, and the evolving role of educators, are critically analyzed. By addressing these barriers, the chapter aims to provide insights into creating a balanced, inclusive, and effective AI-enhanced language curriculum for diverse educational contexts.

DOI: 10.4018/979-8-3693-9606-3.ch008

1. INTRODUCTION

The integration of Artificial Intelligence (AI) into educational contexts has emerged as a transformative force, promising to enhance teaching and learning processes. In the realm of language education, AI technologies hold the potential to personalize learning experiences, improve access to educational resources, and facilitate innovative pedagogical approaches. However, the journey toward integrating AI with language curricula is fraught with challenges that must be addressed to realize its full potential. This chapter explores the multifaceted barriers—pedagogical, technological, and ethical—that hinder the effective integration of AI in language education.

1.1 Pedagogical Challenges

At the core of the pedagogical challenges is the alignment between AI-driven tools and established educational objectives. While AI can automate certain aspects of language learning, it cannot replace the critical human elements of empathy, cultural nuance, and interpersonal interaction that are essential for effective language acquisition. Language learning is inherently social, requiring nuanced communication and contextual understanding that AI systems often struggle to replicate (Almalki, M., & Aziz, M. A. (2022)). Furthermore, the effectiveness of AI tools is contingent upon educators' preparedness to incorporate these technologies into their teaching practices. Many teachers lack the necessary training and support, resulting in resistance to adopting AI-driven methodologies. Consequently, a significant gap exists between the potential benefits of AI and the realities of classroom implementation.

1.2 Technological Challenges

The technological barriers to integrating AI into language curricula are equally substantial. The successful deployment of AI tools requires robust infrastructure, including access to reliable internet and devices, which can be a significant hurdle in under-resourced educational settings. Additionally, the interoperability of AI applications with existing educational platforms poses a challenge (Anderson, T., & Dron, J. (2011)). Educators often find themselves grappling with compatibility issues, which can lead to fragmented learning experiences. Moreover, the development of AI technologies requires vast amounts of quality data. In the context of language education, this can be particularly complex, as the datasets must encompass a diverse range of languages, dialects, and cultural contexts to avoid bias and enhance relevance.

1.3 Ethical Challenges

Incorporating AI into language education also raises pressing ethical concerns that warrant careful consideration. Issues surrounding data privacy, security, and ownership become increasingly salient as AI systems collect and analyze students' personal information to tailor learning experiences. The potential for bias in AI algorithms can exacerbate existing inequalities in education, leading to unequal learning outcomes (Baker, R. S. J. D., & Inventado, P. S. (2014)). For instance, if AI tools are trained on datasets that predominantly feature specific languages or cultural contexts, they may inadvertently marginalize underrepresented groups. This reinforces the need for a critical examination of the ethical implications of AI deployment in educational settings, ensuring that the integration of these technologies aligns with principles of fairness and inclusivity.

1.4 Purpose of the Chapter

This chapter aims to provide a comprehensive overview of the challenges associated with integrating AI into language curricula, highlighting the interplay between pedagogical practices, technological advancements, and ethical considerations. By addressing these barriers, educators, policymakers, and researchers can work collaboratively to create an educational environment that harnesses the power of AI while remaining grounded in humanistic values. The subsequent sections will delve deeper into each category of challenges, offering insights and strategies for overcoming these hurdles and paving the way for a future where AI enriches language education in meaningful ways.

2. UNDERSTANDING AI IN THE CONTEXT OF LANGUAGE EDUCATION

2.1 Definition of AI and Its Relevance to Language Learning

Artificial Intelligence (AI) refers to the simulation of human intelligence processes by computer systems. This includes learning (the acquisition of information and rules for using it), reasoning (using rules to reach approximate or definite conclusions), and self-correction. Within the realm of language education, AI's relevance is profound, as it offers innovative methods to enhance learning experiences, improve outcomes, and increase accessibility for diverse learners (Bennett, S., & Maton, K. (2010)).

In language learning, AI technologies can help address various challenges, such as personalized learning paths, immediate feedback, and scalability of resources. The integration of AI in language education not only facilitates a more engaging learning environment but also allows educators to focus on higher-order teaching activities by automating routine tasks (Blair, C., & Hargreaves, E. (2018)).

2.2 Overview of AI Tools Used in Language Education

AI technologies applicable to language education encompass various tools and applications that harness natural language processing (NLP), machine learning, speech recognition, and other advanced techniques.

- **Natural Language Processing (NLP)**: NLP is a field of AI that enables computers to understand, interpret, and generate human language. In language education, NLP is used in applications such as grammar checkers and writing assistants that help learners refine their language skills. Tools like Grammarly and ProWritingAid leverage NLP algorithms to provide real-time feedback on writing, enhancing learners' understanding of grammar and style.
- **Machine Learning**: Machine learning algorithms are employed to analyze data, identify patterns, and make predictions. In language education, this can be used to personalize learning experiences. For instance, adaptive learning platforms such as Duolingo analyze a learner's performance to tailor exercises that target specific weaknesses, thereby optimizing their learning journey.
- **Speech-to-Text and Text-to-Speech Technologies**: These technologies facilitate the development of listening and speaking skills. Speech recognition tools convert spoken language into text, allowing learners to practice pronunciation and receive immediate feedback on their speech. Conversely, text-to-speech technologies can help learners improve their listening comprehension by converting written text into spoken language, making it accessible for auditory learners.
- **AI-Powered Chatbots**: Chatbots are automated conversational agents that interact with users in natural language. In language learning, chatbots serve as virtual language partners, enabling learners to practice their speaking and writing skills in a low-stakes environment. Applications like Replika allow users to engage in conversation, helping them gain confidence in their language abilities.

- **Intelligent Tutoring Systems (ITS)**: ITS utilize AI to provide personalized instruction and feedback to learners. These systems can assess a student's current knowledge and adapt the curriculum accordingly. For example, platforms like Carnegie Learning use AI algorithms to provide real-time feedback on math and language tasks, promoting personalized learning experiences (Chalmers, C., & Harris, K. (2017)).
- **Automated Essay Scoring**: AI technologies are used to evaluate written assignments, providing instant feedback on grammar, coherence, and overall quality. Tools like ETS's e-rater use NLP to assess essays, allowing educators to efficiently evaluate student writing without compromising the quality of feedback (Dede, C. (2011)).
- **Language Translation Tools**: AI-powered translation applications such as Google Translate leverage deep learning techniques to improve translation accuracy. These tools can help learners understand texts in a foreign language and foster cross-cultural communication, making language learning more inclusive.

2.3 Current Trends in AI Integration within Language Learning Platforms

The integration of AI in language education is experiencing a surge in popularity, driven by advancements in technology and increased demand for personalized learning experiences. Current trends include:

- **Personalization**: AI technologies are increasingly used to create adaptive learning environments that cater to individual learner needs. By analyzing user data, AI systems can adjust content and learning paths to maximize engagement and efficiency.
- **Gamification**: Language learning platforms are incorporating game-like elements powered by AI to make learning more engaging. Features like rewards, challenges, and interactive activities motivate learners and enhance retention (Huang, R. H., & Spector, J. M. (2018)).
- **Multimodal Learning**: Many AI-driven platforms are adopting multimodal approaches, integrating text, audio, and visual elements to provide a richer learning experience. For instance, applications like Babbel use videos and interactive exercises to address different learning styles.
- **Enhanced Assessment**: The use of AI in assessment is evolving, with tools capable of providing formative feedback that is more nuanced than traditional methods. This helps learners understand their progress and areas for improvement in real-time (Luckin, R., & Holmes, W. (2016).

- **Collaborative Learning**: AI technologies are fostering collaborative learning environments where learners can interact with peers and AI tutors. This helps to build communication skills and enhances the learning experience.

2.4 Benefits of AI in Enhancing Language Teaching and Learning Processes

The integration of AI in language education offers numerous benefits that can significantly enhance teaching and learning processes:

- **Immediate Feedback**: AI tools provide instant feedback on language tasks, allowing learners to make adjustments and learn from their mistakes in real time. This promotes a more effective learning process by facilitating self-correction.
- **Scalability**: AI technologies enable educators to reach larger audiences without compromising the quality of instruction. Language learning applications can accommodate thousands of users simultaneously, offering personalized experiences at scale.
- **Accessibility**: AI can help break down barriers to language education by providing resources to learners regardless of their geographical location or socio-economic background. For instance, mobile applications enable learners in remote areas to access quality language instruction.
- **Increased Engagement**: The gamification of language learning through AI applications fosters a more engaging and motivating environment, encouraging learners to persist in their studies.
- **Efficiency**: Automating routine tasks such as grading and providing feedback allows educators to focus more on curriculum development and personalized instruction, leading to improved educational outcomes.
- **Data-Driven Insights**: AI technologies can analyze vast amounts of data to provide insights into learner behavior and performance, helping educators make informed decisions about curriculum design and instructional strategies (Miao, Y., & Zhang, Z. (2020)).

In summary, the integration of AI into language education presents an exciting opportunity to enhance the learning experience through personalized, engaging, and accessible approaches. As these technologies continue to evolve, they hold the potential to transform language learning and teaching processes, making them more effective and inclusive for learners worldwide. Addressing the challenges that accompany this integration will be crucial in harnessing the full potential of

AI in language education, ensuring that its benefits are realized while mitigating associated risks.

3. PEDAGOGICAL CHALLENGES: BALANCING AI WITH HUMAN-LED TEACHING

Language learning is an inherently social process that transcends mere memorization of vocabulary and grammar rules. It encompasses the development of communicative competence, cultural awareness, and emotional intelligence—skills that are vital for effective interaction in diverse linguistic environments (O'Neil, C. (2016)) As educational institutions increasingly turn to Artificial Intelligence (AI) to enhance language instruction, several pedagogical challenges emerge, particularly concerning the balance between AI-driven technologies and human-led teaching. This section delves into these challenges, focusing on the limitations of AI in replicating human interaction, the complexities of contextual learning, and the potential risks of over-reliance on AI tools.

3.1 The Role of Human Interaction in Language Acquisition

Human interaction plays a critical role in language acquisition. Language is not merely a system of signs but a medium of communication that conveys emotions, intentions, and cultural nuances. Face-to-face interactions allow learners to engage in rich, contextually embedded dialogues, where tone, body language, and situational context significantly influence meaning. Research has consistently shown that communicative competence—defined as the ability to use language appropriately in various social contexts—thrives in environments where learners can practice with peers and instructors (Rashid, T., & Asghar, H. M. (2016)).

While AI technologies can automate aspects of language instruction, such as vocabulary drills and grammar exercises, they often struggle to replicate the richness of human interaction. AI systems primarily rely on algorithms and data processing, which may lead to a superficial understanding of language (Selwyn, N. (2016)). For instance, a language model might generate grammatically correct sentences but may not recognize when a phrase could be inappropriate or when sarcasm is being used. Consequently, learners may miss opportunities to develop the subtleties of language that only human interaction can provide.

3.2 The Challenge of Contextual Learning

Contextual learning is another significant challenge when integrating AI into language curricula. Human language is deeply contextual; the meaning of words and phrases can shift dramatically based on situational factors, cultural backgrounds, and interpersonal relationships. AI, however, often relies on vast datasets to identify patterns, which can result in a lack of understanding of nuanced meanings (Stanford University. (2018)). For example, an AI system might struggle to differentiate between formal and informal language use, failing to recognize the social contexts in which different expressions are appropriate.

Moreover, AI systems can have difficulty with idiomatic expressions, regional dialects, and cultural references that are crucial for mastering a language. A learner might receive correct grammar feedback from an AI tool but still lack the ability to engage in authentic conversations due to a gap in contextual understanding. This limitation poses a significant obstacle for language learners who aim to become proficient in real-world communication.

3.3 Balancing AI-Driven Instruction and Teacher-Led Pedagogy

Integrating AI into language education necessitates a delicate balance between technology-driven instruction and traditional teacher-led pedagogy. Educators play a pivotal role in facilitating language learning through personalized feedback, fostering classroom interactions, and creating supportive learning environments. Teachers can adapt their instructional strategies to meet the diverse needs of students, a level of flexibility that AI systems typically lack.

Furthermore, the expertise and intuition of skilled language teachers cannot be replaced by algorithms. For instance, teachers can identify when a student is struggling with a concept and can modify their approach accordingly, providing targeted support that AI may not offer. Effective language instruction often involves understanding the emotional and social dynamics within the classroom—an area where human teachers excel. Thus, while AI can serve as a valuable supplement to language education, it should not replace the essential human element that fosters a deeper understanding of language and culture.

3.4 Concerns about Over-Reliance on AI Tools

The risk of over-reliance on AI tools in language learning raises important concerns about diminished human engagement in the classroom. As educators adopt AI technologies to streamline administrative tasks or provide instant feedback, there is a danger that the human element of teaching could become secondary. Learners might become overly dependent on AI for language practice, relying on automated tools for conversation simulations instead of engaging in meaningful exchanges with their peers and instructors.

This shift toward technology-driven instruction may lead to a reduction in collaborative learning experiences, where students benefit from working together to solve problems and practice language skills. The collaborative aspect of language learning—sharing ideas, negotiating meaning, and engaging in discussions—can significantly enhance language retention and fluency. Therefore, educators must carefully consider the implications of introducing AI tools into the classroom and strive to maintain a balanced approach that emphasizes the importance of human interaction.

4. TECHNOLOGICAL BARRIERS: INFRASTRUCTURE, ACCESSIBILITY, AND INTEROPERABILITY

The successful integration of Artificial Intelligence (AI) in language education is contingent upon a robust technological foundation, which includes access to essential infrastructure, reliable internet connectivity, and digital tools designed to support AI-driven applications. These factors significantly influence how effectively AI can be implemented in language curricula, particularly in diverse educational settings. Unfortunately, many under-resourced areas face significant technological barriers that hinder the adoption of AI, thus limiting its potential to enhance language learning outcomes. This chapter explores the technological barriers to AI integration in language education, focusing on infrastructure requirements, the digital divide, interoperability challenges, and ensuring accessibility and inclusivity.

4.1 Technological Infrastructure Requirements for AI Integration in Language Education

Integrating AI into language education necessitates a comprehensive technological infrastructure. This includes not only hardware, such as computers, tablets, and smartphones, but also software platforms that can support AI applications. Educational institutions must invest in both the physical infrastructure and the necessary software licenses, which can be costly. Moreover, teacher training is essential to ensure that educators are proficient in using these technologies. AI applications often rely on complex algorithms that require substantial computing power and data storage capabilities. For instance, Natural Language Processing (NLP) tools, which are crucial for language learning applications, demand advanced computational resources and large datasets to function effectively.

In addition to hardware and software, reliable internet connectivity is critical. AI applications, particularly those that utilize cloud computing or real-time data processing, require stable and fast internet connections. In regions where internet access is inconsistent or entirely lacking, the effectiveness of AI-driven language learning tools is severely compromised. This issue is further exacerbated in rural or underdeveloped areas, where infrastructural deficits are prevalent.

4.2 The Digital Divide: The Impact of Unequal Access to Technology on AI Adoption

The digital divide poses a significant challenge to the equitable integration of AI in language education. This divide refers to the disparity between individuals who have easy access to digital technology and those who do not. Factors such as socio-economic status, geographic location, and educational disparities contribute to this divide, resulting in unequal opportunities for students to engage with AI-driven language learning tools.

For instance, students in urban centers often have better access to technology, high-speed internet, and advanced educational resources compared to their rural counterparts. This disparity can lead to significant differences in language acquisition outcomes, as students with access to AI technologies can benefit from personalized learning experiences, immediate feedback, and adaptive learning environments. In contrast, students lacking access may miss out on these advancements, perpetuating educational inequalities and limiting their language learning potential.

Addressing the digital divide requires a multifaceted approach. Governments, educational institutions, and private organizations must work collaboratively to increase access to technology in underserved areas. Initiatives such as providing subsidized devices, improving internet infrastructure, and implementing community-based technology training programs can help bridge this gap. Furthermore, raising awareness about the importance of digital literacy and the benefits of AI in education can encourage stakeholders to invest in technology that promotes equitable access.

4.3 Interoperability Challenges between AI Tools and Language Learning Platforms

Another significant technological barrier to integrating AI into language education is the lack of interoperability between different AI tools and language learning platforms. Interoperability refers to the ability of various systems and technologies to communicate and work together seamlessly. In the context of language education, it is essential that AI tools can integrate with existing language learning platforms and curricula.

However, many AI applications are developed independently and may not be compatible with other educational technologies. This fragmentation can lead to disjointed learning experiences, where students and educators must navigate multiple platforms that do not work well together. For example, a language learning app that uses AI for pronunciation feedback may not integrate smoothly with a learning management system (LMS) used to track student progress, resulting in missed opportunities for data sharing and holistic learning experiences.

To address interoperability challenges, developers and educational institutions need to prioritize creating open-source platforms and standards that facilitate collaboration and integration. Encouraging the use of Application Programming Interfaces (APIs) can enable different tools to communicate effectively and share data. Educators should also advocate for systems that allow for seamless integration of various AI tools into existing curricula, making it easier for them to adopt and utilize these technologies.

4.4 Ensuring Accessibility and Inclusivity in AI-Enhanced Language Education

Incorporating AI into language education presents an opportunity to enhance accessibility and inclusivity, yet this potential can only be realized if technological barriers are addressed. Accessibility means ensuring that all students, including those with disabilities, can fully participate in AI-enhanced language learning. This necessitates the development of AI tools that accommodate diverse learning needs and styles.

For example, AI-driven applications should include features such as text-to-speech and speech-to-text capabilities, adjustable font sizes, and customizable learning pathways to support learners with different abilities. Furthermore, AI can be leveraged to provide real-time language support for students who speak multiple languages, facilitating a more inclusive learning environment.

Inclusivity in AI-enhanced language education also involves acknowledging and valuing linguistic diversity. Language learning applications should be designed to reflect the languages and dialects spoken by students, promoting a sense of identity and belonging. This can help to motivate students and make language learning more relevant to their lives.

In summary, the integration of AI in language education faces several technological barriers, including the need for robust infrastructure, the challenges posed by the digital divide, interoperability issues, and the necessity of ensuring accessibility and inclusivity. Addressing these barriers is crucial for the successful implementation of AI-driven language curricula. Stakeholders in education must collaborate to build the necessary technological foundations, advocate for equitable access to resources, and design inclusive AI tools that support diverse learners. By overcoming these technological challenges, we can unlock the transformative potential of AI in language education and enhance learning experiences for all students.

5. TEACHER TRAINING AND PROFESSIONAL DEVELOPMENT

The integration of Artificial Intelligence (AI) into the language curriculum represents a significant shift in educational practices, offering opportunities to enhance learning experiences and outcomes. However, for this transformation to be successful, educators must possess the necessary skills and knowledge to effectively utilize AI tools in their teaching. This section will explore the importance of teacher training and professional development in equipping language educators to navigate AI technologies, adapt their teaching methods, and manage the challenges associated with AI implementation in the classroom.

5.1 The Importance of Teacher Training in AI Literacy and Integration

AI literacy refers to the ability to understand, use, and critically evaluate AI technologies. As AI becomes increasingly prevalent in language education—through tools like chatbots, AI-driven language assessments, and personalized learning platforms—teachers must be well-versed in these technologies to facilitate effective integration. Teacher training programs should focus not only on the technical aspects of AI tools but also on pedagogical strategies that enhance language learning.

Research has shown that educators who receive targeted training in AI are more likely to embrace these technologies in their classrooms. For instance, a study by Smith et al. (2022) found that teachers who participated in AI literacy workshops reported increased confidence in using AI tools, leading to more innovative and engaging language instruction. This highlights the need for comprehensive training programs that address both the theoretical foundations of AI and practical applications within the language curriculum.

5.2 Professional Development Opportunities for Language Educators in the AI Context

Professional development plays a crucial role in helping language educators adapt to the evolving landscape of AI in education. Opportunities for professional growth can take various forms, including workshops, online courses, webinars, and collaborative projects. These initiatives can empower educators to explore AI technologies, share best practices, and develop innovative teaching strategies.

One effective approach is to provide educators with hands-on experience using AI tools in simulated classroom settings. For example, professional development programs could include sessions where teachers practice using AI-driven language apps, analyze student interactions with these tools, and reflect on their effectiveness in promoting language acquisition. Furthermore, fostering communities of practice—where educators can share their experiences and challenges with AI integration—can enhance professional growth and facilitate continuous learning.

5.3 Addressing Teacher Resistance to AI Adoption and Fostering a Culture of Innovation

Despite the potential benefits of AI in language education, some educators may exhibit resistance to adopting these technologies. This resistance can stem from various factors, including fear of the unknown, concerns about job security, and skepticism about the effectiveness of AI tools. To address these challenges, it is essential to foster a culture of innovation within educational institutions.

Creating an environment that encourages experimentation and exploration of AI technologies can help alleviate apprehensions among educators. Institutions should provide support and resources for teachers to trial AI tools in their classrooms, allowing them to observe the impact on student engagement and learning outcomes. Additionally, involving educators in the decision-making process regarding AI tool selection can promote buy-in and ownership of the integration process.

Moreover, leadership support is critical in addressing resistance to AI adoption. School administrators should communicate a clear vision for integrating AI into the language curriculum, highlighting its potential to enhance teaching and learning. By promoting a growth mindset and celebrating successes in AI integration, institutions can inspire educators to embrace innovation.

5.4 Collaboration Between Educators and AI Developers to Create Effective Tools for Language Learning

Collaboration between educators and AI developers is essential for creating effective AI tools tailored to the needs of language learners. AI developers must engage with educators during the design and development process to ensure that the tools align with pedagogical goals and address real classroom challenges.

For instance, educators can provide valuable insights into the specific needs of their students, helping developers create AI applications that are user-friendly and contextually relevant. By conducting focus groups or pilot programs with educators, AI developers can gather feedback on tool functionality and usability, leading to iterative improvements based on classroom experiences.

In addition, interdisciplinary partnerships between educational institutions and technology companies can facilitate the development of innovative AI solutions that enhance language learning. These collaborations can result in the creation of tools that not only support language acquisition but also promote critical thinking, collaboration, and creativity among learners.

6. ETHICAL CONSIDERATIONS: PRIVACY, DATA SECURITY, AND BIAS

The integration of Artificial Intelligence (AI) into language education offers transformative potential for personalized learning and enhanced educational outcomes. However, it simultaneously raises significant ethical concerns that must be addressed to ensure a fair and just educational landscape. This section delves into the ethical challenges associated with AI in language learning, particularly focusing on privacy concerns, data security, and the bias inherent in AI algorithms. It emphasizes the need for robust ethical guidelines to navigate these challenges effectively.

6.1 Privacy Concerns Related to the Use of AI in Language Learning

Privacy is one of the foremost ethical issues surrounding the use of AI in education. Language learning platforms that incorporate AI often collect vast amounts of personal data from students to tailor learning experiences. This data can include sensitive information such as learners' identities, locations, learning habits, and performance metrics. The potential for misuse or unauthorized access to this data poses significant risks. For instance, if language learning applications were to experience data breaches, personal information could be exposed, leading to detrimental consequences for learners.

Moreover, the issue of informed consent is paramount. Students, especially younger learners, may not fully understand the implications of data collection practices associated with AI tools. Educational institutions must ensure that they obtain informed consent in a transparent manner, clearly explaining how data will be collected, used, and protected. Furthermore, there should be a strong emphasis on developing AI systems that prioritize user privacy by design, minimizing data collection to only what is necessary for educational purposes.

6.2 Data Security: Protecting Student Information in AI-Driven Platforms

The security of student information in AI-driven platforms is another critical ethical consideration. Given the increasing reliance on digital tools for language learning, ensuring robust cybersecurity measures is essential to protect sensitive data. This includes implementing encryption protocols, secure user authentication methods, and regular security audits to identify vulnerabilities in AI systems.

Educational institutions must adopt a proactive approach to data security. They should establish policies that mandate the use of secure data management practices and foster a culture of cybersecurity awareness among educators and students alike. Additionally, collaboration with technology providers is vital to ensure that the AI tools being utilized comply with established data protection regulations, such as the General Data Protection Regulation (GDPR) in Europe or similar frameworks in other regions.

6.3 Bias in AI Algorithms: How It Affects Language Learning Outcomes

The potential for bias in AI algorithms is a pressing ethical concern that can significantly impact language learning outcomes. AI systems learn from vast datasets, and if these datasets are unrepresentative or reflect existing social biases, the resulting algorithms may perpetuate these biases in educational contexts. For instance, language learning applications that rely on datasets primarily featuring Standard English may not adequately serve speakers of regional dialects or non-native speakers, thereby disadvantaging certain groups of learners.

Bias can manifest in various forms, including linguistic, cultural, and socioeconomic biases. Students from marginalized communities may find themselves facing additional barriers if AI tools fail to recognize their linguistic diversity or reinforce negative stereotypes. This raises the question of equity in AI-driven language education; biased AI systems can lead to unequal access to learning opportunities, undermining the foundational principles of fairness and inclusivity in education.

To mitigate these risks, it is crucial for educational institutions to conduct thorough bias assessments of the AI tools they adopt. This includes ensuring that the datasets used to train AI algorithms are diverse and representative of the populations they serve. Institutions should actively seek to involve stakeholders from different linguistic and cultural backgrounds in the development and evaluation of AI tools to ensure that diverse perspectives are considered and integrated into AI systems.

6.4 Ethical Guidelines for AI Integration in the Language Curriculum

To address the ethical challenges associated with AI in language education, the establishment of comprehensive ethical guidelines is essential. These guidelines should encompass various aspects, including data privacy, security, and bias mitigation, and should serve as a framework for the responsible integration of AI into language curricula.

- **Data Privacy and Informed Consent:** Educational institutions should develop policies that prioritize student privacy, ensuring that data collection practices are transparent and that informed consent is obtained from all users. This includes clear communication about how data will be used and who will have access to it.
- **Data Security Measures:** Institutions must implement robust security protocols to protect student data from breaches. This includes adopting industry-standard cybersecurity practices, conducting regular audits, and providing training to staff on data security.
- **Bias Detection and Mitigation:** Educational institutions should conduct regular audits of AI algorithms to detect and address potential biases. This includes using diverse datasets for training and involving a wide range of stakeholders in the evaluation of AI tools.
- **Ongoing Professional Development:** Educators should receive training on the ethical implications of AI in education. This includes understanding how to critically evaluate AI tools for potential biases and data privacy issues.
- **Stakeholder Involvement:** Institutions should engage students, parents, and community members in discussions about AI integration in language education, ensuring that a variety of perspectives are considered in decision-making processes.

7. DIGITAL LITERACY: PREPARING STUDENTS AND EDUCATORS FOR AI-INTEGRATED LEARNING

As artificial intelligence (AI) technologies become increasingly embedded in educational frameworks, the necessity for robust digital literacy skills emerges as a critical component of the modern learning experience. Digital literacy in the context of AI-enhanced language learning not only empowers students to use AI tools effectively but also prepares educators to guide their integration into the classroom. This chapter section discusses the imperative of developing digital literacy skills, focusing on responsible AI tool use, enhancing educators' competencies, and promoting critical thinking and ethical considerations in technology utilization.

7.1 The Importance of Digital Literacy in the AI-Driven Language Curriculum

Digital literacy encompasses a broad range of skills necessary for navigating, evaluating, and creating information using digital technologies. In an AI-driven language curriculum, these skills become paramount. Language learning is increasingly reliant on various AI applications, from personalized tutoring systems to automated writing assistants. To harness the potential of these technologies, students must develop digital literacy skills that enable them to engage with AI tools critically and effectively.

Students need to understand how AI technologies operate, including the algorithms that power language processing and the data on which these systems are trained. This knowledge empowers learners to discern between reliable and unreliable sources of information and fosters a deeper comprehension of language nuances and contexts. Furthermore, as students interact with AI tools, they will encounter the limitations inherent in these technologies—such as biases embedded in algorithms and the potential for misinformation. An informed approach to AI usage enhances students' learning experiences while minimizing risks associated with misinformation and cognitive overload.

7.2 Preparing Students to Use AI Tools Responsibly and Effectively

As AI becomes a central element of language education, preparing students to use these tools responsibly is crucial. Digital literacy education should encompass practical training on how to effectively utilize AI-driven language learning applications while fostering an understanding of their ethical implications. For example, students should be taught to evaluate the accuracy and reliability of AI-generated content, encouraging them to approach AI outputs with a critical mindset.

Additionally, promoting responsible AI usage involves instilling a sense of digital citizenship. Students must learn the importance of respectful and ethical behavior in online environments, including the appropriate use of AI tools in academic contexts. This includes avoiding plagiarism and recognizing the value of original thought, ensuring that AI serves as a supportive resource rather than a crutch.

Moreover, awareness of privacy and data security issues is essential. Students should understand how their interactions with AI tools may involve data collection and what implications this has for their personal information. By fostering a culture of responsibility, educators can guide students in leveraging AI tools while navigating potential ethical dilemmas.

7.3 Enhancing Educators' Digital Literacy to Better Integrate AI into Teaching Practices

For effective AI integration in the language curriculum, educators themselves must also enhance their digital literacy. Teacher preparation programs should include comprehensive training on AI technologies relevant to language education. This training should encompass both theoretical knowledge and practical application, enabling educators to design lessons that incorporate AI tools thoughtfully and effectively.

Educators need to become proficient in evaluating AI applications critically, understanding their strengths and limitations. By engaging in continuous professional development focused on digital literacy and AI advancements, teachers can stay abreast of emerging tools and techniques. This ongoing learning is essential for cultivating a learning environment where both educators and students can thrive in an AI-integrated landscape.

Additionally, fostering a collaborative learning culture among educators can enhance the integration of AI tools. Teachers can share best practices, strategies for implementation, and lessons learned from their experiences with AI technologies. This collaborative approach not only promotes digital literacy among educators but also encourages innovation in teaching methods.

7.4 Promoting Critical Thinking and Ethical Considerations in the Use of AI Technologies

Critical thinking is an essential skill that must be emphasized in conjunction with digital literacy when integrating AI into language learning. Students should be encouraged to analyze the content generated by AI tools critically. This involves questioning the accuracy, relevance, and potential biases of AI outputs, fostering a culture of inquiry that extends beyond passive consumption of information.

Promoting ethical considerations in AI usage is equally important. Educators must guide students in reflecting on the implications of AI technologies, including the ethical dilemmas they may encounter. Discussions surrounding topics such as data privacy, algorithmic bias, and the potential impact of AI on language diversity can enhance students' understanding of the broader social and ethical dimensions of technology use.

Furthermore, integrating project-based learning that requires students to explore real-world issues related to AI and language education can foster critical thinking and ethical reasoning. For example, students might investigate the implications of AI-driven language translation tools on cultural understanding and communication. Such projects empower students to apply their digital literacy skills in meaningful ways while developing a nuanced understanding of the intersection between AI technology and language learning.

8. RECOMMENDATIONS AND FUTURE DIRECTIONS

The integration of Artificial Intelligence (AI) into language education presents both opportunities and challenges. To harness the potential of AI while addressing the barriers identified throughout this chapter, several recommendations and future directions should be considered. This section will explore policy recommendations, the potential of AI in promoting multilingual education, the importance of collaborative research, and the opportunities and challenges that lie ahead.

8.1 Policy Recommendations for Successful AI Integration in the Language Curriculum

To ensure the successful integration of AI in language education, policymakers must establish clear guidelines and frameworks that prioritize effective implementation. First and foremost, educational institutions should develop a comprehensive AI strategy that aligns with the overarching goals of the language curriculum. This strategy should encompass teacher training, curriculum design, and the selection of AI tools that support pedagogical objectives.

Additionally, funding mechanisms should be put in place to support research and development in AI-driven educational technologies. Governments should collaborate with private sector companies to create grants and incentives that encourage innovation in AI for language learning. This collaboration will facilitate the creation of adaptive and contextually relevant AI tools that resonate with diverse learner needs.

Lastly, policymakers must address data privacy concerns by implementing robust regulations that protect student information. Establishing guidelines for data collection, storage, and usage will build trust among educators, students, and parents, fostering a conducive environment for AI adoption in language education.

8.2 The Potential of AI in Promoting Multilingual Education and Preserving Linguistic Diversity

One of the most significant benefits of AI integration in language education is its potential to support multilingual education and preserve linguistic diversity. AI tools can facilitate language learning in multilingual contexts, providing personalized experiences that cater to individual learners' needs. For instance, AI-powered language applications can offer tailored feedback and exercises based on learners' proficiency levels, enabling them to progress at their own pace.

Moreover, AI can play a crucial role in the preservation of endangered languages. By utilizing Natural Language Processing (NLP) technologies, developers can create resources that support the documentation and revitalization of minority languages. AI systems can help generate language learning materials, such as textbooks and interactive exercises, which are essential for teaching endangered languages.

In this context, it is crucial to foster partnerships between AI developers, linguists, and cultural organizations to create tools that are not only effective but also culturally sensitive. These partnerships will ensure that AI applications reflect the nuances of diverse languages and cultures, thus promoting linguistic diversity and inclusion.

8.3 The Role of Collaborative Research Between Educators, AI Developers, and Policymakers

To address the challenges of integrating AI into language education effectively, collaborative research among educators, AI developers, and policymakers is essential. Such collaboration can facilitate the development of AI tools that are both pedagogically sound and technologically advanced. Educators can provide valuable insights into the practical needs of language learners and the intricacies of language instruction, while AI developers can leverage their expertise to create tools that enhance learning experiences.

Establishing research consortia that bring together stakeholders from various fields will promote knowledge sharing and innovation. These consortia can focus on identifying best practices, evaluating AI tools' effectiveness, and addressing potential biases in AI algorithms. By fostering an interdisciplinary approach, stakeholders can collaboratively tackle the complex challenges associated with AI integration in language curricula.

Additionally, this collaborative research should prioritize inclusivity, ensuring that marginalized voices, including those of minority language speakers, are represented. This approach will help create AI tools that are sensitive to the linguistic and cultural diversity of learners.

8.4 The Future of AI in Language Education: Opportunities and Challenges Ahead

As AI technologies continue to advance, their potential applications in language education will expand. Future AI tools could utilize more sophisticated machine learning algorithms that better understand context, sentiment, and cultural nuances, providing learners with a more immersive and relevant language learning experience. For instance, AI-driven language platforms could simulate real-life conversations, enabling learners to practice language skills in authentic contexts.

However, several challenges will need to be addressed as we move forward. Ethical concerns surrounding data privacy, bias in AI algorithms, and the risk of replacing human educators must be taken seriously. Continuous monitoring and evaluation of AI tools will be essential to ensure that they serve as a complement to traditional teaching methods rather than a replacement.

Moreover, as AI systems become increasingly capable of understanding language and context, there is a pressing need to develop frameworks that guide their ethical use in educational settings. Ensuring that AI supports rather than undermines human interaction in the learning process will be vital for maintaining the social and emotional aspects of language education.

9. CONCLUSION

The integration of Artificial Intelligence (AI) into the language curriculum presents both significant opportunities and formidable challenges. On the one hand, AI has the potential to revolutionize language learning by offering personalized instruction tailored to individual learners' needs, enhancing accessibility for diverse populations, and automating repetitive tasks that often hinder effective learning. These benefits can facilitate a more engaging and efficient language acquisition process, fostering motivation and retention.

On the other hand, the implementation of AI in education is fraught with pedagogical, technological, and ethical challenges. Pedagogically, there is the risk of undermining the essential human elements of teaching, such as empathy, cultural sensitivity, and social interaction. Technologically, disparities in access to AI tools can exacerbate existing inequalities in education. Ethically, concerns around data

REFERENCES

Almalki, M., & Aziz, M. A. (2022). The Role of Artificial Intelligence in Language Learning: An Overview. *Journal of Language and Linguistic Studies, 18*(1), 122–137.

Anderson, T., & Dron, J. (2011). Human Behavior in a Social Learning Environment. In T. Anderson (Ed.), The Theory and Practice of Online Learning (pp. 95-128). Athabasca University Press.

Baker, R. S. J. D., & Inventado, P. S. (2014). Educational Data Mining and Learning Analytics. In J. A. D. (Ed.), Handbook of Learning Analytics (pp. 101-112). Society for Learning Analytics Research.

Bennett, S., & Maton, K. (2010). Beyond the 'Digital Natives' Debate: Towards a More Nuanced Understanding of Students' Technology Experiences. *Journal of Computer Assisted Learning*, *26*(5), 321–331.

Blair, C., & Hargreaves, E. (2018). The Role of AI in Language Education: A Guide for Educators. *International Journal of Information and Education Technology (IJIET)*, *8*(7), 564–569.

Chalmers, C., & Harris, K. (2017). Machine Learning and Natural Language Processing in Education. *International Journal of Artificial Intelligence in Education*, *27*(4), 703–710.

Chukharev-Hudilainen, E., & Klepikova, T. A. (2016). Automated writing evaluation for formative assessment of second language writing: Investigating the accuracy and usefulness of feedback. *Language Testing*, *33*(3), 307–328.

Dede, C. (2011). Comparing Frameworks for 21st Century Skills. In J. A. Bellanca & R. A. Brandt (Eds.), 21st Century Skills: Rethinking How Students Learn (pp. 51-76). Solution Tree Press.

Huang, R. H., & Spector, J. M. (2018). Educational Technology and the Challenge of Change. *Educational Technology Research and Development*, *66*(4), 973–986.

Kumar, V., & Rose, C. P. (2011). Language learning with technology: Trends, perspectives, and challenges. *AI & Society*, *26*(4), 339–351.

Luckin, R. (2017). Towards artificial intelligence-based assessment systems. *Nature Human Behaviour*, *1*(3), 1–3.

Luckin, R., & Holmes, W. (2016). *Intelligence Unleashed: An Argument for AI in Education*. Pearson.

Miao, Y., & Zhang, Z. (2020). The Application of Artificial Intelligence in Language Learning: Challenges and Opportunities. *Computer Assisted Language Learning, 33*(5), 503–519.

O'Neil, C. (2016). *Weapons of Math Destruction: How Big Data Increases Inequality and Threatens Democracy*. Crown Publishing Group.

Prinsloo, P., & Slade, S. (2017). An ethical framework for learning analytics. *British Journal of Educational Technology*, *48*(1), 160–172.

Rashid, T., & Asghar, H. M. (2016). Technology Adoption and Digital Divide: The Case of Higher Education Institutions in Pakistan. *International Journal of Educational Management, 30*(2), 275–289.

Selwyn, N. (2016). *Education and Technology: Key Issues and Debates*. Bloomsbury Publishing.

Selwyn, N. (2019). Should robots replace teachers? AI and the future of education. *Learning, Media and Technology*, *44*(2), 77–91.

Stanford University. (2018). Ethics of Artificial Intelligence and Robotics. Stanford Encyclopedia of Philosophy. Retrieved from https://plato.stanford.edu/entries/ethics-ai/

Warschauer, M., & Grimes, D. (2007). Automated writing evaluation and its impact on student writing. *Journal of Second Language Writing*, *16*(4), 191–209.

Zawacki-Richter, O., Marín, V. I., Bond, M., & Gouverneur, F. (2019). Systematic review of research on artificial intelligence applications in higher education. *International Journal of Educational Technology in Higher Education*, *16*(1), 39.

ADDITIONAL READING

Bender, E. M., & Gebru, T. (2020). "On the Dangers of Stochastic Parrots: Can Language Models Be Too Big?" *Proceedings of the ACM Conference on Fairness, Accountability, and Transparency*, 12(1), 20-35.

Kukulska-Hulme, A. (2020). Mobile AI for Language Learning: Bridging the Pedagogical Gap. *Educational Technology Review*, *22*(4), 112–130.

Nguyen, D., & Meurers, D. (2022). Natural Language Processing for Language Education: Current Trends and Future Directions. *Computational Linguistics Journal, 48*(1), 85–103.

Pérez, M., & Murray, J. (2021). AI in Language Education: Opportunities and Challenges. *Journal of Applied Linguistics*, *38*(2), 45–62.

Schmidt, P., & Maier, K. (2021). AI and Speech Recognition in Language Learning: Technical Barriers and Solutions. *Journal of AI in Education*, *30*(3), 215–234.

Siddiqui, S., & Jain, R. (2022). AI Ethics in Education: Privacy, Data Security, and Bias. *International Journal of AI Ethics*, *6*(2), 98–120.

KEY TERMS AND DEFINITIONS

Artificial Intelligence (AI): AI refers to the simulation of human intelligence in machines, enabling them to perform tasks such as problem-solving, speech recognition, and learning from data. In education, AI enhances language learning through automated feedback, adaptive learning systems, and natural language processing (NLP).

Language Curriculum: A structured framework that outlines the objectives, content, teaching methodologies, and assessment strategies for language instruction. It includes grammar, vocabulary, communication skills, and cultural contexts in language education.

Pedagogical Barriers: Challenges related to teaching methods and instructional design, such as the lack of AI-integrated teaching strategies, resistance to adopting AI-based learning tools, and the need for teacher training in AI applications for language instruction.

Technological Barriers: Issues arising from infrastructure limitations, digital literacy gaps, and accessibility constraints that hinder the integration of AI tools in language education. These include unreliable internet connectivity, lack of AI-enabled devices, and insufficient institutional support for AI adoption.

Ethical Barriers: Concerns related to bias in AI algorithms, data privacy, academic integrity, and the ethical implications of AI replacing human educators. Ensuring AI tools align with ethical teaching practices and safeguard students' rights is crucial in language curriculum integration.

Natural Language Processing (NLP): A subfield of AI that enables computers to understand, interpret, and generate human language. NLP applications in language learning include AI-powered chatbots, speech recognition, and automated essay grading.

Adaptive Learning Systems: AI-driven platforms that personalize language instruction based on individual student performance, offering real-time feedback and customized learning paths to enhance engagement and proficiency.

Automated Assessment: AI-based evaluation tools that provide instant feedback on writing, speaking, and comprehension skills in language learning. While improving efficiency, automated assessment faces challenges related to contextual understanding and subjectivity in language evaluation.

Teacher AI Readiness: The ability of educators to effectively integrate AI tools into language teaching, including technical skills, pedagogical adaptation, and willingness to embrace AI-enhanced methodologies.

Data Privacy in AI: The protection of students' personal and learning data when using AI-powered language learning platforms. Ethical concerns arise from data collection, algorithmic transparency, and potential misuse of student information.

Human-AI Collaboration in Education: The complementary role of AI in assisting educators rather than replacing them, ensuring that AI supports personalized learning while teachers provide critical thinking, emotional intelligence, and contextual insights in language instruction.

Chapter 9
A Comprehensive Survey on Text Mining From Theory to Practice

Danial Zare
https://orcid.org/0009-0009-8190-328X
University of Alcala, Alcala de Henares, Spain

Luis Fernandez-Sanz
https://orcid.org/0000-0003-0778-0073
University of Alcala, Alcala de Henares, Spain

Vera Pospelova
https://orcid.org/0000-0001-5801-1923
University of Alcala, Alcala de Henares, Spain

Ines López-Baldominos
https://orcid.org/0000-0001-8345-5243
University of Alcala, Alcala de Henares, Spain

ABSTRACT

Text mining refers to the process of extracting useful information from large volumes of unstructured text data. This paper presents a comprehensive survey of text mining, covering foundational theories and practical applications across various domains within the field of Natural Language Processing (NLP). The study begins by examining the core challenges and historical development of text mining, providing context through an exploration of major areas where text mining techniques have significantly evolved. We offer an in-depth, step-by-step analysis of key algorithms in the text mining pipeline, beginning with data collection and preprocessing, moving through feature generation and selection, and highlighting their roles in transforming

DOI: 10.4018/979-8-3693-9606-3.ch009

raw text into valuable insights. This survey serves as a guide for researchers and practitioners by detailing methodological approaches and considerations at each stage of the text mining process. Additionally, Pseudocode and Python implementations of algorithms are provided, facilitating the application of these methods in real-world scenarios.

INTRODUCTION

In the digital age, vast amounts of unstructured data are generated daily, with text being one of the most prevalent forms. From social media posts and news articles to scientific journals and customer feedback, the potential insights contained within textual data are immense. However, extracting meaningful information from such a massive volume of raw text presents significant challenges. This is where text mining becomes crucial. Text mining, widely used in knowledge- based organizations, is the process of examining large sets of documents to discover new information or help answer specific research questions. identifies remaining facts, relationships, and assertions. Once extracted, this information is converted into a structured form that can be further analyzed or presented directly using clustered HTML tables, mind maps, charts, etc. (Abdusalomovna et al., 2023).

Text is the most widely used means of communication today (Ly et al., 2020). By leveraging advanced computational techniques, text mining allows organizations and researchers to turn unstructured data into valuable knowledge, providing a foundation for informed decision-making, predictive analysis, and data-driven innovation. Most of the time, text is analyzed by a human who can read the text and transform it into structured information. It can take a lot of time when it comes to analyzing thousands of sentences. In fact, NLP is a tract of Artificial Intelligence and Linguistics, devoted to make computers understand the statements or words written in human languages. It came into existence to ease the user's work and to satisfy the wish to communicate with the computer in natural language, and can be classified into two parts i.e. Natural Language Understanding or Linguistics and Natural Language Generation which evolves the task to understand and generate the text (Khurana et al., 2023).

Text mining and NLP have rapidly gained traction in both academia and industry, making them some of the most dynamic and intriguing fields in artificial intelligence. The allure of these areas lies in their ability to make sense of the vast amounts of unstructured text data generated daily, from social media posts and blogs to research papers and customer feedback. As these fields evolve, the demand for more sophisticated tools to analyze and understand human language grows, resulting in significant advancements in machine learning models, deep learning, and computational linguistics. The increasing interest in NLP and text mining is also evident in search trends, with data from Google Trends illustrating a consistent rise in searches for related topics over the years. As shown in Figure 1, the popularity of NLP techniques over the past 5 years (from 2019 to 2024) has steadily increased, reflecting a global surge in both academic research and commercial applications.

Figure 1. Popularity of NLP techniques over the past 5 years, based on number searches in Google

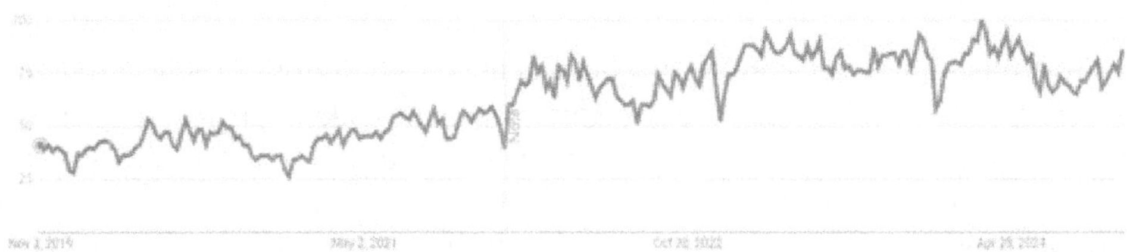

Figure 2, coming from Scopus[1] website illustrates the number of documents published from 2000 to 2024 (the time of writing this paper) containing the term text mining. As it is obvious, the subject of text mining, has been significantly attracted by researchers with a sharp rise in the past ten years.

Figure 2. Number of documents containing term "text mining" published from 2000 to 2024

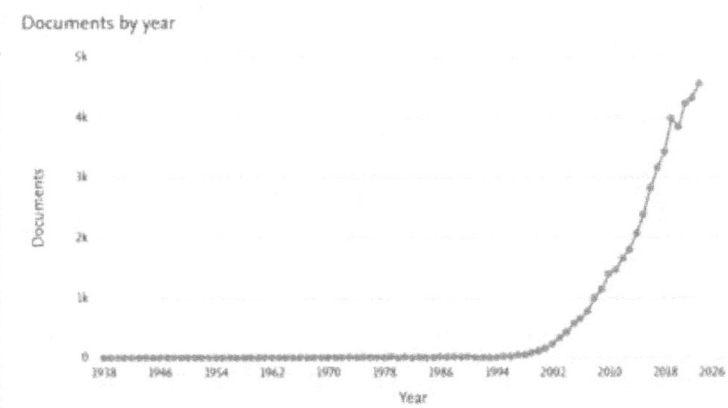

Year	Documents
2023	4563
2022	4324
2021	4237
2020	3828
2019	3982
2018	3413
2017	3353
2016	2824
2015	2380

Therefore, text mining is crucial in extracting valuable insights from vast amounts of unstructured text data. By leveraging natural language processing and machine learning techniques, text mining helps identify patterns, trends, and relationships within textual information. It is widely used in various fields, including business intelligence, healthcare, and social media analysis, enabling organizations to make data-driven decisions. From sentiment analysis to document classification, text mining enhances automation, improves efficiency, and unlocks hidden knowledge, making it an essential tool in the digital age.

1.1 Text mining process

Text mining process starts with a document collection from various resources. Text mining tool would retrieve a particular document and pre-process it by checking format and character sets. Then document would go through a text analysis phase. Text analysis is semantic analysis to derive high quality information from text. Many text analysis techniques are available; depending on goal of organization combinations of techniques could be used. Sometimes text analysis techniques are repeated until information is extracted. The resulting information can be placed in a management information system, yielding an abundant amount of knowledge for the user of that system (VijayGaikwad et al., 2014). Figure 3 simply illustrates the general process of text mining and discovery of knowledge.

Figure 3. Text mining process (VijayGaikwad et al., 2014)

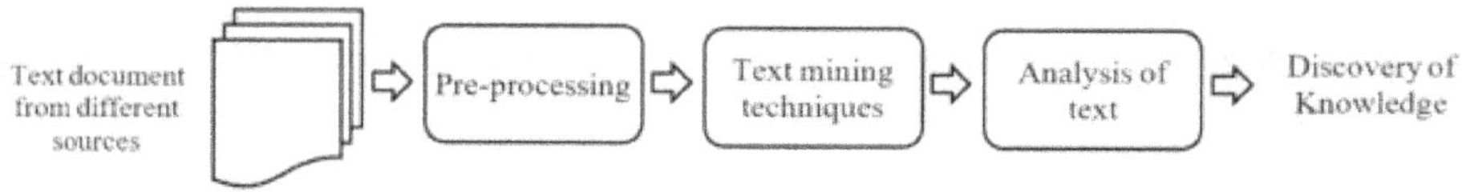

1.2 Text mining methods and models

Traditionally there are so many techniques developed to solve the problem of text mining that is nothing but the relevant information retrieval according to user's requirement. According to the information retrieval basically there are four methods Term Based Method (TBM), Phrase Based Method (PBM), Concept Based Method (CBM) and Pattern Taxonomy Method (PTM) (VijayGaikwad et al., 2014). The **Term-Based Method (TBM)** is one of the simplest and most widely used techniques in text mining. This method relies on individual terms (usually words) as the primary units for extracting meaning and identifying patterns within a text.

Common techniques within this method include term frequency analysis, TF-IDF (Term Frequency-Inverse Document Frequency), and word co-occurrence analysis. Term-based methods often use statistical models to measure the significance of each term based on its frequency and position within a document or corpus. The **Phrase-Based Method (PBM)** extends the term-based approach by analysing phrases instead of individual terms. By focusing on multi-word sequences, or "*n-grams*" (we will discuss *n-grams* more in section 3.3.1 part 3), this method captures additional contextual information, which can be critical for understanding nuanced or idiomatic language. For example, the phrase "*climate change*" has a distinct meaning that differs from the individual words "*climate*" and "*change*". Phrase-based methods identify frequently occurring phrases within a text and measure their importance based on frequency, position, and relevance.

The **Concept-Based Method (CBM)** goes beyond the word and phrase level by analysing the underlying concepts and semantics within a text. This method uses knowledge-based techniques and semantic analysis to understand the meaning behind terms and phrases, focusing on the ideas they represent rather than their literal expressions. For instance, in analysing scientific articles, a concept-based approach would recognize that "*global warming*" and "*climate change*" refer to similar phenomena, even though the terms differ. Finally, the **Pattern Taxonomy Method (PTM)** is a more advanced approach that identifies patterns within a text and organizes them into a hierarchical structure, or taxonomy. Rather than focusing solely on terms or phrases, this method finds frequent patterns or sequences of text, which may include keywords, phrases, or entities, and categorizes them according to their relationships. Pattern taxonomy models often employ data mining techniques like association rule mining or sequence mining to discover these patterns. A major advantage of the pattern taxonomy approach is its ability to handle complex, context-dependent relationships between terms. By structuring patterns hierarchically, this method provides a multi-level view of information within a text corpus, making it especially useful for large-scale information retrieval and categorization in fields like e-commerce, biology, and customer service.

1.3 Text mining steps

Text mining is a powerful tool that turns unstructured textual data into actionable insights. By combining techniques from NLP, machine learning, and data mining, organizations can uncover patterns, sentiments, and trends hidden within vast amounts of text data. The text mining steps - from data gathering and preprocessing to visualization - enable businesses to make data-driven decisions, improve customer experiences, and enhance operational efficiency. Figure 4 illustrates main steps in text mining process all of which are explained in the following sections onwards. The details of each step will be explained from Section 3 onwards.

Figure 4. Text mining steps

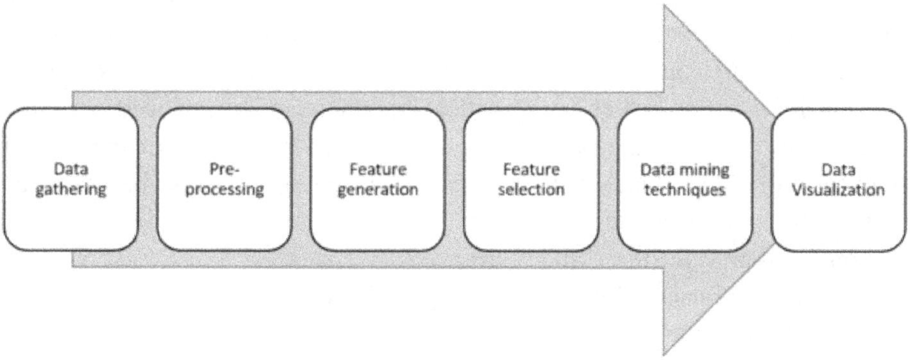

1.4 Objectives

In recent years, text mining has emerged as a pivotal tool in data analysis, enabling the extraction of meaningful insights from unstructured textual data. Despite the proliferation of research in this domain, existing surveys (e.g. (Bijalwan et al., 2014), (Alghamdi & Alfalqi, 2015), (VijayGaikwad et al., 2014), (S. S. Tandel et al., 2019), (Abdusalomovna et al., 2023), (Hotho et al., 2005), (Tabassum & Patil, 2020)) often lacks comprehensive, step-by-step guidance that bridges theoretical concepts with practical implementation. Many surveys provide overviews of algorithms without delving into detailed explanations or offering practical coding examples, leaving practitioners without a clear roadmap for application. Our objectives for writing this paper stems from a desire to fill a gap in the existing literature and provide a truly holistic resource for the field of text mining. This limited scope can leave researchers, practitioners, and newcomers without a clear, in-depth roadmap to effectively understand and apply text mining methods in real-world scenarios.

In response, this contribution aims to go beyond a high-level overview. We strive to explain text mining techniques in a clear, step-by-step manner that not only explores their theoretical underpinnings but also provides practical guidance through Pseudocode and Python code examples which are available in www.zenodo.org repository. By blending theory with hands-on implementation, we hope to bridge the gap between academic knowledge and applied skills, making these techniques accessible to a wider audience. Our survey is designed to cover most of the key concepts within text mining, making it a robust and comprehensive reference for practitioners, researchers, and newcomers alike.

The remaining manuscript is structured as follows: in section 2, we will discuss the previous background of text mining. Section 3 describes different types of data and data collection methods. In section 4, we will explain the most common pre-processing techniques. Feature generation approaches are discussed in section 5 and subsequently, in section 5, we will explain feature selection methods. In each step, we will describe preliminaries and commonly used methods. And finally, in section 6, we conclude by identifying potential challenges and future directions for the development of text mining from both managerial and technological perspectives.

2. LITERATURE REVIEW

Text mining has evolved significantly over the past few decades as researchers have developed diverse techniques such as Information Extraction, Text Classification and Categorization, Clustering and Topic Modelling, Sentiment Analysis and Opinion Mining, Text Summarization and Information Retrieval to extract valuable insights from unstructured text data. Early studies in text mining, often referred to as "text data mining," were rooted in information retrieval and natural language processing (NLP), where the primary focus was on extracting terms and matching text documents to queries based on keywords.

Text mining and NLP encompass a wide range of techniques aimed at extracting meaningful information from unstructured textual data. From identifying entities and relationships in text to classifying documents by topic or sentiment, these methods enable the analysis of large volumes of textual information across various domains. To go deeply through this field, it is recommended to consider different areas of text mining and NLP. The following areas in NLP form the foundation of modern text mining, transforming raw text into structured, actionable insights that support decision-making, automate customer service, enhance search functionality, and more. Then, we will give a summary of previous works in each area separately.

2.1 Information Extraction

Information extraction (IE) is one of the foundational tasks in text mining, focusing on identifying structured data from unstructured text. The goal of information extraction (IE) is to make the text's semantic structure explicit so that we can make use of it. More precisely, IE is the process of analyzing text and identifying mentions of semantically defined entities and relationships within it. These relationships can then be recorded in a database to search for particular relationships or to infer additional information from the explicitly stated facts (Grishman, 2015). Information Extraction (IE) is a long-standing research topic that aims to extract structured factual information from unstructured texts (Andersen et al., 1992), (Crowe, 1995), (Chieu et al., 2003), (Wu & Weld, 2010), (Khot et al., 2017), (Lu et al., 2022). Typically, IE involves a wide range of tasks, such as named entity recognition (NER) (Žukov-Gregorič et al., 2018), (Martins et al., 2019), (X. Li, Feng, et al., 2019), (Das et al., 2021), entity typing (ET) (Choi et al., 2018), (Dai et al., 2021), (K. Pang et al., 2022), (Chen et al., 2022), relation extraction (RE) (X. Li, Yin, et al., 2019), (Fu et al., 2019), (Bian et al., 2024), (D. Ye et al., 2022), relation classification (RC) (Zeng et al., 2015), (W. Ye et al., 2019), (W. Zhou & Chen, 2021), (B. Li et al., 2022), event detection (ED) (Pouran Ben Veyseh et al., 2021), (Lou et al., 2021), (J. Liu et al., 2022), (Zhao et al., 2022), event argument extraction (EAE) (Zhang et al., 2022), (Du & Ji, 2022), (Ma et al., 2022) and event extraction (EE) (Wadden et al., 2019), (Du & Cardie, 2020), (X. Liu et al., 2022), (Hsu et al., 2022) among others. These tasks automatically generate structured factual outputs related to entities, relations and events, and greatly boost the development of NLP community (B. Li et al., 2023).

2.2 Text Classification and Categorization

Text classification is an application of supervised machine learning (SML) used to categorize texts into pre-determined classes, in contrast to unsupervised approaches such as topic modeling, which are used to inductively summarize and group texts (Evans & Aceves, 2016), (Nelson, 2020) and (Molina & Garip, 2019). Text classification is widely used in computer science for tasks such as sentiment analysis (B. Pang & Lee, 2008), spam filtering (Méndez et al., 2006), and hate speech detection (Davidson et al., 2017). Over the past decade, the technique has been adopted by sociologists for a variety of tasks, including the analysis of protest discussion on Twitter (Hanna, 2013), coverage of Large Language Models (LLMs) for text classification inequality in newspaper articles (Nelson et al., 2021), and rhetoric in political speeches (Bonikowski et al., 2022).

Text classification specifically focuses on categorizing and organizing text data to facilitate easier management and analysis (Taha et al., 2024). These techniques leverage natural language processing, machine learning, and data mining to extract meaningful patterns and categorize text data, thereby transforming unstructured text into structured, actionable insights (S. S. Tandel et al., 2019).

Dhar et al. (Dhar et al., 2021) categorized the existing methods into three basic fields: conventional methods, fuzzy logic-based methods, deep learning-based methods. Further, conventional methods have been categorized into three fields: text categorization using handcrafted features, text categorization using nature-inspired algorithms and text categorization using graph-based methods (Figure 5).

The works for categorization of English text documents have received huge recognition across the fields. To name a few, during the '90s, Joachims (Joachims, 1998) introduced the concept of a linear Support Vector Machine (SVM) along with TF-IDF for categorization of text documents. Term-gram, K-Nearest Neighbor (KNN) and Naïve Bayes (NB) have been used in the work of Bijalwan et al. (Bijalwan et al., 2014). In another research, Vinoth et al. (Vinoth et al., 2014) experimented with Reuters and WebKB databases involving 7670 text documents from 8 text domains. The databases were partitioned into 5483 documents and 2187 documents for training and testing purposes. DeySarkar et al. (Dey Sarkar et al., 2014) used a clustering-based method on 13 datasets and classified those using naïve bayes.

Figure 5. The hierarchy of algorithms used for text categorization (Dhar et al., 2021)

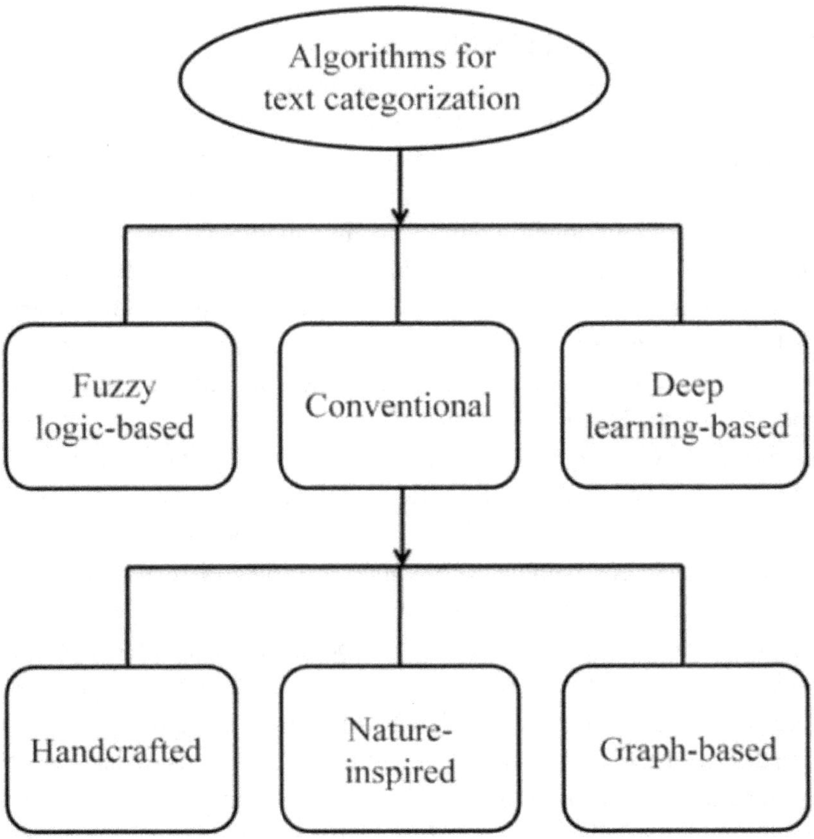

Guru and Suhil (Guru & Suhil, 2015) used Term-Class relevance factor for extracting features along with KNN and SVM for categorizing texts of 20 Newsgroups database. Bag of embeddings model was adopted along with the Stochastic Gradient Descent (SGD) machine learning algorithm in the work of Jin et al. (Kambhampati & Association for the Advancement of Artificial Intelligence, 2016) on 20 Newsgroups and Reuters-21578 text corpora. Two novel feature extraction schemes have been introduced in the work of Wang and Zhang (& , 2013) by involving inverse category frequency (ICF) into term frequency (TF) and for the ICF-based method for text categorization purpose. Dogan and Uysal (Dogan & Uysal, 2019) presented an exhaustive study on the usage of various term frequency component on 7 supervised term-weighting methods among which 6 of the methods were the existing methods and they have derived one from the other. Further information about the history of text classification algorithms could be found in (Dhar et al., 2021).

2.3 Clustering and Topic Modelling

Unlike text classification, which requires predefined labels, clustering and topic modeling are unsupervised learning techniques used to uncover the hidden structure in large collections of text data. The main importance of topic modeling is to discover patterns of word-use and how to connect documents that shared similar patterns. So, the idea of topic models is that term which can be working with documents and these documents are mixtures of topics, where a topic is a probability distribution over words. In other words, topic model is a generative model for documents. It specifies a simple probabilistic procedure by which documents can be generated (Alghamdi & Alfalqi, 2015).

Topic modeling was originally developed in the 1980's and branched off from the subject area of "generative probabilistic modeling" (Vayansky & Kumar, 2020), (L. Liu et al., 2016). This type of modeling assumes that observed variables interact with unobserved, or latent, parameters in a specific probabilistic relationship which then generates the data within a dataset (D. Blei, 2011). The development of these processes arose from the need to briefly describe elements within increasing large collections of data without compromising statistical relationships required to complete more straightforward analyses, like classification and summarization (D. M. Blei et al., 2003) The first method developed for this task was called the TF–IDF reduction scheme and was proposed by two researchers in the field of information retrieval, Salton and McGill, in 1983 (Salton, 1983). TF–IDF reduction was succeeded by another dimensionality reduction method developed by Deerwester et al. (Deerwester et al., 1990a) called latent semantic indexing or analysis (LSI/LSA) in 1990. In LSI, the TF–IDF matrix is factorized by singular value decomposition (SVD). The resulting matrices are used to find a linear subspace within the space of original TF–IDF matrix which describes the majority of the variation in the corpus (Deerwester et al., 1990a).

Clustering groups similar documents together, while topic modeling identifies latent topics within the text. Various kind of topic models, such as Latent semantic analysis (LSA), Probabilistic latent semantic analysis (PLSA), Latent Dirichlet allocation (LDA), Correlated topic model (CTM) have successfully improved classification accuracy in the area of discovering topic modeling (Tarapiah et al., 2013). These algorithms are frequently used in topic modeling to find patterns and themes in textual data. This area is particularly useful in applications like summarizing research trends, organizing large document repositories, and exploring customer reviews.

Further information on topic modeling and clustering could be found in surveys such as (Vayansky & Kumar, 2020) and (Albalawi et al., 2020).

2.4 Sentiment Analysis and Opinion Mining

Sentiment analysis is the process of gathering and analyzing people's opinions, thoughts, and impressions regarding various topics, products, subjects, and services (Wankhade et al., 2022). Sentiment analysis, also known as opinion mining, focuses on identifying and extracting subjective information from text, such as opinions, emotions, and attitudes. This area goes beyond mere classification, providing insights into how people feel about products, events, or issues. Sentiment analysis is often used in marketing and customer service to gauge public opinion on products or brands, as well as in political analysis to track public sentiment over time.

Traditionally, sentiment analysis was performed using machine learning algorithms such as support vector machine (SVM), Naive Bayes, Logistic Regression, and Random Forest (Sharma et al., 2024). However, as the scope of sentiment analysis has widened and new gaps have been identified within sentiment analysis classifications, there has been a shift toward utilizing more complex algorithms to address emerging challenges (Salur & Aydin, 2020). Deep learning algorithms, which are part of the machine learning architecture, offer promising solutions to these challenges, with architectures such as convolutional neural networks (CNNs), long short-term memory networks (LSTMs), and recurrent neural networks (RNNs) demonstrating efficacy in handling complex sentiment analysis tasks (Salur & Aydin, 2020).

The main goal of analyzing sentiment is to analyze the reviews and examine the scores of sentiments. This analysis is divided into many levels (Brown, 2013): document level (Yessenalina et al., 2010), sentence level (Farra et al., 2010), word/term level (Engonopoulos et al., 2011) or aspect level (H. Zhou & Song, 2015). The sequence processes are of sentiment analysis evaluation and detection of the sentiment polarity (Khan et al., 2014). A comprehensive survey on sentiment analysis could be found in (Wankhade et al., 2022), (Khan et al., 2014), (Hussein, 2018), (Medhat et al., 2014) and (Sharma et al., 2024).

2.5 Text Summarization

The main objective of a text summarization (or ATS: automatic text summarization) system is to produce a summary that includes the main ideas in the input document in less space (Radev et al., 2002a) and to keep repetition to a minimum (Moratanch & Chitrakala, 2017). Text summarization aims to create concise versions of longer documents by selecting the most relevant information. ATS is one of the most challenging tasks in NLP and AI in general (El-Kassas et al., 2021a). ATS research began as early as 1958 with Luhn's work (Luhn, 1958) that automatically excerpts abstracts of magazine articles and technical papers. ATS poses many challenges to the research community like: 1) identification of the most informative segments in the input text to be included in the generated summary (Radev et al., 2002b), 2) summarization of long single documents such as books, 3) summarization of multi-documents (Hahn & Mani, 2000), 4) evaluation of the computer-generated summary without the need for the human-produced summary to be compared with, and 5) generation of an abstractive summary (Hahn & Mani, 2000) similar to a human-produced summary.

Summarization techniques are divided into three main categories: extractive, abstractive and hybrid. The extractive approach selects the most important sentences from the input text and uses them to generate the summary. The abstractive approach represents the input text in an intermediate form then generates the summary with words and sentences that differ from the original text sentences. The hybrid approach combines both the extractive and abstractive approaches (El-Kassas et al., 2021b).

Many surveys have been recently published about ATS systems and methodologies. Most surveys focus on techniques and methods of extractive summarization like (nazari & Mahdavi, 2018) because the abstractive summarization needs extensive NLP. In (Kirmani et al., 2019), Kirmani et al. define the common statistical features and some extractive methods. In (Kumar & Sharma, 2019), Kumar and Sharma provide a survey about the extractive ATS systems that apply fuzzy logic methods. In (Mosa et al., 2019), Mosa et al. provide a survey on how the swarm intelligence optimization techniques are applied for ATS. They aim to motivate researchers to use swarm intelligence optimization for ATS especially for short text summarization. Suleiman and Awajan (Suleiman & Awajan, 2019) provide a survey about extractive deep-learning-based text summarization. Some surveys focus on abstractive summarization like (Gupta & Gupta, 2019; Lin & Ng, 2019) for different abstractive methods and Tandel et al (J. Tandel et al., 2019) for abstractive neural-network-based methods. Further information is available in El-Kassas et al survey (El-Kassas et al., 2021b).

2.6 Information Retrieval

An information retrieval (IR) system is a software program that stores and manages information on documents, often textual documents but possibly multimedia. The system assists users in finding the information they need (Hiemstra, 2009). The primary objective is to recognize and retrieve information that is associated with the user's request (Hambarde & Proença, 2023). In today's digital landscape, information retrieval systems are crucial for navigating the vast sea of online information. From using search engines such as Google, Bing, and Baidu, to engaging with question-answering or dialogue systems like ChatGPT and Bing Chat, and discovering content via recommendation platforms like Amazon and YouTube, IR technologies are integral to our everyday online experiences (X. Li et al., 2024).

Modern information retrieval aims to provide users with the most relevant information to their queries. This objective is accomplished in two stages: retrieval and ranking. During the retrieval stage, a collection of initial documents which are potentially relevant to the query is retrieved. After the relevance of these documents is reassessed based on their similarity scores, the ranking is adjusted accordingly. This is done by using various algorithms and models like vector space model (Salton et al., 1975a), Boolean model, Latent Semantic Indexing (Deerwester et al., 1990a), Latent Dirichlet Allocation (LDA) (D. M. Blei et al., 2003), and recent techniques such as pre-trained models like BERT (Devlin et al., 2019). Within the second stage, ranking, the main goal is to adjust the ranking of the initially retrieved documents based on the relevance score. The ranking process typically employs different models than those used in the retrieval stage, as the primary focus is improving the results' effectiveness rather than their efficiency. Traditional models such as BM25 (Connelly, 2018) are used as initial retrievers as they prioritize efficiently recalling relevant documents from a massive document pool.

3. DATA GATHERING

In text mining, various types of data can be analyzed to extract meaningful insights. Understanding these types of data helps in choosing the right text mining techniques and tools to extract meaningful insights and make data-driven decisions. Data can be classified into several types based on its characteristics, structure, and the context in which it is used. To categorize data based on nature, it could be classified into two main groups: Qualitative (categorical) and Quantitative (numerical) data. Another way is to categorize the data based on measurement scales. Nominal scale (i.e., country names or blood types), Ordinal scale (i.e., survey scales: "*good*", "*better*", "*best*"), Interval scale (i.e., temperature in Celsius or Fahrenheit) and Ratio scale (i.e., weight, height, age) are a classification of data based on measurement scales. Categorizing data based on structure is often considered more important than other classifications because it directly impacts how data can be stored, processed, analyzed, and used by modern systems, particularly in data management, analytics, and decision-making. Therefore, we will separately explain this type of data in the following sub-sections. Based on the structure of the data, it can be categorized into three main groups: structured data, unstructured data and semi-structured data.

3.1 Structured Data

Structured text data is organized in a predefined, consistent format, making it easy to process and analyze using tools like SQL or spreadsheet software. Its main characteristics—predefined format, queryability, and consistency—facilitate data management and ensure uniformity. Examples include spreadsheet tables and database tables. The benefits of structured text data include easy access to specific information, reduced errors, and support for automation in tasks like validation and reporting. However, it has limitations such as reduced flexibility, challenges in handling complex or interrelated datasets, and scalability issues as data volume increases, which may require advanced tools to manage effectively.

3.2 Unstructured Data

Unstructured data in text mining refers to information without a predefined format or schema, encompassing diverse formats like text documents, social media content, web pages, multimedia transcriptions, and customer reviews. Unlike structured data, it is free-form and rich in contextual and semantic information but is inherently complex and challenging to analyze. Its variability, ambiguity, and the nuances of natural language require sophisticated techniques and advanced tools for processing and extracting meaningful insights. Challenges include handling large volumes of data, managing noise like typos and irrelevant information, and accurately interpreting context and tone, though successful analysis can yield deep and valuable insights.

3.3 Semi-Structured Data

Semi-structured data lies between structured and unstructured data, combining elements of both by having an inherent but flexible structure, such as in formats like JSON, XML, HTML, or emails. It often follows a hierarchical or self-describing structure, with tags or metadata providing context and relationships. This flexibility allows semi-structured data to adapt to changes, handle large and diverse datasets, and be more manageable than fully unstructured data. However, challenges include complex querying, inconsistent data due to flexible schemas, and performance issues as data volume and diversity grow. Despite these challenges, its adaptability and scalability make it ideal for big data applications.

3.4 Textual data collection methods

Text data serves as a rich source of information and insights for data science projects, yet collecting it in a manner that is both efficient and effective can be challenging. With the right strategies and tools, however, we can gather high-quality text data that will enhance your analysis and drive meaningful outcomes. **Web scraping** is one of the primary methods used to collect text data. It involves automatically extracting data from websites using software tools or scripts. Web scraping is ideal for gathering large volumes of public text data, like news articles, product reviews, or forum discussions. Another method for collecting textual data is using **APIs** (Application Programming Interfaces). Many online platforms (e.g., X, Reddit, news sites) offer APIs, which allow developers to pull data directly. This method is useful when the platform provides structured access to data, such as social media posts, news articles, or other user-generated content. Researchers can create **surveys or questionnaires** to gather specific responses in textual form from participants. It is effective for collecting structured text data on a particular topic, like feedback, opinions, or user experiences.

User-generated content (UGC) includes comments, reviews, and posts created by users on various platforms. This method is often used in sentiment analysis and brand monitoring, as well as studying behaviors and opinions. There are also **social media listening tools** that tracks mentions, keywords, or hashtags across social media platforms to collect relevant posts or comments. They are Valuable for real-time monitoring of trends, sentiment analysis, and understanding public opinion. Another source of text data is **publicly available datasets**. Many organizations and research institutions provide datasets containing textual data for free.

Optical character recognition (OCR) software converts scanned documents, images, or PDFs into editable text. Therefore, this method is useful for digitizing printed materials, historical archives, or scanned books and making them accessible for text analysis. **Transcription of audio and video data** is another way of collecting text data. Transcription tools or services can convert spoken content in audio or video files into written text and they are Ideal for analysing interview responses, speeches, or podcasts in text form. And finally, **Manual Data Entry** could be considered as a collecting text data method by manually inputting or transcribing text from hard-copy sources.

4. PRE-PROCESSING

The preprocessing layer in text mining is crucial as it involves transforming raw, unstructured text into a structured format that can be easily processed and analyzed by algorithms. This step ensures that the data is cleaned, standardized, and ready for the extraction of meaningful patterns and insights. Text preprocessing removes noise, irrelevant information, and inconsistencies from the text while normalizing it to a consistent structure. A good survey of pre-processing methods could be found in (Chai, 2023).

Effective pre-processing can significantly improve the performance of downstream tasks such as sentiment analysis, topic modeling, and text classification. The specific techniques and approaches used during preprocessing depend on the type of analysis to be performed and the characteristics of the dataset. In this part, we will explain some common techniques that are used in pre-processing step in real life.

Figure 6. Pre-processing layers at one glance

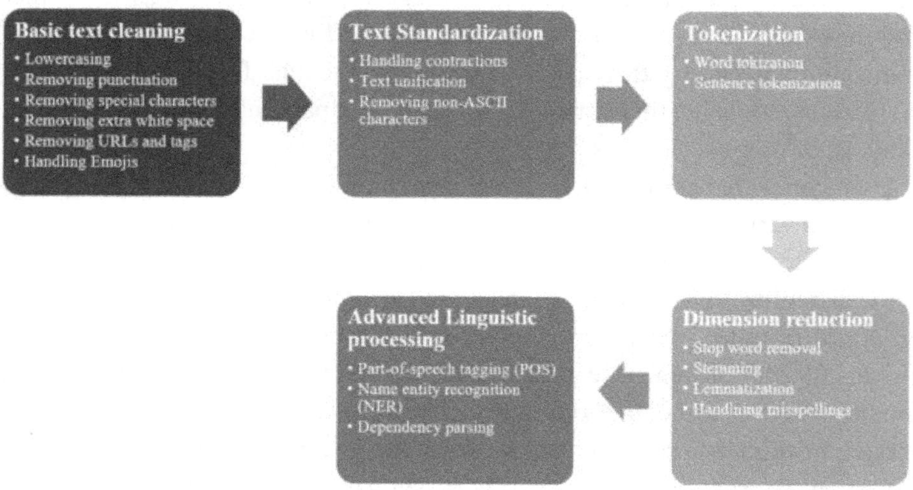

4.1 Basic Text Cleaning

Basic text cleaning is a fundamental step in text preprocessing, aimed at preparing raw text for analysis by removing unnecessary elements and standardizing the data. The primary goal of text cleaning is to ensure that the text is in a consistent and simplified format, making it easier for machine learning models to process and extract meaningful information. Raw text often contains various irregularities, such as special characters, punctuation, or inconsistent formatting, that can introduce noise into the data. By performing basic text cleaning, these issues are addressed early in the pipeline, improving the quality of the text for subsequent stages of analysis.

1. **Lowercasing:** converts text to lowercase for uniformity.
2. **Removing Punctuation:** eliminates punctuation marks that do not convey significant meaning.
3. **Removing Special Characters**: strips out symbols like @, #, &, etc.
4. **Removing Numbers:** deletes numerical data if irrelevant to the task.
5. **Removing Extra Whitespaces**: cleans up multiple or trailing spaces, tabs, or newlines.
6. **Removing URLs and HTML Tags:** strips web addresses and HTML code
7. **Handling Emojis and Emoticons:** removes or converts emojis to textual equivalents.

Many models treat "The" and "the" as different tokens. Lowercasing eliminates this issue by treating them as the same word. The main purpose of the second step is to remove punctuation marks like periods, commas, and question marks. Punctuation typically does not add semantic value for most NLP tasks and can create noise in the data. Subsequently, Special characters may not carry useful meaning and can distract the model. That is why non-alphanumeric characters such as @, #, &, etc are eliminates. The fourth step eliminates numerical digits or sequences from the text. In some contexts, numbers are irrelevant or introduce noise. However, this depends on the use case. Step five gets rid of multiple or trailing whitespaces. Multiple spaces can confuse tokenization and affect the structure of the text. The next step removes hyperlinks, which are usually irrelevant to the core content. URLs typically don't add useful information to text analysis tasks. For example, "<div>Hello, click here: https://example.com</div>" becomes "Hello, click here". And finally, step seven removes or replaces emojis/emoticons with their meaning. Emojis can convey sentiment, but models may not handle them correctly unless they are replaced with meaningful words. As an example, becomes happy.

4.2 Text Standardization

Text standardization is the process of transforming text into a standard and consistent format. The primary goal is to ensure uniformity in the text, which helps reduce the complexity of text data and improve the performance of machine learning and NLP models. It involves several transformations that make the text easier to process by removing or simplifying variations in spelling, format, or structure.

Although researchers consider all the steps in the basic text cleaning layer and the steps in this layer, namely text standardization, to be the same and refer to them as text normalization, we distinguish between these two terms. The second layer converts text into a standardized format, making it easier to process and analyze. Three main steps in this layer are:

1. **Handling Contractions:** expands contractions like “don't” to “do not”.
2. **Text Unification:** unifies text variants.
3. **Removing Non-ASCII Characters:** deletes or normalizes characters that are not part of the standard ASCII set.

Handling contractions involves expanding shortened forms of words (like “don't”, “it's”) into their full versions (“do not”, “it is”). This step is crucial because contractions can introduce ambiguity or inconsistency in the text. Expanding contractions ensures uniformity, improves tokenization, and makes it easier for machine learning models to understand the meaning of the text. For example, “I've” becomes “I have”, which leads to better interpretation and processing of the text. This is particularly important in NLP tasks like sentiment analysis, where nuanced expressions of words can significantly impact model performance. The second step is useful for unifying common abbreviations, symbols, or variants. In fact, it standardizes text by transforming variations into a consistent format. For instance, “U.S.A” becomes “USA” or “ICT” becomes “Information and Communication Technology”.

Removing non-ASCII characters in text preprocessing involves eliminating or converting characters that fall outside the standard ASCII range (which includes common English letters, digits, and basic punctuation). These non-ASCII characters may include accented letters (e.g., “é” in “café”), special symbols, or characters from other languages. This step is important because many NLP models, especially older ones or those designed for English text, may not handle non-ASCII characters well, leading to errors or increased complexity. By removing or replacing them with their ASCII equivalents (e.g., “café” becomes “cafe”), text is standardized, improving model efficiency, and avoiding issues related to encoding mismatches.

4.3 Tokenization

Tokenization simplifies the input data by converting text into manageable and meaningful components that can be processed by algorithms. For example, in word tokenization, the sentence "The cat sat on the mat" would be broken down into ["The", "cat", "sat", "on", "the", "mat"]. This process is fundamental in natural language processing (NLP) tasks like text analysis, machine translation, and sentiment analysis, where it helps structure the data for downstream processes. Two common types of tokenization are:

1. **Word Tokenization:** splits text into individual words.
2. **Sentence Tokenization:** splits text into sentences

This step has a significant impact on the performance of machine learning models. Proper tokenization ensures that relevant patterns and relationships between words are preserved, while incorrect tokenization can lead to loss of information or misinterpretation of the text. It involves splitting a sequence of text into smaller units called tokens. These tokens can be individual words, phrases, or even characters, depending on the specific application. It also affects the size of the vocabulary, which in turn influences memory usage and computational efficiency.

4.4 Stop word Removal

Stop word removal aims at eliminating common words that typically do not contribute much meaning or value in natural language processing (NLP) tasks. Stop words are usually high-frequency words such as "*the*", "*is*", "*in*", "*and*", "*a*", and "*of*". These words appear so frequently in text that they can overshadow more meaningful terms, leading to unnecessary noise in the analysis. By removing stop words, we reduce the dimensionality of the dataset, allowing machine learning models to focus on more informative words that carry significant context or meaning relevant to the task at hand, such as text classification, sentiment analysis, or topic modeling.

The process of removing stop words usually begins by consulting a predefined list of common stop words, which varies depending on the language of the text being processed. Libraries like NLTK (Natural Language Toolkit) or spaCy provide built-in lists for many languages, making it easy to remove these words. For instance, in English text, words like "*the*", "*at*", "*to*", *or* "*on*" are typically removed. However, one challenge with stop word removal is determining the right balance between eliminating irrelevant terms and keeping words that may still hold meaning depending on the context. For example, in some tasks, words like "*not*" or "*very*" may carry important information about sentiment or tone, so they may need to be retained, even though they are commonly categorized as stop words.

Despite its usefulness, stop word removal should be carefully considered for each specific NLP task. In certain cases, stop words can actually provide valuable insights. For instance, in tasks like machine translation or information retrieval, stop words may help maintain sentence structure and coherence. Additionally, if a corpus has very short documents or texts (e.g., social media posts or reviews), removing too many stop words might strip the text of essential context. As a result, it is important to either customize the stop word list based on the task or avoid removing them altogether if they play a crucial role. Ultimately, the decision to remove stop words should be driven by the specific goals of the analysis, the characteristics of the dataset, and the impact on model performance.

4.5 Stemming

Stemming involves reducing words to their base or root form, known as the "*stem*". The goal of stemming is to remove morphological affixes (such as suffixes or prefixes) from words to group together different inflections or variations of a word. For example, the words "*running*", "*runs*", and "*runner*" can all be reduced to the root form "*run*", By simplifying these variations, stemming helps reduce the dimensionality of the text data, allowing models to focus on the core meaning of words rather than their grammatical forms. This process is particularly useful in tasks like information retrieval, search engines, and NLP, where different forms of the same word can clutter the analysis and increase computational complexity.

The most common stemming algorithms include Porter's Stemmer, Snowball Stemmer, and Lancaster Stemmer, each with its own rules for stripping affixes from words. The Porter Stemmer (Porter, 1980), is one of the earliest and most widely used algorithms. It applies a series of rules to iteratively reduce words, ensuring that common inflections like "*-ing*", "*-ed*", and "*-s*" are removed. For instance, "*playing*" is reduced to "*play*" and "*happier*" to "*happi*". However, Porter Stemmer can sometimes produce stems that are not actual dictionary words (e.g., "*happier*" to "*happi*"), and while this approach is computationally efficient, it may result in some loss of meaning. The Snowball Stemmer, also developed by Porter, is an enhanced version of the original and supports multiple languages, making it more versatile for multilingual applications.

One key limitation of stemming is its tendency to be somewhat crude, often resulting in stems that are not actual words. This is because stemming algorithms rely on predefined rules to cut off suffixes, and they do not take into account the full linguistic structure or meaning of words. As a result, some words may be over-stemmed (where too many characters are removed) or under-stemmed (where not enough characters are removed). For example, in over-stemming, both "*university*" and "*universe*" may be reduced to "*universe*", even though they have different meanings. Conversely, under-stemming might result in "*studying*" and "*studies*" being treated as separate stems, even though they are closely related. While stemming is computationally efficient, these errors can sometimes lead to inaccuracies in downstream tasks like text classification or sentiment analysis, where subtle differences in word forms may be important.

4.6 Lemmatization

Lemmatization involves reducing words to their base or canonical form, known as the lemma, while considering the context and linguistic structure. Unlike stemming, which simply chops off word endings, lemmatization is more sophisticated and aims to produce meaningful base forms by considering the grammatical role of the word in a sentence. For example, the word "*better*" has the lemma "*good*", and "*am*", "*is*", and "*are*" all share the lemma "*be*". This method ensures that words with different inflections or variations are reduced to a form that retains the correct meaning in context, making lemmatization particularly useful in NLP tasks where understanding semantic relationships is important.

A key advantage of lemmatization over stemming is its ability to produce linguistically accurate root forms. Lemmatization relies on dictionaries (known as lexical resources) and part-of-speech tagging to determine the correct lemma. For instance, if we consider the word "*saw*", lemmatization will correctly determine whether "*saw*" refers to the verb (past tense of "*see*") or the noun (a tool used for cutting). This attention to context is critical for improving the quality of text data in tasks such as sentiment analysis, text classification, or machine translation, where small changes in word form can significantly impact the meaning of a sentence. Stemming, by contrast, would not distinguish between these variations and might reduce both "*saw*" and "*seen*" to the incorrect base "*s*".

However, the accuracy of lemmatization comes with a trade-off in terms of computational complexity and processing time. Since lemmatization requires analysing the grammatical structure of a sentence and looking up each word in a lexicon to determine its base form, it is generally slower than stemming. This additional computational cost can become significant when dealing with large datasets. Additionally, the effectiveness of lemmatization depends on the quality and completeness of the lexical resources it uses. In some cases, lemmatizers may struggle with rare or specialized terms, and they may not perform as well on informal language such as slang or abbreviations commonly found in social media texts.

5. FEATURE GENERATION (LANGUAGE MODELS)

Feature generation (also known as feature construction, feature extraction or feature engineering) is the process of transforming features into new features that better relate to the target. It also refers to the representation of features in vector forms to make it understandable to the machine. Each of the features that these techniques extract is finally represented in vector form that are then fed to the classifier models (Tabassum & Patil, 2020). Despite its simple data structure without using any explicit semantic information, the vector space model enables very efficient analysis of huge document collections. It was originally introduced for indexing and information retrieval (Salton et al. 1975) but is now used also in several text mining approaches as well as in most of the currently available document retrieval systems (Hotho et al., 2005).

Furthermore, feature generation refers to the process of creating useful representations (or features) particularly when applied to language models, from raw text data that can be used as inputs for machine learning models. These features capture meaningful information about the text, allowing models to perform tasks such as classification, clustering, sentiment analysis, or translation. Methods in this layer can be classified into several categories based on their approach and the type of information they capture. In this paper, we consider four common groups of feature generation methods as statistical, semantic word embedding representation, contextualized word embedding Representation and topic modelling methods.

5.1 Statistical Methods

Statistical methods focus on extracting quantitative properties from text data, converting raw text into structured formats that can be used by machine learning algorithms. These methods rely on the frequency and distribution of words or phrases within documents and across a corpus to generate numerical features. They are some of the most widely used and foundational approaches in NLP due to their simplicity and effectiveness in many text analysis tasks, such as document classification, clustering, and retrieval. Three common statistical methods are BoW (Harris, 1954), TF-IDF (Salton et al., 1975b), N-Grams (Jelinek & Mercer, 1980) which are explained in next sections.

Statistical methods are simple to implement and computationally efficient, making them suitable for a wide range of applications in text mining. They are particularly effective in domains where word frequency and patterns of co-occurrence provide significant insights into document content. However, these methods also come with limitations. One major drawback is the lack of contextual understanding; BoW (Harris, 1954) and TF-IDF (Salton et al., 1975b), for example, treat words independently of their surrounding words, ignoring polysemy (words with multiple meanings) and synonyms.

5.1.1 The Bag of Words (BoW)

BoW (Harris, 1954) model is a simple and commonly used method in text mining and natural language processing to convert text into numerical features that can be used for machine learning tasks. The key idea behind BoW (Harris, 1954) is to treat a text document as an unordered collection of words, disregarding grammar, word order, and context. Each unique word in the text becomes a feature, and the frequency or occurrence of each word is used to represent the document.

Three main steps in this model are **tokenization, vocabulary creation** and **vectorization**. First, the text is split into individual words or tokens (tokenization). Then, a list of all unique words (vocabulary) in the entire corpus is created (vocabulary creation). Subsequently, each document is then represented as a vector. Each position in the vector corresponds to a word in the vocabulary, and the value in that position indicates the word's frequency (or presence/absence) in the document. Here is an example:

Consider the following two simple sentences (documents):

Table 1.

BoW steps	**Document 1**	**Document 2**
	"I love dogs"	*"I love cats"*
Tokenization:	["*I*", "*love*", "*dogs*"]	["*I*", "*love*", "*cats*"]
Vocabulary Creation:	["*I*", "*love*", "*dogs*", "*cats*"]	
Vectorization:	[1, 1, 1, 0]	[1, 1, 0, 1]

The tokenization step is quite clear. Then, we create a vocabulary of unique words from both documents and finally, we represent each document as a vector based on the vocabulary. Each word in the vocabulary becomes a feature (a position in the vector), and the value in the vector represents the frequency of the word in the document. For instance, Document 1 ("*I love dogs*") would be represented as: [1, 1, 1, 0] since,

"*I*" appears once → 1
"*love*" appears once → 1
"*dogs*" appears once → 1
"*cats*" does not appear → 0

Each document is now represented as a fixed-length vector where each entry corresponds to a word in the vocabulary. In this case, the vector shows the presence or absence (or frequency) of each word in the document. After creating vectors in the BoW model (Harris, 1954), these vectors (representing text documents) are used as input features for machine learning algorithms. The BoW vectors serve as the structured, numerical representation of text data that machine learning models require to perform tasks such as classification, clustering, and more.

Although BoW model (Harris, 1954) is widely used in text mining due to its simplicity and effectiveness, it has some limitations. For example, it ignores word order. In fact, it disregards the sequence in which words appear, meaning that "*I love dogs*" and "dogs love I" would have the same representation. Another challenge in this model is context loss meaning that words with different meanings in different contexts are treated the same way. For example, "*bank*" in "*river bank*" and "*money bank*" would be treated identically.

5.1.2 TF-IDF

Originally introduced by Karen Sparck Jones (Salton et al., 1975b), the Term Frequency-Inverse Document Frequency (TF-IDF) (Salton et al., 1975b) serves as a contemporary algorithm in the field of NLP (Zhuohao et al., 2021). TF-IDF (Salton et al., 1975b) is a widely used technique in text mining for feature generation. It refines the basic Bag of Words model (Harris, 1954) by adjusting word frequency to account for the significance of words not just within a single document but across the entire corpus. The main purpose of TF-IDF (Salton et al., 1975b) is to measure how important a word is to a specific document while reducing the weight of common words that are frequent across many documents but carry little unique meaning.

TF-IDF (Salton et al., 1975b) is composed of two parts: **Term Frequency (TF)** and **Inverse Document Frequency (IDF)**. Term Frequency (TF) measures how often a word (term) appears in a document. The idea is that the more frequently a word appears in a document, the more important it is. However, this importance is normalized by the length of the document to avoid bias towards longer documents. The term frequency (TF) of a word *t* in a document *d* is typically defined as:

$$\mathbf{TF(t,d)} = \frac{\textbf{Number of times the term t appears in document d}}{\textbf{Total number of terms in document d}}$$

Equation 5-1. TF formula

Inverse Document Frequency (IDF) measures how important a word is across the entire corpus. Words that appear in many documents (e.g., "*the*", "*is*", "*and*") are considered less informative and are downweighted. Rare words that appear in fewer documents are considered more distinctive and are given more weight. The inverse document frequency (IDF) of a word t is computed as:

$$IDF(t,D) = \log\left(\frac{\textit{Total number of documents in corpus D}}{\text{Number of documents in which the term } t \text{ appears}}\right)$$

Equation 5-2. IDF formula

If the word appears in all documents, the IDF score will be close to zero, indicating that the word is not informative. The TF-IDF score is calculated by multiplying the TF and IDF values as follows:

$$TF - IDF(t,d,D) = TF(t,d) \times IDF(t,D)$$

Equation 5-3. TF-IDF score

Where t is a term (word), d is a document in the corpus and D is the entire corpus.

This score reflects how important a word is in a document relative to its commonality across the entire corpus. Here is an example of how this model works:

Let's say we have three documents in a small corpus:

Document 1: "*I love dogs*"
Document 2: "*I love cats*"
Document 3: "*Dogs love bones*"

Step 1: Term Frequency (TF)

First, we calculate the term frequency for each word in each document. For example, in Document 1 ("*I love dogs*"), the term frequency for the word "*love*" would be:

$$\text{TF}\left(love, \text{Document 1}\right) = \frac{1}{3} = 0.33$$

This process is repeated for all terms in all documents.

Step 2: Inverse Document Frequency (IDF)

Next, we calculate the inverse document frequency for each word across the entire corpus. For example, the word "*love*" appears in all three documents, so the IDF for "*love*" would be:

$$\text{IDF}\left(love, D\right) = \log\left(\frac{3}{3}\right) = log\left(1\right) = 0$$

The IDF for "*dogs*" (which appears in 2 documents) would be:

$$\text{IDF}\left(dogs, D\right) = \log\left(\tfrac{3}{2}\right) = log\left(1.5\right) \approx 0.18$$

And for "*bones*" (which appears in only 1 document), the IDF would be higher:

$$\text{IDF}\left(bones, D\right) = log\left(\tfrac{3}{1}\right) = log\left(3\right) \approx 0.48$$

Step 3: TF-IDF Calculation

Finally, we compute the TF-IDF score for each word in each document. For "*love*" in Document 1, since its IDF is 0 (because it's common across all documents), the TF-IDF score will also be 0. However, for "*dogs*" in Document 1, the TF-IDF score would be:

$$\text{TF-IDF}(dogs, Document\ 1) = 0.33 \times 0.18 = 0.06$$

For "*bones*" in Document 3, the TF-IDF score would be higher because it is rarer across documents:

$$\text{TF-IDF}(bones, Document\ 3) = 0.33 \times 0.48 = 0.16$$

One of the applications of this model is **document classification**. TF-IDF (Salton et al., 1975b) is frequently used as a feature for text classification tasks. By emphasizing words that are significant to a document but rare in the corpus, TF-IDF (Salton et al., 1975b) helps classifiers (like Naive Bayes (Lewis, 1998), Support Vector Machines (Joachims, 1998), or neural networks (Collobert et al., 2011)) distinguish between different classes of documents based on content. On the other hand, search engines use TF-IDF (Salton et al., 1975b) to rank documents by relevance. Documents containing more occurrences of a query term (TF) that are also specific to that term (high IDF) are ranked higher (**information retrieval**). It can also be used to calculate **similarity** between documents. For instance, cosine similarity is often computed between TF-IDF vectors of two documents to measure how similar they are.

Despite advantages and applications of TF-IDF (Salton et al., 1975b), it has some limitations. For instance, like the BoW model (Harris, 1954), TF-IDF (Salton et al., 1975b) treats words as independent features and ignores their order and context within a document. Moreover, it still results in high-dimensional, sparse vectors, particularly for large corpora with diverse vocabularies. However, it is a powerful feature generation technique that improves upon the Bag of Words model by accounting for word frequency both within a document (TF) and across a corpus (IDF). By doing so, it enhances the representation of documents, allowing models to focus on significant and distinctive words while downweighing common, uninformative words. TF-IDF (Salton et al., 1975b) remains a popular and effective tool for text classification, information retrieval, and document similarity tasks.

5.1.3 N-grams

An N-gram model (Jelinek & Mercer, 1980) is a probabilistic language model used in text mining, NLP, and computational linguistics to predict the next word in a sequence of words based on the preceding words. The idea behind the N-gram model (Jelinek & Mercer, 1980) is that the likelihood of a word in a text can be approximated by considering only the previous $N-1$ words, where N is the length of the sequence, or "Gram."

An **N-gram** refers to a contiguous sequence of N words from a given text or speech data. For example:

- **Unigram (1-gram)**: considers individual words (e.g., "*I*", "*love*", "*pizza*").
- **Bigram (2-gram)**: considers pairs of words (e.g., "*I love*", "*love pizza*").
- **Trigram (3-gram)**: considers sequences of three words (e.g., "*I love pizza*").

And so on for higher-order N-grams like 4-grams, 5-grams, etc. The higher the order of the N-gram models, the better the accuracy of the models.

The N-gram model (Jelinek & Mercer, 1980) is based on the **Markov assumption** (Rabiner, 1989), which simplifies language modelling by assuming that the probability of a word depends only on the previous $N-1$ words, not on the entire sentence or history. For example, in a bigram model, the probability of the word w_i depends only on the previous word w_{i-1}, rather than on all preceding words. This model calculates the probability of a word sequence by multiplying the conditional probabilities of each word in the sequence. For instance, in a Bigram model, the probability of a sentence "I love pizza" is calculated as:

$$P(\text{"}I\ love\ pizza\text{"}) = P(\text{"}I\text{"}) \times P(\text{"}love\text{"} \mid \text{"}I\text{"}) \times P(\text{"}pizza\text{"} \mid \text{"}love\text{"})$$

In general, for an N-gram model (Jelinek & Mercer, 1980), the probability of a sequence of words $w_1, w_2, \cdots, w_n$ is approximated as:

$$P(w_1, w_2, \cdots, w_n) = P(w_1) \times P(w_2 w_1) \times P(w_3 w_1, w_2) \times \cdots \times P(w_n w_1, \cdots, w_{n-1})$$

$$= \prod_{i=1}^{n} P(w_i w_1, \cdots, w_{i-1})$$

Equation 5-4. N-Gram model

Since some word combinations may not appear in the training data, the model can suffer from zero probabilities for unseen N-grams. To address this, various smoothing techniques are applied, such as Laplace (Add-One) Smoothing (Manning & Schütze, 1999) which adds 1 to the count of each N-gram to avoid zero probabilities and Good-Turing Smoothing (Good, 1953) which adjusts the probabilities of seen and unseen N-grams based on how frequently other N-Grams appear.

The N-gram model (Jelinek & Mercer, 1980) is widely used in natural language processing for tasks like **text prediction**, **speech recognition**, and **machine translation**. In text prediction, N-gram models (Jelinek & Mercer, 1980) help autocomplete sentences by suggesting the most probable next word based on the previous words typed. This is commonly used in search engines and mobile keyboards, where suggestions improve typing speed and accuracy. In speech recognition, N-gram models (Jelinek & Mercer, 1980) are used to predict the most likely sequence of words that correspond to a spoken phrase. This helps the system choose the correct word sequence from similar-sounding words based on the context, improving the accuracy of speech-to-text systems.

Another significant application of N-gram models (Jelinek & Mercer, 1980) is in machine translation and spelling correction. In machine translation, N-grams predict likely word sequences in the target language, ensuring the translated text maintains proper word order and grammar. N-gram-based spell checkers use word sequences to detect and correct typos by comparing the likelihood of word combinations. For instance, a model can detect that "I love programming" is far more probable than "I love programing," flagging the latter as an error. Moreover, N-grams are applied in information retrieval, where they assist in matching search queries with relevant documents, and in plagiarism detection, identifying repeated or similar phrases between documents.

5.2 Semantic Word Embedding Representation Methods

Semantic Representation Methods in text mining refer to techniques used to capture the meaning and context of words, phrases, and sentences within a text. These methods are designed to move beyond the simple counting of words (like in bag-of-words models) and instead focus on the semantic meaning - or the underlying concept - of the text. Unlike traditional representations like the Bag of Words (Harris, 1954), which simply represent words as isolated tokens, word embeddings encode words in such a way that their contextual relationships and meanings are preserved. In fact, word embeddings are basically representations where contexts and similarities are captured by encoding in a vector space (similar words would have similar representations). Here are the most common semantic representation methods based on word embedding technique.

5.2.1 LSA

Latent Semantic Analysis (LSA) (Deerwester et al., 1990b) is a widely used mathematical model in text mining and natural language processing (NLP) for extracting and representing the underlying relationships between words and documents. The core idea behind LSA is to reduce the dimensionality of a large corpus of text, making it easier to identify patterns and discover hidden semantic structures in the data.

Analysis of latent semantics is done in 3 main steps:

Step 1: Term-Document Matrix (TDM):

The process begins by creating a term-document matrix where each row represents a unique word (term) from the text, and each column represents a document. The values in the matrix are usually word frequencies or some weighted version of term importance (e.g., TF-IDF).

Step 2: Singular Value Decomposition (SVD):

Once the term-document matrix is created, Singular Value Decomposition (SVD) (Eckart & Young, 1936) is applied to decompose it into three matrices:

$$A = U\Sigma V^T$$

Where U is a matrix that represents the term vectors (whose columns are the left singular vectors of A), Σ (Sigma) is a diagonal matrix containing the singular values A, representing the importance of latent topics or concepts and V^T is a matrix that represents the document vectors (whose columns are the right singular vectors of A).

SVD (Eckart & Young, 1936) breaks the high-dimensional matrix into a lower-dimensional space, where latent relationships between words and documents can be more easily identified. The following procedure shows how SVD works:

a) **Compute Singular Values:** calculate the eigenvalues of A^TA and AA^T, which provide the singular values.
b) **Left Singular Vectors:** these are derived from the eigenvectors of A^TA.
c) **Right Singular Vectors:** these are derived from the eigenvectors of AA^T.
d) **Reconstruction:** using U, Σ, and V^T, the original matrix A can be reconstructed.

Step 3: Dimensionality Reduction:

The decomposition essentially projects both words and documents into a lower-dimensional semantic space, where relationships are represented based on concepts or topics instead of direct word-to-word comparisons. This latent space captures the meaning of words even if they do not appear in the same document, based on their co-occurrence patterns across the corpus. The latent space reduces noise and captures key semantic structures. For instance, synonyms or semantically related words will have similar representations in this space, even if they do not occur together in the same document. This makes LSA effective for handling issues like synonymy (different words with the same meaning) and polysemy (words with multiple meanings).

LSA (Deerwester et al., 1990b) has numerous application in text mining, as it helps in uncovering hidden semantic structures in text by representing documents and words in a reduced-dimensional space, improving the understanding of relationships in text data and addressing challenges like synonymy and polysemy.

By reducing the dimensionality of the text, LSA (Deerwester et al., 1990b) can be used to compare documents in a more semantically meaningful way, beyond exact word matches (**Document Similarity** (Deerwester et al., 1990b)). It is also used to improve search engines by matching documents based on latent topics rather than just keyword matching (**Information Retrieval** (Deerwester et al., 1990b)). Furthermore, although LSA (Deerwester et al., 1990b) is not primarily designed as a topic modeling technique, it does reveal latent topics by grouping semantically related terms together (**Topic Modeling** (Bellaouar et al., 2021)). Finally, this technique can be used to extract features that improve the performance of classification algorithms by transforming text into meaningful lower-dimensional representations (**Text Classification** (Kou & Peng, 2015)).

5.2.2 Word2Vec

Word2Vec (Mikolov et al., 2013) is a popular word embedding technique in text mining that transforms words into continuous vectors in a high-dimensional space. These vectors capture both the syntactic and semantic relationships between words based on their context in a corpus. Developed by Google in 2013, Word2Vec (Mikolov et al., 2013) plays a key role in understanding and processing text, as it helps represent words in a way that reflects their meaning and context, rather than just their occurrence.

Word2Vec (Mikolov et al., 2013) starts by taking a large corpus of words as input and generates a vector space, usually consisting of several hundred dimensions. In this space, each unique word from the corpus is represented by a corresponding vector. The positioning of these word vectors is such that words with similar contexts in the corpus are placed near each other in the vector space. Word2Vec operates in two modes as shown in Figure 7. Algorithmically, these modes are similar.

Figure 7. CBOW and Skip-gram models (Mikolov et al., 2013)

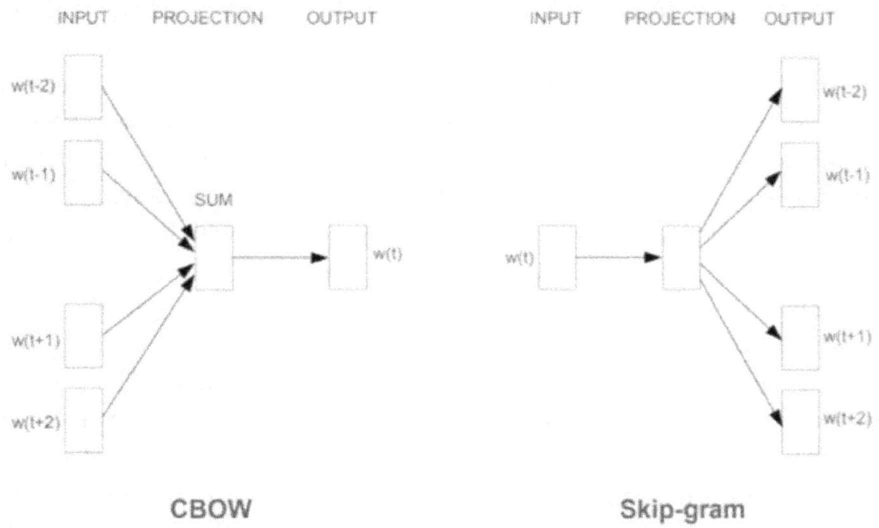

a) **Continuous Bag of Words (CBOW):** predicts a target word based on its surrounding context words. For example, given the sentence "The cat sat on the mat", CBOW will predict the word "*sat*" given the context words "*The*", "*cat*", "*on*", and "*the*".
b) **Skip-gram:** does the opposite of CBOW. It predicts the surrounding context words given a target word. In the example "*The cat sat on the mat*", Skip-gram will try to predict the words "*The*", "*cat*", "*on*", and "*the*" based on the word "*sat*".

Both CBOW and Skip-gram use a simple feedforward neural network with three layers:

I. **Input layer:** which represents the one-hot encoded target (one-hot vector is a $1 \times N$ matrix (vector) used to distinguish each word in a vocabulary from every other word in the vocabulary (Arnaud et al., 2021)) or context words.

II. **Hidden layer:** a single hidden layer where the network learns the word embeddings. The size of this layer corresponds to the size of the embedding vectors (e.g., 100-dimensional, or 300-dimensional).
III. **Output layer:** the final layer where predictions are made for either the target word (in CBOW) or context words (in Skip-gram).

During training, Word2Vec (Mikolov et al., 2013) uses techniques like negative sampling or hierarchical softmax (Koller & Neural Information Processing Systems Foundation, 2009) to efficiently approximate the probabilities of word occurrences. Instead of updating the weights for all words in the vocabulary, Word2Vec (Mikolov et al., 2013) randomly selects a few "negative samples" (words that are not contextually related) and only updates the weights for those words. This reduces computational complexity, especially when dealing with large vocabularies. Subsequently, the second technique replaces the standard softmax function with a hierarchical structure, making it faster to compute the probability distribution over the words, particularly for large vocabularies.

Word2Vec (Mikolov et al., 2013) is trained using a shallow neural network. The input layer represents the target word, and the output layer represents the context words (or vice versa for CBOW). The model then optimizes the word vectors to reduce the error between predicted and actual context words. The training adjusts the word vectors based on their co-occurrence with other words in the text. Each word is transformed into a dense vector (also known as an embedding) in a continuous vector space. For example, the word "*king*" might be represented as a 100-dimensional vector like:

$$king = [0.25, -0.12, 0.84, \ldots, 0.02]$$

The positions of words in the vector space are learned from the training corpus, and words with similar meanings or usage patterns will have similar vectors. Word2Vec (Mikolov et al., 2013) can capture semantic relationships between words. For example, the famous example is:

$$king - man + woman \approx queen$$

This shows that Word2Vec (Mikolov et al., 2013) captures the gender relationship between "*man*" and "*woman*" and "*king*" and "*queen*". On the other hand, Words that appear in similar contexts in the corpus will have similar vector representations. For instance, "*dog*" and "*cat*" might have vectors that are close to each other because they both often appear in similar contexts (e.g., "*pets*," "*animals*").

5.2.3 FastText

FastText (Joulin et al., 2016) is a word embedding model and text classification library developed by Facebook's AI Research (FAIR) team. It is an extension of the word2vec model (Mikolov et al., 2013) but with several enhancements that allow it to handle subword information and out-of-vocabulary words more efficiently. FastText (Joulin et al., 2016) excels at generating high-quality word vectors (embeddings) and performing text classification, especially in cases where computational resources are limited or when dealing with morphologically rich languages.

Unlike models like word2vec that treat each word as an atomic entity, FastText breaks down words into character-level n-grams (subwords). For instance, the word "*where*" can be represented by character-level trigrams: "*whe*", "*her*", "*ere*"]. The full word embedding is the sum of the vectors of these subwords. This enables FastText (Joulin et al., 2016) to:

- **Handle Out-of-Vocabulary (OOV) words**: since FastText learns representations for subwords, it can generate embeddings for words not seen during training, by summing up the embeddings of their subword components.
- **Capture Morphological Information:** by using subwords, FastText can better model words in morphologically rich languages where words can take many forms (e.g., conjugations, inflections).

Similar to word2vec (Mikolov et al., 2013), FastText (Joulin et al., 2016) learns continuous vector representations of words. These embeddings capture semantic relationships between words, so words that appear in similar contexts will have similar vector representations. However, unlike word2vec (Mikolov et al., 2013), FastText (Joulin et al., 2016) can compute embeddings for rare or unseen words thanks to its subword modeling.

FastText (Joulin et al., 2016) can also be used for supervised learning tasks like text classification. It uses hierarchical softmax (Koller & Neural Information Processing Systems Foundation, 2009), which allows for efficient handling of large datasets and fast training. In this mode, FastText (Joulin et al., 2016) trains embeddings alongside a classifier, typically for tasks like sentiment analysis, language identification, or topic classification.

This model uses similar architecture to word2vec's skip-gram or CBOW (Continuous Bag of Words) modes but incorporates subword information. Here is how it works:

- **Skip-gram with subwords:** for each target word, FastText (Joulin et al., 2016) tries to predict the context words (words surrounding the target). However, instead of learning an embedding directly for the word, it learns embeddings for the word's subword n-grams, which are then summed to represent the entire word.

- **Hierarchical Softmax**: when used for classification, FastText (Joulin et al., 2016) utilizes hierarchical softmax (Koller & Neural Information Processing Systems Foundation, 2009) to speed up the training process. Hierarchical softmax (Koller & Neural Information Processing Systems Foundation, 2009) organizes words into a tree structure, reducing the complexity of computing the probability distribution over a large vocabulary.

Consider the word "*jumping*". FastText (Joulin et al., 2016) breaks this word down into a set of character-level n-grams (say trigrams):

Trigrams: ["*jum*", "*ump*", "*mpi*", "*pin*", "*ing*"]

FastText (Joulin et al., 2016) then learns vector representations for each of these subword components, and the final vector representation of the word "*jumping*" is the sum of the vectors for its trigrams. This subword representation allows the model to handle variations like "*jump*", "*jumped*", "*jumping*", etc., more effectively than models like word2vec (Mikolov et al., 2013), which would treat these as completely independent words.

5.3 Contextualized Word Embedding Representation Methods

5.3.1 BERT

BERT (Bidirectional Encoder Representations from Transformers) (Devlin et al., 2018) is a transformative model that has significantly advanced the capabilities of language understanding systems. Developed by researchers at Google AI Language, BERT's (Devlin et al., 2018) architecture and training methodologies address many limitations found in previous models. By leveraging the power of bidirectional context, BERT (Devlin et al., 2018) achieves a nuanced understanding of language that is vital for various applications such as sentiment analysis, question answering, and language inference.

BERT (Devlin et al., 2018) is built upon the Transformer architecture, which was introduced in the paper "Attention is All You Need" by Vaswani et al. in 2017 (Vaswani et al., 2017). The Transformer relies heavily on self-attention mechanisms that allow the model to weigh the relevance of different words in a sentence irrespective of their positions. This self-attention mechanism is crucial for understanding context, enabling the model to consider all words simultaneously rather than sequentially. In contrast to traditional models like recurrent neural networks (RNNs), which process input sequentially, BERT's (Devlin et al., 2018) parallelized approach makes it faster and more efficient for training on large datasets.

BERT's (Devlin et al., 2018) architecture consists of multiple layers of transformers (typically 12 for the base model and 24 for the large model), each containing multiple attention heads. This multi-head attention allows the model to focus on different aspects of the input text simultaneously. The embeddings produced at each layer are contextualized, meaning they are generated based on the entire input rather than a fixed representation, enabling BERT (Devlin et al., 2018) to capture complex word meanings and relationships effectively. There are two steps in this framework, **pre-training,** and **fine-tuning**.

Step 1: Pre-training

The pre-training step of BERT (Devlin et al., 2018) involves training the model on large amounts of unlabelled text data to learn general language representations. This is achieved through two key techniques: **Masked Language Modelling** (MLM) and **Next Sentence Prediction** (NSP). In MLM, a certain percentage (typically 15%) of the input tokens are randomly masked, and the model is tasked with predicting these masked tokens based on the surrounding context. This bidirectional approach allows BERT to consider both the left and right context of each word, enabling it to capture deeper linguistic relationships and nuances. For example, in the sentence "The cat [MASK] on the [MASK]," BERT uses the unmasked words to predict the masked tokens, such as "sat" and "mat." This process helps the model understand context-dependent meanings of words, such as distinguishing between "bank" as a financial institution versus a riverbank.

The NSP task complements MLM by training BERT to understand relationships between sentences. During pre-training, the model is given pairs of sentences and must predict whether the second sentence logically follows the first. Half of the time, the second sentence is the actual next sentence in the text (positive example), and the other half, it is a randomly selected sentence (negative example). For instance, given "The cat sat on the mat" followed by "It was a sunny day," BERT learns to recognize this as a valid sequence. This task is crucial for applications like question answering and natural language inference, where understanding sentence-level relationships is essential. Together, MLM and NSP enable BERT to develop a robust understanding of both word-level and sentence-level context, forming the foundation for its effectiveness in downstream tasks.

Step 2: Fine-tuning

The fine-tuning step in BERT adapts the pre-trained model to specific downstream tasks by training it on labeled task-specific datasets. After pre-training, BERT has already learned general language features, so fine-tuning requires minimal additional training. A task-specific output layer is added on top of the pre-trained model, which varies depending on the task. For example, a softmax layer is added for classification tasks like sentiment analysis, while token-level tasks like named entity recognition (NER) require output layers for each token. In question answering tasks, two output layers are added to predict the start and end positions of the answer within a passage. The entire model, including the pre-trained weights, is then fine-tuned using backpropagation, where the model adjusts its parameters based on the task-specific data and labels.

Fine-tuning is computationally efficient compared to pre-training, as it typically requires only a few epochs of training on the task-specific dataset. Hyperparameters such as the learning rate, batch size, and number of epochs are carefully tuned to optimize performance. A lower learning rate (e.g., 1e-5 or 2e-5) is often used to ensure that the pre-trained weights are adjusted gradually, preventing overfitting, and preserving the general language knowledge learned during pre-training. This process allows BERT to specialize in specific applications, such as sentiment analysis, question answering, or NER, while maintaining its robust understanding of language context. Fine-tuning significantly enhances BERT's performance on these tasks, making it a versatile and powerful tool for a wide range of natural language processing applications.

Figure 8. Overall pre-training and fine-tuning procedures for BERT (Devlin et al., 2018)

6. FEATURE SELECTION

Feature selection is a process in machine learning where the goal is to select the most relevant and important features (or variables) from a dataset while eliminating redundant or irrelevant ones. This step is crucial because it helps improve the performance of machine learning models by reducing overfitting, speeding up model training, and making models more interpretable. By removing unnecessary features, the complexity of the model is reduced, leading to better generalization on unseen data. Figure 9 illustrates the general idea of feature selection step.

Figure 9. Feature selection performance

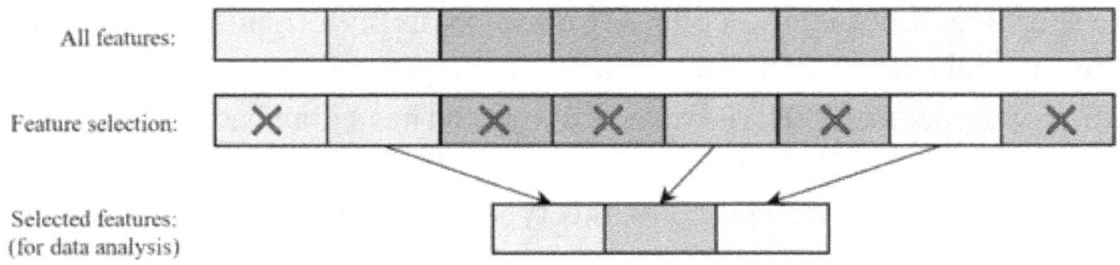

Based on the on information available in the dataset, feature selection approaches can be classified as **supervised** (Aggarwal, 2014), **unsupervised** (Solorio-Fernández et al., 2020) and **semi-supervised** (Sheikhpour et al., 2017). In **supervised** feature selection, the process leverages labeled data (i.e., data with a known target variable) to identify features that are most predictive or informative for the output. By focusing on how each feature influences the target, supervised methods aim to improve the accuracy and performance of machine learning models. For example, in classification tasks, features that contribute most to separating different classes are retained, while irrelevant ones are discarded. In contrast, **unsupervised** feature selection is applied when there are no labels or target variables available. Instead of focusing on predicting a target, the selection process looks for intrinsic properties within the data, such as variance, feature redundancy, or clustering patterns. Unsupervised methods aim to reduce dimensionality by finding the most informative features that capture the underlying structure of the data, even in the absence of a specific target to optimize for. **Semi-supervised** feature selection methods use both labeled and unlabeled data to evaluate feature relevance.

Another classification of feature selection approaches is based on the methods used in them. According to the perspective of the first taxonomy, all supervised, unsupervised, and semi-supervised approaches can be categorized into three common groups: **Filter**, **Wrapper** and **Embedded** methods (Sebastiani, 2002). In the

Filter method features are selected based on statistical measures. It is independent of the learning algorithm and requires less computational time. Information gain (Yang & Pedersen, 1997), chi-square test (Yang & Pedersen, 1997), Fisher score, correlation coefficient, and variance threshold are some of the statistical measures used to understand the importance of the features. The performance of the Wrapper method depends on the classifier. The best subset of features is selected based on the results of the classifier. Wrapper methods are computationally more expensive than filter methods, due to the repeated learning steps and cross-validation. However, these methods are more accurate than the filter method. Some of the examples are Recursive feature elimination (Yan & Zhang, 2015), Sequential feature selection algorithms (Jain & Zongker, 1997), and Genetic algorithms. The third approach is the Embedded method which uses ensemble learning and hybrid learning methods for feature selection. Since it has a collective decision, its performance is better than the other two models. Random forest is one such example. It is computationally less intensive than wrapper methods. However, this method has a drawback of specific to a learning model (Venkatesh & Anuradha, 2019). In this section, we try to explain some feature selection methods based on this type of classification.

6.1 Filter Methods

Filter methods rely on statistical properties of the data to select features independently of the model. They evaluate each feature's relevance based on metrics such as correlation, mutual information, or variance. Features are scored using a statistical measure, and a threshold is applied to retain the most significant ones. These methods are computationally efficient and suitable for high-dimensional datasets like text data. In this section, we will explain some common filter methods and finally describe other filter methods in a table with their advantages and disadvantages.

6.1.1 Information Gain

Information Gain (IG) is frequently employed as a term-goodness criterion in the field of machine learning (Yang & Pedersen, 1997). It is used to measure the reduction in uncertainty about the target variable (e.g., class label) when a specific feature (e.g., a word or term) is known. In text mining, IG evaluates how much information a given word or term contributes toward predicting the class of a document.

- **Entropy:** Entropy is a measure of uncertainty or impurity in a dataset. If a dataset has many different classes with roughly equal probabilities, it has high entropy (i.e., high uncertainty about the class of any given instance). In text mining, entropy helps in determining the randomness of class labels in a document collection, considering a specific feature (word or term).

- **Information Gain Calculation:** Information Gain is calculated by comparing the entropy of the dataset before and after knowing the presence or absence of a specific word or term.

$$IG(t) = -\sum_{i=1}^{m} P(c_i)\log P(c_i)$$

$$+P(t)\sum_{i=1}^{m} P(c_i|t)\log P(c_i|t) + P(\bar{t})\sum_{i=1}^{m} P(c_i|\bar{t})\log P(c_i|\bar{t})$$

Where c_i represents the i-th category, $P(c_i)$ is the probability of the i-th category, $P(t)$ and $P(\bar{t})$ are the probabilities that the term appears or not in the documents, $P(c_i|t)$ is the conditional probability of the i-th category given that term t appeared and $P(c_i|\bar{t})$ is the conditional probability of the i-th category given that term t did not appear.

- **Interpreting Information Gain:** A high *IG* score indicates that knowing the feature (term) significantly reduces the uncertainty about the class label, meaning it is a highly informative term. Words with higher *IG* are generally more relevant for distinguishing between different classes.

6.1.2 Chi-Square Test

Chi-Square (also known as Pearson's Chi-Square) feature selection is a technique that uses statistical theory to test the independence of a term with its class. The Chi-Square values for each term are sorted in descending order to determine the terms or words that will be used as features (Hokijuliandy et al., 2023). The Chi-Square Test assesses the dependency between a feature (e.g., a word, phrase, or token) and the target variable (e.g., class label in classification tasks). For each feature, a contingency table is constructed based on its occurrences across different target categories.

The Chi-Square is calculated according to Equation 6-1

$$\chi^2 = \sum \frac{(O - E)^2}{E}$$

Equation 6-1. The Chi-Square function

Where χ^2 is the chi-square test statistic, Σ is the summation operator, O is the observed frequency and E is the expected frequency. A high Chi-Square statistic or a low p-value indicates that the feature is significantly associated with the target.

Features are ranked based on their Chi-Square statistic and a threshold is applied to select the most relevant features. Principal Component Analysis (PCA)

PCA is a widely used dimensionality reduction technique that transforms data into a new coordinate system. It identifies principal components that capture the most variance in the data, reducing the dataset to a smaller set of components while retaining the most important information. PCA creates a set of orthogonal (independent) components ordered by the amount of variance they capture. Only the top components (based on variance) are retained. Although PCA is primarily a dimensionality reduction technique, it can be used to retain components that capture the most variance. Figure 10 illustrates a 3-dimensional data set (the left figure) mapped to a 2-dimensional data set after using PCA (the right figure).

Figure 10. An example of dimension reduction from 3 to 2 using PCA[2]

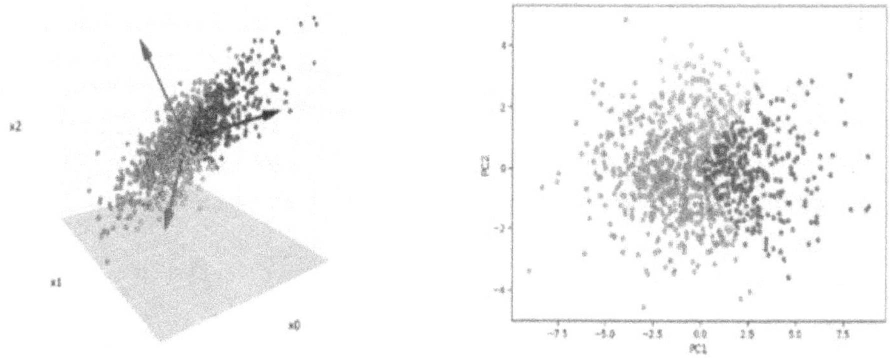

PCA can be summarized in 5 main steps as described below:

1) **Constructing the Covariance Matrix:** PCA begins by creating the covariance matrix, which quantifies the relationships between all pairs of variables within the dataset.
2) **Determining Eigenvalues and Eigenvectors:** Next, the eigenvalues and eigenvectors of the covariance matrix are calculated. The eigenvectors define the directions where the data's variance is maximized, while the eigenvalues indicate the amount of variance along these directions.
3) **Ranking Eigenvalues:** The eigenvalues are then organized in descending order. Larger eigenvalues correspond to eigenvectors that capture greater proportions of the dataset's total variance.

4) **Selecting Principal Components:** A subset of eigenvectors, known as principal components, is selected based on how much total variance they explain. This selection is usually guided by a cumulative variance threshold.
5) **Data Projection:** In the final step, the original dataset is transformed into a lower-dimensional space by projecting it onto the chosen principal components. This projection retains the most significant patterns while reducing dimensionality.

There are still other types of filter methods which we will not discuss them here. However, Table 2 depicts the most common methods and briefly describes their advantages and disadvantages.

Table 2. Comparison of some common filter methods in text feature selection algorithms

Method	Description	Advantages	Disadvantages
Information Gain	Measures the reduction in entropy when a feature is used to split the data.	- Simple to compute - Effective for categorical data - Captures relevance to the target variable	- Ignores feature interdependencies - Can be biased toward features with many unique values
Chi-Square	Evaluates the independence of a feature with respect to the target variable using a Chi-Square test.	- Straightforward to implement - Works well for categorical data - Highlights significant features	- Assumes independence between features - Sensitive to small sample sizes
PCA	Transforms data into a new feature space by maximizing variance along orthogonal components.	- Reduces dimensionality effectively - Captures global variance structure - Model-agnostic	- Requires numerical data - Lacks interpretability of resulting features
Mutual Information	Measures the amount of information a feature shares with the target variable, capturing both linear and non-linear dependencies.	- Effective for both categorical and continuous data - Captures non-linear relationships	- Computationally expensive for large datasets - Can be less intuitive to interpret
Variance Threshold	Removes features with low variance, assuming they provide limited information.	- Simple and computationally efficient - Useful for filtering out irrelevant features	- Ignores the target variable - May remove features with important but rare variations
Correlation Coefficient	Evaluates the linear correlation between features and the target variable (e.g., Pearson or Spearman correlation).	- Useful for continuous target variables - Simple and interpretable	- Only captures linear relationships - Ignores multivariate dependencies

continued on following page

Table 2. Continued

Method	Description	Advantages	Disadvantages
TF-IDF Weighting	Assigns importance to terms based on their frequency in a document relative to their frequency in the entire corpus.	- Well-suited for text data - Highlights unique and significant terms	- Not inherently a feature selection method - Sensitive to noisy data
mRMR (Minimum Redundancy Maximum Relevance)	Selects features that are highly relevant to the target variable but minimally redundant with each other.	- Balances relevance and redundancy - Suitable for multi-class problems	- Computationally intensive for large datasets
CFS (Correlation-based Feature Selection)	Selects features based on their correlation with the target and low inter-correlation with other features.	- Simple and interpretable - Effective in reducing redundancy	- Assumes linear correlations - May overlook complex dependencies
MR (Maximum Relevance)	Focuses solely on selecting features with the highest relevance to the target variable, ignoring redundancy.	- Ensures relevance - Straightforward calculation	- Does not account for feature interdependencies
VIF (Variance Inflation Factor)	Identifies multicollinearity among features by measuring how much variance of a feature is explained by others.	- Detects collinear features effectively - Improves model stability	- Suitable only for numerical features - Computationally expensive for high-dimensional data
Laplace Score	Scores features based on their locality-preserving power, favouring features that preserve local neighbourhood structures in the data.	- Simple and effective for unsupervised problems - Preserves local patterns	- Does not consider global relationships - Limited use in supervised tasks

6.2 Wrapper methods

Wrapper methods evaluate subsets of features based on their predictive performance using a specific machine learning model. They rely on iterative processes to search for the optimal combination of features that maximizes the model's performance. In text mining, these methods are particularly useful when dealing with high-dimensional datasets, as they help in identifying the most informative features for a given task.

6.2.1 Forward Selection

Forward Selection is a stepwise feature selection technique where features are added incrementally to an initially empty feature set. At each step, the algorithm evaluates all potential features not yet in the selected set and adds the one that improves the model's performance the most. This process continues until adding more features does not result in a significant improvement or a pre-defined stopping criterion is met.

Basically, this method is performed in 5 steps as described below:

1) **Start with no features:** Begin with an empty set of features.
2) **Iteratively add features:** At each iteration:
   - Evaluate each feature not already included by adding it temporarily to the current feature set.
   - Train a model using the temporary feature set and evaluate its performance (e.g., using accuracy, precision, recall, or another metric).
3) **Select the best feature:** Add the feature that results in the highest performance improvement to the feature set.
4) **Repeat:** Continue adding features one by one until:
   - There is no significant performance improvement, or
   - A pre-specified number of features is selected.
5) **Final Model:** Use the selected features to train the final model.

6.2.2 Backward Elimination

Backward elimination is a feature selection technique used in text mining and other machine learning tasks to iteratively refine the set of features (variables) by removing those that are least significant. This method aims to simplify models, reduce overfitting, and improve computational efficiency while maintaining or improving predictive performance.

Basically, this method is performed in 5 steps as described below:

1) Start with a full set of features, including all possible variables.
2) Train a model (e.g., regression, decision tree, or another predictive algorithm) on the dataset.
3) Evaluate the significance of each feature based on a chosen criterion, such as:
   - Statistical tests (e.g., p-values in regression models).
   - Model performance metrics (e.g., accuracy, AUC, F1 score).
   - Contribution to the prediction (e.g., feature importance in tree-based models).
4) Remove the least significant feature or the feature contributing the least to the model's performance.
5) Re-train the model on the remaining features and repeat the process until a stopping criterion is met.

In text mining, features are typically represented as text-derived variables such as Bag-of-Words counts, TF-IDF scores, N-grams or embedding dimensions. Backward elimination is applied in the pre-processing or feature generation stage to refine the feature space for instance, removing words or n-grams with minimal impact on classification or regression tasks or identifying and discarding irrelevant topics or dimensions in topic models. The primary goal in text mining is to reduce the number of features without losing the text's essential information needed for the downstream task, improving both the model's interpretability and efficiency.

Due to limitations in space, we will not talk about other wrapper methods. However, Table 3 compares some common wrapper feature selection approaches.

Table 3. Comparison of some common wrapper methods in text feature selection algorithms

Method	Description	Advantages	Disadvantages
Forward Selection	tarts with no features, adds the most significant feature iteratively.	- Simple and intuitive. - Reduces computation by starting with fewer features. - Useful for small datasets.	- Can miss interactions between features. - Greedy approach may lead to suboptimal feature subsets.
Backward Elimination	Starts with all features, removes the least significant feature iteratively.	- Considers the full set of features at the start. - Good for understanding irrelevant features.	- Computationally expensive for datasets with many features. - May remove useful features in interaction.
Recursive Feature Elimination (RFE)	Trains a model and eliminates the least important feature iteratively based on feature importance scores.	- Efficient and works well with models that provide feature importance (e.g., SVM, random forests). - Can capture feature interactions.	- Computationally expensive. - Model-dependent; may not generalize to all algorithms.
Exhaustive Search	Tests all possible combinations of features to find the optimal subset.	- Guarantees the best feature subset (if computational resources allow).	- Extremely computationally expensive; impractical for large datasets. - Not scalable.
Stepwise Selection	Combines forward selection and backward elimination for dynamic feature addition/ removal.	- Balances the pros and cons of forward and backward methods. - Allows bidirectional feature evaluation.	- Greedy approach; may lead to suboptimal subsets. - Computationally intensive for larger datasets.

6.3 Embedded Methods

Embedded methods are feature selection techniques integrated directly into the learning process of a predictive model. These methods leverage the model's training process to identify and prioritize features, making them highly efficient for high-dimensional datasets like those encountered in text mining (e.g., TF-IDF or bag-of-words matrices).

Unlike filter or wrapper methods, embedded methods perform feature selection as part of the model training, reducing the need for separate pre-processing steps. Feature importance is derived from the internal parameters of the model (e.g., weights, splits, or attention scores). These techniques are well-suited for large-scale, sparse text data due to efficient algorithms. In this section, we are going to evaluate some common embedded methods.

6.3.1 Lasso Regression (L1 Regularization)

Lasso Regression, or L1 regularization, is a linear model that introduces a penalty equal to the absolute value of the coefficients of features. This penalty forces some coefficients to become exactly zero, effectively selecting a subset of features. In text mining, where feature matrices (e.g., TF-IDF or bag-of-words) are often high-dimensional and sparse, Lasso is particularly useful to reduce dimensionality and select the most important words or n-grams for predictive tasks. Here, the objective is to minimize the following function:

$$||y - Xw||_2^2 + \alpha \, ||w||_1$$

Where y is the target values (e.g., labels or outputs we want to predict), X is the feature matrix (e.g., a TF-IDF or bag-of-words matrix), w is the weights or coefficients assigned to each feature by the regression model, $||y - Xw||_2^2$ is the squared error (or residual sum of squares). It measures how far the model's predictions are from the true values y, $||w||_1$ is the L1 norm, which sums the absolute values of the weights w (e.g., $|w_1| + |w_2| + \ldots + |w_p|$), α is regularization parameter that controls the trade-off between minimizing error and enforcing simplicity.

In the objective function, as α increases, more coefficients shrink to zero and fewer features are retained.

Larger α causes stronger penalty which means more coefficients are forced to zero and subsequently, smaller α causes weaker penalty which means more features are kept.

6.3.2 Decision Trees

Decision Trees are machine learning algorithms that partition data into subsets based on feature values, forming a tree-like structure. In each split, the tree selects the feature that most effectively reduces uncertainty or impurity, measured by criteria like Gini Impurity or Entropy. This inherent selection process makes Decision Trees an embedded feature selection method. In fact:

- Features that are important for reducing impurity appear higher in the tree.
- Features rarely used for splits are considered less important.

Basically, there are three main steps which clarify how feature importance works in Decision Trees. These three steps are:

1) **Split Criteria:** Decision Trees evaluate how well a feature separates the target variable (e.g., labels in classification tasks). Popular metrics include:
    - Gini Impurity: Measures the likelihood of incorrect classification.
    - Entropy: Measures information gain.

Features that reduce impurity the most are selected for splitting.

2) **Feature Importance:** During training, the tree computes a score for each feature based on how much it contributes to reducing impurity across all splits. Features with higher scores are more important.
3) **Embedded Feature Selection:** By ranking feature importance, Decision Trees identify and prioritize the most relevant features for the prediction task.

Table 4 compares other embedded feature selection methods.

Table 4. Comparison of some common embedded feature selection methods

Method	Description	Advantages	Disadvantages
Lasso Regression (L1)	Adds L1 regularization to a linear model, shrinking irrelevant feature coefficients to zero.	- Automatically selects important features. - Works well with high-dimensional sparse data. - Simple and interpretable.	- Assumes linear relationships. - Sensitive to hyperparameter tuning (α\alphaα). - May not capture feature interactions.
Decision Trees	Splits data by selecting features that reduce impurity (e.g., Gini or Entropy) the most.	- Automatically ranks features. - Captures non-linear interactions. - Intuitive and interpretable.	- Can overfit small or noisy data. - Biased toward features with many unique values.
Random Forests	Aggregates feature importance scores across multiple decision trees.	- Reduces overfitting compared to single trees. - Captures feature interactions. - Robust and scalable.	- Less interpretable than individual trees. - Computationally intensive for very large datasets.
Gradient Boosting Trees	Builds trees iteratively, focusing on reducing errors; computes feature importance as a by-product.	- Highly accurate. - Handles non-linear relationships. - Robust to noise.	- Computationally expensive. - Requires careful tuning of hyperparameters.
Linear SVM	Assigns weights to features, selecting important ones based on their contribution to hyperplane margins.	- Efficient for high-dimensional data. - Works well with sparse text data. - Robust to overfitting.	- Sensitive to scaling of features. - Assumes linear separability of data.
Neural Networks (Attention Mechanisms)	Uses attention weights in models like Transformers to highlight important tokens or words.	- Captures context-sensitive feature importance. - Ideal for sequential data. - Supports transfer learning.	- Computationally expensive. - Requires large datasets for effective training. - Less interpretable.

7. CONCLUSIONS

This chapter has provided a comprehensive survey on the field of text mining, offering a detailed examination of both theoretical foundations and practical applications. By tracing the historical development and challenges of text mining, we have highlighted the significant evolution of key techniques within the domain of Natural Language Processing. The step-by-step analysis of critical algorithms throughout the text mining pipeline has illustrated the importance of data collection, pre-processing, feature generation, and selection in transforming raw text into valuable information. Through this study, we have aimed at bridging the gap between theory and practice, equipping researchers and practitioners with the necessary tools and methodologies for effective text mining applications. Furthermore, the inclusion of Pseudocode and Python implementations ensures that these methods are accessible and reproducible, promoting broader adoption and continued development of text mining solutions in real-world contexts.

As the field of text mining continues to evolve, several promising research avenues emerge. The integration of deep learning models, particularly transformer-based architectures, has shown remarkable potential in enhancing text understanding and extraction. Future research could focus on improving the interpretability and efficiency of these models to ensure their applicability in real-world scenarios. Additionally, the growing availability of multilingual and low-resource language datasets presents opportunities for advancing cross-lingual text mining techniques. Another critical area is the ethical and legal considerations surrounding text mining, including bias mitigation, privacy preservation, and responsible AI development. Exploring these challenges will be crucial in shaping the next generation of text mining applications and ensuring their fair and transparent deployment across industries.

Pseudocode and Python implementations

Pseudocode and Python implementations of algorithms – from pre-processing to feature selection methods mentioned in this paper- are available in the https://zenodo.org/records/14637390 repository,

REFERENCES

Abdusalomovna, T. D., Adhamjon qizi, H. O., Abdukarim qizi, K. O., & Baxtiyor qizi, M. D. (2023). TEXT MINING. *European Journal of Interdisciplinary Research and Development, 13*, 284–289.

Aggarwal, C. C. (Ed.). (2014). *Data Classification* (0 ed.). Chapman and Hall/ CRC., DOI: 10.1201/b17320

Albalawi, R., Yeap, T. H., & Benyoucef, M. (2020). Using Topic Modeling Methods for Short-Text Data: A Comparative Analysis. *Frontiers in Artificial Intelligence, 3*, 42. DOI: 10.3389/frai.2020.00042 PMID: 33733159

Alghamdi, R., & Alfalqi, K. (2015). A Survey of Topic Modeling in Text Mining. *International Journal of Advanced Computer Science and Applications, 6*(1). Advance online publication. DOI: 10.14569/IJACSA.2015.060121

Andersen, P. M., Hayes, P. J., Huettner, A. K., Schmandt, L. M., Nirenburg, I. B., & Weinstein, S. P. (1992). Automatic extraction of facts from press releases to generate news stories. *Proceedings of the Third Conference on Applied Natural Language Processing-*, 170. DOI: 10.3115/974499.974531

Arnaud, E., Elbattah, M., Gignon, M., & Dequen, G. (2021). NLP-Based Prediction of Medical Specialties at Hospital Admission Using Triage Notes. *2021 IEEE 9th International Conference on Healthcare Informatics (ICHI)*, 548-553. DOI: 10.1109/ ICHI52183.2021.00103

Bellaouar, S., Bellaouar, M. M., & Ghada, I. E. (2021). Topic Modeling: Comparison of LSA and LDA on Scientific Publications. *2021 4th International Conference on Data Storage and Data Engineering*, 59-64. DOI: 10.1145/3456146.3456156

Bian, N., Han, X., Sun, L., Lin, H., Lu, Y., He, B., Jiang, S., & Dong, B. (2024). *ChatGPT is a Knowledgeable but Inexperienced Solver: An Investigation of Commonsense Problem in Large Language Models* (No. arXiv:2303.16421). arXiv. http://arxiv.org/abs/2303.16421

Bijalwan, V., Kumari, P., Pascual, J., & Semwal, V. B. (2014). *Machine learning approach for text and document mining* (Versión 1). arXiv. DOI: 10.48550/ARXIV.1406.1580

Blei, D. (2011). Probabilistic topic models. *Proceedings of the 17th ACM SIGKDD International Conference Tutorials*, 1-1. DOI: 10.1145/2107736.2107741

Blei, D. M., Ng, A. Y., & Jordan, M. (2003). *Latent dirichlet allocation. 3*, 993-1022.

Bonikowski, B., Luo, Y., & Stuhler, O. (2022). Politics as Usual? Measuring Populism, Nationalism, and Authoritarianism in U.S. Presidential Campaigns (1952–2020) with Neural Language Models. *Sociological Methods & Research, 51*(4), 1721–1787. DOI: 10.1177/00491241221122317

Brown, T. (2013). *What Consumers Think about brands on social media, and what bunesses need to do about it* (Keep Social Honest). https://www.cim.co.uk/media/1733/ksh_report_.pdf

Chai, C. P. (2023). Comparison of text preprocessing methods. *Natural Language Engineering, 29*(3), 509–553. DOI: 10.1017/S1351324922000213

Chen, Y., Cheng, J., Jiang, H., Liu, L., Zhang, H., Shi, S., & Xu, R. (2022). Learning from Sibling Mentions with Scalable Graph Inference in Fine-Grained Entity Typing. *Proceedings of the 60th Annual Meeting of the Association for Computational Linguistics(*Volume 1*: Long Papers)*, 2076-2087. DOI: 10.18653/v1/2022.acl-long.147

Chieu, H. L., Ng, H. T., & Lee, Y. K. (2003). Closing the gap: Learning-based information extraction rivaling knowledge-engineering methods. *Proceedings of the 41st Annual Meeting on Association for Computational Linguistics - ACL '03, 1*, 216-223. DOI: 10.3115/1075096.1075124

Choi, E., Levy, O., Choi, Y., & Zettlemoyer, L. (2018). Ultra-Fine Entity Typing. *Proceedings of the 56th Annual Meeting of the Association for Computational Linguistics(*Volume 1*: Long Papers)*, 87-96. DOI: 10.18653/v1/P18-1009

Collobert, R., Weston, J., Bottou, L., Karlen, M., Kavukcuoglu, K., & Kuksa, P. (2011). *Natural Language Processing (almost) from Scratch* (Versión 1). arXiv. DOI: 10.48550/ARXIV.1103.0398

Connelly, S. (2018). *Practical BM25—Part 2: The BM25 Algorithm and its variables*. https://www.elastic.co/blog/practical-bm25-part-2-the-bm25-algorithm-and-its-variables

Crowe, J. (1995). Constraint-based event recognition for information extraction. *Proceedings of the 33rd Annual Meeting on Association for Computational Linguistics-*, 296. DOI: 10.3115/981658.981701

Dai, H., Song, Y., & Wang, H. (2021). Ultra-Fine Entity Typing with Weak Supervision from a Masked Language Model. *Proceedings of the 59th Annual Meeting of the Association for Computational Linguistics and the 11th International Joint Conference on Natural Language Processing(*Volume 1*: Long Papers)*, 1790-1799. DOI: 10.18653/v1/2021.acl-long.141

Das, S. S. S., Katiyar, A., Passonneau, R. J., & Zhang, R. (2021). *CONTaiNER: Few-Shot Named Entity Recognition via Contrastive Learning* (Versión 2). arXiv. DOI: 10.48550/ARXIV.2109.07589

Davidson, T., Warmsley, D., Macy, M., & Weber, I. (2017). *Automated Hate Speech Detection and the Problem of Offensive Language* (Versión 1). arXiv. DOI: 10.48550/ARXIV.1703.04009

Deerwester, S., Dumais, S. T., Furnas, G. W., Landauer, T. K., & Harshman, R. (1990a). Indexing by latent semantic analysis. *Journal of the American Society for Information Science, 41*(6), 391–407. DOI: 10.1002/(SICI)1097-4571(199009)41:6<391::AID-ASI1>3.0.CO;2-9

Deerwester, S., Dumais, S. T., Furnas, G. W., Landauer, T. K., & Harshman, R. (1990b). Indexing by latent semantic analysis. *Journal of the American Society for Information Science, 41*(6), 391–407. DOI: 10.1002/(SICI)1097-4571(199009)41:6<391::AID-ASI1>3.0.CO;2-9

Devlin, J., Chang, M.-W., Lee, K., & Toutanova, K. (2018). *BERT: Pre-training of Deep Bidirectional Transformers for Language Understanding* (Versión 2). arXiv. DOI: 10.48550/ARXIV.1810.04805

Devlin, J., Chang, M.-W., Lee, K., & Toutanova, K. (2019). *BERT: Pre-training of Deep Bidirectional Transformers for Language Understanding* (No. arXiv:1810.04805). arXiv. http://arxiv.org/abs/1810.04805

Dey Sarkar, S., Goswami, S., Agarwal, A., & Aktar, J. (2014). A Novel Feature Selection Technique for Text Classification Using Naïve Bayes. *International Scholarly Research Notices, 2014*, 1–10. DOI: 10.1155/2014/717092 PMID: 27433512

Dhar, A., Mukherjee, H., Dash, N. S., & Roy, K. (2021). Text categorization: Past and present. *Artificial Intelligence Review, 54*(4), 3007–3054. DOI: 10.1007/s10462-020-09919-1

Dogan, T., & Uysal, A. K. (2019). On Term Frequency Factor in Supervised Term Weighting Schemes for Text Classification. *Arabian Journal for Science and Engineering, 44*(11), 9545–9560. DOI: 10.1007/s13369-019-03920-9

Du, X., & Cardie, C. (2020). Event Extraction by Answering (Almost) Natural Questions. *Proceedings of the 2020 Conference on Empirical Methods in Natural Language Processing (EMNLP)*, 671-683. DOI: 10.18653/v1/2020.emnlp-main.49

Du, X., & Ji, H. (2022). Retrieval-Augmented Generative Question Answering for Event Argument Extraction. *Proceedings of the 2022 Conference on Empirical Methods in Natural Language Processing*, 4649-4666. DOI: 10.18653/v1/2022.emnlp-main.307

Eckart, C., & Young, G. (1936). The approximation of one matrix by another of lower rank. *Psychometrika, 1*(3), 211–218. DOI: 10.1007/BF02288367

El-Kassas, W. S., Salama, C. R., Rafea, A. A., & Mohamed, H. K. (2021). Automatic text summarization: A comprehensive survey. *Expert Systems with Applications, 165*, 113679. DOI: 10.1016/j.eswa.2020.113679

Engonopoulos, N., Lazaridou, A., Paliouras, G., & Chandrinos, K. (2011). ELS: A word-level method for entity-level sentiment analysis. *Proceedings of the International Conference on Web Intelligence, Mining and Semantics*, 1-9. DOI: 10.1145/1988688.1988703

Evans, J. A., & Aceves, P. (2016). Machine Translation: Mining Text for Social Theory. *Annual Review of Sociology, 42*(1), 21–50. DOI: 10.1146/annurev-soc-081715-074206

Farra, N., Challita, E., Assi, R. A., & Hajj, H. (2010). Sentence-Level and Document-Level Sentiment Mining for Arabic Texts. *2010 IEEE International Conference on Data Mining Workshops*, 1114-1119. DOI: 10.1109/ICDMW.2010.95

Fu, T.-J., Li, P.-H., & Ma, W.-Y. (2019). GraphRel: Modeling Text as Relational Graphs for Joint Entity and Relation Extraction. *Proceedings of the 57th Annual Meeting of the Association for Computational Linguistics*, 1409-1418. DOI: 10.18653/v1/P19-1136

Good, I. J. (1953). The Population Frequencies of Species and the Estimation of Population Parameters. *Biometrika, 40*(3/4), 237. DOI: 10.2307/2333344

Grishman, R. (2015). Information Extraction. *IEEE Intelligent Systems, 30*(5), 8–15. DOI: 10.1109/MIS.2015.68

Gupta, S., & Gupta, S. K. (2019). Abstractive summarization: An overview of the state of the art. *Expert Systems with Applications, 121*, 49–65. DOI: 10.1016/j.eswa.2018.12.011

Guru, D. S., & Suhil, M. (2015). A Novel Term_Class Relevance Measure for Text Categorization. *Procedia Computer Science, 45*, 13–22. DOI: 10.1016/j.procs.2015.03.074

Hahn, U., & Mani, I. (2000). The challenges of automatic summarization. *Computer*, *33*(11), 29–36. DOI: 10.1109/2.881692

Hambarde, K. A., & Proença, H. (2023). Information Retrieval: Recent Advances and Beyond. *IEEE Access : Practical Innovations, Open Solutions*, *11*, 76581–76604. DOI: 10.1109/ACCESS.2023.3295776

Hanna, A. (2013). Computer-Aided Content Analysis of Digitally Enabled Movements. *Mobilization: An International Quarterly (San Diego, Calif.)*, *18*(4), 367–388. DOI: 10.17813/maiq.18.4.m1g180620x7n1542

Harris, Z. S. (1954). Distributional Structure. *Word*, *10*(2-3), 146–162. DOI: 10.1080/00437956.1954.11659520

Hiemstra, D. (2009). Information retrieval models. *Information Retrieval: Searching in the 21st Century*, 1-19.

Hokijuliandy, E., Napitupulu, H., & Firdaniza, . (2023). Application of SVM and Chi-Square Feature Selection for Sentiment Analysis of Indonesia's National Health Insurance Mobile Application. *Mathematics*, *11*(17), 3765. DOI: 10.3390/math11173765

Hotho, A., Nürnberger, A., & Paaß, G. (2005). A Brief Survey of Text Mining. *Journal for Language Technology and Computational Linguistics*, *20*(1), 19–62. DOI: 10.21248/jlcl.20.2005.68

Hsu, I.-H., Huang, K.-H., Boschee, E., Miller, S., Natarajan, P., Chang, K.-W., & Peng, N. (2022). DEGREE: A Data-Efficient Generation-Based Event Extraction Model. *Proceedings of the 2022 Conference of the North American Chapter of the Association for Computational Linguistics: Human Language Technologies*, 1890-1908. DOI: 10.18653/v1/2022.naacl-main.138

Hussein, D. M. E.-D. M. (2018). A survey on sentiment analysis challenges. *Journal of King Saud University. Engineering Sciences*, *30*(4), 330–338. DOI: 10.1016/j.jksues.2016.04.002

Jain, A., & Zongker, D. (1997). Feature selection: Evaluation, application, and small sample performance. *IEEE Transactions on Pattern Analysis and Machine Intelligence*, *19*(2), 153–158. DOI: 10.1109/34.574797

Jelinek, F., & Mercer, R. L. (1980). Interpolated estimation of Markov source parameters from sparse data. *InProceedings of the Workshop on Pattern Recognition in Practice*, 381-397.

Joachims, T. (1998). Text categorization with Support Vector Machines: Learning with many relevant features. In Nédellec, C., & Rouveirol, C. (Eds.), *Machine Learning: ECML-98* (Vol. 1398, pp. 137–142). Springer Berlin Heidelberg., DOI: 10.1007/BFb0026683

Joulin, A., Grave, E., Bojanowski, P., & Mikolov, T. (2016). *Bag of Tricks for Efficient Text Classification* (Versión 3). arXiv. DOI: 10.48550/ARXIV.1607.01759

Kambhampati, S. & Association for the Advancement of Artificial Intelligence (Eds.). (2016). *Proceedings of the Twenty-Fifth International Joint Conference on Artificial Intelligence:New York, NY, USA,9-15 July 2016.* Volume 1. IJCAI, Palo Alto, California. AAAI Press/International Joint Conferences on Artificial Intelligence.

Khan, K., Baharudin, B., Khan, A., & Ullah, A. (2014). Mining opinion components from unstructured reviews: A review. *Journal of King Saud University. Computer and Information Sciences, 26*(3), 258–275. DOI: 10.1016/j.jksuci.2014.03.009

Khot, T., Sabharwal, A., & Clark, P. (2017). *Answering Complex Questions Using Open Information Extraction* (Versión 1). arXiv. DOI: 10.48550/ARXIV.1704.05572

Khurana, D., Koli, A., Khatter, K., & Singh, S. (2023). Natural language processing: State of the art, current trends and challenges. *Multimedia Tools and Applications, 82*(3), 3713–3744. DOI: 10.1007/s11042-022-13428-4 PMID: 35855771

Kirmani, M., Manzoor Hakak, N., Mohd, M., & Mohd, M. (2019). Hybrid Text Summarization: A Survey. In Ray, K., Sharma, T. K., Rawat, S., Saini, R. K., & Bandyopadhyay, A. (Eds.), *Soft Computing: Theories and Applications* (Vol. 742, pp. 63–73). Springer Singapore., DOI: 10.1007/978-981-13-0589-4_7

Koller, D. & Neural Information Processing Systems Foundation (Eds.). (2009). *Advances in neural information processing systems 21: 22nd Annual Conference on Neural Information Processing Systems 2008 ; December 8 - 10, 2008, Vancouver, B. C., Canada ; [proceedings].* Curran.

Kou, G., & Peng, Y. (2015). An Application of Latent Semantic Analysis for Text Categorization. *International Journal of Computers, Communications & Control, 10*(3), 357. DOI: 10.15837/ijccc.2015.3.1923

Kumar, A., & Sharma, A. (2019). Systematic literature review of fuzzy logic based text summarization. *Iranian Journal of Fuzzy Systems, 16*(5). Advance online publication. DOI: 10.22111/ijfs.2019.4906

Lewis, D. D. (1998). Naive (Bayes) at forty: The independence assumption in information retrieval. In Nédellec, C., & Rouveirol, C. (Eds.), *Machine Learning: ECML-98* (Vol. 1398, pp. 4–15). Springer Berlin Heidelberg., DOI: 10.1007/BFb0026666

Li, B., Fang, G., Yang, Y., Wang, Q., Ye, W., Zhao, W., & Zhang, S. (2023). *Evaluating ChatGPT's Information Extraction Capabilities: An Assessment of Performance, Explainability, Calibration, and Faithfulness* (No. arXiv:2304.11633). arXiv. http://arxiv.org/abs/2304.11633

Li, B., Yu, D., Ye, W., Zhang, J., & Zhang, S. (2022). *Sequence Generation with Label Augmentation for Relation Extraction* (Versión 2). arXiv. DOI: 10.48550/ARXIV.2212.14266

Li, X., Feng, J., Meng, Y., Han, Q., Wu, F., & Li, J. (2019). *A Unified MRC Framework for Named Entity Recognition* (Versión 7). arXiv. DOI: 10.48550/ARXIV.1910.11476

Li, X., Jin, J., Zhou, Y., Zhang, Y., Zhang, P., Zhu, Y., & Dou, Z. (2024). *From Matching to Generation: A Survey on Generative Information Retrieval* (No. arXiv:2404.14851). arXiv. http://arxiv.org/abs/2404.14851

Li, X., Yin, F., Sun, Z., Li, X., Yuan, A., Chai, D., Zhou, M., & Li, J. (2019). Entity-Relation Extraction as Multi-Turn Question Answering. *Proceedings of the 57th Annual Meeting of the Association for Computational Linguistics*, 1340-1350. DOI: 10.18653/v1/P19-1129

Lin, H., & Ng, V. (2019). Abstractive Summarization: A Survey of the State of the Art. *Proceedings of the AAAI Conference on Artificial Intelligence, 33*(01), 9815–9822. DOI: 10.1609/aaai.v33i01.33019815

Liu, J., Chen, Y., & Xu, J. (2022). Saliency as Evidence: Event Detection with Trigger Saliency Attribution. *Proceedings of the 60th Annual Meeting of the Association for Computational Linguistics(*Volume 1*: Long Papers)*, 4573-4585. DOI: 10.18653/v1/2022.acl-long.313

Liu, L., Tang, L., Dong, W., Yao, S., & Zhou, W. (2016). An overview of topic modeling and its current applications in bioinformatics. *SpringerPlus, 5*(1), 1608. DOI: 10.1186/s40064-016-3252-8 PMID: 27652181

Liu, X., Huang, H., Shi, G., & Wang, B. (2022). *Dynamic Prefix-Tuning for Generative Template-based Event Extraction*. DOI: 10.18653/v1/2022.acl-long.358

Lou, D., Liao, Z., Deng, S., Zhang, N., & Chen, H. (2021). MLBiNet: A Cross-Sentence Collective Event Detection Network. *Proceedings of the 59th Annual Meeting of the Association for Computational Linguistics and the 11th International Joint Conference on Natural Language Processing(*Volume 1*: Long Papers)*, 4829-4839. DOI: 10.18653/v1/2021.acl-long.373

Lu, Y., Liu, Q., Dai, D., Xiao, X., Lin, H., Han, X., Sun, L., & Wu, H. (2022). *Unified Structure Generation for Universal Information Extraction* (Versión 1). arXiv. DOI: 10.48550/ARXIV.2203.12277

Luhn, H. P. (1958). The Automatic Creation of Literature Abstracts. *IBM Journal of Research and Development*, *2*(2), 159–165. DOI: 10.1147/rd.22.0159

Ly, A., Uthayasooriyar, B., & Wang, T. (2020). *A survey on natural language processing (nlp) and applications in insurance* (Versión 1). arXiv. DOI: 10.48550/ARXIV.2010.00462

Ma, Y., Wang, Z., Cao, Y., Li, M., Chen, M., Wang, K., & Shao, J. (2022). Prompt for Extraction? PAIE: Prompting Argument Interaction for Event Argument Extraction. *Proceedings of the 60th Annual Meeting of the Association for Computational Linguistics(*Volume 1*: Long Papers)*, 6759-6774. DOI: 10.18653/v1/2022.acl-long.466

Manning, C. D., & Schütze, H. (1999). *Foundations of statistical natural language processing*. MIT Press.

Martins, P. H., Marinho, Z., & Martins, A. F. T. (2019). *Joint Learning of Named Entity Recognition and Entity Linking* (Versión 1). arXiv. DOI: 10.48550/ARXIV.1907.08243

Medhat, W., Hassan, A., & Korashy, H. (2014). Sentiment analysis algorithms and applications: A survey. *Ain Shams Engineering Journal*, *5*(4), 1093–1113. DOI: 10.1016/j.asej.2014.04.011

Méndez, J. R., Iglesias, E. L., Fdez-Riverola, F., Díaz, F., & Corchado, J. M. (2006). Tokenising, Stemming and Stopword Removal on Anti-spam Filtering Domain. En R. Marín, E. Onaindía, A. Bugarín, & J. Santos (Eds.), *Current Topics in Artificial Intelligence* (Vol. 4177, pp. 449-458). Springer Berlin Heidelberg. DOI: 10.1007/11881216_47

Mikolov, T., Chen, K., Corrado, G., & Dean, J. (2013). *Efficient Estimation of Word Representations in Vector Space* (Versión 3). arXiv. DOI: 10.48550/ARXIV.1301.3781

Molina, M., & Garip, F. (2019). Machine Learning for Sociology. *Annual Review of Sociology*, *45*(1), 27–45. DOI: 10.1146/annurev-soc-073117-041106

Moratanch, N., & Chitrakala, S. (2017). A survey on extractive text summarization. *2017 International Conference on Computer, Communication and Signal Processing (ICCCSP)*, 1-6. DOI: 10.1109/ICCCSP.2017.7944061

Mosa, M. A., Anwar, A. S., & Hamouda, A. (2019). A survey of multiple types of text summarization with their satellite contents based on swarm intelligence optimization algorithms. *Knowledge-Based Systems, 163*, 518–532. DOI: 10.1016/j.knosys.2018.09.008

nazari, nasrin, & Mahdavi, M. A. (2018). A survey on Automatic Text Summarization. *Journal of AI and Data Mining, Online First.* DOI: 10.22044/jadm.2018.6139.1726

Nelson, L. K. (2020). Computational Grounded Theory: A Methodological Framework. *Sociological Methods & Research, 49*(1), 3–42. DOI: 10.1177/0049124117729703

Nelson, L. K., Burk, D., Knudsen, M., & McCall, L. (2021). The Future of Coding: A Comparison of Hand-Coding and Three Types of Computer-Assisted Text Analysis Methods. *Sociological Methods & Research, 50*(1), 202–237. DOI: 10.1177/0049124118769114

Pang, B., & Lee, L. (2008). Opinion Mining and Sentiment Analysis. *Foundations and Trends® in Information Retrieval, 2*(1–2), 1-135. DOI: 10.1561/1500000011

Pang, K., Zhang, H., Zhou, J., & Wang, T. (2022). Divide and Denoise: Learning from Noisy Labels in Fine-Grained Entity Typing with Cluster-Wise Loss Correction. *Proceedings of the 60th Annual Meeting of the Association for Computational Linguistics(*Volume 1*: Long Papers)*, 1997-2006. DOI: 10.18653/v1/2022.acl-long.141

Porter, M. F. (1980). An algorithm for suffix stripping. *Program, 14*(3), 130–137. DOI: 10.1108/eb046814

Pouran Ben Veyseh, A., Lai, V., Dernoncourt, F., & Nguyen, T. H. (2021). Unleash GPT-2 Power for Event Detection. *Proceedings of the 59th Annual Meeting of the Association for Computational Linguistics and the 11th International Joint Conference on Natural Language Processing(*Volume 1*: Long Papers)*, 6271-6282. DOI: 10.18653/v1/2021.acl-long.490

Rabiner, L. R. (1989). A tutorial on hidden Markov models and selected applications in speech recognition. *Proceedings of the IEEE, 77*(2), 257–286. DOI: 10.1109/5.18626

Radev, D. R., Hovy, E., & McKeown, K. (2002a). Introduction to the Special Issue on Summarization. *Computational Linguistics, 28*(4), 399–408. DOI: 10.1162/089120102762671927

Radev, D. R., Hovy, E., & McKeown, K. (2002b). Introduction to the Special Issue on Summarization. *Computational Linguistics, 28*(4), 399–408. DOI: 10.1162/089120102762671927

Salton, G. (1983). Some research problems in automatic information retrieval. *ACM SIGIR Forum, 17*(4), 252-263. DOI: 10.1145/1013230.511830

Salton, G., Wong, A., & Yang, C. S. (1975a). A vector space model for automatic indexing. *Communications of the ACM, 18*(11), 613–620. DOI: 10.1145/361219.361220

Salton, G., Wong, A., & Yang, C. S. (1975b). A vector space model for automatic indexing. *Communications of the ACM, 18*(11), 613–620. DOI: 10.1145/361219.361220

Salur, M. U., & Aydin, I. (2020). A Novel Hybrid Deep Learning Model for Sentiment Classification. *IEEE Access : Practical Innovations, Open Solutions, 8*, 58080–58093. DOI: 10.1109/ACCESS.2020.2982538

Sebastiani, F. (2002). Machine learning in automated text categorization. *ACM Computing Surveys, 34*(1), 1–47. DOI: 10.1145/505282.505283

Sharma, N. A., Ali, A. B. M. S., & Kabir, M. A. (2024). A review of sentiment analysis: Tasks, applications, and deep learning techniques. *International Journal of Data Science and Analytics*. Advance online publication. DOI: 10.1007/s41060-024-00594-x

Sheikhpour, R., Sarram, M. A., Gharaghani, S., & Chahooki, M. A. Z. (2017). A Survey on semi-supervised feature selection methods. *Pattern Recognition, 64*, 141–158. DOI: 10.1016/j.patcog.2016.11.003

Solorio-Fernández, S., Carrasco-Ochoa, J. A., & Martínez-Trinidad, J. (2020). A review of unsupervised feature selection methods. *Artificial Intelligence Review, 53*(2), 907–948. DOI: 10.1007/s10462-019-09682-y

Suleiman, D., & Awajan, A. A. (2019). Deep Learning Based Extractive Text Summarization: Approaches, Datasets and Evaluation Measures. *2019 Sixth International Conference on Social Networks Analysis, Management and Security (SNAMS)*, 204-210. DOI: 10.1109/SNAMS.2019.8931813

Tabassum, A., & Patil, R. R. (2020). A Survey on Text Pre-Processing & Feature Extraction Techniques in Natural Language Processing. *International Research Journal of Engineering and Technology, 07*(06), 4864.

Taha, K., Yoo, P. D., Yeun, C., Homouz, D., & Taha, A. (2024). A comprehensive survey of text classification techniques and their research applications: Observational and experimental insights. *Computer Science Review, 54*, 100664. DOI: 10.1016/j.cosrev.2024.100664

Tandel, J., Mistree, K., & Shah, P. (2019). A Review on Neural network based Abstractive Text Summarization models. *2019 IEEE 5th International Conference for Convergence in Technology (I2CT)*, 1-4. DOI: 10.1109/I2CT45611.2019.9033912

Tandel, S. S., Jamadar, A., & Dudugu, S. (2019). A Survey on Text Mining Techniques. *2019 5th International Conference on Advanced Computing & Communication Systems (ICACCS)*, 1022-1026. DOI: 10.1109/ICACCS.2019.8728547

Tarapiah, S., AbuHania, R., & Atalla, S. (2013). Smart on-board transportation management system using gps/gsm/gprs technologies to reduce traffic violation in developing countries. *International Journal of Digital Information and Wireless Communications*, *3*(4), 96–105.

Vaswani, A., Shazeer, N., Parmar, N., Uszkoreit, J., Jones, L., Gomez, A. N., Kaiser, L., & Polosukhin, I. (2017). *Attention Is All You Need* (Versión 7). arXiv. DOI: 10.48550/ARXIV.1706.03762

Vayansky, I., & Kumar, S. A. P. (2020). A review of topic modeling methods. *Information Systems*, *94*, 101582. DOI: 10.1016/j.is.2020.101582

Venkatesh, B., & Anuradha, J. (2019). A Review of Feature Selection and Its Methods. *Cybernetics and Information Technologies*, *19*(1), 3–26. DOI: 10.2478/cait-2019-0001

VijayGaikwad, S., Chaugule, A., & Patil, P.VijayGaikwad. (2014). Text Mining Methods and Techniques. *International Journal of Computer Applications*, *85*(17), 42–45. DOI: 10.5120/14937-3507

Vinoth, R. Jayachandran, 2Anjana, Balaji, M., & Srinivasan, R. (2014). A Hybrid Text Classification Approach Using KNN and SVM. *International Journal of Advance Foundation and Research in Computer, 1*(3). https://ijafrc.org/Volumn1/Vol_issue3/3.pdf

Wadden, D., Wennberg, U., Luan, Y., & Hajishirzi, H. (2019). *Entity, Relation, and Event Extraction with Contextualized Span Representations* (Versión 2). arXiv. DOI: 10.48550/ARXIV.1909.03546

Wang, D., & Zhang, H. (2010). Inverse-category-frequency based supervised term weighting scheme for text categorization. arXiv preprint arXiv:1012.2609.

Wankhade, M., Rao, A. C. S., & Kulkarni, C. (2022). A survey on sentiment analysis methods, applications, and challenges. *Artificial Intelligence Review*, *55*(7), 5731–5780. DOI: 10.1007/s10462-022-10144-1

Wu, F., & Weld, D. S. (2010). Open information extraction using Wikipedia. *Association for Computational Linguistics*, 118-127.

Yan, K., & Zhang, D. (2015). Feature selection and analysis on correlated gas sensor data with recursive feature elimination. *Sensors and Actuators. B, Chemical, 212*, 353–363. DOI: 10.1016/j.snb.2015.02.025

Yang, Y., & Pedersen, J. O. (1997). A comparative study on feature selection in text categorization. *In Proceedings of the Fourteenth International Conference on Machine Learning*, 412-420. https://courses.ischool.berkeley.edu/i256/f06/papers/yang97comparative.pdf

Ye, D., Lin, Y., Li, P., & Sun, M. (2022). Packed Levitated Marker for Entity and Relation Extraction. *Proceedings of the 60th Annual Meeting of the Association for Computational Linguistics(*Volume 1*: Long Papers)*, 4904-4917. DOI: 10.18653/v1/2022.acl-long.337

Ye, W., Li, B., Xie, R., Sheng, Z., Chen, L., & Zhang, S. (2019). Exploiting Entity BIO Tag Embeddings and Multi-task Learning for Relation Extraction with Imbalanced Data. *Proceedings of the 57th Annual Meeting of the Association for Computational Linguistics*, 1351-1360. DOI: 10.18653/v1/P19-1130

Yessenalina, A., Yue, Y., & Cardie, C. (2010). Multi-Level Structured Models for Document-Level Sentiment Classification. *In Proceedings of the 2010 Conference on Empirical Methods in Natural Language Processing*, 1046-1056. https://aclanthology.org/D10-1102/

Zeng, D., Liu, K., Chen, Y., & Zhao, J. (2015). Distant Supervision for Relation Extraction via Piecewise Convolutional Neural Networks. *Proceedings of the 2015 Conference on Empirical Methods in Natural Language Processing*, 1753-1762. DOI: 10.18653/v1/D15-1203

Zhang, Z., Strubell, E., & Hovy, E. (2022). Transfer Learning from Semantic Role Labeling to Event Argument Extraction with Template-based Slot Querying. *Proceedings of the 2022 Conference on Empirical Methods in Natural Language Processing*, 2627-2647. DOI: 10.18653/v1/2022.emnlp-main.169

Zhao, K., Jin, X., Bai, L., Guo, J., & Cheng, X. (2022). Knowledge-Enhanced Self-Supervised Prototypical Network for Few-Shot Event Detection. *Findings of the Association for Computational Linguistics: EMNLP, 2022*, 6266–6275. DOI: 10.18653/v1/2022.findings-emnlp.467

Zhou, H., & Song, F. (2015). Aspect-Level Sentiment Analysis Based on a Generalized Probabilistic Topic and Syntax Model. *Proceedings of the Twenty-Eighth International Florida Artificial Intelligence Research Society Conference*. https://cdn.aaai.org/ocs/10382/10382-46113-1-PB.pdf

Zhou, W., & Chen, M. (2021). *An Improved Baseline for Sentence-level Relation Extraction* (Versión 4). arXiv. DOI: 10.48550/ARXIV.2102.01373

Zhuohao, W., Dong, W., & Qing, L. (2021). Keyword Extraction from Scientific Research Projects Based on SRP-TF-IDF. *Chinese Journal of Electronics*, *30*(4), 652–657. DOI: 10.1049/cje.2021.05.007

Žukov-Gregorič, A., Bachrach, Y., & Coope, S. (2018). Named Entity Recognition With Parallel Recurrent Neural Networks. *Proceedings of the 56th Annual Meeting of the Association for Computational Linguistics(*Volume 2*: Short Papers)*, 69-74. DOI: 10.18653/v1/P18-2012

ADDITIONAL READING

Bird, S., Klein, E., & Loper, E. (2009). *Natural language processing with Python: Analyzing text with the natural language toolkit*. O'Reilly Media.

Clark, A., Fox, C., & Lappin, S. (Eds.). (2010). *Handbook of natural language processing* (2nd ed.). CRC Press.

Goldberg, Y. (2017). *Neural network methods in natural language processing*. Morgan & Claypool Publishers. DOI: 10.1007/978-3-031-02165-7

Jurafsky, D., & Martin, J. H. (2021). *Speech and language processing: An introduction to natural language processing, computational linguistics, and speech recognition* (3rd ed.). Prentice Hall.

Manning, C. D., & Schütze, H. (1999). *Foundations of statistical natural language processing*. MIT Press.

ENDNOTES

1 www.scopus.com

2 https://towardsdatascience.com/principal-component-analysis-pca-explained-visually-with-zero-math-1cbf392b9e7d

Compilation of References

Abdusalomovna, T. D., Adhamjon qizi, H. O., Abdukarim qizi, K. O., & Baxtiyor qizi, M. D. (2023). TEXT MINING. *European Journal of Interdisciplinary Research and Development, 13*, 284–289.

Afram, G. K., Benjamin, A. W., & Adebayo, A. F. (2022). Twieng: A multi-domain Twi-English parallel corpus for machine translation of the Twi language, A low-resource African language. *Journal of Mathematical Techniques & Computational Mathematics, 1*(1), 48–57. DOI: 10.20944/preprints202203.0303.v1

Aggarwal, C. C. (Ed.). (2014). *Data Classification* (0 ed.). Chapman and Hall/ CRC., DOI: 10.1201/b17320

Ahmadi, D. M. R. (2018). The use of technology in English language learning: A literature review. *International Journal of Research in English Education, 3*(2), 115–125. DOI: 10.29252/ijree.3.2.115

Ahmad, M., Khalid, A., & Khan, R. (2021). AI-driven tools for language learning: A comprehensive review. *Journal of Educational Technology, 12*(4), 342–360.

Ahsan, M., Nygard, K. E., Gomes, R., Chowdhury, M. M., Rifat, N., & Connolly, J. F. (2022). Cybersecurity threats and their mitigation approaches using machine learning—A review. *Journal of Cybersecurity and Privacy, 2*(3), 527–555. DOI: 10.3390/jcp2030027

Akgun, S., & Greenhow, C. (2022). Artificial intelligence in education: Addressing ethical challenges in K-12 settings. *AI and Ethics, 2*(3), 431–440. DOI: 10.1007/ s43681-021-00096-7 PMID: 34790956

Al-Abdallat, M., & Mansour, A. (2020). The Effect of Teaching Using Artificial Intelligence Software's on the Academic Achievement of the 10th Grade Students in Computer Science Subject and Their Attitudes Towards It in Jordan. In Journal of Education and Practice. DOI: 10.7176/JEP/11-7-10

Alam, A. (2023). Harnessing the Power of AI to Create Intelligent Tutoring Systems for Enhanced Classroom Experience and Improved Learning Outcomes. In *Intelligent Communication Technologies and Virtual Mobile Networks* (pp. 571–591). Springer Nature Singapore. DOI: 10.1007/978-981-99-1767-9_42

Alawneh, Y. J. J., Radwan, E. N. Z., Salman, F. N., Makhlouf, S. I., Makhamreh, K., & Alawneh, M. S. (2024, April). Ethical Considerations in the Use of AI in Primary Education: Privacy, Bias, and Inclusivity. In *2024 International Conference on Knowledge Engineering and Communication Systems (ICKECS)* (Vol. 1, pp. 1-6). IEEE. DOI: 10.1109/ICKECS61492.2024.10616986

Albalawi, R., Yeap, T. H., & Benyoucef, M. (2020). Using Topic Modeling Methods for Short-Text Data: A Comparative Analysis. *Frontiers in Artificial Intelligence*, *3*, 42. DOI: 10.3389/frai.2020.00042 PMID: 33733159

Al-Batineha, M., & Tenaijya, M. (2024). Adapting to technological change: An investigation of translator training and the translation market in the Arab world. *Heliyon*, *10*(7), 1–12. PMID: 38560143

Aldawsari, H. A. (2024). Evaluating Translation Tools: Google Translate, Bing Translator, and Bing AI on Arabic Colloquialisms. *Arab World English Journal (AWEJ)* Special Issue on ChatGPT (April, 2024) 237-251.DOI: https://dx.doi.org/ DOI: 10.24093/awej/ChatGPT.16

Alghamdi, R., & Alfalqi, K. (2015). A Survey of Topic Modeling in Text Mining. *International Journal of Advanced Computer Science and Applications*, *6*(1). Advance online publication. DOI: 10.14569/IJACSA.2015.060121

Alghamdy, R. Z. (2023). Pedagogical and Ethical Implications of Artificial Intelligence in EFL Context: A Review Study. *English Language Teaching*, *16*(10), 87–98. DOI: 10.5539/elt.v16n10p87

Alhaj, A. A. M. (2023). Exploring the Challenges and Obstacles Encountered in Utilizing Artificial Intelligence Tools (AITs) in Translation Teaching from the Perspectives of Faculty Members at Saudi Universities. *Migration Letters : An International Journal of Migration Studies*, *21*(3), 398–412.

Alharbi, K., & Khalil, L. (2023). Artificial Intelligence (AI) In ESL Vocabulary Learning: An Exploratory Study On Students And Teachers' Perspectives. *Migration Letters : An International Journal of Migration Studies*, *20*(S12), 1030–1045.

Alharbi, W. (2023). AI in the Foreign Language Classroom: A Pedagogical Overview of Automated Writing Assistance Tools. *Education Research International*, *2023*, 1–15. DOI: 10.1155/2023/4253331

Al-khresheh, M. H. (2024). Bridging technology and pedagogy from a global lens: Teachers' perspectives on integrating ChatGPT in English language teaching. *Computers and Education: Artificial Intelligence*, *6*(June), 1–12. DOI: 10.1016/j.caeai.2024.100218

Allam, H., Dempere, J., Akre, H., & Flores, P. (2023). Artificial Intelligence in Education (AIED): Implications and Challenges. *Atlantis Highlights in Social Sciences, Education and Humanities*, *13*, 126–140. DOI: 10.2991/978-94-6463-286-6_10

Almaiah, M. A., Yelisetti, S., Arya, L., Christopher, N. K. B., Kaliappan, K., Vellaisamy, P., Hajjej, F., & Alkdour, T. (2023). A novel approach for improving the security of IoT–medical data systems using an enhanced dynamic Bayesian network. *Electronics (Basel)*, *12*(20), 1–15. DOI: 10.3390/electronics12204316

Almalki, M., & Aziz, M. A. (2022). The Role of Artificial Intelligence in Language Learning: An Overview. *Journal of Language and Linguistic Studies*, *18*(1), 122–137.

Alsadoon, R. (2021). Chatting with AI Bot: Vocabulary learning assistant for Saudi EFL learners. *English Language Teaching*, *14*(6), 135–157. DOI: 10.5539/elt.v14n6p135

Alsahafi, M. (2023). The relationship between depth of academic English vocabulary knowledge and academic success of second language university students. *SAGE Open*, *13*(1), 1–9. DOI: 10.1177/21582440231153342

Alshaikhi, T., & Khasawneh, M. A. S. (2024). Investigating the benefits and drawbacks of selected AI-powered instruments employed for foreign language education. *Kurdish Studies*, *12*(2), 2156–2169.

Alwahoub, H. M., Azmi, M. N. L., & Jomaa, N. J. (2020). Teachers' and Students' Perceptions of E-Learning Integration in the Primary Schools of Saudi Arabia. *International Journal of Advanced Research in Education and Society*, *2*(1), 116–126.

Amineh, R. J., & Asl, H. D. (2015). Review of constructivism and social constructivism. *Journal of Social Sciences, Literature, and Languages*, *1*(1), 9–16.

Amin, M. Y. M. (2023). AI and Chat GPT in Language Teaching: Enhancing EFL Classroom Support and Transforming Assessment Techniques. *International Journal of Higher Education Pedagogies*, *4*(4), 1–15. DOI: 10.33422/ijhep.v4i4.554

Andersen, P. M., Hayes, P. J., Huettner, A. K., Schmandt, L. M., Nirenburg, I. B., & Weinstein, S. P. (1992). Automatic extraction of facts from press releases to generate news stories. *Proceedings of the Third Conference on Applied Natural Language Processing*-, 170. DOI: 10.3115/974499.974531

Anderson, T., & Dron, J. (2011). Human Behavior in a Social Learning Environment. In T. Anderson (Ed.), The Theory and Practice of Online Learning (pp. 95-128). Athabasca University Press.

Aoun, J. E. (2017). *Robot-proof: Higher education in the age of artificial intelligence*. MIT Press. DOI: 10.7551/mitpress/11456.001.0001

Aprizal, A. D., & Wachyudi, K. (2024). The Effectiveness of Memrise as a Vocabulary Learning Tool. *Jurnal Ilmiah Wahana Pendidikan, 10*(4), 8–17.

Arnaud, E., Elbattah, M., Gignon, M., & Dequen, G. (2021). NLP-Based Prediction of Medical Specialties at Hospital Admission Using Triage Notes. *2021 IEEE 9th International Conference on Healthcare Informatics (ICHI)*, 548-553. DOI: 10.1109/ICHI52183.2021.00103

Arya, L. (2024). Securing healthcare data and cybersecurity innovations in the era of Industry 5.0. In *Cybersecurity and data management innovations for revolutionizing healthcare* (pp. 132–147). IGI Global., DOI: 10.4018/979-8-3693-7457-3.ch006

Arya, L., & Rastogi, R. (2024). Study on aerial monitoring system in agriculture, forestry, defense, and border protection using artificial intelligence (AI). In *Agriculture and aquaculture applications of biosensors and bioelectronics* (pp. 392–407). Scopus Indexed. DOI: 10.4018/979-8-3693-2069-3.ch021

Arya, L., Sharma, Y. K., & Kumar, R. (2023). Towards a greener tomorrow: IoT-enabled smart environment monitoring systems. *2023 International Conference on Advances in Computation, Communication and Information Technology (ICAICCIT)*, Faridabad, India, 1112-1117. DOI: 10.1109/ICAICCIT60255.2023.10465894

Arya, L., Sharma, Y. K., Kumar, R., Padmanaban, H., Devi, S., & Tyagi, L. K. (2023). Maximizing IoT security: An examination of cryptographic algorithms. *2023 International Conference on Power, Energy, Environment & Intelligent Control (PEEIC)*, Greater Noida, India, 1548-1552. https://doi.org/DOI: 10.1109/PEEIC59336.2023.10451210

Attali, Y., & Burstein, J. (2017). Automated essay scoring with e-rater® V.2. Journal of Language Testing and Assessment.

Attamimi, R. A. (2025). AI and English Language Education: A New Era in the Arab World. In Jomaa, N. (Ed.), *Using AI Tools in Text Analysis, Simplification, Classification, and Synthesis* (pp. 113–130). IGI Global Scientific Publishing., DOI: 10.4018/979-8-3693-9511-0.ch004

Bahari, A., & Gholami, J. (2022). A Systematic review of current research on affordances and challenges of technology-assisted grammar learning. *Computer Assisted Language Learning*, *32*(1), 125–148.

Baidoo-Anu, D., & Ansah, O. L. (2023). Education in the era of generative Artificial Intelligence (AI): Understanding the potential benefits of ChatGPT in promoting teaching and learning. *Journal of Artificial Intelligence*, *7*, 52–62.

Baker, R. S. J. D., & Inventado, P. S. (2014). Educational Data Mining and Learning Analytics. In J. A. D. (Ed.), Handbook of Learning Analytics (pp. 101-112). Society for Learning Analytics Research.

Baker, T., & Smith, L. (2019), Educ-AI-tion rebooted? Exploring the future of artificial intelligence in schools and colleges, Available at: https://media.nesta.org.uk/documents/Future_of_AI_and_education_v5_WEB. Pdf. (Accessed 20 August 2024)

Baker, R. S.. (2020). Designing personalized learning experiences with AI: A framework for language education. *Educational Psychologist*, *55*(3), 121–136.

Baker, T., & Smith, L. (2019). *Education rebooted? Exploring the future of AI in schools and colleges*. NESTA.

Bashir, N. (2021). Impact on student engagement and learning outcomes. EdTechBooks. https://edtechbooks.org/ai_in_education/exploring_the_impact_of_ai_integration_on_student_engagement_and_learning_outcomes

Bassich, A., Foglino, F., Leonetti, M., & Kudenko, D. (2020). Curriculum learning with a progression function. *arXiv preprint arXiv:2008.00511*.

Bates, A. W. (2015). *Teaching in a digital age: Guidelines for designing teaching and learning*. BCcampus.

Bellaouar, S., Bellaouar, M. M., & Ghada, I. E. (2021). Topic Modeling: Comparison of LSA and LDA on Scientific Publications. *2021 4th International Conference on Data Storage and Data Engineering*, 59-64. DOI: 10.1145/3456146.3456156

Bender, E. M., Gebru, T., McMillan-Major, A., & Shmitchell, S. (2021, March). On the dangers of stochastic parrots: Can language models be too big? In *Proceedings of the 2021 ACM conference on fairness, accountability, and transparency* (pp. 610-623). DOI: 10.1145/3442188.3445922

Bennett, E., & Foltz, P. W. (2019). The constructivist ethics algorithm: Value sensitive design for ethical mediation between humans and systems. *Journal of Human-Computer Studies*, *132*, 110–124.

Bennett, S., & Maton, K. (2010). Beyond the 'Digital Natives' Debate: Towards a More Nuanced Understanding of Students' Technology Experiences. *Journal of Computer Assisted Learning*, *26*(5), 321–331.

Bergmann, J., & Sams, A. (2012). *Flip your classroom: Reach every student in every class every day*. International Society for Technology in Education.

Bian, N., Han, X., Sun, L., Lin, H., Lu, Y., He, B., Jiang, S., & Dong, B. (2024). *ChatGPT is a Knowledgeable but Inexperienced Solver: An Investigation of Commonsense Problem in Large Language Models* (No. arXiv:2303.16421). arXiv. http://arxiv.org/abs/2303.16421

Bijalwan, V., Kumari, P., Pascual, J., & Semwal, V. B. (2014). *Machine learning approach for text and document mining* (Versión 1). arXiv. DOI: 10.48550/ARXIV.1406.1580

Bikowski, D. (2018). *Technology for Teaching Grammar*. Wiley. DOI: 10.1002/9781118784235.eelt0441

Blair, C., & Hargreaves, E. (2018). The Role of AI in Language Education: A Guide for Educators. *International Journal of Information and Education Technology (IJIET)*, *8*(7), 564–569.

Blei, D. M., Ng, A. Y., & Jordan, M. (2003). *Latent dirichlet allocation*. *3*, 993-1022.

Blei, D. (2011). Probabilistic topic models. *Proceedings of the 17th ACM SIGKDD International Conference Tutorials*, 1-1. DOI: 10.1145/2107736.2107741

Bonikowski, B., Luo, Y., & Stuhler, O. (2022). Politics as Usual? Measuring Populism, Nationalism, and Authoritarianism in U.S. Presidential Campaigns (1952–2020) with Neural Language Models. *Sociological Methods & Research, 51*(4), 1721–1787. DOI: 10.1177/00491241221122317

Bronstein, B., Wolfe, Z. M., & Ciampa, K. (2023). Transforming digital literacy practices: ChatGPT in education. *International Journal of Educational Technology in Higher Education, 20*(1).

Brown, T. (2013). *What Consumers Think about brands on social media, and what bunesses need to do about it* (Keep Social Honest). https://www.cim.co.uk/media/1733/ksh_report_.pdf

Brown, P., & Smith, J. (2020). Personalized learning and AI: Impacts on K-12 education. *Journal of the Learning Sciences*, *18*(2), 123–135.

Brynjolfsson, E., & McAfee, A. (2014). *The second machine age: Work, progress, and prosperity in a time of brilliant technologies*. WW Norton & Company.

Bulathwela, S., Pérez-Ortiz, M., Holloway, C., & Shawe-Taylor, J. (2021). Could AI Democratise Education? Socio-Technical Imaginaries of an EdTech Revolution. In arXiv (Cornell University). Cornell University. https://doi.org//arxiv.2112.02034DOI: 10.48550

Bulut, O., & Beiting-Parrish, M. (2024). The Rise of Artificial Intelligence in Educational Measurement: Opportunities and Ethical Challenges. In Chinese/English Journal of Educational Measurement and Evaluation (Vol. 5, Issue 3). DOI: 10.59863/MIQL7785

Burden, R. L. (2010). *Psychology for language teachers: a social constructivist approach.* Cambridge University Press.

Burgstahler, S. E., & Cory, R. C. (Eds.). (2010). *Universal design in higher education: From principles to practice.* Harvard Education Press.

Cannix Yau, K., & Chan, K. (2023). *University of Hong Kong temporarily bans students from using ChatGPT.* China News Service.

Cano, C. A. G., & Troya, A. L. C. (2023). AI is applied to teaching and learning processes. *LatIA*, *1*, 2–2. DOI: 10.62486/latia20232

Chai, C. P. (2023). Comparison of text preprocessing methods. *Natural Language Engineering*, *29*(3), 509–553. DOI: 10.1017/S1351324922000213

Chalmers, C., & Harris, K. (2017). Machine Learning and Natural Language Processing in Education. *International Journal of Artificial Intelligence in Education*, *27*(4), 703–710.

Chemnad, K., & Othman, A. (2024). Digital accessibility in the era of artificial intelligence—Bibliometric analysis and systematic review. *Frontiers in Artificial Intelligence*, *7*, 1–17. DOI: 10.3389/frai.2024.1349668 PMID: 38435800

Chen, C.-H., Shiu, M.-F., & Chen, S. (2021). Use Learnable Knowledge Graph in Dialogue System for Visually Impaired Macro Navigation. In Applied Sciences (Vol. 11, Issue 13, p. 6057). Multidisciplinary Digital Publishing Institute. DOI: 10.3390/app11136057

Chen, L., Chen, P., & Lin, Z. (2020). AI in education: A review. *IEEE Access : Practical Innovations, Open Solutions*, *8*, 75264–75278. DOI: 10.1109/ACCESS.2020.2988510

Chen, W., Li, J., & Zha, D. (2021). Artificial intelligence in language education: A review of applications and effects. *Journal of Educational Computing Research*, *59*(3), 507–525.

Chen, X.. (2020). AI in education: The role of teachers in the future classroom. *Journal of Educational Technology & Society*, *23*(2), 40–52.

Chen, X., Xie, H., & Hwang, G. (2020). A multi-perspective study on Artificial Intelligence in Education: grants, conferences, journals, software tools, institutions, and researchers. In *Computers and Education Artificial Intelligence* (Vol. 1, p. 100005). Elsevier BV., DOI: 10.1016/j.caeai.2020.100005

Chen, Y., Cheng, J., Jiang, H., Liu, L., Zhang, H., Shi, S., & Xu, R. (2022). Learning from Sibling Mentions with Scalable Graph Inference in Fine-Grained Entity Typing. *Proceedings of the 60th Annual Meeting of the Association for Computational Linguistics(*Volume 1*: Long Papers)*, 2076-2087. DOI: 10.18653/v1/2022.acl-long.147

Chieu, H. L., Ng, H. T., & Lee, Y. K. (2003). Closing the gap: Learning-based information extraction rivaling knowledge-engineering methods. *Proceedings of the 41st Annual Meeting on Association for Computational Linguistics - ACL '03, 1*, 216-223. DOI: 10.3115/1075096.1075124

Choi, E., Levy, O., Choi, Y., & Zettlemoyer, L. (2018). Ultra-Fine Entity Typing. *Proceedings of the 56th Annual Meeting of the Association for Computational Linguistics(*Volume 1*: Long Papers)*, 87-96. DOI: 10.18653/v1/P18-1009

Chounta, I. A., Bardone, E., Raudsep, A., & Pedaste, M. (2022). Exploring teachers' perceptions of artificial intelligence as a tool to support their practice in Estonian K-12 education. *International Journal of Artificial Intelligence in Education*, *32*(3), 725–755. DOI: 10.1007/s40593-021-00243-5

Chukharev-Hudilainen, E., & Klepikova, T. A. (2016). Automated writing evaluation for formative assessment of second language writing: Investigating the accuracy and usefulness of feedback. *Language Testing*, *33*(3), 307–328.

Cloate, R. (2016). The relationship between international students' English test scores and their academic achievements. *Journal of pedagogic development, 6*(2), 3-8.

Collobert, R., Weston, J., Bottou, L., Karlen, M., Kavukcuoglu, K., & Kuksa, P. (2011). *Natural Language Processing (almost) from Scratch* (Versión 1). arXiv. DOI: 10.48550/ARXIV.1103.0398

Connelly, S. (2018). *Practical BM25—Part 2: The BM25 Algorithm and its variables*. https://www.elastic.co/blog/practical-bm25-part-2-the-bm25-algorithm-and-its-variables

Cotton, D. R., Cotton, P. A., & Shipway, J. R. (2023). Chatting and Cheating: Ensuring academic integrity in the era of ChatGPT. *Innovations in Education and Teaching International*, •••, 1–12.

Crowe, J. (1995). Constraint-based event recognition for information extraction. *Proceedings of the 33rd Annual Meeting on Association for Computational Linguistics-*, 296. DOI: 10.3115/981658.981701

Dabbagh, N., & Kitsantas, A. (2012). Using technology to enhance learning and teaching in the 21st century: The role of teachers as facilitators. *Computers in Human Behavior*, *28*(4), 1167–1175.

Dai, H., Song, Y., & Wang, H. (2021). Ultra-Fine Entity Typing with Weak Supervision from a Masked Language Model. *Proceedings of the 59th Annual Meeting of the Association for Computational Linguistics and the 11th International Joint Conference on Natural Language Processing*(Volume 1*: Long Papers)*, 1790-1799. DOI: 10.18653/v1/2021.acl-long.141

Dale, R., & Viethen, J. (2021). The automated writing assistance landscape in 2021. *Natural Language Engineering*, *27*(4), 511–518. DOI: 10.1017/S1351324921000164

Daller, M. H., & Phelan, D. (2013). Predicting international student study success. *Applied Linguistics Review*, *4*(1), 173–193. DOI: 10.1515/applirev-2013-0008

Das, S. S. S., Katiyar, A., Passonneau, R. J., & Zhang, R. (2021). *CONTaiNER: Few-Shot Named Entity Recognition via Contrastive Learning* (Versión 2). arXiv. DOI: 10.48550/ARXIV.2109.07589

Davidson, T., Warmsley, D., Macy, M., & Weber, I. (2017). *Automated Hate Speech Detection and the Problem of Offensive Language* (Versión 1). arXiv. DOI: 10.48550/ARXIV.1703.04009

De la Vall, R. R. F., & Araya, F. G. (2022). Exploring the Benefits and Challenges of AI-Language Learning Tools. *The International Journal of Social Sciences and Humanities Invention, 10*(1), 7569–7576. DOI: 10.18535/ijsshi/v10i01.02

Dede, C. (2011). Comparing Frameworks for 21st Century Skills. In J. A. Bellanca & R. A. Brandt (Eds.), 21st Century Skills: Rethinking How Students Learn (pp. 51-76). Solution Tree Press.

Deerwester, S., Dumais, S. T., Furnas, G. W., Landauer, T. K., & Harshman, R. (1990a). Indexing by latent semantic analysis. *Journal of the American Society for Information Science*, *41*(6), 391–407. DOI: 10.1002/(SICI)1097-4571(199009)41:6<391::AID-ASI1>3.0.CO;2-9

Denny, P., Gulwani, S., Heffernan, N. T., Käser, T., Moore, S., Rafferty, A. N., & Singla, A. (2024). Generative AI for education (GAIED): Advances, opportunities, and challenges. arXiv preprint arXiv:2402.01580.

Devlin, J., Chang, M.-W., Lee, K., & Toutanova, K. (2019). *BERT: Pre-training ofDeep Bidirectional Transformers for Language Understanding* (No. arXiv:1810.04805). arXiv. http://arxiv.org/abs/1810.04805

Devlin, J., Chang, M.-W., Lee, K., & Toutanova, K. (2018). *BERT: Pre-training of Deep Bidirectional Transformers for Language Understanding* (Versión 2). arXiv. DOI: 10.48550/ARXIV.1810.04805

Dey Sarkar, S., Goswami, S., Agarwal, A., & Aktar, J. (2014). A Novel Feature Selection Technique for Text Classification Using Naïve Bayes. *International Scholarly Research Notices*, *2014*, 1–10. DOI: 10.1155/2014/717092 PMID: 27433512

Dhar, A., Mukherjee, H., Dash, N. S., & Roy, K. (2021). Text categorization: Past and present. *Artificial Intelligence Review*, *54*(4), 3007–3054. DOI: 10.1007/s10462-020-09919-1

Dimitriadou, E., & Lanitis, A. (2023). A critical evaluation, challenges, and future perspectives of using artificial intelligence and emerging technologies in smart classrooms. *Smart Learning Environments*, *10*(12), 1–26. DOI: 10.1186/s40561-023-00231-3

Dogan, T., & Uysal, A. K. (2019). On Term Frequency Factor in Supervised Term Weighting Schemes for Text Classification. *Arabian Journal for Science and Engineering*, *44*(11), 9545–9560. DOI: 10.1007/s13369-019-03920-9

Donnelly-Hermosillo, D., Gerard, L., & Linn, M. C. (2019). Impact of graph technologies in K-12 science and mathematics education. In *Computers & Education* (Vol. 146, p. 103748). Elsevier BV., DOI: 10.1016/j.compedu.2019.103748

Ducar, C., & Schocket, D. H. (2018). Machine translation and the L2 classroom: Pedagogical solutions for making peace with Google translate. *Foreign Language Annals*, *51*(4), 779–795. DOI: 10.1111/flan.12366

Dugošija, T. (2024). Benefits and challenges of artificial intelligence in English language teaching. *Knowledge International Journal*, *62*(2), 275–280.

Du, X., & Cardie, C. (2020). Event Extraction by Answering (Almost) Natural Questions. *Proceedings of the 2020 Conference on Empirical Methods in Natural Language Processing (EMNLP)*, 671-683. DOI: 10.18653/v1/2020.emnlp-main.49

Du, X., & Ji, H. (2022). Retrieval-Augmented Generative Question Answering for Event Argument Extraction. *Proceedings of the 2022 Conference on Empirical Methods in Natural Language Processing*, 4649-4666. DOI: 10.18653/v1/2022.emnlp-main.307

Eckart, C., & Young, G. (1936). The approximation of one matrix by another of lower rank. *Psychometrika, 1*(3), 211–218. DOI: 10.1007/BF02288367

Einarsson, H., Lund, S. H., & Jónsdóttir, A. H. (2024). Application of ChatGPT for automated problem reframing across academic domains. *Computers and Education: Artificial Intelligence, 6*, 100194. DOI: 10.1016/j.caeai.2023.100194

Ejjami, R. (2024). The future of learning: AI-based curriculum development. *Int J Multidiscipline Res, 6*(4).

Elder, C., & Von Randow, J. (2008). Exploring the utility of a web-based English language screening tool. *Language Assessment Quarterly, 5*(3), 173–194. DOI: 10.1080/15434300802229334

El-Kassas, W. S., Salama, C. R., Rafea, A. A., & Mohamed, H. K. (2021). Automatic text summarization: A comprehensive survey. *Expert Systems with Applications, 165*, 113679. DOI: 10.1016/j.eswa.2020.113679

Elkhatat, A. M., Elsaid, K., & Almeer, S. (2023). Evaluating the efficacy of AI content detection tools in differentiating between human and AI-generated text. *International Journal for Educational Integrity, 19*(1), 17. DOI: 10.1007/s40979-023-00140-5

Ellis, R. (2009). The differential effects of three types of task planning on the fluency, complexity, and accuracy in L2 oral production. *Applied Linguistics, 30*(4), 474–509.

Engonopoulos, N., Lazaridou, A., Paliouras, G., & Chandrinos, K. (2011). ELS: A word-level method for entity-level sentiment analysis. *Proceedings of the International Conference on Web Intelligence, Mining and Semantics*, 1-9. DOI: 10.1145/1988688.1988703

Erton, I. (2022). Pragmatic issues in teaching translation and interpretation: A curricular perspective at university level. *Eurasian Journal of Language Teaching and Linguistic Studies, 2*(2), 237–244.

Evans, J. A., & Aceves, P. (2016). Machine Translation: Mining Text for Social Theory. *Annual Review of Sociology, 42*(1), 21–50. DOI: 10.1146/annurev-soc-081715-074206

Fajaruddin, S., Retnawati, H., Setiawan, C., Apino, E., Arlinwibowo, J., & Rachman, D. (2024). Technology's impact on language learning: Meta-analysis on variables and effectiveness. [EduLearn]. *Journal of Education and Learning, 18*(2), 512–525.

Falmagne, J. C., Albert, D., Doble, C., Eppstein, D., & Hu, X. (Eds.). (2013). *Knowledge spaces: Applications in education*. Springer Science & Business Media. DOI: 10.1007/978-3-642-35329-1

Farra, N., Challita, E., Assi, R. A., & Hajj, H. (2010). Sentence-Level and Document-Level Sentiment Mining for Arabic Texts. *2010 IEEE International Conference on Data Mining Workshops*, 1114-1119. DOI: 10.1109/ICDMW.2010.95

Fitria, T. N. (2021). Grammarly as AI-powered English writing assistant: Students' alternative for writing English.Metathesis. *Journal of English Language, Literature, and Teaching*, *1*(5), 65–78. DOI: 10.31002/metathesis.v5i1.3519

Fitzpatrick, T., Alvarado, P., & Tolk, A. (2021). Personalized language learning with AI-powered apps: A case study of Duolingo and Babbel. *International Journal of Education Technology*, *22*(3), 245–259.

Frey, C. B., & Osborne, M. A. (2017). The Future of Employment: How Susceptible are Jobs to Computerization? *Technological Forecasting and Social Change*, *114*, 254–280. DOI: 10.1016/j.techfore.2016.08.019

Fu, J. (2013), "Complexity of ICT in education: A critical literature review and its implications", *International Journal of Education and Development using ICT*, Vol. 9 No. 1, pp. 112-125.

Fu, T.-J., Li, P.-H., & Ma, W.-Y. (2019). GraphRel: Modeling Text as Relational Graphs for Joint Entity and Relation Extraction. *Proceedings of the 57th Annual Meeting of the Association for Computational Linguistics*, 1409-1418. DOI: 10.18653/v1/P19-1136

Fyfe, P. (2022). How to cheat on your final paper: Assigning AI for student writing. *AI & Society*, *38*(4), 1395–1405. DOI: 10.1007/s00146-022-01397-z

Garcia, J. M., & Kelly, T. (2015). *The economics and policy implications of infrastructure sharing and mutualisation in Africa*. World Bank.

Gayed, J. M., Carlon, M. K. J., Oriola, A. M., & Cross, J. S. (2022). Exploring an AI-based writing assistant's impact on English language learners. *Computers and Education: Artificial Intelligence*, *3*, 1–8. DOI: 10.1016/j.caeai.2022.100055

Gbollie, C., & Gong, S. (2013). The Essence of Foreign Language Learning in Today's Globalizing World: Benefits and Hindrances. *New Media and Mass Communication*, *9*, 35–44.

Gligorea, I., Cioca, M., Oancea, R., Gorski, A.-T., Gorski, H., & Tudorache, P. (2023). Adaptive Learning Using Artificial Intelligence in e-Learning: A Literature Review. Education Sciences, 13(12), 1216. Multidisciplinary Digital Publishing Institute. DOI: 10.3390/educsci13121216

Godwin-Jones, R. (2019). Language learning and technology: A new paradigm. *CALICO Journal*, *36*(1), 1–13.

Godwin-Jones, R. (2022). Partnering with AI: Intelligent writing assistance and instructed language learning. *Language Learning & Technology*, *26*(2), 5–24.

Golovatska, I., & Tereshchuk, G. (2024). The use of digital technologies to prepare future translators for the modern requirements of the linguistic services market. *Journal of Educational Technology Development and Exchange*, *17*(1), 175–187. DOI: 10.18785/jetde.1701.10

Gonzales, L., & Martinez, P. (2021). Language learning apps and AI: Tailoring education for better outcomes. *Educational Technology Review*, *9*(3), 245–260.

González, C. (2019). The digital divide and its impact on education: Bridging the gap with technology in language learning. *Journal of Educational Technology & Society*, *22*(3), 156–167.

Good, I. J. (1953). The Population Frequencies of Species and the Estimation of Population Parameters. *Biometrika*, *40*(3/4), 237. DOI: 10.2307/2333344

Grimm, N., Meyer, M., & Volkmann, L. (2015). *Teaching English*. Narr Francke Attempto.

Grishman, R. (2015). Information Extraction. *IEEE Intelligent Systems*, *30*(5), 8–15. DOI: 10.1109/MIS.2015.68

Grubaugh, S., Levitt, G., & Deever, D. (2023). Harnessing AI to Power Constructivist Learning: An Evolution in Educational Methodology [JETM]. *Journal of Effective Teaching Methods*, *1*(3), 81–83. DOI: 10.59652/jetm.v1i3.43

Gu, C., Peng, Y., Nastase, S. A., Mayer, R. E., & Li, P. (2024). Onscreen presence of instructors in video lectures affects learners' neural synchrony and visual attention during multimedia learning. In Proceedings of the National Academy of Sciences (Vol. 121, Issue 12). National Academy of Sciences. DOI: 10.1073/pnas.2309054121

Guerberof-Arenas, A., & Moorkens, J. (2023). Ethics and machine translation: The end user perspective. In *Towards Responsible Machine Translation: Ethical and Legal Considerations in Machine Translation* (pp. 113–133). Springer International Publishing. DOI: 10.1007/978-3-031-14689-3_7

Gupta, S., & Gupta, S. K. (2019). Abstractive summarization: An overview of the state of the art. *Expert Systems with Applications*, *121*, 49–65. DOI: 10.1016/j.eswa.2018.12.011

Guru, D. S., & Suhil, M. (2015). A Novel Term_Class Relevance Measure for Text Categorization. *Procedia Computer Science*, *45*, 13–22. DOI: 10.1016/j.procs.2015.03.074

Guszcza, J., Chui, M., & Patel, S. (2017). *The future of work: How AI will change the way we learn*. McKinsey Global Institute.

Hahn, U., & Mani, I. (2000). The challenges of automatic summarization. *Computer*, *33*(11), 29–36. DOI: 10.1109/2.881692

Haimowitz, S. M. (2014). *U.S. Patent No. 8,666,300*. Washington, DC: U.S. Patent and Trademark Office.

Hambarde, K. A., & Proença, H. (2023). Information Retrieval: Recent Advances and Beyond. *IEEE Access : Practical Innovations, Open Solutions*, *11*, 76581–76604. DOI: 10.1109/ACCESS.2023.3295776

Hamdi, M. (2024, July). How AI is Transforming and Shaping the Future of Education. In *2024 IEEE 28th International Conference on Intelligent Engineering Systems (INES)* (pp. 000115-000116). IEEE. DOI: 10.1109/INES63318.2024.10629089

Han, J., Yoo, H., Kim, Y., Myung, J., Kim, M., Lim, H., Kim, J., Lee, T. Y., Hong, H., Ahn, S.-Y., & Oh, A. (2023). RECIPE: How to Integrate ChatGPT into EFL Writing Education. arXiv preprint arXiv:2305.11583. DOI: 10.1145/3573051.3596200

Hanna, A. (2013). Computer-Aided Content Analysis of Digitally Enabled Movements. *Mobilization: An International Quarterly (San Diego, Calif.)*, *18*(4), 367–388. DOI: 10.17813/maiq.18.4.m1g180620x7n1542

Harrington, M., & Roche, T. (2014). Word recognition skill and academic success across disciplines in an ELF university setting. *Papers in Language Testing and Assessment*, *3*(2), 76–99. DOI: 10.58379/QPEW8104

Harris, Z. S. (1954). Distributional Structure. *Word*, *10*(2-3), 146–162. DOI: 10.1080/00437956.1954.11659520

Hasan, M. K., Fakih, A. H., & Seraj, P. M. I. (2022). The effect of technology-assisted language programme on vocabulary learning among EFL students at the tertiary level. *Heliyon*, *8*(8), 1–6. DOI: 10.1016/j.heliyon.2022.e10313 PMID: 36051275

Healey, J. (2020). [). Thirroul: The Spinney Press.]. *Artificial Intelligence*, *450*, •••.

Heffernan, N. (2019). The evolution of adaptive learning systems in language education. *Educational Technology Review*, *45*(2), 76–88.

Heilala, V., Jääskelä, P., Kärkkäinen, T., & Saarela, M. (2020). Understanding the Study Experiences of Students in Low Agency Profile: Towards a Smart Education Approach. In Lecture notes in electrical engineering (p. 498). Springer Science+Business Media. DOI: 10.1007/978-3-030-53187-4_54

Heil, C., Wu, J. S., Lee, J. H., & Schmidt, T. (2020). A review of mobile language learning applications: Trends, challenges, and opportunities. *The EuroCALL Review*, *28*(1), 20–50.

Hendrawaty, N., Yuliati, Y., & Haryanti, R. P. (2024). EFL Students' Preferences on Vocabulary Learning. *Scope: Journal of English Language Teaching*, *8*(2), 541–550. DOI: 10.30998/scope.v8i2.21876

Hiemstra, D. (2009). Information retrieval models. *Information Retrieval: Searching in the 21st Century*, 1-19.

Hill, R., & Sethi, D. (2023). AI-powered language learning apps: A review of effectiveness. *International Conference of Language Learning*, 15(1), 57-72.

Hipogrosso, S., & Nesmachnow, S. (2020). Analysis of Sustainable Public Transportation and Mobility Recommendations for Montevideo and Parque Rodó Neighborhood. In Smart Cities (Vol. 3, Issue 2, p. 479). Multidisciplinary Digital Publishing Institute. DOI: 10.3390/smartcities3020026

Hockly, N. (2023). Artificial Intelligence in English Language Teaching: The Good, the Bad and the Ugly. In Journal, R. E. L. C. (Ed.), *Issue 2* (Vol. 54, p. 445). SAGE Publishing., DOI: 10.1177/00336882231168504

Hokijuliandy, E., Napitupulu, H., & Firdaniza, . (2023). Application of SVM and Chi-Square Feature Selection for Sentiment Analysis of Indonesia's National Health Insurance Mobile Application. *Mathematics*, *11*(17), 3765. DOI: 10.3390/math11173765

Holmes, W., Bialik, M., & Fadel, C. (2019). *AI in education promises and implications for teaching and learning*. Center for Curriculum Redesign.

Hotho, A., Nürnberger, A., & Paaß, G. (2005). A Brief Survey of Text Mining. *Journal for Language Technology and Computational Linguistics*, *20*(1), 19–62. DOI: 10.21248/jlcl.20.2005.68

Hsu, I.-H., Huang, K.-H., Boschee, E., Miller, S., Natarajan, P., Chang, K.-W., & Peng, N. (2022). DEGREE: A Data-Efficient Generation-Based Event Extraction Model. *Proceedings of the 2022 Conference of the North American Chapter of the Association for Computational Linguistics: Human Language Technologies*, 1890-1908. DOI: 10.18653/v1/2022.naacl-main.138

Huang, K. T., Ball, C., Francis, J., Ratan, R., Boumis, J., & Fordham, J. (2019). Augmented versus VR in education: An exploratory study examining science knowledge retention when using augmented reality/VR mobile applications. *Cyberpsychology, Behavior, and Social Networking*, *22*(2), 105–110. DOI: 10.1089/cyber.2018.0150 PMID: 30657334

Huang, R. H., & Spector, J. M. (2018). Educational Technology and the Challenge of Change. *Educational Technology Research and Development*, *66*(4), 973–986.

Huang, R. H., Spector, J. M., & Yang, J. (2020). Educational technology and the transformation of the classroom: The role of AI in personalized learning. *Journal of Educational Technology & Society*, *23*(4), 1–10.

Huang, Z., Mao, Y., & Zhang, J. (2024). The Influence of Artificial Intelligence Technology on College Learners' Learning Effectiveness from the Perspective of Constructivism — Taking ChatGPT as an Example. *Journal of Education, Humanities and Social Sciences*, *30*, 40–46. DOI: 10.54097/y1x3jj43

Hubackova, S. (2016). The importance of foreign language education. *New Trends and Issues Proceedings on Humanities and Social Sciences*, *5*, 98–101.

Huber, M. (2025). *AI for language education: Project developments 2024. European Centre for Modern Languages*. ECML.

Hubert, K, Elisha B. and Kaledio, P. (2023), Address the potential disparity in access to AI-powered education, Available at: (1) (PDF) Address the potential disparity in access to AI (researchgate.net) (Accessed 05 June 2024).

Hussein, D. M. E.-D. M. (2018). A survey on sentiment analysis challenges. *Journal of King Saud University. Engineering Sciences*, *30*(4), 330–338. DOI: 10.1016/j.jksues.2016.04.002

Hwang, G. J., & Chen, N. S. (2023). Exploring the potential of generative AI in education: Applications, challenges, and future research directions. *Journal of Educational Technology & Society*, *26*(2).

Hwang, G. J., Chen, P. H., & Huang, Y. M. (2020). Integrating AI-based technologies for personalized language learning. *Educational Technology Research and Development*, *68*(4), 2203–2224.

Ilkka, T. (2018). *The Impact of Artificial Intelligence on Learning, Teaching, and Education*. European Union.

International Telecommunication Union (ITU). (2022). Global connectivity and infrastructure for education. https://www.itu.int/dms_pub/itu-d/opb/ind/d-ind-global.01-2022-pdf-e.pdf

Ishak, S. A., Din, R., & Hasran, U. A. (2020). Defining Digital Game-Based Learning for Science, Technology, Engineering, and Mathematics: A New Perspective on Design and Developmental Research. In Journal of Medical Internet Research (Vol. 23, Issue 2). JMIR Publications. DOI: 10.2196/20537

Jain, A., & Zongker, D. (1997). Feature selection: Evaluation, application, and small sample performance. *IEEE Transactions on Pattern Analysis and Machine Intelligence*, *19*(2), 153–158. DOI: 10.1109/34.574797

Jain, S., & Jain, R. (2019). "Role of artificial intelligence in higher education- an empirical investigation", *IJRAR-. International Journal of Research and Analytical Reviews*, *6*(2), 144–150.

Jelinek, F., & Mercer, R. L. (1980). Interpolated estimation of Markov source parameters from sparse data. *InProceedings of the Workshop on Pattern Recognition in Practice*, 381-397.

Joachims, T. (1998). Text categorization with Support Vector Machines: Learning with many relevant features. In Nédellec, C., & Rouveirol, C. (Eds.), *Machine Learning: ECML-98* (Vol. 1398, pp. 137–142). Springer Berlin Heidelberg., DOI: 10.1007/BFb0026683

Johnson, C. I., & Mayer, R. E. (2009). A testing effect with multimedia learning. *Journal of Educational Psychology*, *101*(3), 621–629. DOI: 10.1037/a0015183

Johnson, M., & Lee, W. (2020). AI in language education: Applications in assessment and evaluation. *Educational Assessment Review*, *24*(3), 198–210.

Jomaa, N. J., & Kamal, M. N. (2023). Perspectives of students and teachers towards developing speaking skills by using technology among EFL Iraqi students. In *Integrating TPACK and CALL in English Language Teaching* (pp. 153–173). IGI Global., DOI: 10.4018/978-1-6684-8546-0.ch007

Jomaa, N., Attamimi, R., & Al Mahri, M. (2024). Utilising Artificial Intelligence (AI) in Vocabulary Learning by EFL Omani Students: The Effect of Age, Gender, and Level of Study. *Forum for Linguistic Studies*, *6*(5), 171–186. DOI: 10.30564/fls.v6i5.6968

Jomaa, N., Attamimi, R., & Al Mahri, M. (2025). The Use of Artificial Intelligence (AI) in Teaching English Vocabulary in Oman: Perspectives, Teaching Practices, and Challenges. *World Journal of English Language, 15*(3), 1–13. DOI: 10.5430/wjel.v15n3p1

Jomaa, N., Attamimi, R., & Alghafri, K. (2025). Vocabulary Learning Strategies Utilised by EFL Omani Students in Oman: The Effect of Age, Gender, and Levels of Study. *Forum for Linguistic Studies, 7*(2), 967–987. DOI: 10.30564/fls.v7i2.8450

Jonassen, D. H., & Rohrer-Murphy, L. (1999). Activity theory as a framework for designing constructivist learning environments. *Educational Technology Research and Development, 47*(1), 61–79. DOI: 10.1007/BF02299477

Joulin, A., Grave, E., Bojanowski, P., & Mikolov, T. (2016). *Bag of Tricks for Efficient Text Classification* (Versión 3). arXiv. DOI: 10.48550/ARXIV.1607.01759

Kalyani, L. K. (2023). Revolutionizing Education: AI's Pioneering Role in Shaping Tomorrow's Scholars. *International Journal of Multidisciplinary Research in Arts. Science and Technology, 1*(2), 1–7.

Kambhampati, S. & Association for the Advancement of Artificial Intelligence (Eds.). (2016). *Proceedings of the Twenty-Fifth International Joint Conference on Artificial Intelligence:New York, NY, USA,9-15 July 2016.* Volume 1. IJCAI, Palo Alto, California. AAAI Press/International Joint Conferences on Artificial Intelligence.

Karataş, F., Abedi, F. Y., Gunyel, F. O., Karadeniz, D., & Kuzgun, Y. (2024). Incorporating AI in foreign language education: An investigation into ChatGPT's effect on foreign language learners. *Education and Information Technologies, 29*(15), 1–24. DOI: 10.1007/s10639-024-12574-6

Kashefi, A., & Mukerji, T. (2023). ChatGPT for Programming Numerical Methods. ArXiv, abs/2303.12093.

Keerthiwansha, N. W. B. S. (2018). Artificial intelligence education (AIEd) in English as a second language (ESL) classroom in Sri Lanka. *Artificial Intelligence, 6*(1), 31–36.

Khan, K., Baharudin, B., Khan, A., & Ullah, A. (2014). Mining opinion components from unstructured reviews: A review. *Journal of King Saud University. Computer and Information Sciences, 26*(3), 258–275. DOI: 10.1016/j.jksuci.2014.03.009

Khot, T., Sabharwal, A., & Clark, P. (2017). *Answering Complex Questions Using Open Information Extraction* (Versión 1). arXiv. DOI: 10.48550/ARXIV.1704.05572

Khurana, D., Koli, A., Khatter, K., & Singh, S. (2023). Natural language processing: State of the art, current trends and challenges. *Multimedia Tools and Applications, 82*(3), 3713–3744. DOI: 10.1007/s11042-022-13428-4 PMID: 35855771

Kirmani, M., Manzoor Hakak, N., Mohd, M., & Mohd, M. (2019). Hybrid Text Summarization: A Survey. In Ray, K., Sharma, T. K., Rawat, S., Saini, R. K., & Bandyopadhyay, A. (Eds.), *Soft Computing: Theories and Applications* (Vol. 742, pp. 63–73). Springer Singapore., DOI: 10.1007/978-981-13-0589-4_7

Klein, W. (2001), "Second Language Acquisition", *International Encyclopedia of the Social & Behavioral Sciences*, No. 2001, pp. 13768-13771.

Koller, D. & Neural Information Processing Systems Foundation (Eds.). (2009). *Advances in neural information processing systems 21: 22nd Annual Conference on Neural Information Processing Systems 2008 ; December 8 - 10, 2008, Vancouver, B. C., Canada ; [proceedings].* Curran.

Kou, G., & Peng, Y. (2015). An Application of Latent Semantic Analysis for Text Categorization. *International Journal of Computers, Communications & Control, 10*(3), 357. DOI: 10.15837/ijccc.2015.3.1923

Kuhlman, K. (2017), Best Practices in Foreign Language Learning. Master's thesis. Northwestern College, Iowa. Orange City.

Kukulska-Hulme, A., & Traxler, J. (2019). *Mobile learning: The next generation.* Routledge.

Kulik, J. A., & Fletcher, J. D. (2016). Effectiveness of intelligent tutoring systems: A meta-analytic review. *Review of Educational Research, 86*(1), 42–78. DOI: 10.3102/0034654315581420

Kumar, A., & Sharma, A. (2019). Systematic literature review of fuzzy logic based text summarization. *Iranian Journal of Fuzzy Systems, 16*(5). Advance online publication. DOI: 10.22111/ijfs.2019.4906

Kumar, V., & Patel, N. (2022). Virtual classrooms with AI: Enhancing engagement during the pandemic. *Journal of Online Education, 19*(1), 89–104.

Kumar, V., & Rose, C. P. (2011). Language learning with technology: Trends, perspectives, and challenges. *AI & Society, 26*(4), 339–351.

Labadze, L., Grigolia, M., & Machaidze, L. (2023). Role of AI chatbots in education: Systematic literature review. *International Journal of Educational Technology in Higher Education, 20*(1), 56. DOI: 10.1186/s41239-023-00426-1

Lafleur, L. (2024). The effects of gamified daily awards on digital vocabulary flashcard learning: A case study. *Technology in Language Teaching & Learning, 6*(2), 1–20. DOI: 10.29140/tltl.v6n2.1195

Lai, T., Xie, C., Ruan, M., Wang, Z., Lu, H., & Fu, S. (2023). Influence of artificial intelligence in education on adolescents' social adaptability: The mediatory role of social support. In PLoS ONE (Vol. 18, Issue 3). Public Library of Science. DOI: 10.1371/journal.pone.0283170

Lai, Y., Saab, N., & Admiraal, W. (2022). University students' use of mobile technology in self-directed language learning: Using the integrative model of behaviour prediction. *Computers & Education, 179*, 1–13. DOI: 10.1016/j.compedu.2021.104413

Lantolf, J. P., & Sunderman, G. (2001). The struggle for a place in the sun: Rationalizing foreign language study in the twentieth century. *Modern Language Journal, 85*(1), 5–25. DOI: 10.1111/0026-7902.00094

Lei, X., Fathi, J., Noorbakhsh, S., & Rahimi, M. (2022). The impact of mobile-assisted language learning on English as a foreign language learners' vocabulary learning attitudes and self-regulatory capacity. *Frontiers in Psychology, 13*, 1–14. DOI: 10.3389/fpsyg.2022.872922 PMID: 35800918

Lestari, S., Usadiati, W., & Misrita, M. (2022). The correlation between students' artificial intelligence and theirEnglish reading skills achievement. *Bahasa: Jurnal Keilmuan Pendidikan Bahasa Dan Sastra Indonesia, 3*(2), 103–111. DOI: 10.26499/bahasa.v3i2.110

Leta, F. M., & Vancea, D. P. C. (2023). Ethics in Education: Exploring the Ethical Implications of AI Implementation. *Ovidius University Annals. Economic Sciences Series, 23*(1), 413–421.

Li, B., Fang, G., Yang, Y., Wang, Q., Ye, W., Zhao, W., & Zhang, S. (2023). *Evaluating ChatGPT's Information Extraction Capabilities: An Assessment of Performance, Explainability, Calibration, and Faithfulness* (No. arXiv:2304.11633). arXiv. http://arxiv.org/abs/2304.11633

Li, X., Jin, J., Zhou, Y., Zhang, Y., Zhang, P., Zhu, Y., & Dou, Z. (2024). *From Matching to Generation: A Survey on Generative Information Retrieval* (No. arXiv:2404.14851). arXiv. http://arxiv.org/abs/2404.14851

Li, B., Yu, D., Ye, W., Zhang, J., & Zhang, S. (2022). *Sequence Generation with Label Augmentation for Relation Extraction* (Versión 2). arXiv. DOI: 10.48550/ARXIV.2212.14266

Lim, Ch. P., & Chai, Ch. S. (2004). An activity-theoretical approach to research of ICT integration in Singapore schools: Orienting activities and learner autonomy. *Computers & Education*, *43*(3), 215–236. DOI: 10.1016/j.compedu.2003.10.005

Lin, H., & Ng, V. (2019). Abstractive Summarization: A Survey of the State of the Art. *Proceedings of the AAAI Conference on Artificial Intelligence*, *33*(01), 9815–9822. DOI: 10.1609/aaai.v33i01.33019815

Liu, M. Y. (2023), "Exploring the Application of Artificial Intelligence in Foreign Language Teaching: Challenges and Future Development", *SHS Web of Conferences*, Vol.168, pp. 1-4. DOI: 10.1051/shsconf/202316803025

Liu, J., Chen, Y., & Xu, J. (2022). Saliency as Evidence: Event Detection with Trigger Saliency Attribution. *Proceedings of the 60th Annual Meeting of the Association for Computational Linguistics(*Volume 1*: Long Papers)*, 4573-4585. DOI: 10.18653/v1/2022.acl-long.313

Liu, L., Tang, L., Dong, W., Yao, S., & Zhou, W. (2016). An overview of topic modeling and its current applications in bioinformatics. *SpringerPlus*, *5*(1), 1608. DOI: 10.1186/s40064-016-3252-8 PMID: 27652181

Liu, M., & Yu, D. (2023). Towards intelligent e-learning systems. *Education and Information Technologies*, *28*(7), 7845–7876. DOI: 10.1007/s10639-022-11479-6 PMID: 36532790

Liu, X., Huang, H., Shi, G., & Wang, B. (2022). *Dynamic Prefix-Tuning for Generative Template-based Event Extraction.* DOI: 10.18653/v1/2022.acl-long.358

Li, X., & Deng, Z. (2022). NLP in language tutoring systems: Enhancing feedback and learning outcomes. *Applied Linguistics Research Journal*, *30*(5), 401–417.

Li, X., Feng, J., Meng, Y., Han, Q., Wu, F., & Li, J. (2019). *A Unified MRC Framework for Named Entity Recognition* (Versión 7). arXiv. DOI: 10.48550/ARXIV.1910.11476

Li, X., Yin, F., Sun, Z., Li, X., Yuan, A., Chai, D., Zhou, M., & Li, J. (2019). Entity-Relation Extraction as Multi-Turn Question Answering. *Proceedings of the 57th Annual Meeting of the Association for Computational Linguistics*, 1340-1350. DOI: 10.18653/v1/P19-1129

Loewen, S., Isbell, D. R., & Sporn, Z. (2020). The effectiveness of app-based language instruction for developing receptive linguistic knowledge and oral communicative ability. *Foreign Language Annals*, *53*(2), 209–233. DOI: 10.1111/flan.12454

Long, D., & Magerko, B. (2020, April). What is AI literacy? Competencies and design considerations. In *Proceedings of the 2020 CHI conference on human factors in computing systems* (pp. 1-16). DOI: 10.1145/3313831.3376727

Long, M. H. (1996). The role of the linguistic environment in second language acquisition. In Ritchie, W., & Bhatia, T. (Eds.), *Handbook of second language acquisition* (pp. 413–468). Academic Press.

Lou, D., Liao, Z., Deng, S., Zhang, N., & Chen, H. (2021). MLBiNet: A Cross-Sentence Collective Event Detection Network. *Proceedings of the 59th Annual Meeting of the Association for Computational Linguistics and the 11th International Joint Conference on Natural Language Processing(*Volume 1*: Long Papers)*, 4829-4839. DOI: 10.18653/v1/2021.acl-long.373

Luan, H., Géczy, P., Lai, H., Gobert, J. D., Yang, S. J. H., Ogata, H., Baltes, J., Guerra, R. da S., Li, P., & Tsai, C. (2020). Challenges and Future Directions of Big Data and Artificial Intelligence in Education [Review of Challenges and Future Directions of Big Data and Artificial Intelligence in Education]. Frontiers in Psychology, 11. Frontiers Media. DOI: 10.3389/fpsyg.2020.580820

Luckin, R. (2018). *Machine Learning and Human Intelligence: The future of education for the 21st century*. UCL IOE Press. UCL Institute of Education, University of London, 20 Bedford Way, London WC1H 0AL.

Luckin, R., & Holmes, W. (2016). Intelligence Unleashed: An argument for AI in education.

Luckin, R. (2017). Towards artificial intelligence-based assessment systems. *Nature Human Behaviour*, *1*(3), 1–3.

Luckin, R. (2018). *Machine learning and human intelligence: The future of education for the 21st century*. UCL Institute of Education Press.

Luckin, R., & Holmes, W. (2016). *Intelligence Unleashed: An Argument for AI in Education*. Pearson.

Luckin, R., Holmes, W., Griffiths, M., & Forcier, L. B. (2016). *Intelligence unleashed: An argument for AI in education*. Pearson Education.

Luhn, H. P. (1958). The Automatic Creation of Literature Abstracts. *IBM Journal of Research and Development*, *2*(2), 159–165. DOI: 10.1147/rd.22.0159

Lu, M. (2008). Effectiveness of vocabulary learning via mobile phone. *Journal of Computer Assisted Learning*, *24*(6), 515–525. DOI: 10.1111/j.1365-2729.2008.00289.x

Luo, H., Yang, C., & Li, L. (2021). Immersive virtual reality in foreign language education: A meta-analysis. *Educational Technology Research and Development, 69*(3), 705–729.

Lu, Y., Liu, Q., Dai, D., Xiao, X., Lin, H., Han, X., Sun, L., & Wu, H. (2022). *Unified Structure Generation for Universal Information Extraction* (Versión 1). arXiv. DOI: 10.48550/ARXIV.2203.12277

Ly, A., Uthayasooriyar, B., & Wang, T. (2020). *A survey on natural language processing (nlp) and applications in insurance* (Versión 1). arXiv. DOI: 10.48550/ARXIV.2010.00462

Ma, Y., Wang, Z., Cao, Y., Li, M., Chen, M., Wang, K., & Shao, J. (2022). Prompt for Extraction? PAIE: Prompting Argument Interaction for Event Argument Extraction. *Proceedings of the 60th Annual Meeting of the Association for Computational Linguistics(*Volume 1*: Long Papers)*, 6759-6774. DOI: 10.18653/v1/2022.acl-long.466

Ma, D. T. T., Da, C. V., & Hanh, N. V. (2024). The use of ChatGPT in teaching and learning: A systematic review through SWOT analysis approach. *Frontiers in Education, 9*, 1–17. DOI: 10.3389/feduc.2024.1328769

Maity, S., & Deroy, A. (2024). Generative AI and Its Impact on Personalized Intelligent Tutoring Systems. arXiv preprint arXiv:2410.10650.

Makelenia, S., Mutongoza, B. H., & Linake, M. A. (2023). Language Education and Artificial Intelligence: An Exploration of Challenges Confronting Academics in Global South Universities. *Journal of Culture and Values in Education, 6*(2), 158–171. DOI: 10.46303/jcve.2023.14

Makridakis, S. (2017). The forthcoming Artificial Intelligence (AI) revolution: Its impact on society and firms. *Futures, 90*, 46–60. DOI: 10.1016/j.futures.2017.03.006

Manning, C. D., & Schütze, H. (1999). *Foundations of statistical natural language processing*. MIT Press.

Mardani, A., Devi, S., Alrasheedi, M., Arya, L., Singh, M. P., & Pandey, K. (2023). Hybrid intuitionistic fuzzy entropy-SWARA-COPRAS method for multi-criteria sustainable biomass crop type selection. *Sustainability (Basel), 15*(10), 7765. Advance online publication. DOI: 10.3390/su15107765

Martins, P. H., Marinho, Z., & Martins, A. F. T. (2019). *Joint Learning of Named Entity Recognition and Entity Linking* (Versión 1). arXiv. DOI: 10.48550/ARXIV.1907.08243

Matz, S., Bukow, C. S., Peters, H., Deacons, C., Dinu, A., & Stachl, C. (2023). Using machine learning to predict student retention from socio-demographic characteristics and app-based engagement metrics. In Scientific Reports (Vol. 13, Issue 1). Nature Portfolio. DOI: 10.1038/s41598-023-32484-w

McKinsey & Company. (2020). How artificial intelligence will impact K-12 teachers.

McKinsey. (2022). How technology is shaping learning in higher education. https://www.mckinsey.com/industries/education/our-insights/how-technology-is-shaping-learning-in-higher-education

McKins, W., Bialik, M., & Fadel, C. (2019). *Artificial intelligence in education: Promises and implications for teaching and learning*. Centre for Curriculum Redesign.

Means, B., Toyama, Y., Murphy, R., Bakia, M., & Jones, K. (2009). Evaluation of evidence-based practices in online learning: A meta-analysis and review of online learning studies.

Medhat, W., Hassan, A., & Korashy, H. (2014). Sentiment analysis algorithms and applications: A survey. *Ain Shams Engineering Journal*, *5*(4), 1093–1113. DOI: 10.1016/j.asej.2014.04.011

Méndez, J. R., Iglesias, E. L., Fdez-Riverola, F., Díaz, F., & Corchado, J. M. (2006). Tokenising, Stemming and Stopword Removal on Anti-spam Filtering Domain. En R. Marín, E. Onaindía, A. Bugarín, & J. Santos (Eds.), *Current Topics in Artificial Intelligence* (Vol. 4177, pp. 449-458). Springer Berlin Heidelberg. DOI: 10.1007/11881216_47

Miao, Y., & Zhang, Z. (2020). The Application of Artificial Intelligence in Language Learning: Challenges and Opportunities. *Computer Assisted Language Learning*, *33*(5), 503–519.

Mikolov, T., Chen, K., Corrado, G., & Dean, J. (2013). *Efficient Estimation of Word Representations in Vector Space* (Versión 3). arXiv. DOI: 10.48550/ARXIV.1301.3781

Miller, A., & Young-Jones, A. D. (2012). Academic integrity: Online classes compared to face-to-face classes. *Journal of Instructional Psychology*, *39*(3), 1–8.

Mitchell, R., & Myles, F. (1998). *Second language learning theories*. Oxford Press, Inc.

Moeller, A. J., & Catalano, T. (2015). *Foreign Language Teaching and Learning* (2nd ed.). International Encyclopedia of the Social & Behavioral Sciences. DOI: 10.1016/B978-0-08-097086-8.92082-8

Molina, M., & Garip, F. (2019). Machine Learning for Sociology. *Annual Review of Sociology*, *45*(1), 27–45. DOI: 10.1146/annurev-soc-073117-041106

Mooij, T. (2007). Design of educational and ICT conditions to integrate differences in learning: Contextual learning theory and a first transformation step in early education. *Computers in Human Behavior*, *23*(3), 1499–1530. DOI: 10.1016/j.chb.2005.07.004

Moratanch, N., & Chitrakala, S. (2017). A survey on extractive text summarization. *2017 International Conference on Computer, Communication and Signal Processing (ICCCSP)*, 1-6. DOI: 10.1109/ICCCSP.2017.7944061

Mosa, M. A., Anwar, A. S., & Hamouda, A. (2019). A survey of multiple types of text summarization with their satellite contents based on swarm intelligence optimization algorithms. *Knowledge-Based Systems*, *163*, 518–532. DOI: 10.1016/j.knosys.2018.09.008

Moulieswaran, N., & Kumar, P. N. S. (2022). Education 4.0 – An artificial intelligence technology driven second language learning and teaching. In Karthikeyan, J., & Jin, N. Y. (Eds.), *Neophytes of ELT Research*. Royal Book Publishing.

Moxon, S. (2024). Computer-Assisted Vocabulary Learning for Thai Deaf Students: A Case Study of Sot Suksa School for the Deaf. *Asia Social Issues*, *17*(1), 1–21.

Munday, P. (2016). The case for using DUOLINGO as part of the language classroom experience (Duolingo como parte del curriculum de las clases de lengua extranjera).

Murphy, V. A., Arndt, H., Baffoe-Djan, J. B., Chalmers, H., Macaro, E., Rose, H., Vanderplank, R., & Woore, R. (2020). *Foreign language learning and its impact on wider academic outcomes: A rapid evidence assessment*. University of Oxford.

Mutongoza, B. H., & Olawale, B. E. (2022). Safeguarding academic integrity in the face of emergency remote teaching and learning in developing countries. *Perspectives in Education*, *40*(1), 234–249. DOI: 10.18820/2519593X/pie.v40.i1.14

Nagaraj, S., Kathole, A. B., Arya, L., Tyagi, N., Goyal, S. B., Rajawat, A. S., Raboaca, M. S., Mihaltan, T. C., Verma, C., & Suciu, G. (2022). Improved secure encryption with energy optimization using random permutation pseudo algorithm based on Internet of Thing in wireless sensor networks. *Energies*, *16*(8), 1–16. DOI: 10.3390/en16010008

National Standards in Foreign Language Education Project (NSFLEP). (2014), World Readiness Standards for Learning Languages (WRSLL), Alexandria. VA, Available at: http://actfl/org/publications/all/world-readiness-standards-learninglanguages (Accessed 10 July 2024).

nazari, nasrin, & Mahdavi, M. A. (2018). A survey on Automatic Text Summarization. *Journal of AI and Data Mining, Online First*. DOI: 10.22044/jadm.2018.6139.1726

Nelson, L. K. (2020). Computational Grounded Theory: A Methodological Framework. *Sociological Methods & Research*, *49*(1), 3–42. DOI: 10.1177/0049124117729703

Nelson, L. K., Burk, D., Knudsen, M., & McCall, L. (2021). The Future of Coding: A Comparison of Hand-Coding and Three Types of Computer-Assisted Text Analysis Methods. *Sociological Methods & Research*, *50*(1), 202–237. DOI: 10.1177/0049124118769114

Nunan, D. (2004). *Task-based language teaching*. Cambridge University Press.

O'Neil, C. (2016). *Weapons of math destruction: How big data increases inequality and threatens democracy*. Crown Publishing Group.

O'Neil, C. (2016). *Weapons of Math Destruction: How Big Data Increases Inequality and Threatens Democracy*. Crown Publishing Group.

OECD. (2021). Artificial intelligence and education and skills. https://www.oecd.org/en/topics/sub-issues/artificial-intelligence-and-education-and-skills.html

Oktadela, R., Elida, Y., & Ismail, S. (2023). Improving English Vocabulary through Artificial Intelligence (AI) Chatbot Application. *Journal of English Language and Education*, *8*(2), 63–67.

Özyildirim, İ., & Jomaa, N. J. (2023). Teaching and learning English online: The perspectives of English teachers and students at Karabuk University in Turkey. In *Shaping the Future of Online Learning: Education in the Metaverse* (pp. 220–249). IGI Global., DOI: 10.4018/978-1-6684-6513-4.ch012

Paiva, R., & Bittencourt, I. I. (2020). *Helping Teachers Help Their students: A Human-AI Hybrid Approach*. Springer Switzerland International Publishing.

Pane, J. F., Griffin, B. A., McCaffrey, D. F., & Karam, R. (2014). Effectiveness of cognitive tutor algebra I at scale. *Educational Evaluation and Policy Analysis*, *36*(2), 127–144. DOI: 10.3102/0162373713507480

Pane, J. F., Steiner, E. D., Baird, M. D., & Hamilton, L. S. (2015). *Continued Progress: Promising Evidence on Personalized Learning*. Rand Corporation. DOI: 10.7249/RR1365

Pang, B., & Lee, L. (2008). Opinion Mining and Sentiment Analysis. *Foundations and Trends® in Information Retrieval*, *2*(1–2), 1-135. DOI: 10.1561/1500000011

Pang, K., Zhang, H., Zhou, J., & Wang, T. (2022). Divide and Denoise: Learning from Noisy Labels in Fine-Grained Entity Typing with Cluster-Wise Loss Correction. *Proceedings of the 60th Annual Meeting of the Association for Computational Linguistics(*Volume 1*: Long Papers)*, 1997-2006. DOI: 10.18653/v1/2022.acl-long.141

Perkins, M. (2023). Academic integrity considerations of AI large language models in the post-pandemic era: ChatGPT and beyond. *Journal of University Teaching & Learning Practice*, *20*(2), 7–24. DOI: 10.53761/1.20.02.07

Pokrivcakova, S. (2019). *Preparing teachers for the application of AI-powered technologies in foreign language education*. Sciendo. DOI: 10.2478/jolace-2019-0025

Popescu, A. (2024). AI's secret weapon in education: ChatGPT—the future of personalized learning. *Bulletin of the Transilvania University of Brasov. Series V, Economic Sciences*, *16*(65), 2. DOI: 10.31926/but.es.2023.16.65.2.5

Porter, M. F. (1980). An algorithm for suffix stripping. *Program*, *14*(3), 130–137. DOI: 10.1108/eb046814

Pouran Ben Veyseh, A., Lai, V., Dernoncourt, F., & Nguyen, T. H. (2021). Unleash GPT-2 Power for Event Detection. *Proceedings of the 59th Annual Meeting of the Association for Computational Linguistics and the 11th International Joint Conference on Natural Language Processing(*Volume 1*: Long Papers)*, 6271-6282. DOI: 10.18653/v1/2021.acl-long.490

Prinsloo, P., & Slade, S. (2017). An ethical framework for learning analytics. *British Journal of Educational Technology*, *48*(1), 160–172.

Pusporini, W., & Nurdiyanto, H. (2024). Utilization of AI in Outcome-Based Curriculum Evaluation and Development. *Journal of Research in Social Science and Humanities*, *4*(1), 132–134. DOI: 10.47679/jrssh.v4i1.109

Pylypchuk, M. L. (2021). Structure of professional readiness of future translators for innovative activities. *Professional and Artistic Translation*, *1*, 371–378.

Qasem, F., Ghaleb, M., Mahdi, H. S., Al Khateeb, A., & Al Fadda, H. (2023). Dialog chatbot as an interactive online tool in enhancing ESP vocabulary learning. *Saudi Journal of Language Studies*, *3*(2), 76–86. DOI: 10.1108/SJLS-10-2022-0072

Rabiner, L. R. (1989). A tutorial on hidden Markov models and selected applications in speech recognition. *Proceedings of the IEEE*, *77*(2), 257–286. DOI: 10.1109/5.18626

Radev, D. R., Hovy, E., & McKeown, K. (2002a). Introduction to the Special Issue on Summarization. *Computational Linguistics*, *28*(4), 399–408. DOI: 10.1162/089120102762671927

Radu, I. (2014). Augmented reality in education: A meta-review and cross-media analysis. *Personal and Ubiquitous Computing*, *18*(6), 1533–1543. DOI: 10.1007/s00779-013-0747-y

Rahimi, M., & Fathi, J. (2022). Exploring the impact of wiki-mediated collaborative writing on EFL students' writing performance, writing self-regulation, and writing self-efficacy: A mixed methods study. *Computer Assisted Language Learning*, *35*(9), 2627–2674. DOI: 10.1080/09588221.2021.1888753

Ramírez-Polo, L., & Vargas-Sierra, C. (2023). Translation Technology and Ethical Competence: An Analysis and Proposal for Translators' Training. *Languages (Basel, Switzerland)*, *8*(2), 1–22. DOI: 10.3390/languages8020093

Rao, P. S. (2019). The Impact of Technological Innovations on English Language Teaching in The Modern Era. *International Journal of Engineering Research-Online*, *7*(6), 58–67.

Rashid, T., & Asghar, H. M. (2016). Technology Adoption and Digital Divide: The Case of Higher Education Institutions in Pakistan. *International Journal of Educational Management*, *30*(2), 275–289.

Rhoten, D. (2004). Interdisciplinary research: Trend or transition. *Items & Issues*, *5*(1-2), 6–11.

Rogerson, A. M., & McCarthy, G. (2017). Using internet-based paraphrasing tools: Original work, patchwriting or facilitated plagiarism? *International Journal for Educational Integrity*, *13*(1), 1–15. DOI: 10.1007/s40979-016-0013-y

Roll, I., & Wylie, R. (2016). Evolution and revolution in artificial intelligence in education. *International Journal of Artificial Intelligence in Education*, *26*(2), 582–599. DOI: 10.1007/s40593-016-0110-3

Roschelle, J., Feng, M., Murphy, R. F., & Mason, C. A. (2016). Online mathematics homework increases learner achievement. *AERA Open*, *2*(4), 2332858416673968. DOI: 10.1177/2332858416673968

Rudolph, J., Tan, S., & Tan, S. (2023). ChatGPT: Bullshit spewer or the end of traditional assessments in higher education? *Journal of Applied Learning and Teaching*, *6*(1), 1–22.

Rukiati, E., Wicaksono, J. A., Taufan, G. T., & Suharsono, D. D. (2023). AI on Learning English: Application, Benefit, and Threat. *Journal of Language, Communication, and Tourism*, *2*(1), 32–40. DOI: 10.25047/jlct.v1i2.3967

Rusmiyanto, R., Huriati, N., Fitriani, N., Tyas, N. K., Rofi'i, A., & Sari, M. N. (2023). The role of artificial intelligence (AI) in developing English language learner's communication skills. *Journal of Education*, *6*(1), 750–757.

Sa'd, T., & Hatam, S. (2017). Foreign language learning and identity reconstruction: Learners' understanding of the intersections of the self, the other and power. *CEPS Journal*, *7*(4), 13–36.

Sadiku, M. N., Ashaolu, T. J., Ajayi-Majebi, A., & Musa, S. M. (2021). Artifcial intelligence in education. *International Journal of Scientifc Advances*, *2*(1), 5–11.

Saha, A., Senapati, T., Akram, M., Kahraman, C., Mesiar, R., & Arya, L. (2024). Dual probabilistic linguistic consensus reaching method for group decision-making. *Granular Computing*, *9*(1), 35. Advance online publication. DOI: 10.1007/s41066-024-00458-6

Sajja, R., Sermet, Y., Cikmaz, M., Cwiertny, D., & Demir, I. (2023). Artificial Intelligence-Enabled Intelligent Assistant for Personalized and Adaptive Learning in Higher Education. arXiv preprint arXiv:2309.10892.

Sajja, R., Sermet, Y., Cikmaz, M., Cwiertny, D., & Demir, I. (2024). AI-enabled intelligent assistant for personalized and adaptive learning in higher education. *Information (Basel)*, *15*(10), 596. DOI: 10.3390/info15100596

Salloum, S. A. (2024). AI Perils in Education: Exploring Ethical Concerns. *AI in Education: The Power and Dangers of ChatGPT in the Classroom*, 669-675.

Salton, G. (1983). Some research problems in automatic information retrieval. *ACM SIGIR Forum, 17*(4), 252-263. DOI: 10.1145/1013230.511830

Salton, G., Wong, A., & Yang, C. S. (1975a). A vector space model for automatic indexing. *Communications of the ACM*, *18*(11), 613–620. DOI: 10.1145/361219.361220

Salur, M. U., & Aydin, I. (2020). A Novel Hybrid Deep Learning Model for Sentiment Classification. *IEEE Access : Practical Innovations, Open Solutions*, *8*, 58080–58093. DOI: 10.1109/ACCESS.2020.2982538

Schmid, K.. (2019). Teacher education in the age of AI: Preparing educators for the future classroom. *International Journal of Educational Development*, *67*, 44–53.

Schmidt, T., & Strasser, T. (2022). Artificial intelligence in foreign language learning and teaching: A CALL for intelligent practice. *Anglistik*, *33*(1), 165–184. DOI: 10.33675/ANGL/2022/1/14

Schwendicke, F., Samek, W., & Krois, J. (2020). Artificial intelligence in dentistry: Chances and challenges. *Journal of Dental Research*, *99*(7), 769–774. DOI: 10.1177/0022034520915714 PMID: 32315260

Sebastiani, F. (2002). Machine learning in automated text categorization. *ACM Computing Surveys*, *34*(1), 1–47. DOI: 10.1145/505282.505283

Selwyn, N. (2016). *Education and Technology: Key Issues and Debates*. Bloomsbury Publishing.

Selwyn, N. (2019). Should robots replace teachers? AI and the future of education. *Learning, Media and Technology*, *44*(2), 77–91.

Selwyn, N. (2019). Should robots replace teachers? AI in education. *International Journal of Educational Technology in Higher Education*, *16*(1), 5–15.

Seufert, S., Guggemos, J. and Tarantini, E. (2018), "Digital transformation in schools. Competency requirements for teachers", *Contributions to teacher training*, Vol. 36 No. 2, pp. 175-193.

Shadiev, R., Wen, Y., Uosaki, N., & Song, Y. (2023). Future language learning with emerging technologies. *Journal of Computers in Education*, *10*(3), 463–467. DOI: 10.1007/s40692-023-00285-9

Sharma, N. A., Ali, A. B. M. S., & Kabir, M. A. (2024). A review of sentiment analysis: Tasks, applications, and deep learning techniques. *International Journal of Data Science and Analytics*. Advance online publication. DOI: 10.1007/s41060-024-00594-x

Sharma, S., Gupta, P., & Rao, K. (2021). AI in automated assessment: Transforming language learning. *Journal of Educational AI*, *13*(2), 158–169.

Sharples, M. (2022). Automated essay writing: An AIED opinion. *International Journal of Artificial Intelligence in Education*, *32*(4), 1119–1126. DOI: 10.1007/s40593-022-00300-7

Shatri, Z. G. (2020). Advantages and disadvantages of using information technology in learning process of students. *Journal of Turkish Science Education*, *17*, 420–428. DOI: 10.36681/tused.2020.36

Sheikhpour, R., Sarram, M. A., Gharaghani, S., & Chahooki, M. A. Z. (2017). A Survey on semi-supervised feature selection methods. *Pattern Recognition*, *64*, 141–158. DOI: 10.1016/j.patcog.2016.11.003

Shermis, M. D. (2003). *Automated essay scoring: A cross-disciplinary perspective*. Inc., Publishers. Mahawah. DOI: 10.4324/9781410606860

Shum, S. B., & Ferguson, R. (2012). Social learning analytics. *Journal of Educational Technology & Society*, *15*(3), 3–26.

Skehan, P. (1998). *A cognitive approach to language learning*. Oxford University Press.

Soleimani, H., Mohammaddokht, F., & Fathi, J. (2022). Exploring the effect of assisted repeated reading on incidental vocabulary learning and vocabulary learning self-efficacy in an EFL context. *Frontiers in Psychology*, *13*, 1–11. DOI: 10.3389/fpsyg.2022.851812 PMID: 35250786

Solorio-Fernández, S., Carrasco-Ochoa, J. A., & Martínez-Trinidad, J. (2020). A review of unsupervised feature selection methods. *Artificial Intelligence Review*, *53*(2), 907–948. DOI: 10.1007/s10462-019-09682-y

Stanford University. (2018). Ethics of Artificial Intelligence and Robotics. Stanford Encyclopedia of Philosophy. Retrieved from https://plato.stanford.edu/entries/ethics-ai/

St-Onge, C., Ouellet, K., Lakhal, S., Dubé, T., & Marceau, M. (2022). COVID-19 as the tipping point for integrating e-assessment in higher education practices. *British Journal of Educational Technology*, *53*(2), 349–366. DOI: 10.1111/bjet.13169 PMID: 34898680

Suleiman, D., & Awajan, A. A. (2019). Deep Learning Based Extractive Text Summarization: Approaches, Datasets and Evaluation Measures. *2019 Sixth International Conference on Social Networks Analysis, Management and Security (SNAMS)*, 204-210. DOI: 10.1109/SNAMS.2019.8931813

Sumakul, D. T. Y. G., Hamied, F. A., & Sukyadi, D. (2022) 'Students' Perceptions of the Use of AI in a Writing Class:', in. 67th TEFLIN International Virtual Conference & the 9th ICOELT 2021 (TEFLIN ICOELT 2021), Padang, Indonesia. Available at: DOI: 10.2991/assehr.k.220201.009

Suman, C. and Suman, S. (2023), "Using Artificial Intelligence for Foreign Language Learning", *A Peer Review Research Journal of Language and Human Development*, Vol. 1 No. 1, pp. 57-64.

Sundar, S. S. (2019). Data privacy in AI: Challenges and opportunities for education. *International Journal of Educational Policy*, *24*(2), 143–155.

Sussmann, M. (2024). *AI Tools for the Four Skills in English Language Learning*. Tesol Connections.

Syahrin, S. & Akmal, N. (2024). Navigating the Artificial Intelligence Frontier: Perceptions of Instructors, Students, and Administrative Staff on the Role of Artificial Intelligence in Education in the Sultanate of Oman. *Arab World English Journal (AWEJ) Special Issue on ChatGPT*, (April, 2024) 73-89. DOI: DOI: 10.24093/awej/ChatGPT.4

Tabassum, A., & Patil, R. R. (2020). A Survey on Text Pre-Processing & Feature Extraction Techniques in Natural Language Processing. *International Research Journal of Engineering and Technology*, *07*(06), 4864.

Tafazoli, D. (2023). Critical Appraisal of Artificial Intelligence-Mediated Communication.

Taha, K., Yoo, P. D., Yeun, C., Homouz, D., & Taha, A. (2024). A comprehensive survey of text classification techniques and their research applications: Observational and experimental insights. *Computer Science Review*, *54*, 100664. DOI: 10.1016/j.cosrev.2024.100664

Tahir, M., & Hassan, F. D. (2024). Role of artificial intelligence in education: A conceptual review. *World Journal of Advanced Research and Reviews*, *22*(1), 1469–1475. DOI: 10.30574/wjarr.2024.22.1.1217

Tandel, J., Mistree, K., & Shah, P. (2019). A Review on Neural network based Abstractive Text Summarization models. *2019 IEEE 5th International Conference for Convergence in Technology (I2CT)*, 1-4. DOI: 10.1109/I2CT45611.2019.9033912

Tandel, S. S., Jamadar, A., & Dudugu, S. (2019). A Survey on Text Mining Techniques. *2019 5th International Conference on Advanced Computing & Communication Systems (ICACCS)*, 1022-1026. DOI: 10.1109/ICACCS.2019.8728547

Tarapiah, S., AbuHania, R., & Atalla, S. (2013). Smart on-board transportation management system using gps/gsm/gprs technologies to reduce traffic violation in developing countries. *International Journal of Digital Information and Wireless Communications*, *3*(4), 96–105.

Tegmark, M. (2017). *Life 3.0: Being human in the age of artificial intelligence*. Alfred A. Knopf.

Trilling, B., & Fadel, C. (2009). *21st-century skills: Learning for life in our times*. John Wiley & Sons.

Trivedi, N. B. (2023, November). AI in Education Transformative Force. In *2023 1st DMIHER International Conference on AI in Education and Industry 4.0 (IDICAIEI)* (Vol. 1, pp. 1-4). IEEE. DOI: 10.1109/IDICAIEI58380.2023.10406541

Tunstall, L., Von Werra, L., & Wolf, T. (2022). *Natural language processing with transformers*. O'Reilly Media.

Turaeva, S. (2024), Language, learning and teaching. *Development and Innovations in Science: International scientific-online conference*, pp. 1-4.

UNESCO. (2021). UNESCO strategy on technological innovation in education (2021-2025). https://unesdoc.unesco.org/ark:/48223/pf0000375776

UNESCO. (2022). AI for education: Personalized learning systems report.

University at Buffalo. (2024). *Constructivism: Creating experiences that facilitate the construction of knowledge. North Campus*. University at Buffalo.

VanLehn, K. (2011). The relative effectiveness of human tutoring, intelligent tutoring systems, and other tutoring systems. *Educational Psychologist*, *46*(4), 197–221. DOI: 10.1080/00461520.2011.611369

Vaswani, A., Shazeer, N., Parmar, N., Uszkoreit, J., Jones, L., Gomez, A. N., Kaiser, L., & Polosukhin, I. (2017). *Attention Is All You Need* (Versión 7). arXiv. DOI: 10.48550/ARXIV.1706.03762

Vayansky, I., & Kumar, S. A. P. (2020). A review of topic modeling methods. *Information Systems*, *94*, 101582. DOI: 10.1016/j.is.2020.101582

Venkatesh, B., & Anuradha, J. (2019). A Review of Feature Selection and Its Methods. *Cybernetics and Information Technologies*, *19*(1), 3–26. DOI: 10.2478/cait-2019-0001

Vicsek, L., Vancsó, A., Zajko, M., & Takacs, J. (2024). Exploring LGBTQ+ Bias in Generative AI Answers across Different Countries and Religious Contexts. *arXiv preprint arXiv:2407.03473*.

VijayGaikwad, S., Chaugule, A., & Patil, P.VijayGaikwad. (2014). Text Mining Methods and Techniques. *International Journal of Computer Applications*, *85*(17), 42–45. DOI: 10.5120/14937-3507

Vinoth, R. Jayachandran, 2Anjana, Balaji, M., & Srinivasan, R. (2014). A Hybrid Text Classification Approach Using KNN and SVM. *International Journal of Advance Foundation and Research in Computer, 1*(3). https://ijafrc.org/Volumn1/Vol_issue3/3.pdf

Vogel, D., Stetson, H., & Patel, S. (2019). Advancements in AI for language learning: The promise and potential. *Journal of Computer Assisted Learning*, *35*(5), 488–497.

Vygotsky, L. S. (1984), "The problem of age" in *The collected works of L. S. Vygotsky. Vol. 5. Child psychology*. ed. Rieber R. W. Plenum, New York, NY.

Vygotsky, L. S. (1978). *Mind in society: The development of higher psychological processes*. Harvard University Press.

Wadden, D., Wennberg, U., Luan, Y., & Hajishirzi, H. (2019). *Entity, Relation, and Event Extraction with Contextualized Span Representations* (Versión 2). arXiv. DOI: 10.48550/ARXIV.1909.03546

Walker, T., & Green, J. (2021). Real-time translation and voice recognition: AI in virtual classrooms. *International Journal of Digital Education*, *8*(4), 299–315.

Wang, D., & Zhang, H. (2010). Inverse-category-frequency based supervised term weighting scheme for text categorization. arXiv preprint arXiv:1012.2609.

Wang, N., & Lester, J. C. (2023). K-12 Education in the Age of AI: A Call to Action for K-12 AI Literacy. In International Journal of Artificial Intelligence in Education (Vol. 33, Issue 2, p. 228). Springer Science+Business Media. DOI: 10.1007/s40593-023-00358-x

Wang, Y., Liu, M., & Zhou, Z. (2024). Enhancing ESP Vocabulary Learning through ChatGPT: A Case Study. In J. Cohen & G. Solano (Eds.), *Proceedings of Society for Information Technology & Teacher Education International Conference* (pp. 907-913). Las Vegas, Nevada, United States: Association for the Advancement of Computing in Education (AACE). Retrieved May 29, 2024 from https://www.learntechlib.org/p/224061

Wang, B. T., Teng, C. W., & Chen, H. T. (2015). Using iPad to facilitate English vocabulary learning. *International Journal of Information and Education Technology (IJIET)*, *5*(2), 100–104. DOI: 10.7763/IJIET.2015.V5.484

Wankhade, M., Rao, A. C. S., & Kulkarni, C. (2022). A survey on sentiment analysis methods, applications, and challenges. *Artificial Intelligence Review*, *55*(7), 5731–5780. DOI: 10.1007/s10462-022-10144-1

Warschauer, M., & Grimes, D. (2007). Automated writing evaluation and its impact on student writing. *Journal of Second Language Writing*, *16*(4), 191–209.

Willis, D., & Willis, J. (2007). *Doing task-based teaching*. Oxford University Press.

Wolfram, S. (2023). What is ChatGPT doing . . . and why does it work? http://tinyurl.com/43anvwyb

Woolf, B. P., Lane, H. C., Chaudhri, V. K., & Kolodner, J. L. (2013). AI grand challenges for education. *AI Magazine*, *34*(4), 66–84. DOI: 10.1609/aimag.v34i4.2490

World Economic Forum. (2020). *The Future of Jobs Report 2020*. World Economic Forum. https://www.weforum.org/publications/the-future-of-jobs-report-2020/

World Economic Forum. (2024). The future of learning: How AI is revolutionizing education 4.0. https://www.weforum.org/agenda/2024/04/future-learning-ai-revolutionizing-education-4-0

Wu, F., & Weld, D. S. (2010). Open information extraction using Wikipedia. *Association for Computational Linguistics*, 118-127.

Xiao, Y., & Watson, M. (2019). Guidance on Conducting a Systematic Literature Review. *Journal of Planning Education and Research, 39*(1), 93–112. DOI: 10.1177/0739456X17723971

Yang, Y., & Pedersen, J. O. (1997). A comparative study on feature selection in text categorization. *In Proceedings of the Fourteenth International Conference on Machine Learning*, 412-420. https://courses.ischool.berkeley.edu/i256/f06/papers/yang97comparative.pdf

Yan, K., & Zhang, D. (2015). Feature selection and analysis on correlated gas sensor data with recursive feature elimination. *Sensors and Actuators. B, Chemical, 212*, 353–363. DOI: 10.1016/j.snb.2015.02.025

Ye, D., Lin, Y., Li, P., & Sun, M. (2022). Packed Levitated Marker for Entity and Relation Extraction. *Proceedings of the 60th Annual Meeting of the Association for Computational Linguistics(*Volume 1*: Long Papers)*, 4904-4917. DOI: 10.18653/v1/2022.acl-long.337

Yessenalina, A., Yue, Y., & Cardie, C. (2010). Multi-Level Structured Models for Document-Level Sentiment Classification. *In Proceedings of the 2010 Conference on Empirical Methods in Natural Language Processing*, 1046-1056. https://aclanthology.org/D10-1102/

Ye, W., Li, B., Xie, R., Sheng, Z., Chen, L., & Zhang, S. (2019). Exploiting Entity BIO Tag Embeddings and Multi-task Learning for Relation Extraction with Imbalanced Data. *Proceedings of the 57th Annual Meeting of the Association for Computational Linguistics*, 1351-1360. DOI: 10.18653/v1/P19-1130

Yu, A., & Trainin, G. (2022). A meta-analysis examining technology-assisted L2 vocabulary learning. *ReCALL, 34*(2), 235–252. DOI: 10.1017/S0958344021000239

Zawacki-Richter, O., Marín, V. I., Bond, M., & Gouverneur, F. (2019). A systematic review of research on AI applications in higher education–where are the educators? *International Journal of Educational Technology in Higher Education, 16*(1), 1–27. DOI: 10.1186/s41239-019-0171-0

Zawacki-Richter, O., Marín, V. I., Bond, M., & Gouverneur, F. (2019). Systematic review of research on artificial intelligence applications in higher education. *International Journal of Educational Technology in Higher Education, 16*(1), 39.

Zawacki-Richter, O., Marín, V. I., Bond, M., & Gouverneur, F. (2019). Systematic review of research on artificial intelligence applications in higher education: The state of the art and future research directions. *International Journal of Educational Technology in Higher Education, 16*(1), 1–27.

Zeng, D., Liu, K., Chen, Y., & Zhao, J. (2015). Distant Supervision for Relation Extraction via Piecewise Convolutional Neural Networks. *Proceedings of the 2015 Conference on Empirical Methods in Natural Language Processing*, 1753-1762. DOI: 10.18653/v1/D15-1203

Zhai, X., Chu, X., Chai, C. S., Jong, M. S., Starčič, A. I., Spector, M., Liu, J., Jing, Y., & Li, Y. (2021). A Review of Artificial Intelligence (AI) in Education from 2010 to 2020 [Review of A Review of Artificial Intelligence (AI) in Education from 2010 to 2020]. Complexity, 2021(1). Hindawi Publishing Corporation. DOI: 10.1155/2021/8812542

Zhang, H., Liu, F., & Wang, Y. (2023). Machine learning in K-12 education: A study on personalized learning paths. *The Journal of Educational Research, 20*(3), 185–201.

Zhang, Z., Li, J., Stork, D. G., Mansfield, E., Russell, J., Adams, C., & Wang, J. Z. (2022). Reducing bias in AI-based analysis of visual artworks. *IEEE BITS the Information Theory Magazine, 2*(1), 36–48. DOI: 10.1109/MBITS.2022.3197102

Zhang, Z., Strubell, E., & Hovy, E. (2022). Transfer Learning from Semantic Role Labeling to Event Argument Extraction with Template-based Slot Querying. *Proceedings of the 2022 Conference on Empirical Methods in Natural Language Processing*, 2627-2647. DOI: 10.18653/v1/2022.emnlp-main.169

Zhao, S., Jia, G., Yang, J., Ding, G., & Keutzer, K. (2021). Emotion Recognition From Multiple Modalities: Fundamentals and methodologies. In IEEE Signal Processing Magazine (Vol. 38, Issue 6, p. 59). Institute of Electrical and Electronics Engineers. DOI: 10.1109/MSP.2021.3106895

Zhao, Y., Borelli, A., Martínez, F. J., Xue, H., & Weiss, G. M. (2024). Admissions in the age of AI: detecting AI-generated application materials in higher education. In Scientific Reports (Vol. 14, Issue 1). Nature Portfolio. DOI: 10.1038/s41598-024-77847-z

Zhao, D., Playfoot, J., Nicola, C. D., Guarino, G., Bratu, M., Salvadore, F. D., & Muntean, G. (2021). An Innovative Multi-Layer Gamification Framework for Improved STEM Learning Experience. In Access, I. E. E. E. (Ed.), Vol. 10, p. 3879). Institute of Electrical and Electronics Engineers., DOI: 10.1109/ACCESS.2021.3139729

Zhao, K., Jin, X., Bai, L., Guo, J., & Cheng, X. (2022). Knowledge-Enhanced Self-Supervised Prototypical Network for Few-Shot Event Detection. *Findings of the Association for Computational Linguistics: EMNLP, 2022*, 6266–6275. DOI: 10.18653/v1/2022.findings-emnlp.467

Zhao, Y. (2020). The future of education: The impact of AI on teaching and learning. *Journal of Educational Technology & Society, 23*(4), 130–142.

Zhou, H., & Song, F. (2015). Aspect-Level Sentiment Analysis Based on a Generalized Probabilistic Topic and Syntax Model. *Proceedings of the Twenty-Eighth International Florida Artificial Intelligence Research Society Conference*. https://cdn.aaai.org/ocs/10382/10382-46113-1-PB.pdf

Zhou, W., & Chen, M. (2021). *An Improved Baseline for Sentence-level Relation Extraction* (Versión 4). arXiv. DOI: 10.48550/ARXIV.2102.01373

Zhu, H., & Li, H. (2020). The Construction of Online Education and the Balanced Development of Compulsory Education in the Post-Epidemic Era: A Case Study in China. In Proceedings of the 2021 5th International Seminar on Education, Management and Social Sciences (ISEMSS 2021). https://doi.org/DOI: 10.2991/assehr.k.200826.143

Zhuohao, W., Dong, W., & Qing, L. (2021). Keyword Extraction from Scientific Research Projects Based on SRP-TF-IDF. *Chinese Journal of Electronics, 30*(4), 652–657. DOI: 10.1049/cje.2021.05.007

Zucchet, E. (2023), How artificial intelligence is revolutionizing language learning, Available at: https://www.berlitz.com/blog/artificial-intelligence-ai-language-learning (Accessed 14 July 2024).

Žukov-Gregorič, A., Bachrach, Y., & Coope, S. (2018). Named Entity Recognition With Parallel Recurrent Neural Networks. *Proceedings of the 56th Annual Meeting of the Association for Computational Linguistics(*Volume 2*: Short Papers)*, 69-74. DOI: 10.18653/v1/P18-2012

About The Contributors

Nayef J. Jomaa is an assistant professor in Applied Linguistics at the University of Technology and Applied Sciences-Salalah, Sultanate of Oman. He has several years of teaching experience in Syria, Saudi Arabia, Malaysia, Turkey, and Sultanate of Oman. His research interests focus on L2 writing, academic writing, genre analysis, and Systemic Functional Linguistics (Functional Grammar).

***

Salim Al Maashani is a PhD candidate at Infrastructure University Kuala Lumpur, faculty of Education, Humanities, Social Sciences and Communications in Malaysia. He has long experience in teaching at the University of Technology and Applied Sciences-Salalah, Sultanate of Oman. His research focuses on integrating AI in language learning and teaching.

Ahmed Almaashani is a PhD candidate at University of Bristol, Faculty of Social Sciences and Law, School of Education, United Kingdom. He has long experience in teaching at the University of Technology and Applied Sciences-Salalah, Sultanate of Oman

Leena Arya is working as a Professor at the Department of Computer Science and Engineering at Koneru Lakshmaiah Education Foundation Deemed to be University, Vaddeswaram, 22nd NIRF Ranking University, Guntur, AP, India. She completed her Ph.D. from IIT Roorkee in 2012. She has published over 55 research papers in Scopus and SCI-indexed international journals. She handled a research project for the Department of Science and Technology, DST, New Delhi, as Principal Investigator under the Women Scientists Scheme (WOS-A). She has been granted a UK design and Australian Government Innovation patents. She has been a reviewer of many prestigious international journals and conferences. Her research area includes wireless communication, the Internet of Things (IoT), network security, and artificial intelligence.

Monika Bhatnagar is presently working as an Associate Professor in Galgotia College of Engineering and Technology, Greater Noida. She has 22+yrears of teaching experience in many reputed engineering college of U.P and Life member of ISTE, Dr. Bhatnagar B.E,M. Tech and Ph.D. from reputed state universities. She is academician associated with so many research organization and organizes and attended so many FDP, Seminars, Workshops, conferences etc. and published 20+ research paper and grant patent and Nationally and Internationally. Dr. Bhatnagar is author of 5 Books.

Venkateswara Rao Cheekati is working as Assistant Professor in the Department of Computer Science and Engineering and having 15 years of Teaching experience and Research experience in various areas.

Luis Fernández-Sanz is an associate professor at Dept. of Computer Science of Universidad de Alcala (UAH). He earned a degree in Computing in 1989 at Universidad Politecnica de Madrid (UPM) and his Ph.D. in Computing with a special award at University of the Basque Country in 1997. With more than 20 years of research and teaching experience (at UPM, Universidad Europea de Madrid and UAH), he is also engaged in the management of the main Spanish Computing Professionals association (ATI: www.ati.es) as vicepresident and he is chairman of ATI Software Quality group. He has been vicepresident of CEPIS (Council of European Professional Informatics Societies from 2011 to 2013. With a large number of contributions in refereed impact international journals, conferences and book chapters, his main research interests include technical fields like software quality and engineering and testing and non technical fields like computing education, especially in multinational settings, IT profession and requirements and skills for IT jobs.

Damith Gangodawilage is a practicing scholar and professional with extensive experience in finance and accounting, business management, entrepreneurship, and innovation. Currently serving as the Deputy Dean and the Cluster Head of Accounting, Economics, and Finance of the Qasim Ibrahim School of Business (QISB) at Villa College, Maldives, he has consistently demonstrated leadership in fostering academic excellence and industry engagement. Damith is also the Director of the Centre for Innovation and Entrepreneurship Development (CIED) at Villa College, where he spearheads initiatives such as the VIgnite Business Incubator, driving innovation among youth in the Maldives. With a strong academic foundation, Damith has made significant contributions to teaching, research, and curriculum development. His expertise spans strategic areas such as design thinking, sustainable business practices, and digital transformation. An active researcher, he has authored numerous studies and presentations on topics like corporate sustainability and tax compliance behavior, establishing himself as a thought leader. Dr. Damith is a dedicated mentor and educator, passionately committed to equipping students with critical thinking and problem-solving skills. His innovative approach combines academic rigor with practical insights, making him a distinguished figure in both academia and industry. As a global expert in entrepreneurship and compliance management, he bridges the gap between theory and practice, effectively bringing local solutions to the global stage.

Inés López-Baldominos earned a degree in Information Systems Engineering from the University of Alcalá (UAH) in 2020, followed by a Master's degree in IT Project Management in 2021, receiving several awards for her achievements. She completed her Ph.D. in Information and Knowledge Engineering in 2024. Currently, she is a researcher in the Department of Computer Science at UAH. With over five years of experience, she has actively contributed to multiple EU and national projects focused on digital skills, IT professionalism, digital accessibility and contributing to the development of innovative initiatives. She has also served as an expert for the European Commission, ensuring digital accessibility compliance in the development of DigComp 2.2, and as a consultant for the Spanish Ministry of Finance in digital accessibility. Her main research interests include information quality, digital accessibility, and IT professionalism, aiming to enhance the inclusivity and reliability of digital environments.

K. Pradeep Mohan Kumar is an Associate Professor in the Department of Computing Technology at SRM Institute of Science and Technology. He is doing research in the area of network security and cloud computing. He has published more than 15 paper in SCI indexed journal.

Ali Najeeb is the Vice Rector and Chief Operating Officer (COO) of Villa College, Maldives. He is also a Lecturer at the Faculty of Business Management and heads the Business and Tourism Research Group of the Institute of Research and Innovation at Villa College. He holds a PhD in Management and HR strategy at the University of Wollongong, Australia, a Master's Degree in Human Resource Management at the University of Newcastle, Australia. He is a Chartered Professional Member of Chartered Institute of Personnel and Development (CIPD) and a Certified Professional Member of Australian Human Resource Institute (AHRI). His research interests include higher education governance and management, industrial relations and labour issues in small island states, migrant workers, HRM/ER in tourism and hospitality industry. He has published several research papers in refereed international journals and presented his research work in international scholarly conferences. He is a recipient of the Emerald Literati Award for Excellence 2014 – the outstanding paper award. Dr Najeeb is a former school principal and worked as a Director of the Education and Development Centre in the Ministry of Education. He is also a former fulltime member of the Employment Tribunal, Maldives. Besides his administrative, teaching and research work, he is actively engaged in management and corporate consultancy and training.

Xuan-Hoa Nghiem works at Vietnam National University, Hanoi, Vietnam, and is a dedicated researcher eager and open to collaborate with others in the fields of economics and finance. He is a lecturer committed to ensuring students' welfare and delivering high-quality education.

Joelle Danielle Ngo Ndjama is a Researcher in the field of management. She served as a Research Assistant in the faculty of Management Sciences at the Vaal University of Technology in South Africa. She also served as a lecturer in the Department of Human Resource Management and as a Writing Consultant in the same university.

Damodharan Palaniappan works as an Associate Professor & Head in the Department of Information Technology, Marwadi University, Rajkot, Gujarat. He completed his Ph.D. at Anna University, Chennai, M.E. in Computer Science and Engineering at C.I.E.T, Coimbatore and B.E. in Computer Science and Engineering at CSI College of Engineering, Ketty, Nilgiri. He has 19 years' experience of teaching and research. Currently, he guides 6 Ph.D. research scholars. He has authored 8 book chapters, and he has published research papers in reputed journals. His interested areas of research are Data Mining, Image Processing, Software, Machine Learning and Deep Learning.

Vera Pospelova is an Assistant Professor at Computer Science, University of Alcala, Alcala de Henares, Spain.

M. R. Ramesh is currently affiliated with the Indira Gandhi Centre for Atomic Research in India.

Asanga Ranasinghe, a seasoned industry professional with over 30 years of experience, has assumed the role of Director at the Postgraduate Institute of Management (PIM) with a vision to elevate it into a world-class post-graduate management school.

Ravi Rastogi received his Ph.D. in Computer Science and Engineering in December 2011 from Uttarakhand Technical University, Dehradun, Uttarakhand, India. MS in Computer Science degree in September 2005 from Fairleigh Dickinson University, Teaneck, New Jersey, USA. He is working as a Professor in the Department of Computer Science and Engineering (Honors) at Koneru Lakshmaiah Education Foundation Deemed to be a university. He was a database developer for Microsoft, Seattle, USA, and ING, Philadelphia, USA. His research interests are interconnection networks, stable matching problems, data mining and intelligence in systems, the Internet of Things, and cloud computing. Refereed International Journal publications are 22 and Refereed International Conference Publications are 8.

I**Ridha Rouabhia** is an Algerian academic specializing in English language and literature. He teaches at Ali Lounici University in Blida and conducts research in postcolonial literature, critical discourse analysis, and translation. He authored several books, including The Evolution of Human Communication, Echoes Through Time, and Islamic Wisdom for Modern Living: Timeless Principles in a Changing World, enhancing understanding within the field through his scholarly contributions.

Anandharajah Sagadevan is a graduate in Civil Engineering currently pursuing a Bachelor's in Education. As a prospective student and researcher, they are passionate about exploring the intersections of education and civil engineering. Their academic journey reflects my dedication to contributing to these fields through innovative research and practical applications.

Premavathi T. is working as an Assistant professor in the Department of Computer Engineering—Artificial Intelligence, Marwadi University, Rajkot, Gujarat. She has completed a B.E. in Computer Science and Engineering at Dhanalakshmi Srinivasan Engineering College, Perambalur, Tamil Nadu, and an M.E. in Software Engineering with Distinction at Anna University. Currently, she is pursuing her Ph.D. at Marwadi University. She has 14 years of experience in teaching. She authored 5 book chapters, and she published 3 research papers in national and international seminars and conferences.

Mohit Yadav is an Associate Professor in the area of Human Resource Management at Jindal Global Business School (JGBS). He has a rich blend of work experience from both Academics as well as Industry. Prior to joining JGBS, he taught at reputed institutions like BML Munjal University, Glocal University and Lovely Professional University. He is also guest faculty at Bennett University and Jaypee Business School, Noida. Prof. Mohit holds a Ph.D. from Department of Management Studies, Indian Institute of Technology Roorkee (IIT Roorkee) and has completed Master of Human Resource and Organizational Development (MHROD) from prestigious Delhi School of Economics, University of Delhi. He also holds a B.Com (Hons.) degree from University of Delhi and UGC-JRF scholarship. He has published various research papers and book chapters with reputed publishers like Springer, Sage, Emerald, Elsevier, Inderscience etc. and presented research papers in national and International conferences both in India and abroad. He has many best paper awards on his credit too. He is reviewer of various international journals like Computers in Human Behavior, Policing etc. His areas of interest are Organizational Behavior, HRM, Recruitment and Selection, Organizational Citizenship Behavior, Quality of work life and role.

Rohit Yadav is a seasoned academic and researcher with over six years of teaching experience and nearly three years in industry roles. He holds a Ph.D. from the Indian Institute of Technology (IIT) Roorkee and an MBA in Marketing. His academic expertise lies in Digital Marketing, Integrated Marketing Communication, Social Media and Web Analytics, and International Marketing. Dr. Yadav's scholarly contributions include multiple research papers published in high-impact ABDC A category journals like Journal of Global Information Management and International Marketing Review, multiple B and C category papers. He has also published many other Scopus papers, authored book chapters, and presented papers at international conferences, focusing on digital transformation, marketing innovations, and sustainability. His recent patent on an Investment Simulation Board Game highlights his innovative approach to management education. In addition to academics, Dr. Yadav has successfully organized faculty development programs, coordinated university-level events, and served as an editor for academic journals. His commitment to bridging academia and industry is evident through his consulting projects focusing on market strategy and organizational development. At IILM University, Dr. Yadav is dedicated to fostering a culture of excellence in marketing education, inspiring students to lead with creativity and critical thinking in a rapidly evolving global market.

Index

A

B

C

D

E

F

G

www.ingramcontent.com/pod-product-compliance
Lightning Source LLC
LaVergne TN
LVHW081341300926
849161LV00008B/2037